Women, Children and (Other) Vulnerable Groups
Standards of Protection and Challenges for International Law

Lex et Res Publica

Polish Legal and Political Studies

Edited by Anna Jaroń

Volume 16

Magdalena Półtorak / Ilona Topa (eds.)

Women, Children and (Other) Vulnerable Groups

Standards of Protection and Challenges for International Law

PETER LANG

Bibliographic Information published by the Deutsche Nationalbibliothek
The Deutsche Nationalbibliothek lists this publication
in the Deutsche Nationalbibliografie; detailed bibliographic
data is available online at http://dnb.d-nb.de.

Library of Congress Cataloging-in-Publication Data
A CIP catalog record for this book has been applied for at the
Library of Congress.

This publication was financially supported by the
University of Silesia in Katowice, Poland.

UNIVERSITY OF SILESIA
IN KATOWICE

Cover illustration: Courtesy of Benjamin Ben Chaim

ISSN 2191-3250
ISBN 978-3-631-84152-5 (Print)
E-ISBN 978-3-631-85097-8 (E-Book)
E-ISBN 978-3-631-85127-2 (EPUB)
E-ISBN 978-3-631-85128-9 (MOBI)
DOI 10.3726/b18230

Peter Lang – Berlin· Bern · Bruxelles · New York ·
Oxford · Warszawa · Wien

This publication has been peer reviewed by dr hab. Anna Kosińska, prof. KUL and
dr hab. Iwona Wrońska

www.peterlang.com

Table of contens

Magdalena Półtorak
University of Silesia
e-mail: magdalena.poltorak@us.edu.pl
ORCID ID: 0000-0002-0712-6509
Ilona Topa
University of Silesia
e-mail: ilona.topa@us.edu.pl
ORCID ID: 0000-0001-9004-4071

Introduction: Some remarks on vulnerability in the international human rights law

In the last two decades, the issue of vulnerability has gained significant attention in public policy and academic research. Also, international and national laws relating to human rights have been further developed by the inclusion of particular norms and standards relating to the individuals and groups that have been "traditionally" discriminated (as women, national and ethnic minorities or migrants), which generally require special protection because of their particular condition (children, persons with disabilities, elderly) or who are in need of special treatment due to the hardship situation they found themselves in (as refugees, IDPs).

In the contemporary human rights discourse the notion of vulnerability can be easily found not only in academic research, but also in works of human rights protection bodies, jurisprudence of human rights courts and documents adopted by various international organizations. At the same time, this term is ambiguous and is used in diverse contexts, even if considered only from human rights perspective. C. Hruschka and L. Lebouf confirm explicitly that although terms "vulnerability" or "vulnerable persons" are being used in legal instruments – there is no universal and consistent understanding of this phenomenon.[1] Therefore, it is crucial to identify the character of vulnerability's

1 C. Hruschka, L. Leboeuf, "Vulnerability. A Buzzword or a Standard for Migration Governance?," *Policy Brief No. 20*, Jan. 2019, https://population-europe.eu/sites/default/files/media-documents/pb20_vulnerability_web.pdf (Accessed: 6.11.2020).

notion in international human rights law, to establish why certain individuals or whole groups are "labelled" as vulnerable, and what are the individual and collective outcomes of vulnerability.

1. Notion of and approaches to vulnerability in international human rights' discourse

A fundamental difficulty in dealing with vulnerability is that this category is both universal and particular. M. Albertson Fineman, who describes vulnerability as a useful heuristic device, underlines that vulnerability is an attribute of each human being. It arises "from our embodiment, which carries with it the ever-present possibility of harm, injury, and misfortune from mildly adverse to catastrophically devastating events, whether accidental, intentional, or otherwise."[2] As such, vulnerability has universal character: because of our human embodiment we all are vulnerable and susceptible to harm. Concurrently, everyone experiences this inherited vulnerability in a various manner, because of unique embodiment and different position within the society. As M. Albertson Fineman notes, individual experience of vulnerability considerably depends on the quality and quantity of resources one possesses or can command.[3] The individual experience of vulnerability plainly makes this category particular. Thus, the vulnerability is universal and particular at the same time: all human beings are vulnerable but, in particular circumstances, some of them are vulnerable to the greater extent. This approach appears to be correct; analysis of the jurisprudence of human rights protection bodies reveals that, while dealing with individual cases, they commonly refer to 'particularly vulnerable,' not simply 'vulnerable' individual or group. This observation allows merging the universal-particular approach to vulnerability with the group-based approach,[4] which is also present in human rights discourse relating to this category.

---

2 M. Albertson Fineman, "The Vulnerable Subject: Anchoring Equality in the Human Condition," *Yale Journal of Law and Feminism*, Vol. 20/1, 2008, p. 9. See also: R. Adorno, "Is Vulnerability the Foundation of Human Rights?," [in:] A. Masferrer, E. García Sánchez (eds.), *Human Dignity of the Vulnerable in the Age of Rights*, Springer International Publishing 2016, p. 257, available from: https://www.researchgate.net/publication/303564783_Is_Vulnerability_the_Foundation_of_Human_Rights (Accessed 15.11.2020).

3 M. Albertson Fineman, "The Vulnerable Subject", p. 10.

4 L. Peroni, A. Timmer, "Vulnerable groups: The promise of an emerging concept in European Human Rights Convention Law," *International Journal of Constitutional Law*, Vol. 11.3, 2013, pp. 1060–1061.

The group-based approach on vulnerability distinguishes particular groups, which are "labelled" as vulnerable because of certain reasons: their weakness and susceptibility to harm or structural discrimination and historical, systematic violations of their rights, and therefore requiring special protection.[5] The first explanation associates particular vulnerability with perpetuated, institutionalized cultural patterns considering some groups as subordinated, excluded, completely different or simply invisible and therefore excluded as partners in social relations. Here, the particular vulnerability is a consequence of historical, rooted in collective consciousness biases and subsequent stigmatization followed by negative social attitudes resulting in social exclusion. In other words, vulnerability is the resultant of broaden social, political and institutional circumstances. In this sense, vulnerability relates to national and religious minorities, indigenous people, persons with disabilities, elderly people, persons living with HIV or members of the LGBT+ group, but also women. The second explanation of assigning a group as vulnerable relates to exceptionally difficult group situations that preclude the ability of self-satisfaction of basic material needs and make them dependent from external assistance. This source of vulnerability is often indicated in relation to asylum seekers, refugees, migrant workers and internationally displaced persons, mainly because of their experience of migration,[6] but also same additional factors play the role: health conditions, age, disabilities or trauma. It is necessary to mention also the third possible basis of group vulnerability following some physical and mental conditions, which relates especially to children whose particular vulnerability is uncontested, but also is visible regarding elderly persons or persons with disabilities.

As can be seen from the above, a group may be considered vulnerable because of variety and – often coexisting – reasons. On the other hand, not each member of a group recognized as vulnerable *prima facie*, is and should be individually seen as such. Therefore, the discussed category should be used carefully because of a high risk of subsequent stigmatization, victimization

---

5 A. Grear, "Challenging Corporate "Humanity:" Legal Disembodiment, Embodiment and Human Rights," *Human Rights Law Review*, Vol. 7.6, 2007, pp. 511–543.

6 Nevertheless, as stressed in OHCHR-GMG *Principles and Guidelines* "migrants are not inherently vulnerable," but in their case due multiple and intersecting forms of discrimination, inequality and other factors full enjoyment of human rights is limited. More on the conception of "migrant in vulnerable situations" [in:] OHCHR – GMG (2017), *Principles and Guidelines, supported by practical guidance, on the human rights protection of migrants in vulnerable situations*, https://www.ohchr.org/Documents/Issues/Migration/PrinciplesAndGuidelines.pdf (Accessed: 6.11.2020).

and paternalistic approach,[7] and the emphasis should be put on the factors that place an individual in a particular vulnerability position.

The last issue relates to the role, which vulnerability plays in the assessment of the enjoyment of human rights and freedoms. Implicitly, the assumption that vulnerable groups and individuals do exist, necessitates the introduction of legal solutions that provide for increased protection of their special needs and facilitate escaping future discrimination and neutralization of harm resulting from membership of certain, unprivileged group. Thus, it helps to close the lacunas in the international system of human rights (including regional solutions) and determines effective protection to those who undoubtedly require it.

In the first part of the book above-mentioned general aspects of vulnerability are discussed in more detail.

A. Gliszczyńska-Grabias and G. Baranowska in the chapter entitled **"The concept of vulnerability in the United Nations human rights treaty bodies protection system"** present the comprehensive analysis of treaty provisions under which certain groups are named and recognized as vulnerable, offering also a general overview of the invocation of the concept of vulnerability in the decisions of selected UN treaty bodies. Next, the authors review who so far has been considered vulnerable by the treaty bodies and conclude with defining the attitude of selected UN treaty bodies towards the notion of vulnerability.

The chapter on **"The European Court of Human Rights towards group vulnerability: an open-ended approach"** by E. Morawska focuses on establishing the basic characteristics of currently developing in ECHR jurisprudence approach to vulnerability, and thus on defining and assessing its personal and material scope. After thorough analysis of the groups recognized by the Court as vulnerable and discussion of factors decisive for such a determination, the author concludes by evaluating the relationship between vulnerability and the effectiveness of the rights and freedoms of individual members of these groups, and the overall efficiency of the Convention system and the preservation of its key foundations.

The last chapter included in the first part of the book by S. Kowalska on **"Protection of individuals and groups especially vulnerable to discrimination**

7 L. Peroni, A. Timmer, *Vulnerable groups*, p. 1070. See also: J. Freedman, "The uses and abuses of "vulnerability" in EU asylum and refugee protection: protecting women or reducing autonomy?," *Papeles del CEIC*, Vol. 2019/1, papel 204, pp. 1–15 (http://dx.doi.org/10.1387/pceic.19525) or E.C. Gilson, "Vulnerability and Victimization: Rethinking Key Concepts in Feminist Discourses on Sexual Violence. Signs," *Journal of Women in Culture and Society*, 42(1), 2016, pp. 71–98.

and unequal treatment in the context of transformations of social life" considers the question of the protection and the legal status of individuals and groups – those especially vulnerable to discrimination and unequal treatment. The author demonstrates that dignity is both a fundamental value and the goal of protection, while law-making and implementation, without due regard to the standards that stem from dignity lead to arbitrariness and discrimination. S. Kowalska uses an example of racial discrimination and notes the current rise in covert discrimination, but also new, emerging forms of discrimination. Her conclusions strongly corelates with M. Albertson Fineman's findings that society and its institutions can ameliorate, compensate, and lessen our vulnerability by creating the possibility of layered opportunities and support for individuals.[8]

2. Women as a particularly vulnerable group

The universal system of human rights protection, which encompasses guarantees of rights and freedoms for all human beings in the same way does not consider that, there is a striking difference of certain individual from the "ideal" one in some cases. Therefore, in order to encompass the distinct situation of some individuals, particular human rights obligations are undertaken. Thus, the special protection in human rights law have been established for particular groups, among them – women.

The inferior status of women is deep-rooted in culture, tradition and history of humankind. Although the main documents of universal human rights protection such as the 1948 *Universal Declaration on Human Rights* or the 1966 *International Covenant on Civil and Political Rights and the International Covenant on Economic, Social and Cultural Rights* proclaims equal rights for men and women and prohibit discrimination on the grounds of sex, the inequality is still common, and women continuously are subjected to discrimination in various aspects of life. Moreover, they are particularly vulnerable to specific violations such as gender-based violence, also in the form of traditional practices, trafficking and sex discrimination.

The 1979 *Convention on the Elimination of All Forms of Discrimination against Women* has been adopted in order to overcome this structural mistreatment. As a preamble to CEDAW states, the concern that "discrimination against women continues to exist," and

8 M. Albertson Fineman, "The Vulnerable Subject", p. 10.

> violates the principles of equality of rights and respect for human dignity, is an obstacle to the participation of women, on equal terms with men, in the political, social, economic and cultural life of their countries, hampers the growth of the prosperity of society and the family and makes more difficult the full development of the potentialities of women in the service of their countries and of humanity,

was the factor which led to adoption of this treaty. The same concern resulted in the adoption on international level of other treaties dealing with particular faces of inequality and discrimination of women, just to mention the *UN Convention on the Political Rights of Women* (1952) and the *UN Convention on the Nationality of Married Women* (1957). A great number of treaties on maternity protection, equal renumeration, social security standards have been adopted by the International Labour Organization.[9] It is also worth to mention regional treaties that aim in the protection of the rights of women, as the *Optional Protocol to the African Charter on Human and Peoples' Rights on the Rights of Women in Africa*, so-called *Maputo Protocol* (2003), *the Inter-American Convention on the Granting of Political Rights to Women* (1948), *the Inter-American Convention on the Granting of Civil Rights to Women* (1948) and the 1994 *Inter-American Convention on the Prevention, Punishment and Eradication of Violence against Women* (Convention of Belém do Pará).

As can be easily inferred from the number of treaties that deal with the distinct aspect of the vulnerability of women, the number of problematic areas is overwhelming and therefore, it is impossible to cover them all in one publication. That is why the second part of the book covers up-to-date, comprehensive analysis of international legal responses towards carefully selected problems of women as particularly vulnerable.

This part starts with the chapter by B. Stępień **"On the road to political equality in Mexico: gender-based political violence and electoral justice."** The author analyses political violence against women on the example of the electoral processes in Mexico, presents the international legal framework pertaining to gender discrimination and gender equality, as well as national Mexican regulations relating to this field, and offers insight into selected cases concerning gender-based political violence. The conclusion is positive: the

9 E.g. 1935 Underground Work by Women in Mines Convention (No. 45), 1848 Night Work by Women in Industrial Employment Convention (No. 89), 1951 Equal Remuneration for Men and Women Workers for Work of Equal Value Convention (No. 100), 1952 Minimum Standards of Social Security Convention (No. 102), 1958 Discrimination in Respect of Employment and Occupation Convention (No. 111), 2000 Maternity Protection Convention (No. 183).

author notes a very strong movement supporting gender equality in Mexico, aiming to eradicate discrimination and political violence against women.

Next, M. Myl deals with **"Increased vulnerability of women to enforced disappearances."** The author evaluates the situation of women in the context of enforced disappearance and determines the reasons of the increased vulnerability of women-victims to enforced disappearances. It is underlined that women are at the forefront of the struggle against the act and, at the same time, are in a situation of particular vulnerability in the case of enforced disappearances.

This is followed by the chapter by A. Szczerba entitled **"Protection of women with respect to pregnancy and maternity in European Union law – between paternalism and equality."** It offers a critical analysis of selected protective measures stipulated in the European Union secondary legislation through the gender equality glass. As author notes, the EU normative standard on pregnant workers and workers adopted lately, contributes to ensuring equal opportunities for women implying changes to social and legal attitude towards pregnancy. Nevertheless, as based on stereotypical assumptions, it also interferes with women's autonomy and results in less favorable treatment of women as defined in terms of *substantive* equality.

Also, the chapter by U. Torbus **"Facilitating the work of mothers. How to diminish female vulnerability in the labour market?"** deals with the desired protection framework for women at work. The author discusses particularly the solutions introduced on the EU level by the brand-new *Directive 2019/1158 on work life balance*, which she considers as having a great potential to facilitate the work of women and diminish their vulnerability in the labour market.

Next chapter touches upon the protection of women with respect to pregnancy and maternity, but is devoted to women in a specific situation. A. Jaworska-Wieloch provides for the analysis on **"Pregnant women and those serving a prison sentence with a child under international law."** It is obvious that isolation in prison is of great difficulty for pregnant women and women, who raise their children in prisons. The author research relates to the international, European and Polish legal standards in order to establish if afforded protection is sufficient.

The last chapter in this part, written by K. Jędrzejczyk-Kuliniak discusses another aspect of women's particular vulnerability. The author in **"Double discrimination of immigrant women in Poland in the context of world migration trends. Ukrainian case"** on the basis of a country specific case-study analyses the situation of immigrant women who, because of their gender and origin, may experience double discrimination. The chapter deals also with the issues of tolerance of otherness, coexistence model and factual observance of the rights of particularly vulnerable groups.

3. Children's (and motherhood) vulnerability

The special needs and the unique situation of children have been already reflected in the provisions of many international agreements on the protection of their rights. The general rules concerning the rights of all children are contained primarily in the 1989 *Convention on the Rights of the Child*, but also in regional treaties, just to mention the 1990 *African Charter of the Rights and Welfare of the Child*. However, the general reason for recognizing the children vulnerable as such differs from other particularly protected group. It is not structural discrimination or specially difficult situation, but the belief – citing the preamble to the CRC – that "the child, by reason of his physical and mental immaturity, needs special safeguards and care including appropriate legal protection, before as well as after birth." It is because their fragile construction and sensitivity, that children requires and are granted special protection. At the same time, children are highly dependent on others to satisfy their basic needs, what also is indicated as the source of their vulnerability.[10] These factors make children exceptionally exposed to violence, abuse and exploitation, which takes various forms – from domestic violence and child labour, through trafficking, child marriage or female genital mutilation to recruitment into armed groups.

Due to the almost unlimited ways in which children can be subjected to mistreatment of various kind, international community – on both universal and regional levels – has adopted specific treaties dealing with these particular issues, just to mention some of them, as (1973) *Minimum Age Convention*, (1980) *Hague Convention on the Civil Aspects of International Child Abduction*, (1999) *Worst Forms of Child Labour Convention*, (2000) *Optional Protocol to the CRC on the Sale of Children, Child Prostitution, and Child Pornography*, (2000) *Optional Protocol to the CRC on the Involvement of Children in Armed Conflict*, (1996) *European Convention on the Exercise of Children's Rights* or (1984) *Inter-American Convention on Conflict of Laws Concerning the Adoption of Minors.*

As the international obligations, also the legal scholarship on children protection is immense. Even though, the number of possible topics seems to be

10 A. Bagattini, "Children's well-being and vulnerability," *Ethics and Social Welfare*, 2019, Vol. 13, No. 3, available at: https://doi.org/10.1080/17496535.2019.16479 (Accessed: 15.11.2020), p. 211.

infinite. Therefore, in this book only some selected issues of their particular situation are discussed.

The part on children vulnerability starts with the chapter by A. Wedeł-Domaradzka entitled **"Between need and desire – the vulnerability of woman and child in surrogacy proceedings."** The author analyses the existing variety of legal solutions and the lack of coherent international regulations from the perspective of possible violations of women's and children's rights in the surrogacy proceedings. She notes the need for comprehensive, world-wide treaty that could help to overcome possibility of abuses with regard to child's needs and his best interests, including the introduction of aa system of sanctions against intermediaries, recruiters or other entities benefiting from illegal activities.

It is followed by O. Sitarz contribution on **"International law and national law of selected countries on the issue of infanticide."** The chapter addresses the issue of the normative approach to the crime of infanticide in the light of each child's right to life. The dogmatic and criminological analysis carried out allows to pose the thesis that the concept of infanticide as a privileged type is a systemic, even normative discrimination against the weaker, which contradicts the principle of the best interests of the child.

Next chapter, authored by J. Markiewicz-Stanny on **"Age assessment procedures and the protection of children's rights: an analysis of international standards"** considers the relationship between the procedures for assessing the age of foreigners and enjoying by children of their rights guaranteed in international documents. The recognition of a person as being a child is fundamental for benefitting of this status, yet, on the other hand, age assessment requires the use of measures that involve interference with the privacy and autonomy of individuals. Therefore, the author claims that the age assessment procedures should be applicable only to the foreigners whose age is doubtful, and such individuals should be treated as children until it is estimated that they are the adults.

J. Gumuła-Kędracka in her chapter **"Protection of children's rights in cases of international parental abduction"** analyses the provisions of the 1980 *Hague Convention on the Civil Aspects of International Child Abduction* in the light of the realization of the best interest of child, while this principle has its specific understanding under this treaty. The general assumption that each return of a child to a place of his habitual residence is in the child's best interests, cannot be always considered correct. The "best interest of child" is interpreted outside the 1980 Hague Convention and thus put the most vulnerable actors of the Hague proceedings – children – at risk of their rights to be breached.

Finally, K. Kamińska deals with the issue of **"Welfare of adopted children in international legal Acts in the 20th and 21st century."** The author analyses the international legal standard of protection for a child adopted in order to establish how the welfare of an adopted child is protected under international law, and noting the dangers that occur in the adoption proceedings, as illegal child trafficking.

4. Other faces of vulnerability

The sole number of groups recognized as particularly vulnerable indicates that the topic is enormous and can be assessed from divergent perspectives. As different are the reason for the vulnerability of women, children, migrants, elderly persons, asylum seekers or persons HIV positive, the scientific attitude also varies. Therefore, the last part of the book, in order to show the apparent connection between law and other spheres of human life, includes contributions undertaking a different approach, mostly a sociological one. On the one hand, it allows us to present further perspectives on vulnerability, and – on the other – helps to realize that vulnerability always is simultaneously multidimensional and contextual and in every moment of life, for plentiful reasons, each human being may be "labelled" vulnerable.

This part begins with D. Bek chapter on **"Cultural determinants of the victimization of vulnerable groups in the Roma community."** The author analyses those aspects of Roma culture that may favour the victimization of women. Although this contribution deals with a particular minority, its findings are applicable to a broad spectrum of cases of discrimination and inequality. The thesis that traditional beliefs in the inferiority of women to men, their objectification and the related exposure of women to various forms of discrimination are encountered in numerous cultures, reflects the reality of many women all over the world.

Next chapter by I. Delekta examines the difficulties that are often unavoidable in elder age. In **"Senior consumer's dilemma: what does my warranty actually say? Or, once again, on exclusion and warranty readability"** the issues of the consumer warranty and elderly consumers are analyzed from a sociolinguistic perspective. The study reveals some tendencies, characteristics and potential problem areas related to the consumer warranty, shows linguistic and non-linguistic sources of problems and provides some remedies to make the consumer warranty more senior friendly.

Finally, J. Klimczak and D. Nowalska-Kapuścik in the chapter on **"Local senior policy as a tool of combating discrimination of the elderly on the**

basis of the situation in Bogucice district." discuss the ongoing process of ageing of society, that results in tendency to create negative attitudes, prejudices and stereotypes causing marginalization, exclusion and discrimination of seniors. The authors analyse senior policy on local level, underling the need of coordination and constant supervision of the processes of implementation of elderly persons' human rights.

***

The purpose of this publication is to present to the international academic community a detailed analysis on the current scope of the international legal protection of vulnerable persons in thoughtfully selected material. It must be mentioned that there are appreciated publications on this topic, but their scope differs significantly from the present book: they either deal solely with the notion of vulnerability in general terms or present the wide-ranging description of the international legal response to the position of certain groups, without raising the specific problems as indicated above. The monograph is not intended to deal with the entire spectrum of questions and concerns that comprise vulnerability, it would be simply unbearable. On the contrary, it deals with the specific aspects of vulnerable individuals and groups' legal position, nevertheless preceded by the insight into the overall concept of vulnerability in international law.

We hope that this publication will meet the interest of both "traditional" human rights researchers, as well as focused on vulnerability phenomenon academics from other than law disciplines in the framework of social sciences.

Taking the opportunity let us express our deep gratitude to the reviewers: dr hab. Anna Kosińska, prof. KUL and dr hab. Iwona Wrońska, whose sense of subject matter, valuable experience and extremely precise suggestions helped to give this book its final shape.

Finally, we would like to say a simple "thank you" to our personal "Human Rights Mentor" – prof. dr hab. Barbara Mikołajczyk, whose advice, real help and mental support (especially in "vulnerable situations") we can always count on.

Editors

PART I The concept of vulnerability

Aleksandra Gliszczyńska-Grabias

Poznań Human Rights Center, Institute of Law Studies, Polish Academy of Sciences

e-mail: a.gliszczynska-grabias@inp.pan.pl

ORCID ID: 0000-0002-0578-6669

Grażyna Baranowska

Poznań Human Rights Center, Institute of Law Studies, Polish Academy of Sciences

e-mail: g.baranowska@inp.pan.pl

ORCID ID: 0000-0001-6614-9121

The concept of vulnerability in the United Nations human rights treaty bodies protection system[1]

Abstract: The universal concept of human rights protection assumes that individual rights and freedoms must be protected from unlawful interference by the state and other – private – entities. However, when it comes to groups that are distinguished by features for which they are particularly discriminated against, this standard protection very often proves to be insufficient. Thus, the human rights protection systems has to come up with and advocate a formula under which these groups, particularly susceptible to violations of their rights and freedoms, would be more strongly protected in and by the relevant instruments of international law. The identification of these sensitive groups, the evolution of protection granted to them and the reflection of the protection trends in the jurisprudence of international human rights control institutions and organizations, such as the United Nations (UN) treaty bodies – all remain topical issues to this day. Also vital in this context is how the various UN treaty bodies approach the concept of vulnerability. Even though some treaty bodies are called upon to deal with

1 Research for the article has been funded by the Polish National Science Center (NCN), Grant No. 2019/33/B/HS5/01634.

specific vulnerable groups (children, people with disabilities or refugees, to name but some), little attention has so far been paid to just how these bodies relate to and shape the concept of vulnerability itself.

This chapter offers some general remarks and observations on all these issues, starting with a brief introduction to the UN system of human rights protection and to the concept of vulnerability, indicating groups historically recognized by this system as sensitive, and sketching the evolution of the relevant protection mechanisms. This is followed by an analysis of treaty provisions under which certain groups are named and recognized as vulnerable, offering also a general overview of the invocation of the concept of vulnerability in the decisions of selected UN treaty bodies. Next comes a review of who so far has been considered vulnerable by the treaty bodies, and the chapter concludes with an attempt to define the attitude of selected UN treaty bodies towards the notion of vulnerability.

Keywords: vulnerability, United Nations treaty bodies, discrimination, minorities, human rights protection

Desperation, weakness, vulnerability – these things will always be exploited. You need to protect the weak, ring-fence them, with something far stronger than empathy.

Zadie Smith[2]

1. Introductory remarks

The human rights protection system operating within the United Nations is referred to as the universal system. Its creation is a direct consequence of the transfer of the issue of human rights from the exclusive domain of individual states to the sphere of international law.[3] This fundamental change was brought about by the dramatic events of the Second World War that, as never before, made the international community aware of the need to guarantee and respect human rights. As one author noted, the consensus around the need to provide and impose on states legally binding obligations to protect human rights emerged after the world became aware of the destruction of morality that took place in concentration camps.[4]

2 Interview with Z. Smith, *The New Yorker*, 3 February 2013, [online:] https://www.newyorker.com/books/page-turner/this-week-in-fiction-zadie-smith-2 [available: 04.05.2020].

3 For a comprehensive study on the UN human rights protection system see: P. Alston (ed.), *The United Nations and Human Rights. A Critical Appraisal*, Oxford 1992.

4 J. Morsink, "The Universal Declaration and the Conscience of Humanity," [in:] *Human Rights and History. A Challenge for Education*, R. Huhle (ed.), Berlin 2010, p. 36.

This new approach to the protection of human rights understood as a political and legal obligation was expressed in the UN Charter of 26 June 1945 by the commitment of the UN member states to undertake, independently and jointly with other states within this organization, efforts to respect the rights and freedoms of each individual, regardless of his or her race, gender, language or religion.[5] The implementation of this commitment began with the adoption of the Universal Declaration of Human Rights on 10 December 1948.[6] The UN General Assembly thus established the first universal international instrument for the protection of human rights, containing provisions on unacceptable grounds of discrimination and differentiation in the exercise of human rights and freedoms. According to its Article 2:

> [e]veryone is entitled to all the rights and freedoms set forth in this Declaration, without distinction of any kind, such as race, colour, sex, language, religion, political or other opinion, national or social origin, property, birth or other status.

Furthermore, Article 7 stipulates that

> [a]ll are equal before the law and are entitled without any discrimination to equal protection of the law. All are entitled to equal protection against any discrimination in violation of this Declaration and against any incitement to such discrimination.

These general instruments of human rights protection were further developed in the form of the treaty system, based on the various international human rights treaties and special treaty bodies guarding their observance. The treaty bodies system addresses primarily issues related to the protection of the rights and freedoms of specific groups. The selection of these groups is closely related to the historical momentum of the drafting and implementing the subsequent treaties. They were initially created to protect groups traditionally (and historically) exposed to increased discrimination and hatred: ethnic, racial, national and religious minorities. Article 27 of the International Covenant on Civil and Political Rights (ICCPR)[7] can serve as an example here:

> In those States in which ethnic, religious or linguistic minorities exist, persons belonging to such minorities shall not be denied the right, in community with the other members of their group, to enjoy their own culture, to profess and practise their own religion, or to use their own language.

---

5 Charter of the United Nations, opened for signature in San Francisco on 26 June 1945. It came into force for Poland on 24 October 1945 (Dz.U. 1947, No. 23, item 90).

6 Universal Declaration of Human Rights of 10 December 1948.

7 International Covenant on Civil and Political Rights of 16 December 1966. It came into force for Poland on 18 June 1977 (Dz.U. 1977, No. 38, item 167).

Even though nowhere in what are historically known as the core UN human rights treaties is there any mention of vulnerability as such, the then understanding of this term seems to refer to individuals and groups defined by their race, colour, sex, language, religion and national or ethnic origin. Thus, from the beginning of the formation of the universal system of human rights protection, particularly vulnerable groups were defined as those most often discriminated against. For a long time members of the LGBTQ groups, people with disabilities and refugees, among others, were left out of this category. Today, when social reality is much more complex than before, human rights protection mechanisms must respond to the challenges they face in a much more appropriate and coherent way, including in-depth protection of an ever-growing number of individuals who today belong to distinct groups which remain particularly vulnerable. Obviously, this challenge has to be taken up not only by the universal system. In fact, the most progressive in this regard seems to be the European system, built around the European Convention on Human Rights, with the European Court of Human Rights proving to be a precursor in expanding the scope of groups that deserve increased protection and should be perceived as vulnerable. The Court did this, for example, by recognizing that protection against hate speech should apply not only to racist and xenophobic statements, but also to those of a homophobic nature.[8]

Extending the scope of human rights law and arming systems of human rights protection with new instruments often involves introducing novel concepts and designations into legal circulation to name phenomena that so far went unnoticed or unacknowledged. And so, for example, in recent years we witnessed the addition of the concepts of multiple discrimination or discrimination by association to European anti-discrimination law.[9] At the same time, this kind of 'activism' in the area of human rights law is very often met with resistance from those who for various reasons contest the need for it.[10] One of the arguments raised in discussions is that it is impossible to encapsulate certain phenomena within sufficiently detailed and specific legal definitions. This is certainly the case with the concept of 'vulnerability.' Nonetheless, the looming conceptual and definitional difficulties do nothing to eliminate the obvious need to address this issue, also within the UN treaty bodies system.

---

8 ECtHR Judgment of 9 February 2012 in 1813/07, *Vejdeland and others v. Sweden*.

9 For a detailed analysis of these phenomenon see: U. Belavusau, K. Henrard (eds.), *EU Anti-Discrimination Law beyond Gender*, Oxford 2018.

10 W. Osiatyński, *Human rights and their limits*, Cambridge 2009.

2. Vulnerability in the UN treaty-based system of human rights protection

As already mentioned, the concepts of 'vulnerability' or 'vulnerable groups' do not appear in the treaties of the universal system of human rights protection constituting its oldest core, such as both the Covenants, namely the ICCPR and the International Covenant on Economic, Social and Cultural Rights (ICESCR),[11] and the International Convention on the Elimination of All Forms of Racial Discrimination (ICERD),[12] although in fact many of the provisions of the ICCPR, and essentially the entire ICERD concern guarantees of protection of the rights of persons belonging to groups particularly vulnerable to various, multiple and intense forms of undertreatment and discrimination. In ICERD in particular we can see that in addition to religion and belief, it is exactly race and skin colour that historically remain features that most often makes minorities particularly vulnerable in a given environment.[13]

That said, direct references to vulnerability do in fact exist in the UN treaty system. The Preamble to the International Convention on the Protection of the Rights of All Migrant Workers and Members of Their Families[14] (adopted in 1990, and thus not a first-generation UN human rights treaty) mentions

> the situation of vulnerability in which migrant workers and members of their families frequently find themselves owing, among other things, to their absence from their State of origin and to the difficulties they may encounter arising from their presence in the State of employment.

In turn, the Preamble to one of the additional protocol to the Convention on the Rights of the Child recognizes "the special needs of those children who are particularly vulnerable to recruitment or use in hostilities contrary to the

11 International Covenant on Economic, Social and Cultural Rights of 16 December 1966, opened for signature in New York on 19 December 1966. It came into force for Poland on 18 June 1977 (Dz.U. 1977, No. 38, item 169).

12 International Convention on the Elimination of All Forms of Racial Discrimination of 21 December 1965, opened for signature in New York on 7 November 1966. It came into force for Poland on (Dz.U. 1969, No. 25, item 187).

13 T. van Boven, "Combating Racial Discrimination in the World and in Europe," *Netherlands Quarterly of Human Rights* 1993, Vol. 11, no 2.

14 International Convention on the Protection of the Rights of All Migrant Workers and Members of Their Families of 18 December 1990.

present Protocol owing to their economic or social status or gender."[15] However, much more attention is paid to vulnerability in the Optional Protocol to the Convention on the Rights of the Child on the sale of children, child prostitution and child pornography[16] which recognizes that:

- children are especially vulnerable to sex tourism, as it directly promotes the sale of children, child prostitution and child pornography;
- girl children, who are at greater risk of sexual exploitation, belong to particularly vulnerable group;
- States Parties shall adopt appropriate measures to protect the rights and interests of child victims of the practices prohibited under the Protocol, by recognizing the vulnerability of child victims;
- States Parties shall adopt or strengthen, implement and disseminate laws, administrative measures, social policies and programmes to prevent the offences referred to in the Protocol and particular attention shall be given to protect children who are especially vulnerable to such practices;
- States Parties shall promote the strengthening of international cooperation in order to address the root causes, such as poverty and underdevelopment, contributing to the vulnerability of children.

In addition, the International Convention for the Protection of All Persons from Enforced Disappearance (ICPPED)[17] provides that "in respect of pregnant women, minors, persons with disabilities or other particularly vulnerable persons" each State Party to the Convention may establish so-called aggravating circumstances.

It is already very clear at this point that references to vulnerability are very rare in UN treaties, and one is even tempted to say that they hardly exist in them at all. Moreover, when present – and they made their appearance at a relatively late stage, in 1990 – they serve mostly to highlight the particularly difficult situation of a given group or category within a group rather than to add any specially tailored rights or other mechanisms of rights protection. What should be

15 Optional Protocol to the Convention on the Rights of the Child on the involvement of children in armed conflict of 25 May 2000. It came into force for Poland on 7 May 2005 (Dz.U. 2007, No. 91, item 608).

16 Optional Protocol to the Convention on the Rights of the Child on the sale of children, child prostitution and child pornography of 25 May 2000. It came into force for Poland on 24 December 2004 (Dz.U. 2007, No. 76, item 494).

17 International Convention for the Protection of All Persons from Enforced Disappearance of 20 December 2006.

noted though is that it follows from the ICPPED that pregnant women, minors and persons with disabilities are legally qualified as vulnerable.

Due to the specific manner of functioning of international human rights protection systems, in which treaty provisions are interpreted and developed in the case-law of the relevant control bodies – for the UN this is the system of treaty bodies – it is in fact the latter where the most frequent and detailed references to vulnerability are to be found. This is because treaty bodies manifest flexibility and readiness for a progressive interpretation of the treaty provisions which were very often established decades earlier. Nevertheless, in this case too references to vulnerability are not numerous, and they vary deeply in character. Statistically, references to 'vulnerability' or 'vulnerable individual or group' appear in 51 views of the treaty bodies,[18] including eight references made by the Committee against Torture (CAT), nine by the Committee on the Elimination of Discrimination against Women (CEDAW), of which three were in admissibility decisions; three references by the Committee on Economic, Social and Cultural Rights (CESC), including in one admissibility decision; three references by the Committee on the Rights of the Child (CRC), one reference by the Committee on the Rights of Persons with Disabilities (CRPD), and as many as 27 references by the Human Rights Committee (HRC). It must be stressed that the wide discrepancies in the numbers of references are not due to differences in attitudes of the various treaty bodies but to the scope and number of cases the treaty bodies are generally examining, with the HRC being the undisputed leader within the UN treaty bodies system of human rights protection.

References to vulnerability first appeared in a CAT decision issued in 1999, concerning attempts to prevent the applicant's deportation to Somalia: "the Committee considers that two factors support the author's case that he is particularly vulnerable to the kind of acts referred to in article 1 of the Convention." The CAT also pointed out that belonging to a specific, more vulnerable ethnic clan, exposed the applicant to additional harassment.[19] From that moment on, more than a decade had to pass, until 2011, before vulnerability became noticeably more present in decisions of treaty bodies, with the CEDAW[20] and HRC becoming

18 This applies to all cases of invoking the notion of vulnerability, both in the reasoning of the treaty bodies and arguments of the applicants and/or state parties.

19 CAT Views of 14 May 1999 in 120/1998, *S.S. Elmi v. Australia*.

20 CEDAW Views of 27 September 2011 in 17/2008, *Maria de Lourdes da Silva Pimentel v. Brasil*.

pioneers in championing the concept.[21] Statistical analyses show that the majority of views referring to vulnerability date to after 2016.

Clearly, the manner in which vulnerability is invoked is closely tied to the nature of each treaty body, which in a way hinders the development of a single coherent understanding and application of this concept in the case-law of all treaty bodies. And so, the CAT refers to vulnerability practically exclusively in its deportation decisions[22] (examples of which include *Elmi*,[23] *N.P.*,[24] *Y.H.A*,[25] *L.P*,[26] *A.N.*[27] and *Adam Harun*[28]). The concept of vulnerability also appears in the context of deportation and forced expulsions in decisions by the HRC, which refers to vulnerability in other circumstances in just a handful of its other decisions that will be discussed in more detail below. All the CESCR decisions in which vulnerability is mentioned have so far concerned evictions and stress that states have particular obligations in this context with regard to vulnerable persons (*Ben Djazia and Bellili*;[29] *Alban*[30] *and S.S.R.*[31]). Finally, the CEDAW, when dealing with violations of women's rights, has so far noted the vulnerability of women as a phenomenon resulting from combinations of several co-existing factors.

Although the treaty bodies' deliberations in their decisions are the most important element co-creating standards for human rights protection in specific areas, if a more coherent picture of the situation is to be presented, it may also be worthwhile to look at cases where the treaty bodies make no mention of vulnerability but the concept nevertheless appears in arguments brought by the applicants and/or state parties.[32] Here are a few examples to illustrate this point.

---

21 HRC Views of 26 July 2010 in 1959/2010, *Jama Warsame v. Canada*.

22 Both CAT and the ECtHR are using vulnerability to calibrate acceptable treatment and living conditions, see a comparison on non-refoulement cases: B. Çalı, C. Costello, S. Cunnigham, "Hard Protection through Soft Courts? Non-Refoulement before the United Nations Treaty Bodies," *German Law Journal* 2020, Vol. 21, pp. 381–383.

23 CAT Views of 14 May 1999 in 120/1998, *S.S. Elmi v. Australia*.

24 CAT Views of 6 May 1999 in 106/1998, *N.P. v. Australia*.

25 CAT Views of 23 November 2001 in 162/2000, *Y.H.A. v. Australia*.

26 CAT Views of 1 December 2016 in 666/2015, *L.P. v. Australia*.

27 CAT Views of 3 August 2018 in 742/2016, *A.N. v. Switzerland*.

28 CAT Views of 6 December 2018 in 758/2016, *Adam Harun v. Switzerland*.

29 CESCR Views of 20 June 2017 in 5/2015, *Mohamaed Ben Djazia and Naouel Bellili v. Spain*, para. 15.2.

30 CESCR Views of 20 June 2019 in 37/2018, *Alban v. Spain*.

31 CESCR Decision of 11 October 2019 in 51/2018, *S.S.R. v. Spain*.

32 See UN treaty bodies views and decisions in cases: CAT Views of 6 May 1999 in 106/1998, *N.P. v. Australia*; CAT Views of 8 May 2009 in 261/2005, *Osmani v. Serbia*;

In *D.G. v. Netherlands*, adjudicated by the CEDAW, the issue of recognizing the applicant as a vulnerable person constituted one of the cornerstones of discussion and dispute in the case between the applicant and the State party.[33] Vulnerability appears in the very centre of the complaint, where a claim against the state is being defined:

> The author claims that the State party has violated her rights under articles 2, 5, 11, 12 and 16 of the Convention owing to its failure to comply with its positive obligation to protect her as a vulnerable person and a victim of gender-based violence (human trafficking). She considers that the procedural requirements imposed on her (residence permit, being homeless, the completion of certain forms) and the lack of proper assessment of her status as a victim violated her rights under the Convention because they prevented her from gaining access to social benefits and shelter.[34]

The state, in its turn, maintained that the guarantees of special protection for vulnerable persons – both in national law provisions and in the procedures for their implementation themselves – were preserved. An interesting exchange of arguments also concerned the very nature of state obligations in the context of vulnerability: the author of the complaint rejected the State party's argument that the positive obligation to protect vulnerable persons relates only to the procedural requirements, arguing that it is the vulnerability itself that triggers the obligation. It is thus regrettable that in settling the case the CEDAW did not refer to these discussions, ignoring the discussion on vulnerability of the author of the complaint. Similarly, the HRC disregarded the debate on vulnerability when considering the case against Canada, where the State party gave some indication in its argument of its understanding of the category of vulnerable persons, arguing that the applicant did not belong to the category considered vulnerable, such as women and children.[35] It is clear from treaty bodies' decisions that not only women and children can be considered vulnerable, and the HRC could have reacted to the state's argumentation by stating that.

CEDAW Views of 21 July 2017 in 75/2014, *Reyna Trujillo Reyes and Pedro Arguello Morales v. Mexico*; CEDAW Decision of 16 July 2019 in 102/2016, *J.D.* et al. *v. Czech Republic*; CEDAW Decision of 25 February 2019 in 98/2016, *K.K. v. Russian Federation*; CRC Views of 18 September 2019 in 17/2017, *M.T. v. Spain*; HRC Decision of 29 March 2016 in 2402/2014, *A.A.I. and A.H.A. v. Denmark*; HRC Views of 7 November 2017 in 2594/2015, *K.S. and M.S. v. Denmark.*

33 CEDAW Views of 21 July 2015 in 52/2013 *D.G. v. The Netherlands.*

34 Ibidem, para. 3.

35 HRC Views of 21 July 201 in 1959/2010, *Jama Warsame v. Canada.*

In another case considered by the HRC, regarding deportations and also taking into account the situation of children,[36] the issue of vulnerability appears both in the arguments of the parties and in separate opinions of individual HRC members (critical towards the HRC's failure to see this aspect of the case), but not in the considerations of the HRC which eventually declared the case inadmissible.[37] What is more, in a very similar case which the HRC considered a year earlier, there were references to vulnerability, including some that consequently led to the finding of a violation of the Convention.[38]

The general picture of the attitude of treaty bodies to the concept of vulnerability presented above proves it to be basically incidental and ambiguous in its construal and recall. It is to be noted that the concept of vulnerability appears in different contexts and can be treated differently even by one and the same treaty body. Therefore, in anticipation of a more coherent position and to better understand the nature of vulnerability as seen by the UN treaty bodies, one should perhaps rely primarily on reviews of individual cases brought to the treaty bodies for their consideration.

3. Who has been so far considered vulnerable by the UN treaty bodies?

One of the key issues of the functioning of the concept of vulnerability in international human rights law is the distinction between the vulnerable character of entire specific groups and vulnerability arising from specific, individual characteristics of a person which may or may not be associated with belonging to a particular group. Here, treaty bodies resort to different methods of assessment and there is certainly no established practice in this regard. That notwithstanding, it is worth pointing out a few noticeable trends in the practice of the UN treaty bodies in relation to criteria for classifying individuals and / or groups as vulnerable.

---

36 HRC Decision of 29 March 2016 in 2402/2014, *A.A.I. and A.H.A. v. Denmark*.

37 The applicants cite in their complaint, *inter alia*, ECtHR case-law in similar cases, in which the aspect of vulnerability was raised and taken into account when establishing a violation of the rights and freedoms guaranteed in the ECHR. See para. 31 of the decision.

38 HRC Views of 22 July 2015 in 2360/2014, *Warda Osman Jasin v. Denmark*.

In the case-law of UN treaty bodies, references were made to the following groups found to be vulnerable:

- in the context of indigenous and tribal populations, the CAT considered specific clan communities, weaker than other clans, as being vulnerable;[39]
- victims of torture: in one of the cases considered by the CAT, the applicant claimed that, "[t]he notion of "situation of vulnerability" should not be limited to families with children but should include persons belonging to a particularly vulnerable group, like victims of torture, such as the complainant" (para. 5.7). This view was accepted by the CAT which went on to say that, "the Committee also notes that the complainant has provided three medical reports with very detailed information regarding his vulnerability as a victim of torture" (para. 8.7).[40] Also in another case concerning human rights violations suffered by an individual subjected to torture, the applicant argued that he is a vulnerable person due to being a torture victim (para. 5.3), which was supported in CAT's decision that the state should consider his vulnerability as a victim of torture (para. 9.9);[41]
- the Roma, in the context of the brutal attacks on Roma settlements. In this case CAT referred directly to the vulnerability of the Roma, stating that, 'the burning and destruction of houses constitute, in the circumstances, acts of cruel, inhuman or degrading treatment or punishment. The nature of these acts is further aggravated by the fact that some of the complainants were still hidden in the settlement when the houses were burnt and destroyed, the particular vulnerability of the alleged victims and the fact that the acts were committed with a significant level of racial motivation;[42]
- ethnic minorities in the context of ethnic conflicts;[43]
- persons of African descent,[44] with one particularly interesting aspect in this case being the applicant's reference to her vulnerability as a result of two combined factors: African descent and low social-economic background.

---

39 CAT Views of 14 May 1999 in 120/1998, *S.S. Elmi v. Australia;* CAT Views of 23 November 2001 in 162/2000, *Y.H.A. v. Australia.*

40 CAT Views of 3 August 2018 in 742/2016, *A.N. v. Switzerland.*

41 CAT Views of 6 December 2018 in 758/2016, *Adam Harun v. Switzerland.*

42 CAT Views of 21 November 2002 in 161/2000, *Hajrizi Dzemajl* et al. *v. Yugoslavia*, para. 9.2.

43 CAT Views of 1 December 2016 in 666/2015, *L.P. v. Australia.*

44 CEDAW Views of 27 September 2011 in 17/2008, *Maria de Lourdes da Silva Pimentel v. Brasil.*

However, the CEDAW did not confirm that both of these factors were equally qualifying the applicant as vulnerable. Instead, it rather unclearly stated that women of African descent belong to the most vulnerable sectors of society and that the discrimination they face was exacerbated by regional, economic and social disparities;[45]
- unaccompanied child migrants, being considered a particularly vulnerable group.[46]

The positions expressed by the UN treaty bodies in the abovementioned decisions may suffice to draw the preliminary conclusion that the vulnerable status of the mentioned groups is not fundamentally challenged, irrespective of the particular circumstances of each individual case. Often, however, vulnerability is being recognized by the treaty bodies based purely on the individual situation of persons, very often requiring this to include multiple factors enhancing vulnerability.

The CEDAW found that the vulnerable position of the author of the complaint being reviewed was due to her being an "illiterate migrant woman without a command of Bulgarian or relatives in the State party, and dependent on her husband" (para. 8.5).[47] In another case, vulnerability was based on the combination of two aspects: gender discrimination and discrimination through association of the author of the complaint with her severely disabled child, whom she had been taking care of for 20 years (para. 7.11).[48] One may wonder whether, at least in the former of the two cases just mentioned, only one of the aspects cited should suffice to recognize vulnerability. However, the CEDAW did not touch upon this question.

Although the status of single parenthood alone is not considered a vulnerability, it has been recognized as such in the context of deportation, where the author of the complaint was a 'single mother with no education, with a 5-year-old child, and with no previous integration into Italian society'[49] and where the case concerned a single mother, severely mistreated by her spouse, facing great poverty, with no help from the authorities (in the place where she was supposed to be deported to).[50] This aspect of the assessment by the UN treaty bodies of the situation of asylum

45 Ibidem, para. 7.7.

46 CRC Views of 31 May 2019 in 22/2017, *J.A.B. v. Spain*, para. 13.11.

47 CEDAW Views of 23 July 2012 in 32/2011, *Isatou Jallow v. Bulgaria*.

48 CEDAW Views of 3 May 2016 in 104/2016, *Natalia Ciobanu v. Republic of Moldova*.

49 HRC Views of 29 July 2017 in 2470/2014, *Hibaq Said Hashi v. Denmark*, para. 9.10.

50 HRC Views of 10 March 2017 in 2512/2014, *Raziyeh Rezaifar v. Denmark*, para. 9.9.

seekers/refugees with small children is particularly interesting because it indicates very clearly the lack of transparency in the criteria for recognizing vulnerability.[51] There have been a couple of cases of a family not found to be vulnerable where a father was present:

> The fact that they may possibly be confronted with serious difficulties upon return, in the light of the past traumas suffered by all members of the family, in particular the children, by itself does not necessarily mean that they would be in a special situation of vulnerability – and in a situation significantly different to many other refugee families – such as to conclude that their return to Bulgaria would constitute a violation of the State party's obligations under article 7 of the Covenant.[52]

At the same time, a family with four children who had residence permit in Italy but was homeless there was found to be vulnerable.[53]

Another situation where vulnerability would be intuitively expected to appear as a rule is the deprivation or/and restriction of liberty. In this context, however, the UN treaty bodies do not recognize vulnerability as a matter of course, but they did in fact see as vulnerable a person with disabilities being imprisoned and minorities in criminal proceedings.[54]

More examples of finding vulnerability in specific individual circumstances include a transgender person in the context of arbitrary arrest and detention, deportation and forcible return;[55] a minor who was a refugee and suffering from psychological problems;[56] a pregnant woman after learning that her much-wanted pregnancy was not viable,[57] and human rights defenders whom the HRC described, in the drastic circumstances of the particular case, as "vulnerable as a group."[58]

The UN treaty bodies' case-law contains many other examples of references to vulnerability which, however, complicate even further the attempts to etermine

51 HRC Views of 22 July 2015 in 2360/2014, *Warda Osman Jasin v. Denmark*; HRC Views of 13 July 2018 in 2575/2015, *Bayush Alemseged Araya v. Denmark.*

52 HRC Views of 8 November 2017 in 2585/2015, *M.A.S and L.B.H v. Denmark*, para. 8.12.

53 HRC Views of 10 March 2017 in 2681/2015, *Y.A.A. and F.H.M. v.* Denmark, para. 7.9.

54 HRC Views of 28 October 2016 in 2107/2011, *Berezhnoy v. Russian Federation.*

55 HRC Views of 20 March 2017 in 2593/2015, *MZBM v. Denmark*, para. 6.6.

56 HRC Views of 7 November 2017 in 2770/2016, *O.A. v. Denmark*, para. 8.6.

57 HRC Views of 31 March 2016 in 2324/2013, *Amanda Jane Mellet v. Ireland*, para. 7.4. HRC Views of 17 March 2017 in 2425/2014, *Siobhan Whelan v. Ireland.*

58 HRC, Views of 10 November 2017 in 2610/2015, *Yelitze Lisbeth Moreno de Castillo v. Venezuela*, para. 9.2.

the position of these bodies in relation to this phenomenon. And so, in the HRC's decisions, we find references to someone finding himself or herself "in a situation of great vulnerability"[59] or "in a particular vulnerable situation."[60] It is unclear whether this way of referring to vulnerability carries the same weight as direct applications of this concept: an individual is not referred to as "vulnerable" so only the situation in which this person finds him- or herself in was defined as such. '*The family's vulnerable status*' is yet another unclear term.[61] It would appear from the review of the relevant cases that family members are vulnerable. In the same context, the HRC also stated that it

> considers that the mere fact that the authors may be possibly confronted with difficulties upon their return to Bulgaria does not in itself mean that they would be in a special situation of vulnerability and in a situation significantly different to many other families.[62]

Moreover, the CAT on several occasions noted that the status of vulnerability can change over time – while a group should have been considered vulnerable in the past, this can change as the situation in the country changes.[63]

Another difficulty in interpreting the approach of treaty bodies to vulnerability is the kind of grading they use to assess vulnerability. In the case of an unprotected, unaccompanied migrant child who was ill, the CRC considered them "highly vulnerable."[64] In turn, in a concurring opinion by the HRC's member Yuval Shany we see the expression '*extremely vulnerable person*' in a reference to the deportation of a person suffering from schizophrenia to Jamaica, while all his family and access to medical assistance were associated

---

59 HRC Views of 7 July 2016 in 2379/2014, *Obah Hussein Ahmed v. Denmark*, para. 13.4.

60 HRC Views of 7 July 2016 in 2379/2014, *Obah Hussein Ahmed v. Denmark*, para. 13.8.

61 HRC Views of 22 July 2015 in 2360/2014, *Warda Osman Jasin v. Denmark*, para. 8.9; HRC Views of 7 July 2016 in 2379/2014, *Obah Hussein Ahmed v. Denmark*, para.13.8; HRC Views of 29 March 2016 in 2409/2014, *Abdilafir Abubakar Ali and Mayul Ali Mohamad v. Denmark*, para. 7.8.

62 HRC Views of 28 October 2016 in 2569/2015, *B.M.I. and N.A.K. v. Denmark*, para. 8.6.

63 CAT Views of 23 November 2001, 162/2000, *Y.H.A. v. Australia* para. 7.4; CAT Views of 1 December 2016 in 666/2015, *L.P. v. Australia*, para. 8.9.

64 CRC Views of 31 May 2019 in 22/2017, *J.A.B. v. Spain*, para. 13.11. Interestingly, the CRC in another case, which also concerned a child in migration procedures (the main problem was the use of procedures by the state as for adult migrants), CRC, although it found a violation of the Convention, did not state that the applicant was a vulnerable person or found himself in a vulnerable situation. CRC Views of 18 September 2019 in 17/2017, *M.T. v. Spain*.

with Canada. There was also this said regarding the special situation of pregnant women who should generally be considered a vulnerable group: "a pregnant woman in a highly vulnerable position after learning that her much-wanted pregnancy was not viable."[65]

4. Conclusions

The eminent Polish writer and 2018 Literature Nobel Prize Winner Olga Tokarczuk observed that "[t]enderness is deep emotional concern about another being, its fragility, its unique nature, and its lack of immunity to suffering."[66] In saying that Tokarczuk also masterfully defined the very notion of vulnerability which is what she sees fragility, unique nature, and lack of immunity to suffering, caused by discrimination, hatred and other forms of human rights violations to be.

There can be no doubt that the notion of vulnerability is gaining popularity not only in the discussions on the social dimensions of discrimination and disadvantaged groups but also in legal scholarship, in conversations about proposed changes and amendments to the international human rights protection treaties or in the case-law of international human rights protection bodies.[67] At the same time it must be stressed that there is as yet no legally binding definition of the term, which makes it that much more ambiguous and confusing.[68] Furthermore, disputes abound concerning the very meaning, scope and implications of the concept of vulnerability and the consequences of including

---

65 HRC Views of 31 March 2016 in 2324/2013, *Amanda Jane Mellet v. Ireland*, para. 7.4.

66 O. Tokarczuk, *The Tender Narrator*, Nobel Lecture by Olga Tokarczuk, Nobel Laureate in Literature 2018, [online:] https://www.nobelprize.org/uploads/2019/12/tokarczuk-lecture-english-2.pdf, p. 24 [available: 23.10.2020].

67 E.g. A.H.E, Morawa, "Vulnerability as a Concept of International Human Rights Law," *Journal of International Relations and Development* 2003, Vol. 6. No. 2; A. Chapman, B. Carbonetti, "Human Rights Protections for Vulnerable and Disadvantaged Groups: The Contributions of the UN Committee on Economic, Social and Cultural Rights," *Human Rights Quarterly* 2011, Vol. 33; L. Peroni, A. Timmer, "Vulnerable groups: The promise of an emerging concept in European Human Rights Convention law," *International Journal of Constitutional Law* 2013, Vol. 11, No. 4; O. M. Arnardóttir, "Vulnerability under Article 14 of the European Convention on Human Rights. Innovation or Business as Usual?," *Oslo Law Review* 2017, Vol. 3; D. Estrada – Tanck, *Human Security and Human Rights under International Law: The Protections Offered to Persons Confronting Structural Vulnerability*, Oxford 2016.

68 L. Peroni, A. Timmer, "Vulnerable groups," p. 1058.

the notion in the catalogue of international human rights protection tools aimed at advancing the protection of rights and freedoms of the most disadvantaged groups and individuals. This is also fully confirmed in the current position and understanding of the concept of vulnerability within the UN human rights protection treaty system. Another great writer, cited at the beginning of this chapter, Zadie Smith, stresses the need to use instruments for protection of vulnerable persons which are "far stronger than empathy." And yet the UN treaty bodies human rights protection system has not yet created a sufficiently strong basis for building an effective and law-based protective shield for vulnerable individuals and groups.

The research into the concept of vulnerability in the UN human rights treaty bodies protection system reported in this chapter shows, above all else, the continuing absence of consolidated and uniform reference by UN human rights treaty bodies to vulnerability. The relatively recent introduction of the category of vulnerable groups into the language of human rights law results in it having found its way into only a very limited number of treaty provisions, and in a highly variegated approach of the various treaty bodies to classifying and even referring to vulnerable in relation to particular situations of individuals or groups. Thus, the notion and category of vulnerability still needs strengthening and systematization. At present only an extremely limited number of features warrants the definition of an individual or group as particularly vulnerable in a manner that would not generate major controversy. Based on the existing *acquis* of the treaty system, it cannot be said with confidence that the construal and functioning of the concept of vulnerability in the area of human rights law is as postulated and formulated in the emerging scholarship on the subject[69] where, in general, the following is acknowledged and distinguished: (a) vulnerability related to personal constraints where some groups are identified as vulnerable due to their fragile physical or mental condition, e.g. children, persons with disabilities, older people and pregnant women. This kind of vulnerability is closely connected to the physical fragility of the persons belonging to these groups, but also (which should be treated as one of the distinguishing features of vulnerability) because of the social perception of such persons as weaker, more prone to become victims of human rights violations, as not being able to protect themselves from various forms of abuse; and (b) vulnerability related to

69 Based on research proposal concerning the notion of vulnerability in international human rights law authored by A. Gliszczyńska-Grabais, G. Baranowska, K. Sękowska-Kozłowska, A.Hernandez-Pełczyńska (unpublished).

social position where some groups are identified as vulnerable due to structural discrimination or disadvantage they experience (e.g. the Roma people, indigenous people and religious minorities) or the critical situation they face (e.g. refugees, migrants and internally displaced persons). This classification seems to reliably and rationally reflect the essence of the concept of vulnerability, but its legal sanctioning and rooting in the universal human rights protection system is for now still a matter of the future.

The unprecedented crisis caused by the current global pandemic creates new challenges for the entire universal system of human rights protection – probably the most serious since its inception, and subjects its functioning to a serious test. Situations of the kind we are now seeing always result in restrictions of the rights and freedoms of individuals – extremely sever in this case – and very often tend to be exploited in an abusive manner by authorities with authoritarian leanings. In such circumstances, the protection of the rights of the most vulnerable groups remains the basic obligation of not just human rights activists but also of legal scholars and researchers studying human rights protection systems. We hope that this chapter will turn out to be one modest step on the road to the fulfilment of this obligation.

Bibliography:

Alston P. (ed.), *The United Nations and Human Rights. A Critical Appraisal*, Oxford 1992.

Arnardóttir O. M., "Vulnerability under Article 14 of the European Convention on Human Rights. Innovation or Business as Usual?," *Oslo Law Review* 2017, Vol. 3.

Belavusau U., Henrard K. (eds.), *EU Anti-Discrimination Law beyond Gender*, Oxford 2018.

Çalı B., Costello C., Cunnigham S., "Hard Protection through Soft Courts? Non-Refoulement before the United Nations Treaty Bodies," *German Law Journal* 2020, Vol. 21.

Chapman A., Carbonetti B., "Human Rights Protections for Vulnerable and Disadvantaged Groups: The Contributions of the UN Committee on Economic, Social and Cultural Rights," *Human Rights Quarterly* 2011, Vol. 33.

Estrada – Tanck D., *Human Security and Human Rights under International Law: The Protections Offered to Persons Confronting Structural Vulnerability*, Oxford 2016.

Morawa A.H.E., "Vulnerability as a Concept of International Human Rights Law," *Journal of International Relations and Development* 2003, Vol. 6. No. 2.

Morsink J., "The Universal Declaration and the Conscience of Humanity," [in:] *Human Rights and History. A Challenge for Education*, R. Huhle (ed.), Berlin 2010.

Osiatyński W., *Human rights and their limits*, Cambridge 2009.

Peroni L., Timmer A., "Vulnerable groups: The promise of an emerging concept in European Human Rights Convention law," *International Journal of Constitutional Law* 2013, Vol. 11, No. 4.

van Boven T., "Combating Racial Discrimination in the World and in Europe," *Netherlands Quarterly of Human Rights* 1993, Vol. 11, No. 2.

Elżbieta Hanna Morawska

Cardinal Stefan Wyszynski University

e-mail: e.morawska@uksw.edu.pl

ORCID ID: 0000-0001-7299-0320

The European Court of Human Rights towards group vulnerability: an open-ended approach

Abstract: The subject matter of this chapter has been inspired by the ECtHR's granting of the status of particularly vulnerable groups to certain groups. It focuses on establishing the basic characteristics of this new approach to vulnerability, and thus on defining and assessing its personal and material scope. It therefore identifies the key issues for this approach and then analyses them in detail. One of these issues is the prohibition of discrimination against particularly vulnerable groups. It should be stressed that the ECtHR, when assessing an allegation of violation of this prohibition, does not take into account the personal status or personal characteristics of that group, but refers to the social context of complex and deeply rooted disadvantages for that groups.

A review of the case-law of the ECtHR indicates that this approach to vulnerability is not sufficiently well established to be regarded as consistent. The analysis also shows that it is difficult to consider this approach as sufficiently well as being structured and transparent. What is more, it does not dominate the case-law; in fact, the approach in question is limited in many respects. This inconsistency, as well as the caution in developing it, seems to be due to the lack of a common concept of vulnerability, because it is diverse and multi-faceted.

Keywords: European Convention on Human Rights, European Court of Human Rights, group vulnerability, determinants of vulnerability, prohibition of discrimination, socio-economic dimension of the ECHR

1. Introductory remarks

In 1981, the European Court of Human Rights (hereinafter: Court/ECtHR) examined the complaint of Mr. Dudgeon,[1] which concerned the existence in

1 The relevant judgments of the Court referred to in this paper can be found in the HUDOC database at www.echr.coe.int.

the criminal law of Northern Ireland of various offenses related to the homosexual behavior of men and police investigation. In his view, the provisions constituted an unjustified interference with his right to respect for his privacy life based on the violation of art. 8 (Article 8) of the European Convention of Human Rights[2] (hereinafter: Convention/ECHR), and violated the prohibition of discrimination within the meaning of art. 14 (Article 14) of the Convention on grounds of sex, sexuality and place of residence.[3] While considering this case, the Court drew attention to persons "who are young, weak in body or mind or inexperienced or in a state of physical, moral or economic dependence" and then recognized them as "especially vulnerable."[4] In doing so, the Court referred for the first time in case-law to the concept of vulnerability. However, it did not define it, but only indicated its determinants, such as age, physical condition, mental abilities, experience and physical, moral and social dependence.[5]

The Court then applied vulnerability determinants in the case of *Stubbings and Others v. the UK* of 1996, examining the applicants' allegations regarding the infringement of Article 8 of the ECHR in connection with acts of sexual abuse in childhood. In its response, the Court stated that

> sexual abuse is undoubtedly a disgusting type of crime that destroys its victims. Children and other vulnerable persons are entitled to State protection in the form of effective deterrence, against such grave types of interference with essential aspects of their private lives.[6]

The separation of children from vulnerable persons is part of the Court's case-law initiated in *Dudgeon*. For, as C. Dröge rightly points out, the need to protect children against sexual abuse is becoming increasingly apparent as it may harm their health or physical, mental, moral or social development and their sense of personal dignity in a special and extremely durable way.[7]

---

2 Convention for the Protection of Human Rights and Fundamental Freedoms, CETS: No. 005, opened for signature in Rome on 4 November 1950. Commonly known as the European Convention on Human Rights.

3 ECtHR, *Dudgeon v. the UK* (App. No. 7525/76), judgment of 22 November 1981, para. 49; 62.

4 Ibidem.

5 Ibidem.

6 ECtHR, *Stubbings and Others v. the UK* (App. No. 22083/93 22095/93), judgment of 22 October 1996, para. 64.

7 C. Dröge, *Positive Verpflichtungen der Staaten in der Europäischen Menschenrechtskonvention*, Berlin 2003, p. 324; see also ECtHR, *Mubilanzila Mayeka*

Moreover, since the early years of the twenty-first century, the Court has begun to recognize clearly selected groups of persons as particularly vulnerable. In this way, it embraced a distinction between group and individual vulnerability.[8]

With this in mind, the chapter examines the main elements of the "group vulnerability case-law" developed by the Court. This analysis is legal and therefore omits the philosophical and political aspects of vulnerability. In addition, this analysis is intended to provide a thorough insight into the ECtHR's case-law in order to determine how the Court applies group vulnerability in its case-law. At the same time, this analysis is not intended to provide a detailed description of the ECtHR's case-law as such. Rather, it seeks to answer the questions concerning the process of categorizing particularly vulnerable groups, the types of justifications for their differentiation, and the implications of these distinctions, both in the field of human rights and fundamental freedoms and the obligations of States Parties.

It is important to emphasize that the chapter places a primary focus on the group approach, meaning it does not deal with those cases in which the Court finds that the applicant is in a vulnerable position individually, especially in cases concerning prisoners or children, as these are not based on a group-centred analysis.[9]

To properly address these research problems, a number of detailed research questions needed to be posed; they were definitional, praxeological, and explanatory, not least as these are general problems that go beyond the implicit, concrete facts of the case. Given that, on the one hand, the concept of vulnerable groups has a specific meaning in the Court's case-law, and on the other hand, the meaning of vulnerability is "imprecise and questioned,"[10] this will not be an easy task.

---

and Kaniki Mitunga v. Belgium (App. No. 13178/03), judgment of 12 November 2006, para. 5.

8 ECtHR, *Uzan v. Ukraine* (App. No. 51243/08), judgment of 18 February 2010, para. 34.

9 A similar approach was followed by A. Timmer, "A Quiet Revolution: Vulnerability in the European Court of Human Rights," [in:] *Vulnerability: Reflections on a New Ethical Foundation for Law and Politics*, eds. M. Fineman, A. Grear, Farnham 2013, pp. 152–161; see also, M. Bossuyt, "Categorical rights and Vulnerable Groups: Moving Away from the Universal Human Being," *The George Washington International Law Review* 2016, Vol. 48.

10 L. Peroni, A. Timmer, "Vulnerable groups: The promise of an emerging concept in European Human Rights Convention law," *International Journal of Constitutional Law* 2013, Vol. 11, No. 4, p. 1058.

2. Categories of vulnerable groups in the case law of the ECtHR

At the present stage of the development of the Strasbourg case-law, several vulnerable groups can be distinguished, but seven of them are leading. They include the Roma population, mentally disabled persons, people living with HIV, persons with a physical disability, and finally, asylum seekers.

Nevertheless, the above list is by no means a sealed catalog and the Court holds that other populations may be considered vulnerable if there are good reasons for it. It can therefore be said that the catalog of vulnerability groups is neither closed-ended or homogeneous.[11]

Hence, in order to obtain a more complete picture of the Court's case-law, other vulnerability groups are considered below alongside the leading ones.

2.1. Roma population

As regards the first group, the Roma population, the 2001 Grand Chamber judgment in *Chapman v. the UK* of 2001 is of key importance.[12] In this case, the applicant called on the Court to consider then recent international events in limiting the margin of appreciation granted to States in the light of the examination problems of particularly vulnerable groups such as Gypsies.[13] The Court responded as follows:

> [T]here may be said to be an emerging international consensus amongst the Contracting States of the Council of Europe recognising the special needs of minorities and an obligation to protect their security, identity and lifestyle. . ., not only for the purpose of safeguarding the interests of the minorities themselves but to preserve a cultural diversity of value to the whole community.[14]

The above statement requires two brief comments. First, immediately after, the Court added that the above consensus did not seem detailed enough for it to formulate any guidance on ensuring "the specific needs of minorities and the

---

11 L. Peroni and A. Timmer underline: "what exactly ties all these groups together is still not entirely clear, as the Court has not (yet) fully developed a coherent set of indicators to determine what renders a group vulnerable." See, L. Peroni, A. Timmer, "Vulnerable groups: The promise of an emerging concept in European Human Rights Convention law", *International Journal of Constitutional Law* 2013, Vol. 11, No. 4, p. 1064.

12 ECtHR, *Chapman v. the UK* (App. No. 27238/95), judgment of 18 January 2001.

13 Ibidem, para. 93.

14 Ibidem.

obligation to protect their security, identity and lifestyle."[15] As a consequence, the Court reaffirmed its view of the complexity and sensitivity of political issues balancing the interests of the general public, in particular in the field of environmental protection, and the interests of minorities with potentially conflicting requirements, which reduces its role to one that is strictly supervisory.[16] Additionally, the Court's reference to the European consensus and the requirement of a fair balance of the interests of the individual with the interest of the community indicates that the Court made the above findings assessing whether the interference with the right to respect for private and family life (Article 8 ECHR) was "necessary in a democratic society" for legitimate purposes and responded to the "pressing social need," in particular whether it was proportionate to the legitimate aim pursued.[17]

Secondly, it is worth noting that the main documents of international law regarding the protection of human rights or minorities usually do not define the term "minorities." It is assumed in the academic literature that it is up to each state to make its own decisions in this regard, depending on the social context and internal political situation. The Court has nevertheless provided the decisive elements of the specific characteristics of ethnic groups, stating that "ethnicity has its source in the ideas of social groups marked by a common nationality, tribal affiliation, religious faith, common language or cultural and traditional origin and backgrounds."[18]

2.2. Ethnic Uzbeks in the southern regions of Kyrgyzstan

At the same time, the Court has so far pointed to the need to preserve the cultural diversity of the entire community only in relation to the Roma population. This aspect of the Court's group approach to the Roma population was, however, due to the nature of the allegations of Roma people. In other words, the Court's main objective is not to build a comprehensive, theoretical concept of group vulnerability, but to verify the existence of a particular violation of

15 Ibidem, para. 93.

16 See also ECtHR, *Beard v. the UK* (App. No. 24882/94), judgment of 18 January 2001; ECtHR, *Coster v. the UK* (App. No. 24876/94), judgment of 18 January 2001; ECtHR, *Jane Smith v. the UK* (App. No. 25154/94), judgment of 18 January 2001; ECtHR, *Lee v. the UK* (App. No. 25154/94), judgment of 18 January 2001.

17 ECtHR, *Chapman v. the UK* (App. No. 27238/95), judgment of 18 January 2001, para. 90.

18 ECtHR, *Timishev v. Russia* (App. No. 55762/00 55974/00), judgment of 13 December 2005, para. 55.

the Convention. Hence, in examining the alleged violation of the Convention, which is different from previous violations, the Court may indicate another aspect of the group's vulnerability. This was the case with the allegations of violation of the Convention put forward by ethnic Uzbeks living in southern Kyrgyzstan.

The Court's findings showed that ethnic Uzbeks were a group that had been systematically exposed to torture and other ill-treatment by law-enforcement agencies.[19] This was associated with the ethnic riots that broke out at the Kyrgyz-Uzbek border on June 10, 2010. The riots began in Osh and quickly spread throughout the region, also reaching the Jalat-Abad region. Importantly, they soon became violent, a fact which prompted the government to declare a state of emergency and issue a shoot-to-kill policy to stop the violence. However, it was not until June 14 that the situation was brought under control and sporadic clashes continued in the following days. As many as 470 people were killed during the riots while thousands were injured and displaced.[20]

The Court examined the above circumstances in its judgments regarding the complaints submitted by ethnic Uzbeks against the Russian Federation on its refusal to grant refugee status and decision on expulsion or extradition to Kyrgyzstan or Uzbekistan. The standard formula in the judgments reads as follows:

> Given the widespread use by the Kyrgyz authorities of torture and ill-treatment in order to obtain confessions from ethnic Uzbeks charged with involvement in the inter-ethnic riots in the Jalal-Abad Region, which has been reported by both UN bodies and reputable NGOs [Amnesty International and Human Rights Watch], the Court is satisfied that the applicant belongs to a particularly vulnerable group, the members of which are routinely subjected in Kyrgyzstan to treatment proscribed by Article 3 of the Convention.[21]

19 ECtHR, *R. v. Russia* (App. No. 11916/15), judgment of 26 January 2016, para. 61–62.

20 K. Toktomushev, *Kyrgyzstan – Regime Security and Foreign Policy*, Routledge: 2017, p. 114.

21 ECtHR, *Turgunov v. Russia* (App. No. 15590/14), judgment of 22 November 2015; *R. v. Russia* (App. No. 11916/15), judgment of 26 January 2016; *Khamrakulov v. Russia* (App. No. 68894/13), judgment of 16 April 2015; *Gayratbek Saliyev v. Russia* (App. No. 39093/13), judgment of 17 April 2014; *Nabid Abdullayev v. Russia* (App. No. 8474/14), judgment of 15 November 2015; *Kadirzhanov and Mamashev v. Russia* (App. No. 42351/13 47823/13), judgment of 17 July 2014.

It should be added that the Court has generalized this approach, both in relation to the ethnic riots of June 2010 and to ethnic Uzbeks.[22] A similar stance can be observed in the case of *Mukhitdinov v. Russia* of 2015, where

> constant position that the individuals, whose extradition was sought by the Uzbek authorities on charges of religiously or politically motivated crimes, constituted a vulnerable group, running a real risk of treatment contrary to Article 3 of the Convention in the event of their transfer to Uzbekistan.[23]

Although in the case at issue, the Court refers to a vulnerable group, and not to a particularly vulnerable group, it is, after all, an insignificant difference that does not seem to change the essence of the Court's position.

2.3 Political opposition in Belarus, Kazakhstan, and Uzbekistan

Moreover, the review of the case-law shows that terminological inconsistency is somewhat characteristic of Strasbourg practice. This can also be seen in those judgments in which the Court addresses the political opposition in Belarus, referring to it as "widely recognized as a particularly vulnerable group in Belarus."[24]

Although the Court attributes vulnerability to the political opposition in Belarus without any justification, it can be concluded from the context of the case that the key to this attribution is the serious risk of ill-treatment or an unfair trial in the future.[25] This threat is also essential for adding the political opposition in Kazakhstan and Uzbekistan to particularly vulnerable groups.[26]

All in all, it can be said that since the *Saadi v. Italy* case, the Court has been increasingly inclined to generally recognize "a group systematically exposed

---

22 ECtHR, *Egamberdiyev v. Russia* (App. No. 34742/13), judgment of 26 June 2014; ECtHR, *Akram Karimov v. Russia* (App. No. 62892/12), judgment of 28 May 2014; ECtHR, *Nizamov and Others v. Russia* (App. Nos. 22636/13, 24034/13, 2403334/13 and 24528/13), judgment of 7 May 2014, with further references.

23 ECtHR, *Mukhitdinov v. Russia* (App. No. 20999/14), judgment of 21.05.2015, para. 45.

24 ECtHR, *Puzan v. Ukraine* (App. No. 51243/08, of 18 February 2010, para. 34; ECtHR, *Kamyshev v. Ukraine* (App. No. 3990/06), 20 May 2010, para. 41.

25 ECtHR *Padalevicius v. Lithuania* (App. No. 12278/03), judgment of 7 July 2009, para. 71.

26 ECtHR, *Dzhaksybergenov v. Ukraine* (App. No. No. 12343/10), 10 February 2011, para. 37; ECtHR, *Elmuratov v. Russia* (App. No. 66317/09), judgment of 3 March 2011.

to the practice of ill-treatment" in a third country as particularly vulnerable, although it retains to this day a level of restraint in this respect.[27]

2.4 Asylum seekers as particularly underprivileged and vulnerable

As for today, asylum seekers are the last group that the Court has recognized as vulnerable. The leading case regarding the vulnerability of asylum seekers is *M.S.S. v. Belgium and Greece*. Essentially, it concerns Afghan asylum seekers who were forwarded by the Belgian authorities to Greece under the EU Dublin II Regulation. Regarding his detention, the Court emphasized that "the applicant, who was an asylum seeker, was particularly vulnerable because of everything he had undergone during the migration and the traumatic experiences he probably had before."[28]

In the case of that population group, the Court speaks of "a particularly underprivileged and vulnerable population group."[29] The analysis of the case-law shows that this group approach is used by the Court in a strictly defined context, namely in relation to the material conditions of detention of asylum seekers.[30]

The Court seems to use the term 'asylum-seeker' deliberately. This means that the beneficiaries of this protection are not only refugees. This, in turn, has far-reaching implications. The notion 'refugee' is defined by the 1951 Refugee Convention, the key legal document of International Refugee Law. It also outlines refugee rights, as well as the general obligations of States to protect them. Refugee status is, however, obtained only if the person is recognized as such by the authority that has determined that the relevant conditions laid out in the Geneva Convention are met. On the other hand, no conditions need to be met, and no procedure followed, to become an asylum seeker, for anyone seeking asylum in a country other than his or her own is an asylum seeker.

It should also be added at this point that categories of persons other than asylum seekers can be considered a particularly underprivileged and vulnerable group, meaning this is not a homogeneous category. At least two such groups should be distinguished; these are children seeking asylum and

---

27 ECtHR, *M.S. v. Slovakia and Ukraine* (App. No. 17189/11), 11 June 2020, paras. 113–120.

28 ECtHR, *M.S.S. v. Belgium and Greece* (App. No. 30696/09), judgment of 21 January 2011, para. 232.

29 Ibidem, para. 251.

30 Ibidem, para. 161.

internally displaced persons. Let us first have a look at the status of asylum-seeking children.

2.4.1 Asylum-seeking children

As already remarked above, the Court explicitly identifies children as vulnerable persons, but it generally applies an individual approach to them. In the context of asylum, however, the Court seems to combine the individual vulnerability approach with the group approach, stating that "it is important to bear in mind that the child's extreme vulnerability is the decisive factor and takes precedence over considerations relating to the status of illegal immigrant," while also asserting that "children have specific needs that are related in particular to their age and lack of independence, but also to their asylum-seeker status."[31]

This seems to be a deliberate strategy aimed at strengthening the protection of the child's rights and fundamental freedoms in the asylum procedure, in particular in cases of child detention. However, from the point of view of constructing the concept of group vulnerability, such statements are misleading and introduce ambiguity.

2.4.2. Internally displaced persons

The second group of persons recognized as particularly underprivileged and vulnerable consists of internally displaced persons (IDP). However, the Court has ruled so only in two cases concerning persons resettled to their new place of residence in Baku during the armed conflict between Azerbaijan and Armenia over the Nagorno-Karabakh.[32]

The context of these cases is therefore completely different from the *M.S.S.* case. Also, the subject of the Court's examination is not the conditions of detention, but the loss of home, possessions, and sources of income due to applicants' displacement.

31 ECtHR, *Tarakhel* v. *Switzerland* (App. No. 29217/12), judgment of 4 November 2014, para. 99; ECtHR, *Popov v. France* (App. No. 39472/07 39474/07), judgment of 19 January 2012, para. 91; ECtHR, *Abdullahi Elmi and Aweys Abubakar v. Malta* (App. No. 25794/13 28151/13), judgment of 22 November 2016, para. 103.

32 ECtHR, *Chiragov and Others v. Armenia* (App. No. 13216/05) decision of 14 December 2011, para. 146; *Sargsyan v. Azerbaijan* (App. No. 40167/06) decision of 14 December 2011, para. 145.

2.5 Persons with mental disorders and people living with HIV

Before turning to the presentation of the last two groups considered by the Court to be particularly vulnerable, let us first go back to the issue of "extreme vulnerability." In the case of *Centre For Legal Resources On Behalf Of Valentin Vâmpeanu v. Romania*, the Court stated the following:

> Extreme vulnerability of a person is a broad concept that should include, for the above purposes, people of tender age, or elderly, gravely sick or disabled people, people belonging to minorities, or groups subject to discrimination based on race, ethnicity, sex, sexual orientation or any other ground.[33]

This statement is important in determining the scope and application of the group vulnerability approach. Not only does the Court explicitly apply this approach, but it also links it with the prohibition of discrimination in exercising the rights and fundamental freedoms. Therefore, it could be assumed that art. 14 ECHR becomes the normative basis for the analyzed approaches to vulnerability, although this is not the only such basis. On the other hand, the review of the case-law shows that the Court expressly uses the term 'vulnerability' in relation to the prohibition of discrimination only in the case of persons with mental disorders and those living with HIV. This issue is examined in more detail below, but for now, it is reasonable to identify this particularly problematic and important aspect and indicate the Court's practice in relation to it.[34]

2.5.1 Persons with mental disorders

As stated above, persons with mental disorders are one of the groups explicitly recognized by the Court as particularly vulnerable in the context of the prohibition of discrimination. The Court confirmed this stance in 2010 when resolving the complaint of *Alajos Kiss v. Hungary*.[35] This recognition is not surprising given that the vulnerability of persons with disabilities has been present in Strasbourg case-law for many years. It is now a broadly understood,

---

33 ECtHR, *Centre For Legal Resources On Behalf Of Valentin Vâmpeanu v. Romania* (App. No. 47848/08), judgment of 17 July 2014, para. 11.

34 In the *Y v. Turkey* case, the Court examined whether the applicant had suffered degrading and discriminatory treatment due to his HIV status because of the hospital medical staff of the emergency and intensive care units in the Istanbul Teaching and Research Hospital, and was therefore treated in a manner inconsistent with the art. 8 EKPC and 14: ECtHR, *Y. v. Turkey* (App. No. 648/10), decision of 17 February 2015.

35 ECtHR, *Alajos Kiss v. Hungary*, (App. No. 38832/06), judgment of 20 May 2010.

multidimensional topic providing an important pivot for state responsibility under the ECHR and the Protocol.[36] Therefore, this group approach to vulnerability is not just about mental disability, although mental disabilities are indeed subject to special consideration under it. Strasbourg case-law can therefore be regarded in this respect as well established.[37]

It is worth emphasizing, however, that the Court applies this approach both towards disabled persons remaining "under the exclusive control of domestic authorities"[38] and to persons living outside this control, i.e. at home with their family.[39] Nevertheless, in the latter case, the ECtHR applies a group approach to vulnerability only in extreme and exceptional circumstances, which can be explained by its doubts about the legitimacy of the excessive extension of the social dimension of the Convention.[40]

In turn, detention is an example of the place where disabled persons are subject to the exclusive control of domestic authorities. As a result, the Court's approach to the vulnerability of detainees is becoming increasingly diverse and complex, as the group approach is not the only approach used by the Court. On the contrary, the Court usually takes an individual approach to the vulnerability of persons in detention or speaks of their vulnerable position.[41]

There is one more important thing to note here and that is detention being understood in a broad sense, the consequence of which is that a group approach to persons with mental disorders in criminal detention ends up applying to non-criminal forms of detention as well, such as compulsory psychiatric hospitalization.[42]

36 ECtHR, *Z.H. v. Hungary* (App. No. 28973/11), judgment of 8 November 2012, para. 29.
37 ECtHR, *Cînța v. Romania* (App. No. 3891/19), judgment of 18 February 2020, para. 41.
38 ECtHR, *O'Keeffe v. Ireland* (App. No. 35810/09), judgment of 28 January 2014, para. 145.
39 ECtHR, *Guberina v. Croatia* (App. No. 23682/13), judgment of 22 March 2016.
40 C. Dröge, *Positive Verpflichtungen der Staaten in der Europäischen Menschenrechtskonvention*, Springer, Berlin 2003, pp. 109–114.
41 ECtHR, *Z.H. v. Hungary* (App. No. 28973/11), judgment of 08 November 2012, para. 42; ECtHR, *Mihailovs v. Latvia* (App. No. 35939/10), judgment of 22 January 2013, para. 149; ECtHR, *Schweizerische Radio- Und Fernsehgesellschaft SRG v. Switzerland* (App. No. 34124/06), judgment of 21 June 2012.
42 ECtHR, *Fernandes de Oliveira v. Portugal* (App. No. 78103/14), judgment of 31 January 2019, para. 113.

2.5.2 People living with HIV

As already established, 'persons living with HIV' are another particularly vulnerable population. Here, special attention should be drawn to the judgment in *Kiyutin v. Russia* of 2011, in which the Court adopted this stance for the first time. Although the Court's argumentation drew from the *Alajos Kiss* case,[43] currently it is the case *Novruk and Others v. Russia* of 2016 that seems to be the leading one in case-law.

In that case, the Court ruled that art. 14 was violated in connection with art. 8 because of the discriminatory treatment of HIV-infected foreigners under the residence permit procedure (since, due to the HIV virus, they were permanently banned from returning to Russia). The decisions made by the Russian authorities, including by Russia's domestic courts, assumed that HIV-positive non-nationals would engage in specific unsafe behaviors and that nationals would also fail to protect themselves. According to the Court, that assumption is an unjustified generalization having no basis in fact and failing to consider the specific situation of the applicants.[44]

3. The determinants of particular groups vulnerability in the case law of the ECtHR

The above findings show that, despite the predominance of the individual approach to the protection of vulnerable groups in today's international law, the Court is gradually, on a case-to-case basis, developing a separate approach to specific groups.

Unfortunately, the Court avoids formulating the general definition of group vulnerability and does not indicate its premises, making it difficult to establish general principles determining whether a group can be considered vulnerable or is excluded from such recognition.[45] Let us consider the example of persons covered by social security. To date, the Court has not once applied the group

43 ECtHR, *Kiyutin v. Russia* (App. No. 2700/10), judgment of 10 March 2011, para. 63–64.

44 ECtHR, *Novruk and Others v. Russia* (App. No. 31039/11 48511/11 76810/12 et *al*, judgment of 15 March 2016.

45 According to Peroni and Timmer, the case-law reveals "some blanks or inconsistencies," because "there are more groups that could have fallen within the notion of vulnerable groups" such as "national minorities, religious minorities and LGBT people." See, L. Peroni, A. Timmer, "Vulnerable groups: The promise of an emerging concept in European Human Rights Convention law," *International Journal of Constitutional Law* 2013, Vol. 11, No. 4, p. 1056.

approach to any such persons, although it has stressed their vulnerability on many occasions.[46] The Court tends to state the following:

> [I]n considering whether the interference imposed an excessive individual burden the Court will have regard to the particular context in which the issue arises, namely that of a social-security scheme. Such schemes are an expression of a society's solidarity with its vulnerable members.[47]

The case-law analysis also shows that the Court uses different approaches to vulnerability towards the same group of persons. This is demonstrated by the example of "particular vulnerability of the victims of domestic violence."[48] While in the *Opuz* case, and subsequently in the *Bevacqua and S.* case, the Court adopted a group approach,[49] in the *Valiulienė* case it assessed the problem of women as victims of domestic violence in terms of individual vulnerability.[50] It did the same in *Volodin,*[51] despite stressing that

> [T]he issues of domestic violence, which can take various forms – ranging from physical assault to sexual, economic, emotional, or verbal abuse – transcends the circumstances of an individual case. It is a general problem which affects, to a varying degree, all member States and which does not always surface since it often takes place within personal relationships or closed circuits and affects different family members, although women make up an overwhelming majority of victims.[52]

Furthermore, in the *Opuz* case, the Court coined a new term to refer to the victims of domestic violence, namely "the group of «vulnerable individuals» entitled to State protection."[53] This inconsistent approach to the vulnerability of victims of domestic violence proves that the Court has not yet developed a

---

46 See, Y. Al Tamimi, "The protection of Vulnerable Groups and Individuals by the European Court of Human Rights," *European Journal of Human Rights* 2016, Vol. 5, p. 23.

47 ECtHR, *Iwaszkiewicz v. Poland*, (App. No. 30614/06), judgment of 26 July 2011, para. 49; ECtHR, *Fábián v. Hungary* (App. No. 78117/13), judgment of 05/09/2017, para. 118.

48 ECtHR, *Bevacqua and S. v. Bulgaria* (App. No. 71127/01), judgment of 12 June 2008, para. 65.

49 ECtHR, *Opuz v. Turkey* (App. No. 33401/02), judgment of 9 June 2009, para. 132; ECtHR, *Bevacqua, and S.* (App. No.71127/01), judgment of 12 June 2008, para. 65.

50 ECtHR, *Valiulienė v. Lithuania* (App. No. 33234/07), judgment of 26 March 2013.

51 ECtHR, *Hajduová V. Slovakia* (App. No. 2660/03), judgment of 30 November 2010; ECtHR, *B. v. The Republic of Moldova* (App. No. 61382/09), judgment of 16 July 2013.

52 ECtHR, *Volodina v. Russia* (App. No. 41261/17), judgment of 9 July 2019, para. 71.

53 ECtHR, *Remetin v. Croatia* (App. No. 29525/10), judgment of 11 December 2012, para. 91.

uniform approach to this issue.[54] Similar conclusions can be drawn regarding the Court's approach to children's vulnerability: although their vulnerability is recognized in the individual approach, cases can be identified where the Court refers to "vulnerable groups such as children."[55]

The determinants of vulnerability of given groups is another research problem. Generally, the legal literature tends to accuse the Court for often failing to specify the determining factors of a group's vulnerability. This assessment is confirmed by the case-law review. For example, in the *Chapman* case, the Court did not indicate the reason why the Roma are considered vulnerable. This lack of justification is not limited just to the group approach, because the Court has not yet explained the determinants of vulnerability, e.g. in relation to children. In its judgments, the Court quite often does not mention the reasons for the recognition of a given group as vulnerable, even if such fact has already been established in earlier cases. It also happens that the Court uses different terms in the 'new' justifications of group vulnerability or omits certain aspects. Moreover, if the Court indicates the reasons for vulnerability, it almost never explains why they should be considered a constitutive premise for the vulnerability of a group. Thus, the identification of vulnerability determinants requires a thorough case-law analysis. As a rule, however, the first cases tend to be the source of key findings in this regard.

In the light of the case-law analysis, five main types of justification for recognizing a given population as a vulnerable group can be identified. Just like the catalog of these groups, they are not internally uniform. The predominant position has a justified reasoning containing a specific historical aspect, i.e. exposure in the past to prejudices with lasting consequences causing the social exclusion of a group. As part of that justification, the Court refers to "turbulent

---

54 See also strong criticism of the Court's position contained in the separate opinion of judge Pinto de Albuquerque, joined by judge Dedov, on the judgment by the ECtHR of 9 July 2019 in the *Volodina v. Russia* (App. No. 41261/17). Interestingly, in proposing a list of vulnerable groups in *Kiyutin* and including the gender criterion, the Court did not mention the line taken in *Opuz* but referred to the judgments under Article 14 of the ECHR and consequently its classic approach as laid down in *Abdulaziz, Cabales and Balkandali v. the UK*, (App. No 921480 et al), judgment of 28 May 1985.

55 ECtHR, *Cevrioğlu v. Turkey* (App. No. 69546/12), judgment of 4 November 2016, para. 67; ECtHR, *Zinatullin v. Russia* (App. No. 10551/10), judgment of 28 January 2020, para. 27.

history and constant uprooting," to "suffering considerable discrimination in the past," and to "suffering due to less favorable treatment than others."

For these last two lines of justification, the historical aspect is important, but it is not conclusive, unlike "traumatic experiences during migration" and an increasingly broad consensus at the European and international level reaffirmed in specific legal documents.

3.1 Turbulent history and constant uprooting

Considering the above remarks, it can be said that the analysis of the leading cases for group vulnerability points to historical conditioning as the main indicator of the vulnerability of a given group, with this very factor being further addressed by the Court in the context of the history of prejudice, discrimination, and stigmatization. Having said that, this aspect of a group's history can only constitute the basis for recognizing it as particularly vulnerable. In other words, in the Court's view, discrimination, marginalization, and segregation in the past seem to be historical indicators that render a group vulnerable. Citing history, prejudice, stereotypes or other adverse social situation of the groups, the Court shows that understanding of their vulnerability is embedded in a specific social context.

The Grand Chamber used this reasoning in 2007 in the *D.H. and Others* case, stating that "as a result of their turbulent history and constant uprooting the Roma have become a specific type of disadvantaged and vulnerable minority."[56] It should be added that the Court did not indicate which concrete historical events it had in mind regarding the "turbulent history and the continued escaping of the Roma," nor did it explain how to understand the term "a particular type of disadvantaged and vulnerable minority." Furthermore, this justification was criticized by Judge H. Borrego Borrego. In his dissenting opinion, he raised doubts as to the Court's assessment of the broader historical and social context of the Roma. In his view, the Court should not make general statements about all members of a vulnerable group, but rather examine the individual applications that were presented to it.[57]

---

56 ECtHR, *D.H. and Others v. the Czech Republic*, (App. No. 57325/00), judgment of 13 November 2007, para. 182.

57 Dissenting opinion of judge H. Borrego Borrego, on the judgment of the ECtHR of 13 November 2007 in the *D.H. and Others v. the Czech Republic*, (App. No. 57325/00).

Despite this criticism, the Court has continued applying this historical reasoning in Roma cases after *D.H. and Others*, in particular in the case of *Oršuš and Others v. Croatia* and *Horváth and Kiss v. Hungary*.[58]

3.2 Suffering considerable discrimination in the past

Historical conditioning has also been applied by the Court towards vulnerable populations other than the Roma. The first such group is persons with mental disorders. In the Court's opinion, these persons are a particularly vulnerable social group because they have "suffered considerable discrimination in the past."[59]

Then, building upon the justification for the special vulnerability of people with mental disorders, the Court uses the same method as for the Roma population: it refers to the past without indicating specific events and then generalizes the past simply because it applies to every individual in question. In doing so, the Court goes beyond the individual dimension of the case being studied. Not only that, the Court reinforces the above observations, stating that "such groups have in the past been exposed to prejudices with lasting consequences, resulting in their social exclusion."[60]

For clarity, it is worth acknowledging that the Court also relies on the above findings to establish a violation of Article 8 ECHR without a link to Article 14 ECHR. More specifically, the Court's objective here is to find out whether the interference with the applicant's right to respect for his or her private life was disproportionate to the legitimate aim pursued.[61]

Finally, another important issue to be considered is the flexible approach of the ECtHR to the classification of mental disorders. The Court does not seek to obtain full confirmation of the occurrence of specific symptoms of a mental illness, meaning its objective is not to make a medical diagnosis. That is why the Court generally refers to the term "mental disorder."[62]

---

58 ECtHR, *Oršuš and Others v. Croatia* (App. No. 15766/03), judgment of 16 March 2010, para. 147. ECtHR, *Horváth and Kiss v. Hungary* (App. No. 11146/11), judgment of 29 January 2013, para. 102 ECtHR, *Aksu v. Turkey* (App. Nos. 4149/04 and 41029/04), judgment of 15 March 2012, para. 44; ECtHR, *Balázs v. Hungary* (App. No. 15529/124), judgment of 20 November 2015, para. 53.

59 ECtHR, *Kiyutin v. Russia* (App. No. 2700/10), judgment of 10 March 2011, para. 63.

60 Ibidem.

61 ECtHR, *A.N. v. Lithuania* (App. No. 17280/08), judgment of 31 May 2016, para. 113.

62 ECtHR, *Guberina v. Croatia* (App. No. 23682/134), judgment of 22 March 2016, para. 73 (multiple physical and mental disabilities).

Let us recall that the Court has generalized the above determinants of group vulnerability and therefore also applies them to persons with intellectual disabilities[63] as well as those living with HIV.

3.3 Suffering due to less favorable treatment than others

In *Kiyutin,* the Court noted that it had previously identified

> [A] number of such vulnerable groups that suffered different treatment on account of their sex (see *Abdulaziz, Cabales and Balkandali*, para. 78, and *Burghartz v. Switzerland*, para. 27), sexual orientation (see *Schalk and Kopf v. Austria*, para. 97; *Smith and Grady v. the United Kingdom*, para. 90), race or ethnicity (see *D.H. and Others*, para. 182; *Timishev v. Russia*, para. 56), mental faculties (see *Alajos Kiss*, para. 42; *Shtukaturov v. Russia*, para. 95), or disability (see *Glor*, para. 84).[64]

The above statement appears to establish, on the sole basis of the prohibition of discrimination (Article 14), the general principle for determining the vulnerability of groups. However, upon careful review, it becomes clear that this assumption is not entirely well grounded.

Firstly, the Court referred to the prohibition of discrimination and focused on groups distinguished by certain identity markers, such as gender, sexual orientation, race and ethnicity, mental abilities, and disability. However, while doing so, the Court omitted some of the grounds of the prohibition on discrimination, such as skin color, language, religion, political or other views, property, and birth. Moreover, it also omitted the ground "other status," which is understanding that art. 14 may include any grounds for discrimination and "is not limited to traits that are personal in the sense that they are innate or inherent."[65] In turn, the indicated identity markers of a vulnerable group are not the same as those indicated in the context of extremely vulnerable groups. At that time, the Court indicated four such markers, namely: race, ethnicity, gender, sexual orientation or 'any other ground.'[66] In relation to this, it should be stressed that, after the *Clift v. the UK* case, the words "other status" have a broad meaning in general . . . and their interpretation is not limited to different treatment based on characteristics which are personal in the sense that they

---

63 ECtHR, *A.-M.V. v. Finland* (App. No. 53251/13) of 23 March 2017.

64 ECtHR, *Kiyutin v. Russia* (App. No. 2700/10), judgment of 10 March 2011, para. 63.

65 Ibidem, para. 56; see also the leading case: *Clift v. the UK* (App. No. 7205/07), judgment of 13 July 2010, paras. 56–58.

66 ECtHR, *Centre For Legal Resources On Behalf Of Valentin Câmpeanu v. Romania* (App. No. 47848/08), judgment of 17 July 2014, para. 11.

are innate or inherent."[67] Therefore, the non-discrimination guarantee covers a wide range of grounds for discrimination.

Secondly, in cases assigned to particular identity markers, the Court examined *expresis verbis* the issue of group vulnerability only in two cases, namely in *D.H. and Others* and *Alajos Kiss*. Additionally, the Court did not define the vulnerable groups only by reference to the four discrimination grounds identified in *Kiyutin* judgment but did so by clearly pointing also to historical prejudices that had led to the social exclusion and negative stereotypes of these groups' members.

At the same time, it should not be assumed that the Court (Chambers) refers to the vulnerability of groups willingly. On the contrary, case-law studies have shown that in most cases – even those that relate to *Kiyutin* or the subgroups that the Court previously recognized as vulnerable – the Court extremely rarely refers to the concept of the vulnerability of groups.[68] The Grand Chamber approaches this concept with caution, too. In fact, the Grand Chamber still seems to avoid referring to a group's vulnerability and focuses instead on analyzing the allegations only in light of art. 14.[69] The exception is the cases concerning the education of Roma children, but even there, the Grand Chamber relied on Roma population's vulnerability with regard to children only as one of the many arguments and resolved these cases prior to the *Kiyutin* judgment.[70]

The approach of the Grand Chamber in this respect can be illustrated by the statement of the Court sitting in the plenary session of the *Abdulaziz, Cabales and Balkandali v. the UK* case, according to which:

---

67 ECtHR, *Clift v. the UK* (App. No. 7205/07), judgment of 13 July 2010, para. 59.

68 See e.g. the following judgments in which the Court found violations of Article 14: *Kurić and Others v. Slovenia* (App. No. 26828/06), judgment of 26 June 2012, concerning the discrimination ground of race/ethnic origin; *Vallianatos and Others v. Greece* (App. No. 29381/09) of 7 November 2013, concerning the discrimination ground of sexual orientation; *Boacă and Others v. Romania* (App. No. 40355/11, of 12 January 2016, concerning individuals of Roma origin and the discrimination ground of race/ethnic origin; *Carvalho Pinto de Sousa Morais v. Portugal* (App. No. 17484/15) of 25 July 2017, concerning the discrimination ground of sex/gender.

69 There are, however, individual cases in which the GC invokes Chambers' findings regarding group vulnerability; see: *Tarakhel v. Switzerland* (App. No. 29217/12), judgment of 4 November 2014, para. 97.

70 ECtHR, *D.H. and Others v. the Czech Republic* (App. No. 57325/00), judgment of 13 November 2007, para. 181.

> [T]he notion of discrimination within the meaning of Article 14 (art. 14) includes in general cases where a person or group is treated, without proper justification, less favourably than another, even though the more favorable treatment is not called for by the Convention.[71]

3.4 Traumatic experiences during migration

The social-contextual definition of justification for group vulnerability is not the only one found in Strasbourg case-law. As already hinted at in our previous remarks, the Court identified in 2011, in the case of *M.S.S.*, asylum seekers as a new category of a vulnerable group.[72] Noting the applicant's detention conditions, the Court found that "the applicant, being an asylum-seeker, was particularly vulnerable because of everything he had been through during his migration and the traumatic experiences he was likely to have endured previously."[73]

In the Court's view, the applicant was being detained in unacceptable conditions. It expressed its conviction that the conditions generated the feeling of arbitrariness together with the feeling of inferiority and anxiety, and undoubtedly infringed deeply upon the applicant's dignity. As a result, they constituted degrading treatment contrary to Article 3 of the Convention. The above findings led the Court to state that the applicant's distress was accentuated by the vulnerability inherent to his situation as an asylum-seeker."[74] Finally, the Court asserted for the first time that the applicant's status "as an asylum-seeker and, as such, a member of a particularly underprivileged and vulnerable population group in need of special protection."[75]

In analysing the above justification, at least two factors should be addressed, namely the recognition of asylum-seekers as a group and then the inherent character of their vulnerability. Consequently, their vulnerability does not stem from history, social structure or social exclusion due to marginalization and

---

71 ECtHR, *Abdulaziz, Cabales and Balkandali v. the UK* (App. Nos. 9214/80, 9473/81, 9474/81) of 28 May 1985, para. 82.

72 ECtHR, *M.S.S. v. Belgium and Greece* (App. No. 30696/09), judgment of 21 January 2011, para. 255; 251; M. Bossuyt, "Categorical rights and Vulnerable Groups: Moving Away from the Universal Human Being," *The George Washington International Law Review* 2016, Vol. 48, p. 721.

73 ECtHR, *M.S.S. v. Belgium and Greece* (App. No. 30696/09), judgment of 21 January 2011, para. 232.

74 Ibidem, para. 233.

75 Ibidem, para. 251.

stigmatization and is instead an already integral part of their identity as asylum seekers.

It is worth noting here that in a separate (partly concurring and partly dissenting) opinion, Judge A. Sajó stressed these two factors. First, Sajó objects to the recognition by the Court of asylum seekers as a homogeneous social group. He emphasizes that they are not socially classified, and therefore, cannot be viewed as a homogeneous social group. Secondly, he puts in doubt the rationale of recognizing asylum seekers as inherently vulnerable, citing in his argumentation the fact that asylum seekers, unlike the Roma, are not a pre-emptive group at risk of social exclusion. According to Sajó, asylum seekers cannot therefore be considered a group whose every member is inherently vulnerable.

Last but not least, Judge Sajó criticizes the Court from a different position than Judge H. Borrego Borrego. While Borrego Borrego disputes the Court's competence to make general statements about all members of a vulnerable group, Sajó seems to adopt a less critical stance towards the Court and the concept of group vulnerability, merely stating that asylum seekers cannot be truly referred to as a "vulnerable" group." It seems that the way Sajjó sees it, the sufficient homogeneity of a potentially vulnerable group is crucial. Having said that, he does not explain what this group homogeneity means, or which conditions must be met for a group to be considered vulnerable. This is evidenced by the fact that Sajó recognizes people with mental disabilities as an "undeniably vulnerable group" in his partly concurring and partly dissenting opinion.[76]

3.5. Broad consensus at the international and European level

Analyzing the case of *M.S.S.*, the Court seems to have been aware that its findings could stir controversy. Anticipating that criticism, the Court cited international documents to better justify its position, noting, for example,

> the existence of a broad consensus at the international and European level concerning this need for special protection, as evidenced by the Geneva Convention, the remit and the activities of the UNHCR and the standards set out in the Reception Directive.[77]

---

76 See partly concurring and partly dissenting opinion of Judge A. Sajó on the judgment of the ECtHR of 21 January 2011, in the *M.S.S. v. Belgium and Greece* (App. No. 30696/09).

77 ECtHR, *M.S.S. v. Belgium and Greece* (App. No. 30696/09), judgment of 21 January 2011, para. 251.

In the same way, the Court has used international legal documents in other cases to justify its recognition of a group as vulnerable. For example, in the *Kiyutin* case, the Court referred to the United Nations Declaration of Commitment on HIV/Aids. In turn, in the *A.-M.V.* case, it pointed out the United Nations Convention on the Rights of Persons with disabilities while also acknowledging the interpretation given by the UN Committee on the Rights of Persons with Disabilities (CRPD), as well as the related recommendations, resolutions and strategy statements adopted by the Council of Europe bodies.[78]

The Court also relied on the Council of Europe documents to substantiate its reasoning of the Roma vulnerability in the *D.H. and Others v. the Czech Republic* case. In addition to the instruments of the Council of Europe bodies, the Court referred there to the Framework Convention for the Protection of National Minorities, and then to EU law instruments and the case-law of the Court of Justice of the European Communities (CJEC). Subsequently, it cited the relevant UN instruments, namely the International Covenant on Civil and Political Rights, the International Convention on the Elimination of All Forms of Racial Discrimination and the Convention on the Rights of the Child while acknowledging the contributions of the UN Human Rights Committee, the Committee on the Elimination of Racial Discrimination, and UNESCO legal instruments.

Of course, the Court recalled the documents to demonstrate the "existence of a broad consensus" in terms of its findings and thus deprive them of the characteristics of *originality* and anticipate allegations of extensive judicial activism. In addition, the construction of the European consensus is closely linked to the evolutionary interpretation of the Convention. This is because the existence of a consensus on a given issue is part of the ECHR quest to indicate a common European standard of human rights, which is to meet the present-day conditions and as such is intended to reflect changes in European societies.[79]

---

78 ECtHR, *A.-M.V. v. Finland* (App. No. 53251/13), judgment of 23 March 2017, para. 74.

79 In this way, the criterion of *European consensus* is connected with the rules of evolutionary interpretation. An example of using this connection could be the case *of Dudgeon v. the UK* (App. No. 7525/76), judgment of 22 November 1981, para. 60; see also *Y. Y. v. Turkey* (App. No. 14793/08) of 10 March 2015, paras. 100–111. See also, E. H. Morawska, *Zobowiązania pozytywne państw Konwencji o ochronie praw człowieka i podstawowych wolności [Positive obligations of States Parties to the Convention for the Protection of Human Rights and Fundamental Freedoms]*, Warszawa 2016, pp. 129–134.

Moreover, the construction of the European consensus is connected with the doctrine of margin of appreciation, which is important from the standpoint of one of the legal implications of the group vulnerability approach described below. And so, wherever there is a consensus, the Court generally either grants the State a narrow margin of appreciation or excludes it altogether.[80] On the other hand, where there is no such consensus, the Court assumes that this margin is broad.[81]

4. The Implications of the ECtHR Group Approach to Vulnerability

It seems that the remarks and comments made so far leave no doubt that recognition of group vulnerability entails a number of legal consequences.[82] Some of these consequences can be considered logical and obvious, e.g. the asylum-seeker status is particularly important in determining whether the threshold of severity required by Article 3 has been attained. That means, belonging to the 'particularly underprivileged and vulnerable population group' is a factor to be taken into account in determining whether a case falls within the ambit of Article 3 ECHR.[83]

The introduction of group vulnerability to Strasbourg case-law, however, also comes with a number of more far-reaching implications and its very existence promotes the development of some general statements and doctrines that have been long present. Firstly, they relate to the development of the doctrine of

---

80 ECtHR, *Sunday Times v. the UK* of 1979, para. 59; *Kincses v. Hungary* (App. No. 66232/10), judgment of 27 January 2015, para. 30.

81 ECtHR, *Rasmussen v. Denmark* (App. No. 8777/79) of 28 November 1984; *Engel and Others v. the Netherlands* (App. No. 5100/71, et al), judgment of 8 June 1976.

82 See, generally, L. Peroni, A. Timmer, "Vulnerable groups: The promise of an emerging concept in European Human Rights Convention law," *International Journal of Constitutional Law* 2013, Vol. 11, No. 4, pp. 1056–1085; A. Timmer, "A Quiet Revolution: Vulnerability in the European Court of Human Rights," [in:] *Vulnerability: Reflections on a New Ethical Foundation for Law and Politics*, eds. M. Fineman, A. Grear, Farnham 2013, pp. 147–170; Y. Tamini, *The protection of vulnerable groups and individuals by the European Court of Human Rights,* University of Amsterdam (Master's Thesis – May 2015), [on line:] http://njb.nl/Uploads/2015/9/Thesis-The-protection-of-vulnerable-groups-and-individuals-by-the-European-Court-of-Human-Rights.pdf [available: 20 June 2020].

83 ECtHR, *Oršuš and Others v. Croatia* (App. No. 15766/03), judgment of 17 July 2008, para. 39.

positive obligations, and secondly, to the burden of proof, and more precisely, to shifting the burden of proof onto the respondent State.

4.1 Special positive obligation

The most obvious consequence of considering a group as particularly vulnerable is the imposition of special positive obligations on the State.

Positive obligations, regardless of the nature and level of detail of their normative bases, are the product of the Convention bodies. Therefore, although they have been present in Strasbourg case-law since the late 1970s, they are still perceived as something special and their direct legitimacy raises doubts to this day.[84]

Being the brainchild of the ECHR bodies,[85] their implicit nature is clearly emphasized in the literature,[86] where they are often described as implied positive obligations of the High Contracting Parties.[87] This approach stems from the original role of the ECHR, i.e. the defense of every person against state interference with rights and fundamental freedoms.[88] As a matter of principle,

---

84 See, J. Christoffersen, *Proportionality, Subsidiarity and Primarity in the European Convention on Human Rights*, Leiden 2009, p. 95.

85 See, F. Sudre, *Droit européen et international des droits de l'homme*, 6th ed, Paris 2003, p. 228.

86 ECtHR, *Osman v. the UK* (App. No. 23452/94), judgment of 28 November 1998, para. 128. See also, dissenting opinion of judge P. van Dijka on the ECtHR judgment of 30 July 1998 in the *Shefield and Horsham v. the UK* (App. No. 22985/93, 23390/94), para. 2.

87 See, P. van Dijk, "Positive Obligations Implied in the European Convention on Human Rights: Are the States Still the "Master" of the Convention," [in:] *The Role of the Nation State in the 21st Century: Human Rights, International Organisations, and Foreign Policy: Essays in Honour of Peter Baehr*, eds. P.R. Baehr, M.C. Castermans-Holleman, G.J.H. van Hoof, J. Smith, The Hague 1998, pp. 17–33; D. Xenos, *The Positive Obligations of the State under the European Convention of Human Rights*, London 2011, p. 65; A. Mowbray, *The Development of Positive Obligations under the European Convention on Human Rights by the European Court of Human Rights*, Oxford 2004, p. 100; A. Mowbray, "A Study of the Principle of Fair Balance in the Jurisprudence of the European Court of Human Rights," *Human Rights Law Review* 2010, Vol. 10, is. 2, pp. 289–317.

88 See, dissenting opinion of judge G. Fitzmaurice on the judgment of the ECtHR of 13 June 1979 in the *Marckx v. Belgium* (App. No. 6833/74), para. II.7; see also E. Palmer, *Judicial Review, Socio-Economic Rights and the Human Rights Act*, Oxford 2007, p. 51.

objective obligations arising from the Convention for States Parties, are *predominantly negative*),[89] while positive obligation were added to them.[90]

The Court also held that the subject of positive obligations must be defined in such a way so they would not be impossible for states to fulfill or overly burden them.[91] As a result, the Court rarely approaches the effectiveness of these obligations with a view to maximizing them but rather emphasizes the need for their optimization.[92] In addition, as early as 1985, the Court stated that the manner of their implementation fell within the discretion of states,[93] which subsequently developed into the principle of a margin of appreciation, the scope of which varies depending on a range of factors, including the type of rights infringed, severity or rights significant for the applicants.[94]

A similar situation occurs with the positive obligations linked to group vulnerability, whose structure is not homogeneous but is adapted to different situations and to the specificity of the rights with which they are correlated. Furthermore, their basis can be found in the Court's finding that vulnerable groups are in need of special protection.[95]

Thus, the Court has found that States are obliged to provide special protection to the members of vulnerable groups with a history of discrimination and stigmatization. In *Chapman*, the Court recognized "a positive obligation imposed on the Contracting States by virtue of Article 8 to facilitate the Gypsy way of life."[96] In the *V.C.* case, the Court spoke of a positive obligation "under Article 8 to secure through its legal system the rights guaranteed by that Article,

---

89 EComHR, *W. v. the UK* (App. No. 10871/84) of 10.07.1986 r.; ECtHR, *Özgür Gündem v. Turkey* (App. No. 23144/93), of 16 March 2000, para. 42.

90 ECtHR, *Marckx v. Belgium* (App. No. 6833/74), judgment of 13 June 1979, para. 31.

91 ECtHR, *Osman v. the UK* (App. No. 23452/94), judgment of 28 November 1998, para. 116.

92 This method is criticized by E. Palmer, "A Wrong Turning: Article 3 ECHR and Proportionality," *Cambridge Law Journal* 2006, Vol. 65, No. 2, pp. 438–452.

93 ECtHR, *Abdulaziz, Cabales and Balkandali v. the UK* (App. No. 9214/80 et al) of 28 May 1985, para. 82; 67.

94 A. Wiśniewski, *Koncepcja marginesu oceny w orzecznictwie Europejskiego Trybunału Praw Człowieka [The concept of margin of appreciation in the case law of the European Court of Human Rights]*, Gdańsk 2008, p. 173.

95 ECtHR, *M.S.S. v. Belgium and Greece* (App. No. 30696/09), judgment of 21 January 2011, para. 251.

96 ECtHR, *Chapman v. the UK* (App. No. 27238/95), judgment of 18 January 2001, para. 96.

by putting in place effective legal safeguards to protect the reproductive health of women of Roma origin in particular."[97]

Then, the Court confirmed the existence of positive obligations in Roma cases under Art. 2 of Protocol No. 1 in connection with art. 14 ECHR. These cases deal with the right to education of Roma children. Accordingly, the Court required to establish sufficient guarantees that the special needs of Roma children as members of a disadvantaged group are adequately addressed in school curricula.[98] In *Horvath and Kiss,* the Court even pointed out "the positive obligations of the State to undo a history of racial segregation in special schools"[99]

The Court derived a similar far-reaching positive obligation from art. 8 ECHR in *Aksu*. Given that the Roma are a group particularly vulnerable due to the history of racial discrimination, the Court cited the findings of the *Nachova* case where, under art. 8 the Convention, States have the obligation to "use all available means to combat racism, thereby reinforcing democracy's vision of a society in which diversity is not perceived as a threat but as a source of enrichment."[100]

However, from the point of view of developing positive obligations, imposing positive obligations on asylum seekers seems crucial because they strengthen the social dimension of the Convention. For in *M.S.S.* the Court found that States are obliged to provide accommodation and decent material conditions to impoverished asylum seekers.[101] This statement may be all the more surprising because it differed from the case-law established in the case of *Müslim v. Turkey*

---

97 ECtHR, *V.C. v. Slovakia* (App. No. 18968/07), judgment of 08 November 2011, para. 145.

98 ECtHR, *D.H. and Others v. the Czech Republic* (App. No. 57325/00), judgment of 13 November 2007, para. 207; *Oršuš and Others v. Croatia* (App. No. 15766/03), judg ment of 16 March 2010, para. 182; *Horváth and Kiss v. Hungary* (App. No. 11146/11), judgment of 29 January 2013, para. 127.

99 ECtHR, *Horváth and Kiss v. Hungary* (App. No. 11146/11), judgment of 29 January 2013, para. 127.

100 ECtHR, *Nachova and Others v. Bulgaria* (App. Nos. 43577/98 and 43579/98), judgment of 6 July 2005, para. 145; *Aksu v. Turkey* (App. Nos. 4149/04 and 41029/04), judgment of 27 July 2010, para. 49; Aksu v. *Turkey* (App. Nos. 4149/04 and 41029/04), judgment of 15 March 2012, para. 44; ECtHR, *Horváth and Kiss v. Hungary* (App. No. 11146/11), judgment of 29 January 2013, para. 101.

101 See, The European Parliament and the Council Directive 2013/33/EU of 26 June 26, 2013 laying down standards for the reception of applicants for international protection.

of 2005, according to which "Article 3 does not entail any general obligation to give refugees financial assistance to enable them to maintain a certain standard of living."[102]

In *M.S.S.*, the Court obliges States to take concrete action towards asylum seekers. These measures can have a social, financial, property or living dimension, and therefore refer to the provision of certain material goods by the State. Imposing these obligations on States is associated with a process that can be called the socialization of the ECHR and also something that is not consistent with the ECHR's *travaux préparatoires.*[103] Judge A. Sajó referred to this issue in his separate opinion to the judgment in M.S.S, when he states that the position of the Court on an applicant's living conditions are

> perfectly compatible with the concept of the Social Welfare State and social rights, at least for a constitutional court adjudicating on the basis of a national constitution that has [constitutionalized] the Social Welfare State.[104]

In Judge Sajó's opinion,

> [t]here seems to be only a small step between the Court's present position and that of a general and unconditional positive obligation of the State to provide shelter and other material services to satisfy the basic needs of the 'vulnerable.'[105]

On the other hand, however, it should be noted that the findings of the *M.S.S.* (M.S.S. test) can be used only in extremely difficult living conditions and only to meet the basic – essential needs of the asylum seekers.[106] So, it is about

---

102 ECtHR, *Müslim v. Turkey* (App. No. 53566/99), judgment of 26 April 2005, para. 85; *M.S.S. v. Belgium and Greece* (App. No. 30696/09), judgment of 21 January 2011, para. 249.

103 Judge G. Fitzmaurice and judge T. Vilhjálmsson pointed out the similar remarks in their separate opinions. See, respectively *Marckx v. Belgium* (App. No. 6833/74), judgment of 13 June 1979 and *Airey v. Ireland* (App. No. 6289/73), judgment of 9 October 1979.

104 In the opinion of judge A. Sajó, the applicant in the *M.S.S.* case was not particularly vulnerable, since "the applicant was in possession of considerable means" (he had paid his smuggler 12,000 United States dollars, para. 15), and "as a former interpreter he was capable of communicating in a foreign environment" (para. 106). The applicant himself alleged that he "spent months living in a state of the most extreme poverty… and the ever-present fear of being attacked and robbed." (para. 254). See, para. II. Alleged violation of article 3 of the Convention by Greece.

105 Ibidem.

106 ECtHR, *M.S.S. v. Belgium and Greece* (App. No. 30696/09), judgment of 21 January 2011, para. 263.

homelessness and the illegal occupation of public places, such as streets, parks, and abandoned buildings, without resources and access to sanitary facilities, associated with the constant fear of attack and robbery and complete destruction caused by the situation (difficulty finding food, obtaining a work permit and lack of access to free medical care, etc.).[107]

In addition, this high threshold of 'extreme poverty' occurs in cases concerning the living conditions of children who are seeking asylum, although the Court emphasizes specific needs and their extreme vulnerability.[108] For example, the Court used this test in the case of *V.M. and Others v. Belgium*, which concerned the applicants' living conditions, including a baby and a disabled child. After rejecting the asylum application, they had to live in the streets. They stayed there for four weeks – barring two nights – without any resources, no access to sanitary facilities, and no means of providing for their essential needs. Only such extreme conditions "attained the level of severity required to fall within the scope of Article 3 of the Convention and amounted to degrading treatment.[109]

4.2 Burden of proof

As indicated earlier, classifying a given group as a vulnerable population also results in significant changes in the burden of proof. A review of the case-law makes it possible to pinpoint two types of cases in which these changes usually occur: first, these are cases dealing with the prohibition of discrimination, and second, those focusing on the restrictions but without reference to this prohibition.

One of the elements linking these cases is the very weighty reasons test. In cases on the discriminatory, this test is used in connection with the doctrine of margin of appreciation. In the literature, it is emphasized that the margin of appreciation is a broad and multifaceted concept. In what concerns the analysis at hand, however, its primary meaning seems to be the most important. In it, it is assumed that the margin of appreciation contains two related dimensions: one indicates the extent of the State's discretion in a particular case, and the other indicates 'the level of scrutiny' applied by the Court. Regarding the burden of

107 Ibidem.

108 ECtHR, *Tarakhel v. Switzerland* (App. No. 29217/12), judgment of 4 November 2014, para. 119.

109 ECtHR, *V.M. and Others v. Belgium* (App. No. 60125/11), judgment of 07 July 2015, para. 158.

proof, it can be assumed that the scope of the margin of appreciation determines the degree of discretion in which the State must prove compliance with the ECHR of its acts or omissions in order to be accepted by the Court. In turn, it provides a "level of scrutiny" over the Court, which G. Letsas terms "the limits or the intensity of the audit of the European Court of Human Rights in the light of its status as an international court."[110]

In general, under Art. 14 ECHR, the State "enjoys a margin of appreciation in assessing whether and to what extent differences in otherwise similar situations justify a different treatment,"[111] and yet in *Kiyutin*, the Court stated that

> [I]f a restriction on fundamental rights applied to a particularly vulnerable group in society that had suffered considerable discrimination in the past, the State's margin of appreciation was substantially narrower, and it must have very weighty reasons for imposing the restrictions in question.[112]

Given these statements, it is clear that in the event of discrimination against the member of a vulnerable group, the Court decided to limit the margin of appreciation.[113] This approach is similar to that used by the Court in cases involving discrimination based solely or to a decisive extent on sex, race (ethnicity), sexual orientation, disability, nationality, and birth outside marriage (the so-called 'suspect grounds').[114] In these cases, the Court, by using the reference to the test of very important reasons when assessing the justification of the differences in treatment submitted by the respondent State, reduces the margin of appreciation accordingly. If the respondent State oversteps its margin of appreciation, the Court may find the applicant has been the victim of discrimination and thus of a violation of the Convention.[115]

---

110 G. Letsas, "Two Concepts of the Margin of Appreciation," *Oxford Journal of Legal Studies* 2006, Vol. 26, pp. 720–721; A. Mowbray makes a similar distinction, which he refers to as the principle of fair balance and the margin of appreciation doctrine. A. Mowbray, "A Study of the Principle of Fair Balance in the Jurisprudence of the European Court of Human Rights," *Human Rights Law Review* 2010, Vol. 10, is. 2, p. 316. See also, M. Ambrus, "The European Court of Human Rights and Standards of Proof in Religion Cases," *Religion and Human Rights* 2013, Vol. 8, No. 2, pp. 107–137.

111 ECtHR, *Abdulaziz, Cabales and Balkandali v. the UK* (App. No. 9214/80 et al), judgment of 28 May 1985, para. 82, para. 72.

112 ECtHR, *Kiyutin v. Russia* (App. No. 2700/10), judgment of 10 March 2011, para. 63.

113 ECtHR, *I.B. v. Greece* (App. No. 552/10), judgment of 3 November 2013, para. 81.

114 See, J. Gerards, "The Discrimination Grounds of Article 14 of the European Convention on Human Rights," *Human Rights Law Review* 2013, Vol. 13, pp. 99–124.

115 ECtHR, *Kiyutin v. Russia* (App. No. 2700/10), judgment of 10 March 2011, para. 74.

The above remarks lead to *D.H. and Others v. the Czech Republic* and *Biao v. Denmark*, in which the Court shifted the burden of proof from the applicants onto the respondent State. These are cases where discrimination was based solely or decisively on the ethnicity and in which the Court confirmed the group vulnerability of the Roma population. In *D.H. and Others*, the Court held that

> [T]he evidence provided by the applicants can be considered sufficiently reliable and meaningful to lead to a strong presumption of indirect discrimination. The burden of proof must therefore be transferred to the government, which must show that the difference in influence of legislation was due to objective factors unrelated to ethnicity.[116]

In the above quote, the Court refers to "shifting the burden of proof to government" because, in principle, the applicant must first prove the difference in treatment based on a particular ground of discrimination ("causation"). He or she should also convince the Court that he or she is in a situation similar to another person/group who is treated more favorably ('comparability'). After determining these elements, the burden of proof lies with the respondent State, which must show that the disputed treatment was justified. It should be added, however, that this must be an "objective and reasonable" justification, i.e. it pursues a "legitimate aim" and there is a "reasonable relationship of proportionality" between the means employed and the aim sought to be realized.[117]

It follows that in *D.H. and Others* the burden of proof was shifted when the Court found, on the basis of an assessment of the evidence submitted by the applicants, that there was a 'strong presumption' of discrimination. Next, it can be assumed that the respondent State must rebut that presumption by presenting to the Court objective factors unrelated to ethnicity.

However, in the *Biao* case, the Court did not refer to the notion of presumption of discrimination. Instead, it reaffirmed that "the burden of proof must shift to the government to demonstrate that the difference in influence of legislation serves a legitimate purpose and results from objective factors unrelated to ethnicity," and then added that

> the government must give compelling or very weighty reasons unrelated reasons with ethnicity, if such indirect discrimination is to be in accordance with art. 14 in connection with art. 8 Conventions.[118]

116 ECtHR, *D.H. and Others v. the Czech Republic* (App. No. 57325/00), judgment of 13 November 2007, para. 195.

117 *ECtHR, S.A.S. v. France* (App. No. 43835/11), judgment of 1 July 2014, para. 161.

118 ECtHR, *Biao v. Denmark* (App. No. 38590/10), 24 May 2016, para. 114.

This brings us to the abovementioned reasonability and objectivity of the justification for the differences in treatment, and consequently, to the second form of the doctrine margin of appreciation in case-law which G. Leads referred to as *substantive*. This form focuses on "the relationship between individual freedoms and collective goals," given that, in this case, it is a matter of balancing, "between the requirements of the general interest of the community and the requirements for the protection of fundamental rights of the individual" can be described as the principle of fair balance.[119]

In light of the above, the requirement for the respondent State to provide "compelling or very weighty reasons unrelated reasons with ethnicity" means that only such reasons for differential treatment of a member of a vulnerable group can be considered satisfactory: first, the requirement for fair balance, and second, the required justification for this differentiation. This also applies to the measures adopted by the respondent State in a case, which must be proportionate to the needs of the general interest being implemented. Their disparity may lead to discrimination, thus violating the Convention. The Court confirmed this in *Kiyutin,* stating that

> People living with HIV are a vulnerable group with a history of prejudice and stigmatization and that the State should be afforded only a narrow margin of appreciation in choosing measures that single out this group for differential treatment on the basis of their HIV status.[120]

As can be seen, the Court applies the increased test of proportionality of aims and means not only in cases concerning the discrimination of a vulnerable group.

It is used in the assessment of "interference with the rights of persons belonging to particularly vulnerable groups," for such interference "required strict control" and "only very valid reasons can justify all restrictions" (legitimate purpose). An example of this type of case is *Z.H. v. Hungary* of 2012.[121] It concerned detaining a person suffering from many disabilities and unable to communicate with the outside world. In examining the conditions of this detention, the Court emphasized the following:

> Given that the applicant undoubtedly belongs to a particularly vulnerable group ... and that as such he should have benefited from reasonable steps on the side of the authorities to prevent situations likely to result in inhuman and degrading treatment,

119 ECtHR, *Sporrong and Lönnroth v. Sweden* (App. No. 7151/75 7152/75), judgment of 23 September 1982, para. 69.

120 ECtHR, *Kiyutin v. Russia* (App. No. 2700/10), judgment of 10 March 2011, para. 64.

121 ECtHR, *Z.H v. Hungary* (App. No. 28973/11), judgment of 8 November 2012.

> . . . it was incumbent on the Government to prove that the authorities took the requisite measures.[122]

The Court's observations showed that, in such situations, the State had positive due diligence obligations, i.e. due diligence in ensuring protection against ill-treatment. In the context of the burden of proof, this means that it is the respondent State, and not the applicant, who must provide satisfactory proof that it has fulfilled their obligation.[123]

This shift of the burden of proof was modeled on the one which occurs in cases where a person is taken to police custody in good health, but it appears that he or she is injured at the time of release. It is also in this situation that the State has a duty to provide a credible explanation of how these injuries occurred, otherwise a clear issue arises under Article 3 of the Convention.[124]

Regardless, it should be kept in mind that the Court does not apply the margin of appreciation doctrine in a consistent and transparent manner. Its contextual aspect, i.e. placing it within the circumstances of the examined case, is extremely important. The Court approaches the burden of proof similarly.

Thus, the systematization and generalization of the Court's findings is a very difficult and sometimes impossible task.

5. Conclusions

In the summary of the above analysis, it should be emphasized, once again, that the Court has not so far developed a coherent set of determinants of group vulnerability. In justifying the recognition of a given group of persons as vulnerable, the Court tends to focus essentially on discrimination and historically shaped stereotypes. Instead of providing a general definition of a vulnerable group, the Court, by examining the individual applications of the Roma, HIV-positive persons, persons with mental disorders, and asylum seekers, to give just a few examples, developed a special interpretative technique. However, the question arises whether, and to what extent, it bears a departure from the current rules of interpretation of the Convention.

First of all, one would need to answer whether this approach falls within the evolutionary (dynamic) interpretation of the Convention, or in other words, whether the vulnerability of a particular group can be considered part of social

122 Ibidem, para. 31.
123 Ibidem, para. 33.
124 Ibidem, para. 31.

and economic change and whether, as such, it should be included in the evolutionary interpretation of the ECHR.

Subsequently, in the light of the analysis, the question seems justified whether a group approach to vulnerability actually strengthens the effectiveness of the rights and freedoms of individual members of these groups. This is especially true when we consider that belonging to a vulnerable group does not prejudge the admissibility of any application by a member of that group or the finding of a violation of his or her rights and fundamental freedoms. Rather, for each case separately, the Court takes into account the applicant's individual situation, where belonging to a vulnerable group is just one among many factors. Moreover, in many of the cases, this fact was not mentioned at all, while in others it was deemed irrelevant. This is due to the Court's contextual approach to vulnerability.

Additional considerations arise from concern about the effectiveness of the Convention system and the preservation of its key foundations. First of all, these are related to the subject and purpose of the Convention, given that the Convention is an instrument to protect the rights and fundamental freedoms of individual human beings, not groups – even the most vulnerable.[125] The academic literature underlines that the Convention is shaped by the liberal rights theory, with the consequence being that its subject is an abstract legal subject who is invulnerable.[126] This theory, also called the traditional concept of human rights, refers to civic and political rights, whose original task was to defend dignity and autonomy against state interference. That is why it is the individual who is the original and primary subject entitled to enjoy the rights and freedoms guaranteed under the Convention.[127] As a result, the gradual increase in the use of the group approach, especially towards particularly vulnerable groups, may be considered contrary to the provisions of the Convention and its Protocols.

Similar objections result from the analysis of the approach to particularly vulnerable groups in the context of the socio-economic dimension of the ECHR, especially considering that the confirmation of the socio-economic dimension of the ECHR is crucial to developing a vulnerable groups approach.

---

125 ECtHR, *Soering v. the UK* (App. No. 14038/88), judgment of 7 July 1989, para. 87.

126 A. Grear, *Redirecting Human Rights: Facing the Challenge of Corporate Legal Humanity*, London 2010, p. 43.

127 M. Bossuyt, "Categorical rights and Vulnerable Groups: Moving Away from the Universal Human Being," *The George Washington International Law Review* 2016, Vol. 48, p. 718.

The socio-economic dimension of the ECHR obviously goes beyond the Court's concept of group vulnerability. The Court has established that many civil and political rights guaranteed by the Convention have "implications of a social or economic nature."[128] It further stressed that there could be 'no water-tight division' between social and economic rights and civil and political rights.[129] On the other hand, however, the ECtHR sets specific limits for these implications[130] and makes clear that "the Convention is essentially directed at the protection of civil and political rights."[131] The Court, thus, does not precisely indicate the extent of these social and economic implications. This practice creates certain confusion and uncertainty, which are a matter of serious concern.[132] It seems that the vulnerable-groups approach raises the same objections, since the Court's approach is strongly criticized for overstretching the ECHR socio-economic obligations and for profoundly altering the nature of the Convention.[133]

Lastly, let us point out the uncertainty arising from the current overload of the Court and the perceived inefficiency of the Convention mechanism. With this in mind, the question arises whether it would not be better to strengthen the existing Council of Europe mechanisms aimed at protecting vulnerable groups rather than develop a questionable and objectionable new case-law doctrine within the ECHR legal order.

Bibliography:

Ambrus M., "The European Court of Human Rights and Standards of Proof in Religion Cases," *Religion and Human Rights* 2013, Vol. 8, No. 2.

---

128 ECtHR, *Airey v. Ireland* (App. No. 6289/73), judgment of 9 October 1979, para. 26.

129 Ibidem, para. 26.

130 ECtHR, *Mohammed Hassan and Others v. the Netherlands and Italy* (App. No. 40524/10 et al), judgment of 27 August 2013, paras. 70–71.

131 ECtHR, *N. v. the UK* (App. No. 26565/05), judgment of 27 May 2008, para. 44.

132 See: I. Leijten, *Defining the Scope of Economic and Social Guarantees in the Case Law of the ECtHR,* [in:] *The Role of the European Court of Human Rights in Determining the Scope of Human Rights*, eds. E. Brems, J. Gerards, Cambridge 2014, p. 115; E. Koch, "Justiciability of Indivisible Rights," *Nordic Journal of International Law* 2003, Vol. 72, is. 1, p. 25.

133 Partly concurring and partly dissenting opinion of Judge A. Sajó on the judgment of the ECtHR of 21 January 2011, in the *M.S.S. v. Belgium and Greece* (App. No. 30696/09).

Bossuyt M., "Categorical Rights and Vulnerable Groups: Moving Away from The Universal Human Being," *The George Washington International Law Review* 2016, Vol. 48.

Christoffersen J., *Proportionality, Subsidiarity and Primarity in the European Convention on Human Rights*, Leiden 2009.

Dröge C., *Positive Verpflichtungen der Staaten in der Europäischen Menschenrechtskonvention*, Berlin 2003.

Gerards J., "The Discrimination Grounds of Article 14 of the European Convention on Human Rights," *Human Rights Law Review* 2013, Vol. 13.

Grear A., *Redirecting Human Rights: Facing the Challenge of Corporate Legal Humanity*, London 2010.

Koch E., "Justiciability of Indivisible Rights," *Nordic Journal of International Law* 2003, Vol. 72.1.

Leijten I., "Defining the Scope of Economic and Social Guarantees in the Case Law of the ECtHR," [in:] *The Role of the European Court of Human Rights in Determining the Scope of Human Rights*, eds. E. Brems, J. Gerards, Cambridge 2014.

Letsas G., "Two Concepts of the Margin of Appreciation," *Oxford Journal of Legal Studies* 2006, Vol. 26.

Morawska E., *Zobowiązania pozytywne państw-stron Konwencji o ochronie praw człowieka i podstawowych wolności* [Positive obligations of States Parties to the Convention for the Protection of Human Rights and Fundamental Freedoms], Warszawa 2016.

Mowbray A., "A Study of the Principle of Fair Balance in the Jurisprudence of the European Court of Human Rights," *Human Rights Law Review* 2010, Vol. 10, is. 2.

Mowbray A., *The Development of Positive Obligations under the European Convention on Human Rights by the European Court of Human Rights*, Oxford 2004.

Palmer E., "A Wrong Turning: Article 3 ECHR and Proportionality," *Cambridge Law Journal* 2006, Vol. 65, No. 2.

Palmer E., *Judicial Review, Socio-Economic Rights and the Human Rights Act*, Oxford 2007.

Peroni L., Timmer A., "Vulnerable groups: The promise of an emerging concept in European Human Rights Convention law," *International Journal of Constitutional Law* 2013, Vol. 11. No. 4.

Sudre F., *Droit européen et international des droits de l'homme*, 6th ed, Paris 2003.

Tamimi Y. Al, "The protection of Vulnerable Groups and Individuals by the European Court of Human Rights," *European Journal of Human Rights* 2016, Vol. 5.

Tamimi Y. Al, *The protection of vulnerable groups and individuals by the European Court of Human Rights,* University of Amsterdam (Master's Thesis – May 2015), [on line:] http://njb.nl/Uploads/2015/9/Thesis-The-protection-of-vulnerable-groups-and-individuals-by-the-European-Court-of-Human-Rights.pdf [available: 20 June 2020].

Timmer A., "A Quiet Revolution: Vulnerability in the European Court of Human Rights," [in:] *Vulnerability: Reflections on a New Ethical Foundation for Law and Politics*, eds. M. Fineman, A. Grear, Farnham 2013.

Toktomushev K., *Kyrgyzstan – Regime Security and Foreign Policy,* Routledge 2017.

Van Dijk P., "Positive Obligations Implied in the European Convention on Human Rights: Are the States Still the "Master" of the Convention," [in:] *The Role of the Nation-State in the 21st Century: Human Rights, International Organisations and Foreign Policy: Essays in Honour of Peter Baehr,* eds. P.R. Baehr, M.C. Castermans-Holleman, G.J.H. van Hoof, J. Smith, The Hague 1998.

Wiśniewski A., *Koncepcja marginesu oceny w orzecznictwie Europejskiego Trybunału Praw Człowieka* [The concept of margin of appreciation in the case law of the European Court of Human Rights], Gdańsk 2008.

Xenos D., *The Positive Obligations of the State under the European Convention of Human Rights*, London 2011.

Samanta Kowalska

The President Stanisław Wojciechowski Academy in Kalisz

e-mail: skowalska13@interia.pl

ORCID ID: 0000-0002-8803-3901

Protection of individuals and groups especially vulnerable to discrimination and unequal treatment in the context of transformations of social life

Abstract: The non-discrimination principle is closely related to equality, which plays a significant role in the human moral-ethical system. This paper is devoted to considerations on the protection and the legal status of individuals and groups – those especially vulnerable to discrimination and unequal treatment. It demonstrates that dignity is both a fundamental value and the goal of protection. Law-making and application of the law that are implemented without regard for the standards that stem from dignity lead to arbitrariness and discrimination. The above issue has been discussed using a striking example of a violation of human rights – racial discrimination, which, in the case of the Republic of South Africa (RSA), took the form of exercise of authority based on segregation policy. The social mechanism that engendered the tragic events in RSA is currently making an alarming return. Many areas of the world are witnessing a rise in covert discrimination and, in addition, new, previously unknown forms of discriminations are emerging. This question has been addressed in the context of Article 14 of European Convention on Human Rights, which is structured as an "open-model non discrimination clause," which means that the list of possible grounds for discrimination discussed in this paper is not finite. The current dynamics of social life result in the non-discrimination clause being increasingly often addressed in the complaints reviewed by the European Court of Human Rights. Differential treatment based on "sensitive grounds" is more difficult to justify. The issue has been discussed based on the example of selected applications brought before the European Court of Human Rights, with the view to development of more effective and efficient mechanisms of protection of vulnerable individuals and groups.

Keywords: human rights, *vulnerable* individuals *and* groups, non-discrimination clauses, Apartheid, European and international law

1. Introductory remarks

The phenomenon of discrimination is one of the most persistent threats to the rights and freedoms of man. Over the course of time, emergence of conflicts, progressing social diversification and rivalry on various grounds reveal the deepening disparities in the legal and factual status of individuals. There arises the need for effective and efficient actions to prevent arbitrariness. This call is especially relevant in the case of people particularly vulnerable to discrimination and unequal treatment. Such a situation may come as a result of poor health, age, a fortuitous event, criminal acts or natural disasters. The problem is exceedingly complex and requires discernment as well as multidimensional remedial actions.

Discrimination manifests itself as a negative social phenomenon that can destabilise the functioning of a particular social group or the entire country. Therefore, an analysis of the existing legal regulations in this matter ought to be preceded by a discussion of the sociological context. The scope of the term "social life" extends to include the factors that determine personal and social growth, transformations in the way of life, the properties of structures, social behaviours and their underlying causes.[1] This is the general definition, which shows that discrimination, as one of the aspects of social life with negative connotations, may exert a negative influence on the horizontal and the vertical sphere alike. The denotations of the term "social life" also encompass ethnicity, origins, the study of the genesis and the dynamics of the emergence of social phenomena. Perceiving ethnicity and origin aside from the axiology of human rights and a commonsense approach to the issue may lead to discrimination of people from a certain country or nation. The perspective of legal sciences on the subject of social life is primarily focused on the prevention of negative social phenomena and the analysis of the reception and the impact of legal norms.[2] The law, as a phenomenon of social nature itself, must be a reflection of timeless values, not merely declaratory in nature. Legal regulations should stimulate to concrete action characterised by empathy and care for others. The current paper presents an analysis of a phenomenon that many people consider a thing of the past. However, as it will be demonstrated, apartheid continues into the

1 A. Harrington, "Introduction. What is Social Theory?," [in:] *Modern Social Theory. An Introduction*, ed. A. Harrington, Oxford 2005, p. 1.

2 See: R.H. Brescia, "Creative Lawyering for Social Change," *Georgia State University Law Review* 2019, Vol. 35.3, pp. 529–604; A. Woolhandler, "Rethinking the Judicial Reception of Legislative Facts," *Vanderbilt Law Review* 1988, Vol. 41.1, pp. 111–126.

21st century in a modified form, manifesting itself as vicious and dangerous forms of discrimination. The reflections, therefore, need to be preceded by an exposition of the essence of anti-discrimination legal mechanisms. Indeed, the law in this area constitutes a safeguard against discrimination, not only on the grounds of race but also against other forms of discrimination that threaten the dignity and the rights of man.

2. The genesis of anti-discrimination law in the light of the axiology of human rights

The norms of anti-discrimination law concentrate on the personified values aimed at the protection of human dignity. Throughout the ages, people have searched for touchstones of positive law. The Second World War was a turning point in hitherto history of humanity. In response to the measureless tragedy, terror and cruelty, people united in efforts to forge a multilateral agreement that would comprise the main principles and norms for the international community lifting itself up from the destruction of war. The Charter of the United Nations[3] was an expression of committed will and faith in restoration of fundamental human rights, dignity and the inherent value of the human being. In accordance with the Charter, the United Nations commenced its operation, serving the role of a 'watchman' over peace and security, advancement and preservation of human rights. Hope was placed in the United Nations to achieve what the League of Nations had not been able to do.[4] The creation of the UN sparked the vision of restoration of social justice also in institutionalised forms of international activity. Time has shown, however, that the UN had to face, and continues to face new challenges. The current issues of public interest include the problem of the enforcement of the rulings of the principal judicial organ of the UN, that is the International Court of Justice,[5] the emergence of new disputes

3 The Charter of the United Nations was signed in San Francisco on 26 June 1945.

4 J. Eloranta, "Why did the League of Nations fail?," Paper presented at the Sixth European Historical Economics Society Conference, 9–10 September 2005, Istanbul, pp. 1–39. See: J.C. Ebegbulem, "The Failure of Collective Security in the Post World Wars I and II International System," *Transcience* 2011, Vol. 2.2, pp. 23–29; S. Wertheim, "The League of Nations: a Retreat from International Law?," *Journal of Global History* 2012, Vol. 7.2, pp. 210–232.

5 M. Štulajter, "Problem of Enforcement of an International Law – Analysis of Law Enforcement Mechanisms of the United Nations and the World Trade Organization," *Journal of Modern Science* 2017, Vol. 33.2, pp. 325–326. See also: R.J. Delahunty, "Paper Charter: Self-Defense and the Failure of the United Nations Collective

and new threats to order and stability, e.g. hybrid warfare, trans-sectoral and amorphous nature of the phenomenon of terrorism. Nonetheless, it is beyond a doubt that the UN continues to undertake efforts aimed at the preservation of peace and security, improvement of living conditions, development of culture and education, promoting equality between men and women, providing aid for children, refugees and other groups at the risk of social exclusion, discrimination and unequal treatment.

The Universal Declaration of Human Rights[6] is the foundation upon which international protection of human rights is established, stating that human rights apply to every person, regardless of their race, gender, nationality, social origin, religion, worldview or any "other status" (Article 2). Even though the Declaration does not have biding force, it influences legislation, judicature and administration throughout the world.

Recognition of the inherent dignity and equal and inalienable rights of all members of the human family is expressed in the legally binding International Covenant on Civil and Political Rights[7] and in the International Covenant on Economic, Social and Cultural Rights.[8] The ICCPR is characterised by a traditional conception of human rights and freedoms. The Covenant specifies them and provides norms which had not been included in the Declaration, e.g. prohibition of incitement to national, racial and religious hatred, incitement of discrimination, hostility or violence [Article 20(2)]; the rights of national, ethnic, linguistic or religious minorities to use their language, to profess and practise their own religion, to enjoy their culture (Article 27). To take advantage of these rights, a person also needs suitable and secure living conditions. Therefore, the second Covenant was adopted, which guarantees economic,

---

Security System," *Catholic University Law Review* 2007, Vol. 56.3, pp. 871–957; A. Gilmour, "The Future of Human Rights: A View from the United Nations," *Ethics & International Affairs* 2014, Vol. 28.2, pp. 239–250.

6 The Universal Declaration of Human Rights was proclaimed by the United Nations General Assembly in Paris on 10 December 1948.

7 International Covenant on Civil and Political Rights (ICCPR) adopted and opened for signature, ratification and accession by General Assembly Resolution 2200A (XXI) of 16 December 1966, entry into force 23 March 1976, in accordance with Article 49.

8 International Covenant on Economic, Social and Cultural Rights (ICESCR) adopted and opened for signature, ratification and accession by General Assembly Resolution 2200A (XXI) of 16 December 1966, entry into force 3 January 1976, in accordance with Article 27.

social and cultural rights. The axiom that is shared by all of the rights included in the ICESCR is the freedom from interference, the right to demand specific actions from the obliged entities, benefits for the entitled subjects,[9] e.g. assurance of safe and healthy working conditions [Article 7(ii)(b)]; enjoyment of the highest attainable standard of physical and mental health [Article 12(1)]; participation in cultural life [Article 15(1)(a)]; enjoyment of the benefits of scientific progress and its applications [Article 15(1)(b)].

The importance and the value of human rights have been further emphasised in regional treaties on human rights. On the basis of Article 1 of the American Convention on Human Rights[10] has been guaranteed that all persons subject to jurisdiction the free and full exercise of rights and freedoms recognized herein without any discrimination, and in Article 24 has been ensured the right to equal protection. In turn, the African Charter on Human and Peoples' Rights[11] in Article 2 includes the right to enjoyment of the rights and freedoms without distinction of any kind, while Article 3 specifies the right to be equal before the law and the right to equal protection of the law. In Europe, the cornerstone for the formation of the system of human rights has been found in the Convention for the Protection of Human Rights and Fundamental Freedoms,[12] adopted by the Council of Europe. One of the main goals behind the above international treaty was to reinforce human rights, to prevent the atrocities of World War II from being repeated and to counteract the spread of communist rule in Europe.

Human rights, as a point of reference for law-making and application of law, should be perceived through the lens of human dignity. In the light of the above, another conclusion emerges, namely that dignity in national systems of law and in international law alike functions not only as an instrument of human rights protection, but also an interpretative indication that facilitates identification of aberrations from sound legislature. John Finnis pointed to the meaning of practical reasonableness, stating that its expressions are conducive to actualisation

---

9 Z. Kędzia, "Wprowadzenie do Międzynarodowego Paktu Praw Gospodarczych, Socjalnych i Kulturalnych," [in:] *Międzynarodowy Pakt Praw Gospodarczych, Socjalnych i Kulturalnych. Komentarz*, eds. Z. Kędzia, A. Hernandez-Połczyńska, Warszawa 2018, pp. 2–3.

10 American Convention on Human Rights adopted in San José, Costa Rica on 22 November 1969.

11 African Charter on Human and Peoples' Rights adopted in Nairobi on 27 June 1981.

12 The Convention for the Protection of Human Rights and Fundamental Freedoms (European Convention on Human Rights) opened for signature in Rome on 4 November 1950, entered into force on 8 September 1953.

of and upholding respect for "all the basic forms of human good."[13] This question takes on special importance when it comes to counteracting arbitrariness and the protection of subjectivity, particularly that of vulnerable social groups and individuals, e.g. the elderly, people with disabilities, victims of crimes.

In connection with the above, it should be emphasised that human rights belong to everyone, from a moral and legal standpoint alike. People differ with regards to physical appearance, character traits and personality. It is necessary to draw a distinction between characteristics that constitute one's individuality, bestow a personal aspect on their life and existence, and the ones that serve as factors that create artificial divisions in society. Interaction with people coming from different cultures may help teach empathy, mutual understanding and tolerance. The existence of differences is characteristic of every social group. Majority, however, is relative in nature. Luís Roberto Barroso wrote: "human dignity . . . protects the equal intrinsic worth of all human beings and the special place of humanity in the universe."[14] If a person desires to live in secure conditions and in harmony with others, they ought to attain an appropriate perception of their position in the universe and of the needs and desires of other people. Hence the conclusion that human rights do not exist merely as a concept or a metaphysical truth, but also as common values which, if respected, ensure safety as well as personal and social growth.

In every ethical system that concerns itself with the value of the human being, the right to equal treatment occupies a central role. Taking into consideration constitution and anatomical structure, or individual abilities and psychophysical predispositions, it is impossible to treat every person according to the same 'measure.' However, there are circumstances in which special treatment of e.g. children and pregnant women will not be considered discrimination. Symmetric equality exists in situations where similar circumstances are treated equally, and differently in different situations.[15] People who are unable to properly defend their rights require special protective measures and support. In the case of persons with special needs, there emerges equality in an asymmetric sense, e.g. protection and care of people with disabilities. Special protective measures may be different depending on the special needs of the individual

---

13 J. Finnis, *Natural Law & Natural Right*, Oxford 2011, p. 410.

14 L.R. Barroso, "Here, There, and Everywhere: Human Dignity in Contemporary Law and in the Transnational Discourse," *Boston College International & Comparative Law Review* 2012, Vol. 35.2, p. 393.

15 S. Besson, "The Principle of Non-Discrimination in the Convention on the Rights of the Child," *The International Journal of Children's Rights* 2005, Vol. 13.4, p. 438.

or the group in question. The diversity of the protective measures is dictated by the kind of special need displayed by the person at an increased risk of discrimination. The term "positive discrimination" represents legal means and actions aimed at diminishing the factual inequality that affects people who belong to minority groups.[16] In the words of Samantha Besson, measures within positive discrimination can be implemented if they are

> necessary to correct past discrimination in practice.[17] They should, moreover, be accompanied by other measures which focus on other levels of the discrimination process than on its results. Finally, they should be targeted at a special group and never be absolute.[18]

Affirmative action directed towards disadvantaged individuals ought to be temporary and continue until the point of resolution of a given manifestation of inequality, e.g. insufficient number of women employed at a workplace or a public institution. These solutions and legal measures should not result in the discrimination of the majority group.

3. Apartheid: an egregious racial discrimination

Discrimination is a term that is widely construed as having a negative connotation. Actions in favour of non-discrimination are central to international human rights law. However, it is necessary to develop public awareness and a positive moral attitude towards the intensification of such efforts with a view to increasing the practicality of anti-discrimination law on a national and international stage. There ought to be an attitude of alertness, because at any given time, there may emerge circumstances that require immediate reaction and inspection to determine whether discriminative treatment or arbitrary exclusion from legal protection of persons on the basis of specific characteristics, orgin or world-view has taken place. One such example of flagrant violation of human rights was the introduction of a political system based on racial segregation in the Republic of South Africa (RSA) – the apartheid,

---

16 Based on Strasbourg case law, e.g. Application *Ayten Ünal Tekeli v. Turkey*, 2005, No. 29865/96, § 51; *D.H. and Others v. Czech Republic*, 2007, No. 57325/00, § 175; *J.D. and A. v. United Kingdom*, 2020, No. 32949/17, 34614/17, § 86.

17 On the subject of "the context of transitional measures designed to correct historic inequalities" the European Court of Human Rights has spoken, e.g. in Application *J.D. and A. v. United Kingdom*, 2020, No. 32949/17, 34614/17, § 89.

18 S. Besson, "The Principle of Non-Discrimination in the Convention on the Rights of the Child," *The International Journal of Children's Rights* 2005, Vol. 13.4, p. 439.

which brought about great suffering, white supremacy and marginalisation of Blacks and Coloureds. Racial discrimination dominated every area of public and personal life. Introduction of differential treatment on the basis of race started with institutionalisation through arbitrary regulations which were rigorously enforced, e.g. the Prohibition of Mixed Marriages Act, No. 55 of 1949, Population Registration Act, No. 30 of 1950, Group Areas Act, No. 41 of 1950. The consequences of the above-mentioned legislation could be felt for years after it was formal repealed.

The roots of the segregationist politics of the RSA trace back not only to Afrikaner nationalism inspired by Dutch Calvinism (later referred to as Afrikaner Calvinism),[19] but also to the preceding age of colonialism and slavery. On the territory of the present day Republic of South Africa, Dutch colonisation begun in 1652.[20] The settlers would bring their culture, customs, beliefs. From this idealogical ground, the foundation myth of the Afrikaner nation grew over time, which was to be rekindled at a later period. In the 1930s, the South African Bureau of Race Relations (SABRA) designed a plan of separate development of the races, which assumed maintaining differences in the society.[21] In 1948, after the Nationalist Party assumed power, it operated according to the ideology of 'baasskap,' which held that the white race ("white power") was to dominate in all social and institutional structures. The supporters of this destructive ideology claimed that

> the imposition of white rule was necessary to prevent the outbreak of 'a racial holocaust,' where competing tribal interests would inevitably precipitate the country into a state of violence and anarchy.[22]

Along with the installation of the Nationalist Party, apartheid became the official form exercise of power by the government at the time. Cristina Buarque de Holland used the wording in this context "the regime's racial."[23] This example

19 J. Dobošová, "Calvinism in the Context of the Afrikaner Nationalist Ideology," *Asian and African Studies* 2009, Vol. 18, No. 2, pp. 305–323.

20 J. Fourie, *Slaves as Capital Investment in the Dutch Cape Colony, 1652–1795*, Stellenbosch University, The Department of Economics and the Bureau for Economic Resarch, Stellenbosch Economic Working Papers 21/11, December 2011, p. 2.

21 C. Lingaas, "The Crime against Humanity of Apartheid in a Post-Apartheid World," *Oslo Law Review* 2015, No.2, p. 88.

22 M. Susser, "Apartheid and the Causes of Death: Disentangling Ideology and Laws from Class and Race," *American Journal of Public Health* 1983, Vol. 73.5, p. 581.

23 C.B. De Hollanda, "Human Rights and Political Transition in South Africa: the Case of the Truth and Reconciliation Commission," *Brazilian Political Science Review* 2013, Vol. 7, No. 1, p. 9.

illustrates how harmful and dangerous ideology may inspire a political movement that will cause suffering, exclusion and persecution of innocent people. This leads to the conclusion that safeguarding and promoting human rights must also involve action against destructive, hateful ideology.

The apartheid resulted in a discriminative social 'architecture.' Disparities in the financing of the education system, and the exclusion of black people and other people included in the ban from participation in business activities had long-lasting consequences on social life, health and welfare. The introduced prohibitions and arbitrary regulations left their mark on the social and economic state of the entire country.

In the context of the issues under discussion, it is important to mention a provision from the Convention on the Non-Applicability of Statutory Limitations to War Crimes and Crimes Against Humanity,[24] which states that "inhuman acts resulting from the policy of apartheid" are not subject to a statutory limitation "irrespective of the date of their commission" [Article I(b)]. The Convention was not received enthusiastically by certain Western countries. Nonetheless, this had no bearing on its validity, because of the universality of the norm of the Convention.[25]

It must be noted that the United Nations Security Council condemned apartheid multiple times. In the Resolutions, it was argued that cessation of arbitrary arrests, bloodshed, persecutions and racial discrimination in the RSA is only possible on the condition of complete abolishment of the apartheid through peaceful resolution and establishment of a society where all people could enjoy their rights.[26] The Resolutions of the United Nations Security Council clearly stated that the policy of apartheid is an assault on dignity of mankind and conscience.[27]

---

24 Convention on the Non-Applicability of Statutory Limitations to War Crimes and Crimes Against Humanity adopted and opened for signature, ratification and accession by General Assembly Resolution 2391 (XXIII) of 26 November 1968. Entry into force 11 November 1970, in accordance with article VIII.

25 D. Dróżdż, *Zbrodnia ludobójstwa w międzynarodowym prawie karnym*, Warszawa 2010, p. 76.

26 See, e.g. UN Security Council, Security Council Resolution 473 (1980) [South Africa], 13 June 1980, S/RES/473 (1980), item 4; UN Security Council, Security Council Resolution 556 (1984) [South Africa], 23 October 1984, S/RES/556 (1984), item 4.

27 UN Security Council, Security Council Resolution 392 (1976) [South Africa], 19 June 1976, S/RES/392 (1976), item 3; UN Security Council, Security Council Resolution 473 (1980) [South Africa], 13 June 1980, S/RES/473 (1980), item 3.

Apartheid was outlawed as a crime against humanity on the basis of the Convention adopted by the United Nations General Assembly on 30 November 1973.[28] Article II states that the crime of apartheid may take the form of legislative measures aimed at the exclusion of a racial group or groups from participation in political, socio-cultural or economic life as well as intentional creation of conditions preventing their full development. The policy of apartheid was realized "in particular by denying to members of a racial group or groups basic human rights and freedoms" (subparagraph "c"). This serves as a warning against facade laws and the infiltration of anti-values into legal practice. The Convention was developed in the Cold War period. As a result, some believed that it was politicised and that its content was "selective" since it neglected to address the forms of state governance based on discrimination and racial segregation that existed at that time in other parts of the world.[29]

Formally, the apartheid in RSA lasted for over four decades. According to the constitution adopted in 1996,[30] the Republic of South Africa is a democratic state founded on values such as: "human dignity, the achievement of equality and the advancement of human rights and freedoms; non-racialism and non-sexism" [Section 1(a-b)]. Based on Section 9, subsection 1, everyone is equal before the law and has the right to equal protection and benefit of the law. Subsection 2 addresses this issue in more detail:

> Equality includes the full and equal enjoyment of all rights and freedoms. To promote the achievement of equality, legislative and other measures designed to protect or advance persons, or categories of persons, disadvantaged by unfair discrimination may be taken.[31]

In order to counteract the phenomenon in question, the South African Promotion of Equality and Prevention of Unfair Discrimination Act No. 4 of 2000 (PEPUDA) was adopted. The prohibition also covered harassment and hate speech, regardless of whether it is committed by government officials or private individuals.

---

28 International Convention on the Suppression and Punishment of the Crime of Apartheid adopted and opened for signature, ratification by General Assembly Resolution 3068 (XXVIII) of 30 November 1973.

29 C. Lingaas, "The Crime against Humanity of Apartheid in a Post-Apartheid World, *Oslo Law Review* 2015, No. 2, p. 89.

30 The Constitution of the Republic of South Africa adopted on 8 May 1996 and amended on 11 October 1996 by the Constitutional Assembly.

31 See also: Section 9, subsection 3–5 of the Constitution of the Republic of South Africa.

It must be noted that there still remains the necessity for decisive and harmonised action because, as stated by the South Africa Public Service Commission Report, in the time period covered by the analysis,[32] there was still an observable preference to employ white people, especially for managerial positions, while black people were less likely to be employed and received lower wages.[33] The above situation can be attributed to the mentality and the systemic inequalities that come as a 'legacy' of colonialism, apartheid and a social system built on patriarchy. Increasingly often students[34] participate in protests for the elimination of unequal distribution of resources and against socio-economic injustice in public and private life. Progressing unemployment in the RSA, inflation and recession feed into populism built on black nationalism. Nelson Mandela, Nobel Peace Prize laureate and the first black President of the RSA, worked towards the abolishment of apartheid through peaceful means and establishment of a state founded on democratic values. Growing social dissatisfaction, poverty, corruption give cause for the concern that the "demons of the past" may return in a new form. These fears seem to be valid, given that Julius Malema, the founder of Economic Freedom Fighters and the leading populist activist has put forth a slogan of making the RSA "black." His rhetoric involves demands of dispossession of white farmers from their lands without any compensation. Instigation of social unrest, in connection with the socio-economic situation in the country, has left the government under great pressure. Calls for "redress for the wrongs of the past" have intensified.[35]

Keeping in mind the past suffering of millions of children, women and men, the victims of "unimaginable atrocities that deeply shock the conscience of humanity," the International Criminal Court (ICC) was established. The Statue of the Court,[36] although not free from lacunas and ambiguities, is considered

32 The research was conducted in the years 1995–2002.

33 South Africa Public Service Commission, An Audit of Affirmative Action in Public Service 42 (2006).

34 A. Kok, "The Promotion of Equality and Prevention of Unfair Discrimination Act 4 of 2000: How to Balance Religious Freedom and Other Human Rights in the Higher Education Sphere," *South African Journal Of Higher Education* 2017, Vol. 31, No. 6, p. 25.

35 A. Żukowski, "Land Reform In The Republic Of South Africa: Social Justice Or Populism?," *Werkwinkel. Journal of Low Countries and South African Studies* 2017, Vol. 12.1, p. 78.

36 Rome Statute of the International Criminal Court adopted on 17 July 1998 by the United Nations Diplomatic Conference of Plenipotentiaries on the Establishment of an International Criminal Court.

"the most important institutional innovation" since the UN started to operate.[37] According to Article 25, paragraph 1, the ICC has jurisdiction over natural persons. In many African countries, adoption of individual criminal responsibility has become a hope for putting a stop to the spread of "the culture of impunity,"[38] making it possible to practice "public account of justice"[39] with regards to individuals who, regardless of their public function or social status, have committed crimes as defined by the Statute.

The International Criminal Court is the first permanent international court with jurisdiction over natural persons, competent to judge them for "the most serious crimes of concern to the international community as a whole" (Preamble). According to Article 7, paragraph 1, subparagraph "j,' apartheid is counted among crimes against humanity. However, in draft of the Statute did not initially make mention of apartheid. Inclusion of apartheid in the Statute's list of crimes against humanity was met with criticism on the part of some scholars.[40] They voiced the opinion that acts included under this definition had already been condemned as crimes against humanity on the basis of previous International Convention on the Elimination of All Forms of Racial Discrimination and International Convention on the Suppression and Punishment of the Crime of Apartheid.

In 1992, the International Law Commission (ILC) presented its Draft Code of Crimes against the Peace and Security of Mankind, which did include apartheid. At the time of the ILC's development of the project, the apartheid regime in the RSA was formally coming to an end. The Commission justified inclusion of apartheid in the jurisdiction of International Criminal Court in the following words: "certain crimes because of their particular gravity, heinous nature, and the considerable detriment they cause to mankind, must come within the purview of an international criminal court ... it is possible to make a distinction between the most serious crimes, such as genocide and apartheid, which involve

37 W.A. Schabas, *An Introduction to the International Criminal Court*, Cambridge 2017, p. ix. The above issue was also recalled in the monograph: M. Jorgensen, *American Foreign Policy Ideology and the International Rule of Law. Contesting Power through the International Criminal Court*, Cambridge 2020, p. 13.

38 M. du Plessis, *The International Criminal Court and its Work in Africa. Confronting the Myths*, 1 November 2008, Institute for Security Studies Paper 173, p. 2.

39 Ibidem, p. 3.

40 M. Klamberg (ed.), *Commentary on the Law of the International Criminal Court*, Brussels 2017, p. 59.

mass and systematic violations of universal values, and other crimes."[41] In the opinion of Roger Clark's, listing apartheid among crimes against humanity in the Rome Statute of the International Criminal Court is rather symbolic in nature, given the existing international contracts that address this matter.[42] Similar perspectives surfaced in discourse years earlier regarding the crime of genocide. Later tragic events, such as these in Rwanda, have nonetheless shown that the legal-legislative perspective ought to be characterised by mindfulness of the currently existing phenomena and emerging social transformations. Humanity continues to face wars, conflicts, discrimination, social exclusion. This inspires deeper reflection on the condition of the people of today.

In the discourse of the past, there arose the question of whether apartheid as a crime against humanity has the status of customary law. Judge *Kōtarō* Tanaka issued a dissenting opinion to the judgment of the International Court of Justice in the South West Africa (Ethiopia v. South Africa, Liberia v. South Africa), where he presented arguments demonstrating that: "the norm of non-discrimination or non-separation on the basis of race has become a rule of customary international law."[43] In the light of the above, apartheid appears as a qualified form of racial discrimination that stands in conflict with fundamental principles of international law. At present, the status of apartheid as a norm of *ius cogens* is beyond a doubt.[44]

41 Para. 38, 40, [in:] *Draft Code of Crimes against the Peace and Security of Mankind. Tenth Report on the Draft Code of Crimes against the Peace and Security of Mankind*, by Mr Doudou Thiam, Special Rapporteur, 20 March 1992 (A/CN. 4/442), p. 55.

42 Evocation: C. Lingaas, "The Crime against Humanity of Apartheid in a Post-Apartheid World," *Oslo Law Review* 2015, No. 2, p. 93.

43 International Court of Justice, Reports of Judgment, Advisory Opinions and Orders, *South West Africa, Ethiopia V. South Africa, Liberia V. South Africa*, Judgment of 18 July 1966, Second Phase, Dissenting Opinion of Judge *Kōtarō* Tanaka, p. 293. See also: International Court Of Justice, Reports of Judgment, Advisory Opinions And Orders, *Case Concerning The Barcelona Traction, Light And Power Comapny, Limited, Belgium V. Spain*, Judgment of 5 February 1970, Second Phase, § 34.

44 International Law Commission, Formation and Evidence of Customary International Law, 14 March 2013 (A/CN. 4/659), § 35. See: W. Kälin, J. Künzli, *The Law of International Human Rights Protection*, Oxford 2019, p. 60.

4. Modern manifestations of apartheid based on the example of North Korea

Apartheid has been mostly discussed in the context of the Republic of South Africa. However, there are other regions of the world, where the authorities exercise methods directly or covertly based on racial discrimination and its other sinister, arbitrary emanations. The legal definition of 'apartheid' is now applied to the situation that currently exists for example in North Korea.[45] Since the 1950s, there has been a caste system in the South Korean regime called 'songbun.' Social status is hereditary and, as a result, people may get arrested for the 'crimes' of their distant relatives they had never met. The Human Rights Council of the United Nations, pursuant to the Resolution of 21 March 2013, established the Commission of Inquiry.[46] The Commission found egregious, widespread and systematic violations of human rights in North Korea. People are persecuted for their political and religious views, sex and race, etc. There is human trafficking, exterminations, forced abortions, forced disappearances and deliberate deprivation of livelihood.

Michael Kirby, during his statement at the 25th session of the Human Rights Council, spoke in such suggestive words:

> Satellite images show the Democratic People's Republic of Korea, at night, immersed in darkness in stark contrast to the blazing lights of its neighbours. This visual impression epitomises the accounts conveyed to the Commission by the brave witnesses who came before it. Their country is a dark abyss where the human rights, the dignity and the humanity of the people are controlled, denied .... Contending with the scourges of Nazism, apartheid, the Khmer Rouge and other affronts required courage by great nations and ordinary human beings alike. It is now your duty to address the scourge of human rights violations and crimes against humanity in the Democratic People's Republic of Korea.[47]

---

45 C. Lingaas, "The Crime against Humanity of Apartheid in a Post-Apartheid World," *Oslo Law Review* 2015, No. 2, p. 108.

46 UN Human Rights Council, Situation of Human Rights in the Democratic People's Repubilc of Korea: Resolution, adopted by the Human Rights Council, 14 July 2013 (A/HRC/RES/22/13). Adopted without a vote on 21.03.2013, 48th meeting, item 5.

47 Statement by Mr Michael Kirby, Chair of the Commission of Inquiry on Human Rights in the Democratic People's Republic of Korea to the 25th Session of the Human Rights Council, Geneva, 17 March 2014.

Inclusion of apartheid in the jurisdiction of the Rome Statute of the ICC is an expression of foresight in preventive measures that reaches well beyond the territory of the Republic of South Africa.

These facts gain special significance in the light of the new forms of racial discrimination and unequal treatment that are emerging, often times very insidious ones, to which the international community must not be indifferent. Formerly unknown forms of discrimination and unequal treatment may lead to reformulation of hitherto expressions of apartheid and cause the paradigm under analysis to develop new elements characteristic of other criminal acts that pose a threat to human dignity, existence and security.

5. Protection of social and cultural diversity

Legal acts from the field of legal protection of human rights widely condemn the phenomenon of discrimination. The Convention of 7 March 1966[48] voiced the necessity of decisive action for the elimination of racial discrimination in all its forms. Undoubtedly, discrimination on the basis of race is one of the most grievous ones. The European Court of Human Rights spoke up regarding this issue. In the application of D.H. and Others against the Czech Republic,[49] it was emphasised that discrimination *inter alia* on the grounds of origin is a manifestation of racial discrimination, a phenomenon with dangerous and hurtful consequences.[50] The effects of discrimination may be felt many generations into the future, also destabilising the functioning of the society as a whole. It needs to be kept in mind that thought, as the place where every action originates, may spark a hate campaign that threatens personal psycho-physical integrity as well as the identity of a given national or ethnic group. Therefore, all acts of discrimination call for dynamic and decisive action on the part of the state. Cultural diversity should not be perceived as a threat, but rather as a source of harmonious development and coexistence. Strasbourg case-law has demonstrated

48 International Convention on the Elimination of All Forms of Racial Discrimination, 7 March, New York, adopted and opened for signature and ratification by General Assembly Resolution 2106 (XX) of 21 December 1965, entry into force 4 January 1969, in accordance with Article 19.

49 Application *D.H. and Others v. the Czech Republic*, 2007, No. 57325/00, § 176.

50 See also, e.g. Application *Anelia Kunchova Nachova, Aksiniya Hristova, Todorka Petrova Rangelova, Rangel Petkov Rangelov v. Bulgaria*, 2005, No. 43577/98, 43579/98, § 145; *Ilyas Yakubovich Timishev v. Russia*, 2006, No. 55762/00, 55974/00, § 56; *Spiridon Sampanis and Others v. Greece*, 2008, No. 32526/05, § 68.

that both criminal acts on the grounds of race and acts of racial discrimination without the use of force are to be considered a threat.[51] The latter phenomenon may manifest itself e.g. in education. It should be noted that regardless of the existing regulations, the practice may prove different from the declared goals. Therefore, the European Court of Human Rights emphasised the need to take into account the *de facto* situation when considering the problem of discrimination.[52] This demand should be heeded also with respect to the way that studies on the phenomenon of discrimination are conducted. They ought to be comprehensive rather than fragmentary or limited in scope to a narrow time period or a selected geographic region. Cultural diversity in turn creates a diverse world where people can freely develop their skills, make choices, be creative, exchange opinions and ideas. The richness of forms of cultural expression contributes to the growth of the society as a whole. Despite the cultural differences among people, countries and nations are united by a common legacy, heritage and values. These aspects also serve as a positive factor in the prevention of pathological phenomena that carry the danger of harming the identity and the social cohesion of humanity.

6. Equality as a principle of social justice

The role of comprehensive and coordinated laws in counteracting discrimination and propagating equality was highlighted in the Declaration of Principles on Equality.[53] The declaration stresses the role of equality as a fundamental principle of social justice. One of the main goals is the prevention of disparities in the understanding of equality and in the existing attitudes towards it that may lead to the trivialization of legal regulations or to arbitrariness in their application. In the light of the Declaration, the meaning of the term "full and effective equality" and "equality" itself are wider in scope than "non-discrimination." The right to equality is the right of all people "to be equal in dignity, to be treated with respect."[54] As stated in Principle 1 of the Declaration, each person has the right to participate on equal basis in all areas related to political, social, economic and civil life. It can therefore be seen that the Declaration departs from the model of division of rights used by ICCPR and ICESCR. However,

---

51 Application *D.H. and Others v. the Czech Republic*, 2007, No. 57325/00, § 130.

52 Application *Maurice Zarb Adami v. Malta*, 2006, No. 17209/02, § 76.

53 The Equal Rights Trust launched the Declaration of Principles on Equality on 21 October 2008.

54 Principle 1 of the Declaration of Principles on Equality.

equal treatment is not the same as identical treatment. It follows from the Declaration that in order to achieve effective equality and ensure social justice the remedial actions must suited to the particular circumstances of a given person, which in turn points to the need for an individualised decision process. The right to equality belongs to every person staying in or under the jurisdiction of a country, including refugees and stateless persons.

Positive action for the assurance of the right to equality includes "a range of legislative, administrative and policy measures to overcome past disadvantage and to accelerate progress towards equality of particular groups" (Principle 3). This is especially important in the context of neutralisation of processes and phenomena with historical connotations, which may be a significant factor in generating new forms of discrimination and unequal treatment. It should be noted that positive action as presented in Principle 3 does not constitute an exception from the principle of equal treatment, but as part of implementation. In the Declaration, the right to non-discrimination has been framed as a free-standing right, "subsumed in the right to equality" (Principle 4 *in fine*). Adoption of this legal construct may help improve the effectiveness of prevention of various forms of discrimination that could otherwise arise as an undesirable outcome of the positive action implemented by the state.

The legal act under discussion lists grounds of discrimination such as race, sex, age, ethnicity, civil and family status, pregnancy, maternity, language, religion, disability, gender identity, economic status.[55] It is noteworthy that the factors may exist in combination, e.g. when a child is arbitrarily denied admission to school because of their sex and nationality or ethnicity. Principle 6 emphasises that legislation must ensure equal protection from discrimination regardless of the grounds of discrimination or their combination.

Analysis of Principle 8 leads to the observation that the right to equality pertains to regulations in this matter in both domestic law and in areas bound by the norms of international human rights law. The Declaration may serve as a basis for the development of regulations for the prevention of discrimination in public and private sphere in the spirit of mutual understanding and shared values. The above Principle also applies to non-national legal entities. The Human Rights Committee has unequivocally demonstrated that the right

55 Further described: Principle 5 of the Declaration of Principles on Equality.

to equality before the law and freedom from discrimination "requires States to act against discrimination by public and private agencies in all fields."[56]

In the realm of the activity of states, it is increasingly frequent to observe the influence of international corporations. To give an example, in South Asia and Sub-Saharan Africa there are concerns whose production is built on child exploitation. According to United Nations Children's Fund (UNICEF), up to 168 million children aged 5–17 may be victims of such practices worldwide.[57] Children are forced to work beyond their capabilities and often in dangerous conditions, e.g. in factories, industrial facilities and mines. The Human Rights Committee emphasised that ensuring equal treatment pertains to girls and boys alike. The responsibility of the state in this regard is not limited to legal measures but extends to abolishment and neutralisation of practices that could pose a threat to the development, liberty and well-being of children.[58] Undoubtedly, this should apply equally to other persons regardless of their origin, age, sex or nationality.

Intergenerational relations is another area that calls for application of regulations based on anti-discrimination law. Ageism is a threat to the subjectivity of the elderly.[59] Societal ageing is becoming a problem of sociology, demographics and medicine, but also ethics and law. The elderly should not be perceived through the lens of conventional social roles. According to more than half of all Europeans, discrimination on the basis of age or disability is a widespread phenomenon in member states.[60] Gender discrimination is an exceedingly harmful form of discrimination.[61] Gender stereotypes may have an adverse impact on every sphere of life and human activity. Victims of crime are

---

56 UN Human Rights Committee (HRC), CCPR General Comment No. 28: Article 3 (The Equality of Rights Between Men and Women), 29 March 2000, CCPR/C/21/Rev.1/Add.10, § 31. See also: § 4.

57 *Child Labour and UNICEF in Action: Children at the Centre*, New York 2014, p. 3.

58 See: e.g. UN Human Rights Committee (HRC), CCPR General Comment No. 28: Article 3 (The Equality of Rights Between Men and Women), 29 March 2000, CCPR/C/21/Rev.1/Add.10, § 28.

59 B. Mikołajczyk, *Międzynarodowa ochrona praw osób starszych*, Warszawa 2012, p. 39 and following.

60 *Communication from the Commission to the European Parliament, the Council, the European Economic and Social Committee and the Committee of the Regions, European Disability Strategy 2010–2020: A Renewed Commitment to a Barrier-Free Europe*, Brussels, 15.11.2010 [COM (2010) 636 final], p. 6.

61 M. Półtorak, "EIGE jako przykład działalności wspierającej równe traktowanie kobiet i mężczyzn w UE," *Roczniki Administracji i Prawa* 2014, Vol. 14, No. 1, pp. 57–73.

also vulnerable to discrimination.[62] "Polska Karta Praw Ofiary" ("The Polish Charter of Victim Rights") dictates that the victim must not be blamed for the acts of the perpetrator, nor should the perpetrator be excused or justified because of stereotypes, his or her culture or tradition (II, item 5). In this context, the role of the axiology of human rights is evident as a constructive factor in formulation of legally binding regulations (*hard law*) or reinforcement of the performativity of the already existing laws concerning the protection of individuals and groups that are particularly vulnerable to discrimination.

It must be pointed out that inactivity/desistance may constitute a form of 'acquiescence' to discrimination, as does abuse of authority. A legal act with great bearing on this issue is the UN Declaration of Basic Principles of Justice for Victims of Crime and Abuse of Power.[63] The declaration became a stimulus for the development of mechanisms of protection of victims of crime under the UN as well as in regional systems of human rights protection. The measures aimed at the improvement of the status of victims include ensuring the factual dimension of subjective rights, adequate redress for the suffered wrongs and suffering, access to the judicial system and the right to a fair trial. Separation of state authority from the private lives of individuals is a significant factor in constructing reasonable legislation and in the practical realisation of the guarantee function of the law. Actualisation of the above function is crucial, since it ensures protection from violence (physical, psychological) from public authorities and other parties.

7. Prospective take on anti-discrimination clauses

In the ICCPR, the anti-discrimination clause is found in Article 2, paragraph 1. The prohibition of discrimination applies to transposition and to application of regulations in the area of personal, political, social, cultural and economic rights.[64] This leads to the conclusion that the scope of the rights included under the protection from discrimination as established by Article 2 encompasses the rights named by the Pact. In turn, article 26 is a free-standing nature, which

62 K. Sękowska-Kozłowska, "Międzynarodowe prawo antydyskryminacyjne – między tworzeniem standardów a skuteczną ochroną ofiar," [in:] *Różni, ale równi. Prawo a równe traktowanie cudzoziemców w Polsce*, ed. W. Klaus, Warszawa 2013, pp. 21–39.

63 Declaration of Basic Principles of Justice for Victims of Crime and Abuse of Power adopted by General Assembly Resolution 40/34 of 29 November 1985.

64 R. Wieruszewski (ed.), *Międzynarodowy Pakt Praw Obywatelskich (Osobistych) i Politycznych. Komentarz*, Warszawa 2012, pp. 636–637, 642, 643.

forbids "discrimination in law or in fact in any field regulated and protected by public authorities."[65] The content of Article 26 points to the duties of the State Parties. One of the crucial measures is sound legislation, which should guarantee effective protection from discrimination. According to the UN Human Rights Committee, "when legislation is adopted by a State party, it must comply with the requirement of article 26 that its content should not be discriminatory."[66] Practices of law implementation should mitigate inequalities between people rather than exacerbate them. In the light of the above, introduction of new protective measures must not lead to ghettoisation of individuals and groups susceptible to discrimination and unequal treatment but, on the contrary, facilitate social integration.

It is worth noting that there exist forms of discrimination that require synergistic action based on the combination of legal regulations and educational programs that are suited to the local conditions, traditions and customs. To provide an example, societies characterised by male dominance demonstrate a higher 'tolerance' for violence towards women. Cultural norms, religious traditions and superstitions are among the factors that can create complacency in the face of violence. Victims of domestic abuse should not stop at merely registering complaints or testimonies, because keeping record of the incidents does not amount to a genuine resolution of the problem.

In the European Convention on Human rights, the prohibition of discrimination is expressed in Article 14 in the form of the principle of equality.[67] Article 14 applies to the rights and freedoms listed in the Convention and in the Additional Protocols. Its accessory character means that the European Court of Human Rights, while evaluating whether there has been a case of discrimination as defined in Article 14, bases its an assessment on the scope of the substantial rights recognised by the Convention. However, it must be stressed that the Court may make an assessment on the basis of Article 14 in conjunction with other substantive rights named in the Convention, even if the substantive

65 UN Human Rights Committee (HRC), CCPR General Comment No. 18: Non-discrimination, 10 November 1989, § 12.

66 UN Human Rights Committee (HRC), CCPR General Comment No. 18: Non-discrimination, 10 November 1989, § 12.

67 J. Gerards, "The Discrimination Grounds of Article 14 of the European Convention on Human Rights," *Human Rights Law Review* 2013, Vol. 13.1, p. 117; J. Sobczak, W. Sobczak, "Ograniczanie człowieka w jego prawach ze względu na przynależność wyznaniową albo bezwyznaniowość," *Annales Universitatis Mariae Curie-Skłodowska. Sectio K: Politologia* 2012, Vol. 19, No. 1, p. 67.

right itself has not been violated.[68] The range of unlawful grounds for discrimination is non-enumerative. Article 14 has been formulated as an open-model non-discrimination clause.[69] Certainly, it is more difficult to justify differential treatment on the basis of sensitive grounds, e.g. gender, ethnicity. It is to be kept in mind that the characteristics that once represented the most frequent grounds for discrimination may subside and be replaced by factors and forms that were previously lesser-known or not as impactful. The non-exhaustive nature of the bases for discrimination named in Article 14 is also intended to preserve the values which are of such great importance to society that certain practices have been prohibited in order to protect the essence of said values from depreciation.

Furthermore, referring to the European Convention on Human rights as a "living instrument" implies the need for interpretation of the conventional norms in the context of the events surrounding a given application,[70] and in the light of the changing circumstances.[71] This postulate ought to be analysed in a wider context, taking into consideration scientific and technological progress and the evolution of ethical views. The process of interpretation should also be marked by the awareness of new developments in international law.[72]

Based on Strasbourg case-law, there emerged a perception that Article 14, with regards to the substantive rights guaranteed by the Convention, prohibits discrimination whose basis or cause can be traced to a "personal characteristic ('status') by which persons or groups of persons are distinguishable from each other."[73] Over the course of time, the line of jurisprudence evolved to include

---

68 Applications examined by the European Court of Human Rights, e.g. *Karlheinz Schmidt v. Germany*, 1994, No. 13580/88, § 22; *Anton Gerard van Raalte v.* the Netherlands, 1997, § 33; *Antun Petrovic v. Austria*, 1998, No. 20458/92, § 22; *Kevin David Willis v. the United Kingdom*, 2002, No. 36042/97, § 29; *Ettien Laurent Koua Poirrez v. France*, 2003, No. 40892/98, § 36; *E.B. v. France*, 2008, No. 43546/02, § 47; *Manfred Sommerfeld v. Germany*, 2003, No. 31871/96, § 84.

69 O.M. Arnardóttir, "Non-discrimination Under Article 14 ECHR: the Burden of Proof," *Scandinavian Studies in Law* 2007, Vol. 51, pp. 14, 25.

70 Application, e.g. *Claude Mazurek v. France*, 2000, No. 34406/97, § 49; *Philippe Fretté v. France*, 2002, No. 36515/97, § 34; *Sven Glor v. Switzerland*, 2009, No. 13444/04, § 76.

71 Application *Ayten Ünal Tekeli v. Turkey*, 2005, No. 29865/96, § 54; *Lajos Weller, Dániel and Máté Weller v. Hungary*, 2009, No. 44399/05, § 28.

72 See, e.g. Application *Marlène Kress v. France*, 2001, No. 39594/98, § 70; *Kemal Demir and Vicdan Baykara v. Turkey*, 2008, No. 34503/97, § 146.

73 Application *Viking and Annemarie Kjeldsen, Arne and Inger Busk Madsen, Hans and Ellen Pedersen v. Denmark*, 1976, No. 5095/71, 5920/72, 5926/72, § 56.

other factors that are objective in nature[74] and can be reasonably argued, e.g. the geographical location[75] of the arrest by an officer. This approach makes it possible to account for the territorial scope of legal regulations, since these may differ based on the territorial system used in a given country. Another potential criterion is the place of residence of a person receiving a pension or another benefit.[76] The above facts give more consequence to the question of the responsibility of a State Party for actions committed outside of its territory in the event that they lead to violations of the rights and liberties guaranteed under the European Convention on Human Rights.[77]

In the application of Sean Clift v. United Kingdom,[78] in the context of the country determining a political and economic strategy, an appeal was made to the state's "direct knowledge of their society and its needs."[79] The phrasing

---

74 European Court of Human Rights indicated that "a difference of treatment is discriminatory if it has no objective and reasonable justification, in other words, if it does not pursue a legitimate aim or if there is not a reasonable relationship of proportionality between the means employed and the aim sought to be realised," [in:] *Sean Clift v. United Kingdom*, 2010, No. 7205/07, § 73. The position frequently expressed in other applications, e.g. *Claude Mazurek v. France*, 2000, No. 34406/97, § 48; *J.M. and S.D. Burden v. United Kingdom*, 2006, No. 13378/05, § 55; *Annette Carson and Others v. United Kingdom*, 2010, No. 42184/05, § 61; *Abduladhim Maktouf and Goran Damjanović v. Bosnia and Herzegovina*, 2013, Nos. 2312/08, 34179/08, § 81; *J.D. and A. v. United Kingdom*, 2020, Nos. 32949/17, 34614/17, § 83. Strasbourg caselaw has emphasised: "the Contracting States enjoy a certain margin of appreciation in assessing whether and to what extent differences in otherwise similar situations justify a different treatment. The scope of the margin of appreciation will vary according to the circumstances, the subject matter and the background," [in:] *Sven Glor v. Switzerland*, 2009, No. 13444/04, § 74. The above issue also called in Application, e.g. *Philippe Fretté v. France*, 2002, No. 36515/97, § 40; *Ayten Ünal Tekeli v. Turkey*, 2005, No. 29865/96, § 52; *Lajos Weller, Dániel and Máté Weller v. Hungary*, 2009, No. 44399/05, § 28; *Konstantin Aleksandrovich Markin v. Russia*, 2012, No. 30078/06, § 126.

75 Application, e.g. *Gerard Magee v. United Kingdom*, 2000, No. 28135/95, § 50.

76 Among applications examined by the European Court of Human Rights one can note down, e.g. *Natālija Andrejeva v. Latvia*, 2009, No. 55707/00, § 75; *Annette Carson and Others v. United Kingdom*, 2010, No. 42184/05, § 62.

77 I. Topa, "Ewolucja podejścia Europejskiego Trybunału Praw Człowieka do eksterytorialnego stosowania Konwencji," [in:] *Europejska Konwencja Praw Człowieka i jej system kontrolny – perspektywa systemowa i orzecznicza*, eds. M. Balcerzak, T. Jasudowicz, J. Kapelańska-Pręgowska, Toruń 2011, pp. 373–393.

78 Application *Sean Clift v. United Kingdom*, 2010, No. 7205/07.

79 Application *Sean Clift v. United Kingdom*, 2010, No. 7205/07, § 73.

"other status" in article 14 means that European Court of Human Rights may consider factors other than innate or inherent characteristics.[80] Janneke Gerards explained this issue in the following manner:

> The equal treatment rationale implies that all forms of different treatment should be subjected to review, regardless of their grounds . . .. If the Court would only accept cases based on 'suspect' personal characteristics, it is more difficult for it to deal with cases that relate to 'hidden' forms of unequal treatment and to stimulate states to eliminate deeply rooted, nearly invisible discrimination . . .. Article 14 does not only mention 'other status' (on which the 'personal characteristic' branch of the Court's case law relies), but it also prohibits expressly discrimination on 'any ground' . . .. The Court could thereby offer important protection against unjustified unequal treatment that is complementary to the protection currently offered by EU law.[81]

The open model of the non-discrimination clause may help identify differences in treatment that are not listed in Article 14, including intersectional discrimination, discrimination based on cumulative grounds.[82] On 4 November 2000, Protocol No. 12 to the European Convention on Human Rights[83] was signed, which contained a general prohibition of discrimination. To ensure equality, there must a stronger focus on the realisation and activation of the "control benchmark" based on dignity.

---

80 S. Fredman, "Emerging from the Shadows: Substantive Equality and Article 14 of the European Convention on Human Rights," *Human Rights Law Review* 2016, Vol. 16.2, p. 5.

81 J. Gerards, "The Discrimination Grounds of Article 14 of the European Convention on Human Rights," *Human Rights Law Review* 2013, Vol. 13.1, pp. 118, 123. See: O. De Schutter, *The Prohibition of Discrimination under European Human Rights Law*, European Commission 2005.

82 J. Gerards wrote for example about "discrimination based on multiple or cumulative grounds" and "discrimination based on 'semi-suspect' grounds" in "The Discrimination Grounds of Article 14 of the European Convention on Human Rights," *Human Rights Law Review* 2013, Vol. 13.1, pp. 119, 122. In turn, on the subject of multiple and overlapping discrimination: A. Śledzińska-Simon, "Zasada równości i zasada niedyskryminacji w prawie Unii Europejskiej," *Studia Biura Analiz Sejmowych* 2011, No. 2 (26), p. 44.

83 Protocol No. 12 to the Convention for the Protection of Human Rights and Fundamental Freedoms adopted in Rome on 4 November 2000.

8. Conclusions

Equality, as a principle that is deeply rooted in the human sense of justice and morality, has become one of the fundamental values of a democratic society. After the Second World War, the principles of equality and non-discrimination became the focus of the attention of the international community. The aim of the universal system of human rights protection and its regional emanations is to protect human dignity, ensure peace and security. In the early 21st century, migrations, scientific and technological progress, globalisation, changes in world-view, economic and cultural transformations create new challenges to the safeguarding of human rights. While part of the inhabitants of the Earth enjoy freedom and stability, others face poverty, hunger, conflicts of various kinds, social exclusion, acts of violence and discrimination. It must be remembered that obvious displays of discrimination and arbitrariness can also take place in countries that are considered fortresses of democracy and safety. The current analysis included a retrospective legal-historical look at the problem of apartheid and its modern manifestations to serve as an illustration and as a warning against the consequences of illusory laws combined with destructive ideology. Even though international cooperation has resulted in numerous conventions and documents designed to counter discrimination, frequently it is their practical implementation that proves problematic. Law-making and application of the law ought to be carried out with an awareness of the transformations taking place in social life, so as to establish future-minded, coherent, not declaratory anti-discrimination law. The axiology of human rights supports modernisation of the frameworks of social policy for the purpose of effective neutralisation of cases of marginalisation and countering the propagation of ideological and cultural homogeneity in place of pluralism. Adopting the above perspective helps to identify phenomena that could lead to the questioning subjectivity, especially that of vulnerable groups and individuals. Effective protection of people who are at an increased risk of suffering discrimination and unequal treatment requires not only on the guarantee of equality before the law, but especially on the efforts to establish factual equality built on dialogue, empathy and cooperation of all the members of the society.

Bibliography:

Arnardóttir O.M., "Non-discrimination Under Article 14 ECHR: The Burden of Proof," *Scandinavian Studies in Law* 2007, Vol. 51.

Barroso L.R., "Here, There, and Everywhere: Human Dignity in Contemporary Law and in the Transnational Discourse," *Boston College International & Comparative Law Review* 2012, Vol. 35.2.

Besson S., "The Principle of Non-Discrimination in the Convention on the Rights of the Child," *The International Journal of Children's Rights* 2005, Vol. 13.4.

Brescia R.H., "Creative Lawyering for Social Change," *Georgia State University Law Review* 2019, Vol. 35.3.

Child Labour and UNICEF in Action: Children at the Centre, New York 2014.

De Hollanda C.B., "Human Rights and Political Transition in South Africa: the Case of the Truth and Reconciliation Commission," *Brazilian Political Science Review* 2013, Vol. 7, No. 1.

Delahunty R.J., "Paper Charter: Self-Defense and the Failure of the United Nations Collective Security System," *Catholic University Law Review* 2007, Vol. 56.3.

De Schutter O., *The Prohibition of Discrimination under European Human Rights Law*, European Commission 2005.

Dobošová J., "Calvinism in the Context of the Afrikaner Nationalist Ideology," *Asian and African Studies* 2009, Vol. 18, No. 2.

Dróżdż D., *Zbrodnia ludobójstwa w międzynarodowym prawie karnym*, Warszawa 2010.

Du Plessis M., The International Criminal Court and its Work in Africa. Confronting the Myths, 1 November 2008, Institute for Security Studies Paper 173.

Ebegbulem J.C., "The Failure of Collective Security in the Post World Wars I and II International System," *Transcience* 2011, Vol. 2.2.

Eloranta J., "Why did the League of Nations fail?," Paper presented at the Sixth European Historical Economics Society Conference, 9–10 September 2005, Istanbul.

Finnis J., *Natural Law & Natural Right*, Oxford 2011.

Fourie J., *Slaves as Capital Investment in the Dutch Cape Colony, 1652–1795*, Stellenbosch University, The Department of Economics and the Bureau for Economic Resarch, Stellenbosch Economic Working Papers 21/11, December 2011.

Fredman S., "Emerging from the Shadows: Substantive Equality and Article 14 of the European Convention on Human Rights," *Human Rights Law Review* 2016, Vol. 16.2.

Gerards J., "The Discrimination Grounds of Article 14 of the European Convention on Human Rights," *Human Rights Law Review* 2013, Vol. 13.1.

Gilmour A., "The Future of Human Rights: A View from the United Nations," *Ethics & International Affairs* 2014, Vol. 28.2.

Harrington A., "Introduction. What is Social Theory?," [in:] *Modern Social Theory. An Introduction*, ed. A. Harrington, Oxford 2005.

Jorgensen M., *American Foreign Policy Ideology and the International Rule of Law. Contesting Power through the International Criminal Court*, Cambridge 2020.

Kälin W., Künzli J., *The Law of International Human Rights Protection*, Oxford 2019.

Kędzia Z., "Wprowadzenie do Międzynarodowego Paktu Praw Gospodarczych, Socjalnych i Kulturalnych," [in:] *Międzynarodowy Pakt Praw Gospodarczych, Socjalnych i Kulturalnych. Komentarz*, eds. Z. Kędzia, A. Hernandez-Połczyńska, Warszawa 2018.

Klamberg M. (ed.), *Commentary on the Law of the International Criminal Court*, Brussels 2017.

Kok A., "The Promotion of Equality and Prevention of Unfair Discrimination Act 4 of 2000: How to Balance Religious Freedom and other Human Rights in the Higher Education Sphere," *South African Journal of Higher Education* 2017, Vol. 31, No. 6.

Lingaas C., "The Crime against Humanity of Apartheid in a Post-Apartheid World," *Oslo Law Review* 2015.2.

Mikołajczyk B., *Międzynarodowa ochrona praw osób starszych*, Warszawa 2012.

Półtorak M., "EIGE jako przykład działalności wspierającej równe traktowanie kobiet i mężczyzn w UE," *Roczniki Administracji i Prawa* 2014, Vol. 14, No. 1.

Schabas W.A., *An Introduction to the International Criminal Court*, Cambridge 2017.

Sękowska-Kozłowska K., "Międzynarodowe prawo antydyskryminacyjne – między tworzeniem standardów a skuteczną ochroną ofiar," [in:] W. Klaus (ed.), *Różni, ale równi. Prawo a równe traktowanie cudzoziemców w Polsce*, Warszawa 2013.

Śledzińska-Simon A., "Zasada równości i zasada niedyskryminacji w prawie Unii Europejskiej," *Studia Biura Analiz Sejmowych* 2011, No. 2 (26).

Sobczak J., Sobczak W., "Ograniczanie człowieka w jego prawach ze względu na przynależność wyznaniową albo bezwyznaniowość," *Annales Universitatis Mariae Curie-Skłodowska. Sectio K: Politologia* 2012, Vol. 19, No. 1.

Štulajter M., "Problem of Enforcement of an International Law – Analysis of Law Enforcement Mechanisms of the United Nations and the World Trade Organization," *Journal of Modern Science* 2017, Vol. 33.2.

Susser M., "Apartheid and the Causes of Death: Disentangling Ideology and Laws from Class and Race," *American Journal of Public Health* 1983, Vol. 73.5.

Topa I., "Ewolucja podejścia Europejskiego Trybunału Praw Człowieka do eksterytorialnego stosowania Konwencji," [in:] *Europejska Konwencja Praw Człowieka i jej system kontrolny – perspektywa systemowa i orzecznicza*, eds. M. Balcerzak, T. Jasudowicz, J. Kapelańska-Pręgowska, Toruń 2011.

Wertheim S., "The League of Nations: a Retreat from International Law?," *Journal of Global History* 2012, Vol. 7.2.

Wieruszewski R. (ed.), *Międzynarodowy Pakt Praw Obywatelskich (Osobistych) i Politycznych. Komentarz*, Warszawa 2012.

Woolhandler A., "Rethinking the Judicial Reception of Legislative Facts," *Vanderbilt Law Review* 1988, Vol. 41.1.

Żukowski A., "Land Reform In The Republic Of South Africa: Social Justice Or Populism?," *Werkwinkel. Journal Of Low Countries And South African Studies* 2017, Vol. 12.1.

Part II Women as a particularly vulnerable group

Barbara Stępień

Iberoamerican University (Universidad Iberoamericana) in Mexico; Research and Analysis Executive in the Electoral Court of Mexico City, Mexico.

E-mail: barbara.stepien@hotmail.com

ORCID ID: 0000-0002-2430-5445

On the road to political equality in Mexico: gender-based political violence and electoral justice

Abstract: The main purpose of this article is to reflect on the phenomenon of gender-based political violence. The issue of political violence against one of the most vulnerable groups in society – women – is herein analysed based on the example of the electoral processes in one of the largest Latin American countries: Mexico. Insomuch, the author presents the international legal framework pertaining to gender discrimination and gender equality, as well as national Mexican regulations relating to this field. Consequently, this article offers insight into selected cases concerning gender-based political violence resolved by the Supreme Chamber of the Electoral Court in Mexico. In conclusion, it is stated that there is currently a very strong movement supporting gender equality in Mexico; aiming to fully eradicate the issue of discrimination and political violence against this vulnerable group. Thus, many mechanisms (the strongest among them being parity and affirmative actions) have been introduced to equalize the opportunities of women and men (both in private and political life).

Keywords: gender-based political violence, equality, gender discrimination, vulnerable groups, women' rights.

The ideal of domestic life is a miniature despotism. One supreme head, to whom all the other members of the family are subject. This ideal would be destroyed if the equality of women with men were recognised by extending the suffrage to women.[1]

Millicent Garret Fawcett

1 In 1871, Millicent Garret Fawcett presented this famous lecture in the New Hall, Tavistock (United Kingdom), on the political-electoral rights of women – wherein

1. Introductory remarks

When, at the turn of the XIX and XX century, women such as Millicent Garret Fawcett and Emmeline Pankhurst started the suffragist movement, they probably could not have ever imagined that women would still be fighting for their political-electoral rights around the world more than a hundred years later. The strong suffragist movement achieved the right to vote for women, and, as a result, society has taken a step forward towards gender equality in all realms of human activity. Nonetheless, women still suffer a structural discrimination, which is especially visible in the political sphere. Consequently, women remain categorized as a minority[2] and as a vulnerable group: both in terms of social and political power.[3]

Hence, twenty-first century women continue to engage themselves in direct action, often displaying civil disobedience – as was in the case of their predecessors – with the aim of achieving a respectful position in society and thus in the political arena. The twentieth century slogan "Votes for Women"[4] is still current and, regardless of the fact that women share a universal suffrage, they still face numerous barriers in the endeavour of exercising their rights; this time in a somewhat more 'passive' manner – while being elected.

Nonetheless, the social and political changes among recent years have increased the general participation of women in politics (which undoubtedly must be considered a positive tendency),[5] yet, at the same time, it has exposed

---

she summarized twelve of the most common objections regarding women's right to vote, as given by their opponents. M.G. Fawcett, *Electoral Disabilities of Women*, London 1872, p. 4.

2 R. Osbürne, "¿Son las mujeres una minoría?," *ISEGORÍA: Revista de Filosofía Moral y Política* 1996, No. 14, p. 79.

3 J. A. González, M. del Pilar Hernández and A. Sánchez-Castañeda, "La pluralidad de los grupos vulnerables: un enfoque interdisciplinario," [in:] *Derechos humanos: Memoria del IV Congreso Nacional de Derecho Constitucional*, eds. D. Valadés, R. Gutiérrez Rivas, Mexico City 2001, p. 227.

4 *Votes for Women* was also the official newspaper of the leading suffragist organization: the Women's Social and Political Union, founded in 1907. M. Chandler, *Votes for Women C. 1900–28*, Oxford 2001, p. 17.

5 For example, female participation in national parliaments in the world increased over the last 25 years by 13 % (from 11.3 % in 1994 to 24.3 % in 2019). Source: https://www.unwomen.org/en/what-we-do/leadership-and-political-participation/facts-and-figures [available: 14.02.2020].

female candidates and politicians to another, one could say, new type of gender violence; this time political.[6]

Therefore, the purpose of this article is to analyse the phenomenon of gender-based political violence, to present its characteristics and the applicable legal regulations which may prevent it (both at international and national levels). The presented considerations will be conducted based on the example of Mexico, where the issue of political violence against women has been identified during several electoral processes over the last few years. Thus, selected cases resolved by the Supreme Chamber of the Electoral Court of Mexico will be analysed, together with the applicable case law. Additionally, the particular mechanisms (such as parity measures and affirmative actions) employed by the Mexican legislative power and electoral bodies in order to eradicate the phenomenon of gender-based political violence will be presented.

2. The international legal framework regarding the prohibition of discrimination

Firstly, it must be explained that the legal framework pertaining to the issue of gender-based political violence is strictly related to all documents and mechanisms adopted with the aim of equalizing the position of women and men – thereby preventing discrimination of the former.

Therefore, throughout the XX century, various conventions and declarations fundamental to founding the equal position of women and men in society have been adopted, aiming, *inter alia*, to establish appropriate mechanisms protecting women from any form of discrimination. The first worldwide document recognizing the equal position of individuals, regardless of their gender, was the Universal Declaration of Human Rights, adopted in 1948. Within, Article 1 states that all human beings are born equal in their dignity and rights.[7] Consequently, in 1966, two International Covenants were adopted, one

6 Five main types of gender political violence can be distinguished, namely: symbolic, psychological, economic, sexual and physical. Centro de Investigaciones para. la Equidad Política Pública y Desarrollo, *Igualdad y Justicia: La violencia política por razón de genero durante el proceso electoral 2018 en México*, Mexico City 2018, pp. 22–34.

7 Initially, the first draft of the Universal Declaration of Human Rights used the wording "all men," which was changed to "all people" and finally to "all human beings," thanks to the work and efforts of Eleanor Roosevelt and the Commission on the Status of Women. T. Lindbolm, "Article 1," [in:] *The Universal Declaration of*

on Economic, Social and Cultural Rights and the other on Civil and Political Rights. Both Covenants prohibited any form of discrimination, however, it was not until 1979 that women received their own international "Bill of Rights."

The most important legal act explicitly forbidding any form of discrimination against women – the "Bill of Rights of Women"[8] – is the Convention on the Elimination of All Forms of Discrimination against Women (CEDAW), which was adopted by the United Nations General Assembly on December 18th, 1979.[9] According to CEDAW, all States Parties are obligated to guarantee to women equal – with men – social, economic, cultural, civil and political rights.[10] CEDAW provides a definition of discrimination against women, which should be understood as:

> any distinction, exclusion or restriction made on the basis of sex which has the effect or purpose of impairing or nullifying the recognition, enjoyment or exercise by women, irrespective of their marital status, on a basis of equality of men and women, of human rights and fundamental freedoms in the political, economic, social, cultural, civil or any other field.[11]

Therefore, State Parties should pursue concrete actions in order to eliminate any form of discrimination against women.[12] These measures encompass, *inter alia*, the adoption of appropriate legislative regulations, sanctions, and furthermore establish legal protection in relation to the rights of women as on an equal basis with men.

Subsequently, during the Fourth World Conference on Women (September 1995, Beijing), the Beijing Declaration and Platform for Action were adopted: indicating twelve crucial areas for women and specifying the necessary commitments to be implemented and realized by the World States.[13]

Human Rights: A Common Standard of Achievement, eds. A. Gudmundur, E. Asbjorn, The Hague 1999, p. 45.

8 Readers interested in extensive analysis of CEDAW may consult: A. Byrnes, J. Connors, *The International Bill of Rights for Women: The Impact of the CEDAW Convention*, Oxford 2018.

9 It entered into force on 03.09.1981 after its ratification by the twentieth country. As of 12.02.2020 there are 189 State Parties to the Convention. (https://treaties.un.org/Pages/ViewDetails.aspx?src=TREATY&mtdsg_no=IV-8&chapter=4&clang=_en, available: 12.02.2020).

10 Article 3 of the CEDAW.

11 Article 1 of the CEDAW.

12 Article 2 of the CEDAW.

13 Such as: poverty, education and training, health, violence, armed conflict, economy, power and decision-making, institutional mechanisms, human rights,

The importance of equal rights and the human dignity of women and men (as underlined in all the aforementioned documents) were also highlighted by the Declaration.[14]

Insomuch that the analysis conducted in this article is based on the example of Mexico, it is also important to briefly present the regional – American – framework of protection of the rights of women. By the year 1948, the Organization of American States had already adopted the Inter-American Convention on the Granting of Political Rights to Women,[15] stating that the passive and active right to vote cannot be denied nor abridged on the grounds of sex.[16]

Years later, on September 6th, 1994, the Inter-American Convention on the Prevention, Punishment and Eradication of Violence against Women was adopted in Belem Do Pará in Brazil (widely known as the "Convention of Belem Do Pará").[17] According to the Convention, a woman has the right, *inter alia*, to "equal access to the public service of her country and to take part in the conduct of public affairs, including decision-making processes."[18] The Convention further recognizes the right of every woman to a life free from violence,[19] including, *inter alia*,

> the right of women to be free from all forms of discrimination; and . . . to be valued and educated free of stereotyped patterns of behaviour and social and cultural practices based on concepts of inferiority or subordination.[20]

---

media, environment, and the rights of the girl child (https://beijing20.unwomen.org/~/media/headquarters/attachments/sections/csw/pfa_e_final_web.pdf, available: 28.02.2020).

14 Paragraph 8 of the Beijing Declaration.

15 The Convention entered into force on 29.12.1954. As of 13.02.2020 there are 24 States Parties to the Convention (http://www.oas.org/juridico/english/sigs/a-44.html, available: 13.02.2020).

16 Article 1 of the Inter-American Convention on the Granting of Political Rights to Women, 1948.

17 It entered into force on 03.05.1995 and as of 12.02.2020 there are 32 States Parties to the Convention (https://www.oas.org/juridico/english/sigs/a-61.html, available: 12.02.2020).

18 Article 4 letter j of the Convention of Belem do Pará.

19 According to article 1 of the Convention of Belem do Pará, violence against women denotes "any act or conduct, based on gender, which causes death or physical, sexual or psychological harm or suffering to women, whether in the public or the private sphere."

20 Article 5 letters a and b of the Convention of Belem do Pará.

To provide women with the proper conditions to exercise their rights, as described in the Convention, State Parties should undertake appropriate measures, such as the introduction of national legislation, procedures, and institutions in order to prevent, punish and eradicate any form of violence against women.[21]

3. The Mexican normative road to parity

Mexico has been a member state of the two main international and regional organizations, that is the United Nations[22] and the Organization of the American States[23] and forms part of the Universal and Inter-American system of Human Rights.[24] Therefore, for many years, Mexico has been complying with international legal frameworks and endeavouring to improve the situation of women in Mexico in many areas, including in the political sphere.[25]

---

21 Article 7 letters a-h of the Convention of Belem do Pará.

22 Mexico has been one of the 51 original members of the United Nations since 1945 (https://www.un.org/en/member-states/#gotoM, available: 21.02.2020).

23 Mexico has been one of the 21 original members of the Organization of the American States since 1948 (http://www.oas.org/en/member_states/default.asp, available: 21.02.2020).

24 The main international documents, which form the basis of the Inter-American system of Human Rights are as follows: the American Declaration of the Rights and Duties of Man (1948), the Charter of the Organization of American States (1948), the American Convention on Human Rights (1969), the Protocol of San Salvador: "An additional Protocol to the American Convention on Human Rights in the Area of Economic, Social and Cultural Rights" (1988), the Protocol to the American Convention on Human Rights to Abolish the Death Penalty (1990), the Inter-American Convention to Prevent and Punish Torture (1985), the Inter-American Convention on the Forced Disappearance of Persons (1994), the "Convention of Belem do Pará:" the Inter-American Convention on the Prevention, Punishment and Eradication of Violence against Women (1994), the Inter-American Convention on the Elimination of All Forms of Discrimination against Persons with Disabilities (1999) along with others. Y. Pérez Fernández Ceja, *La incorporación de la jurisprudencia internacional de derechos humanos por los Tribunales de Derecho Interno*, Mexico City 2017, p. 72.

25 Besides Mexico, there are another four countries in Latin America which have developed laws against political violence and harassment, namely: Bolivia, Costa Rica, Honduras and Peru. L. Albaine, "Marcos normativos contra el acoso y/o violencia política en razón de género en América Latina," [in:] *Cuando hacer política te cuesta la vida. Estrategias contra la violencia política hacia las mujeres en América Latina*, eds. F. Freidenberg, G. del Valle Pérez, Mexico City 2017, p. 121.

The first important step in Mexico regarding gender equality in terms of political rights can be dated back to the federal elections on July 3rd, 1955, when, for the first time, women could execute their right to vote, granted as a result of the 1953 constitutional amendment.[26] Over the following years, there have been various reforms at both federal and local levels,[27] undertaken to equalize the position of women and men in politics. Among the most important, it is worth mentioning:

a) Amendments to the Federal Code of Electoral Institutions and Procedures (Código Federal de Instituciones y Procedimientos Electorales):[28]
   1) in 1990, the Federal Electoral Code changed its name to the Federal Code of Electoral Institutions and Procedures (DOF 15/08/1990) and urged political parties to "promote" greater participation of women in political life in Mexico through the nomination of female candidates[29] (however it did not introduce any sanctions nor require specified percentage adherence of female candidates to comply with it);
   2) in 1996, an affirmative action was introduced to the aforementioned Federal Code (DOF 22/11/1996), which stated that the political parties would "consider" in their statutes that nominations for deputies and

26 The constitutional amendment of February 1947 had already granted women the right to vote in Mexico. However, such a right was then limited only to municipal elections (article 115, section I, paragraph 2). Article 115 of the Federal Constitution stated that: "Women will participate in municipal elections, on equal condition with men, with the right to vote and be voted" (DOF 12/02/1947). C. Licona Vite, *Un Siglo de Participación Política de la Mujer en México (1916–2016)*, Mexico City 2016, p. 10. For further analysis regarding the fight for women's political-electoral rights – see P. Galeana, "Lucha de las mujeres por sus derechos políticos," [in:] *Perspectivas sobre las mujeres en México: Historia, administración pública y participación política*, eds. A. Pérez Correa, G.L. Ramírez, Mexico City 2018, pp. 27–30.

27 Readers interested in extensive analysis of public policies on gender equality promoted by the governments of Mexico City may consult V. R. Ávila García, *Análisis Comparativo de las Políticas Publicas en materia de Igualdad de Género promovidas por los Gobiernos de la Ciudad de México en los Periodos de 2000–2006, y 2006–2012*, Mexico City 2018.

28 V.C. de Dios, "Violencia política contra las mujeres en México," *Derechos Fundamentales a Debate*, No. 3, Guadalajara 2017, p. 67.

29 Article 175, section III of the Federal Code of Electoral Institutions and Procedures.

senators could not exceed 70 percent of the same gender[30] (however still no sanctions were established);[31]

3) in 2002, another reform of the aforementioned Federal Code was introduced. The amendments obliged parties to comply with the 70/30 gender quota[32] in relation to candidates for deputies and senators and included the criterion of gender alternation in the plurinominal lists (articles 175 A and 175 B were introduced). Furthermore, for the first time, it introduced a sanction (very timidly configured[33]) for not fulfilling the quota, which was a refusal to register the proposed list of candidates in proportional representation should the gender quota not be met. Uninominal candidates were exempted from the requirement;[34]
4) in 2008, a new Federal Code of Electoral Institutions and Procedures was published (DOF 14/01/2008). The new Code not only maintained

30 Article 5, transitional section XXII of the Federal Code of Electoral Institutions and Procedures.

31 S. Nava, "Igualdad de género en las sentencias del Tribunal Electoral del Poder Judicial de la Federación. Avances progresivos para. su consolidación," [in:] *La Justicia Electoral*, eds. M. Zavala, F. Zertuche, Mexico City 2015, p. 341.

32 Readers interested in an early debate regarding the constitutionality of such requirements may see: M. Iglesias, "La acción positiva en la forma de cuotas electorales rígidas: algunas reflexiones en torno a los casos de Coahuila y Veracruz," [in:] *Tópicos electorales: un diálogo judicial entre América y Europa*, eds. L. Ríos, Madrid 2011, pp. 382–399.

33 Article 175 C stated the set procedure. In the first instance, the inability to comply with the gender quota was to be notified to political parties by the Federal Electoral Institute. Upon such notifications, the parties had 48 hours to correct the proposed list. Failure to comply with this implied only a "public admonition," upon which the Federal Electoral Institute would again grant a further 24 hours to comply with the gender quota. Only failure to comply with the electoral regulations upon this last instance was indeed sanctioned with the refusal to register the list.

34 It must be noted that the Mexican Parliament, at the Federal level, is composed of a Senate and a Chamber of Deputies. In the Senate (comprising 128 members) 64 members are elected in a "first-past-the-post" system in the Federal Entities. The other 32 members are elected among the "first minority" (best loser) of the said elections and the remaining 32 members are elected in a single national district under proportional representation. Regarding the Chamber of Deputies (comprising 500 members), 300 members are elected in uninominal districts by a "first-past-the-post" system while the remaining 200 members are elected under proportional representation in 5 regional lists. M.A. Rivera León, "¿Abrir o desbloquear? El debate de las listas electorales en México," *Revista Mexicana de Derecho Electoral* 2012, No. 2, pp. 165–168.

but raised the gender quota to 60/40 in nominations for deputies and senators of proportional representations (the sanction procedure was also upheld, as described in *supra note 34*). Simultaneously, it still exempted nominations for uninominal districts from the fulfillment of the quota.[35]

b) In the year 2014, as a result of the 2014 amendment,[36] three new laws were adopted which remain in force to date:
   1) the General Law on Electoral Institutions and Procedures (Ley General de Instituciones y Procedimientos Electorales), which replaced the aforementioned Federal Code of Electoral Institutions and Procedures;[37]
   2) the General Law on Political Parties (Ley General de Partidos Políticos);[38]
   3) the General Law on Electoral Crimes (Ley General en Materia de Delitos Electorales[39]).

In such a way, the constitutional requirement of gender parity was reflected in article 232.4 of the General Law on Electoral Institutions and Procedures. This article granted faculties to local and national institutes to reject the registration of nominations which did not comply with parity (upon a previous requirement to comply with the regulations within 24 hours, as stipulated by article 235). Moreover, article 233 of the above-mentioned law stated that, without any exception, all nominations should respect gender parity. Furthermore, article 3.5 of the General Law on Political Parties forbade the practice of nominating in uninominal districts a single gender in low-competitive districts. In other words, a political party was not allowed to nominate female candidates exclusively in districts in which historically it had obtained low results (and consequently reserve high-competitive districts for the nomination of male candidates).

35 Article 221.1 and 221.2 of the Federal Code of Electoral Institutions and Procedures (DOF 14.01.2008).

36 The constitutional reform of 2014 (DOF 10/02/2014), introduced to the Federal Constitution (article 41 of the Constitution), stipulates gender parity in connection with the composition of the federal and local congresses. It stated that political parties must "guarantee parity between genders in nominations to federal and local legislators" and that the general law (upon a centralization of competences to regulate electoral processes or the electoral process) would regulate the above-mentioned parity.

37 DOF 23.05.2014.

38 DOF 23.05.2014.

39 DOF 23.05.2014.

Additionally, in the years 2003 and 2006 respectively, two important legislations in terms of gender discrimination were adopted; that is – the Federal Law to Prevent and Eliminate Discrimination (Ley Federal para. Prevenir y Eliminar la Discriminación[40]) and the General Law for Equality between Women and Men (Ley General para. la Igualdad entre Mujeres y Hombres[41]).

4. The phenomenon of gender-based political violence

4.1. How can it really be defined?

All the aforementioned reforms and legislations constituted important aids in targeting the issue of gender discrimination in Mexico. Paradoxically, the constitutional and legal framework introduced in 2014 seems to have triggered gender-based political violence in Mexico more than ever. A possible explanation is that the introduction of a 50 percent requirement made political parties and male politicians feel that political spaces, which prototypically had belonged to them, were being displaced in favour of women. Until 2008, only a 70/30 quota had been employed and only between 2008–2014 did the 60/40 quota take place. In such a way, political parties had, until 2014, managed to work under a favourable legal framework and avoid the application of electoral normativity when the quotas were raised; men, as a political entity, were not prepared for the serious legal revolution that the new 2014 framework introduced in terms of the enforcement of the provision.

Therefore, to combat the phenomenon of gender-based political violence, in 2016 a specialized document was adopted at the federal level explicitly addressing this problem – the Protocol to Address Political Violence against Women (Protocolo para Atender la Violencia Política contra las Mujeres). In the following year (2017) the 2016 Protocol was revised and renamed the Protocol for the Attention of Political Violence against Women Due to Gender Reasons (Protocolo para la Atención de la Violencia Política contra las Mujeres en Razón de Género), which is applicable to date.

The 2017 Protocol defines gender political violence as:

> all those actions or omissions of people, servants or public servants who address a woman for being a woman (based on gender) which have a differentiated impact on

40 DOF 11.06.2003.

41 DOF 02.08.2006.

them or affect them disproportionately, with the object or result of undermining or annulling their political-electoral rights, including the exercise of office.[42]

The main objectives of the 2017 Protocol are to: facilitate the identification of political violence against women based on gender, serve as a guide in the federal sphere for the identification of political violence, promote adequate coordination between federal institutions in order to eradicate violence, and guide victims of political violence on the basis of gender at all levels of government in respect to what is and is not such violence, as well as inform them regarding the authorities they can contact for assistance.[43]

4.2. Case Study – The "Juanitas"

The phenomenon "Juanitas" refers to an electoral practice employed in Mexico which meant that political parties nominated female candidates for popular elections or public positions, but after the female candidates took office they were immediately forced to resign (or such a resignation had been agreed beforehand), and consequently, they were replaced by male substitutes from the same political party. The objective of this practice was to comply with the gender quota established by law yet still retain power in the hands of men. It

42 The author's own translation of the Spanish original version of the Protocol.

43 Tribunal Electoral del Poder Judicial de la Federación, *Protocolo para. la Atención de la Violencia Política Contra las Mujeres en Razón de Género*, Mexico City 2017, p. 19. Due to space limitation of this article only brief analysis of the Protocol are presented. Readers interested in the topic may further consult: F. Freidenberg, "La violencia política hacia las mujeres: el problema, los debates y las propuestas para. América Latina," [in:] *Cuando hacer política te cuesta la vida. Estrategias contra la violencia política hacia las mujeres en América Latina*, eds. F. Freidenberg, G. del Valle Pérez, Mexico City 2017, pp. 3–42. For more practical examples consult: E. A. Iglesias Gutiérrez, "Violencia política de género," [in:] *Temas Selectos Sobre Violencia Política de Género*, eds. C. A. Vázquez Azuara, C. García Méndez, Xalapa, Veracruz, Mexico City 2019, pp. 53–64; I. Castro Apreza, "Paridad y violencia política. Los retos de las mujeres indígenas de Chiapas," [in:] *Cuando hacer política te cuesta la vida. Estrategias contra la violencia política hacia las mujeres en América Latina*, eds. F. Freidenberg, G. del Valle Pérez, Mexico City 2017, pp. 309–339; R.B. López Vences, "Violencia política hacia las mujeres indígenas en los municipios de Oaxaca," [in:] *Cuando hacer política te cuesta la vida. Estrategias contra la violencia política hacia las mujeres en América Latina*, eds. F. Freidenberg, G. del Valle Pérez, Mexico City 2017, pp. 341–356.

was not until the year 2009 that such a *modus operandi* was discovered by the public, stemming from a series of resignations by different women.[44]

The name "Juanitas" itself has an origin suitable to Latin-American magical realism and comes from the well-known case of Rafael Acosta Ángeles (whose nickname was "Juanito"). In 2009, a female politician – Clara Brugada – had won the right to be nominated by a political party to contend for Jefatura Delegacional (District President) in Iztapalapa, Mexico. However, a few days before the election, her candidacy was annulled by the Electoral Court, who deemed it discordant with internal regulations. The former Presidential Candidate, López Obrador, supported Brugada by offering to have the position taken *via* the election of a 'puppet' District President. In order to achieve this, López Obrador supported Rafael Acosta's nomination for District President, representing a different political party. Acosta, who did not have a strong political background nor any real chance of winning the election on his own merit, accepted and during the campaign openly declared that, if he won, he would immediately resign in favour of Brugada. In that way, Brugada would be appointed Jefa Delegacional by the local parliament. The combined support of López Obrador's political base and Brugada's popularity won the election for the 'puppet' – Acosta. "Juanito" kept his promise initially and immediately asked for a leave of absence (not a resignation) and thus Brugada was proclaimed Jefa Delegacional. However, in an unexpected turn of events, Acosta decided to return to the office, as was his right – being on leave and not having resigned from the position. After great political tension, Brugada was finally appointed Jefa Delegacional as "Juanito" was forced to resign due to strong accusations of falsifying documents. Hence, the name "Juanito," in Mexico, describes a political puppet or a person without merit who is used merely to fulfill a formality, as his/her seat is reserved for someone else.

The most important case pertaining to the "Juanitas" issue was resolved by the Supreme Chamber of the Electoral Court of Mexico in the year 2011. Ten women[45] appealed Resolution CG327/2011 of the General Council of the

44 In the first session of the LXI Legislature of the Chamber of Deputies in 2009, eight female deputies requested leave (*licencia*) and were substituted by their fellow male party members (which was a clear violation of the principle of gender quotas).

45 Initially it was brought by a group of eight women on 7th November 2011, and then by another two women on 8th November 2011. The total number of ten cases was accumulated and proceeded together as one case, as permitted by the procedural rules of the General Law on Appeal Procedures on Electoral Matters (Ley General del Sistema de Medios de Impugnación en Materia Electoral), article 31.1.

Federal Electoral Institute (Instituto Nacional Electoral) – which specified the applicable criteria for the registration of candidates for the various positions of popular election presented by political parties and, where appropriate, coalitions before the Councils of the Institute, for the federal electoral process 2011–2012 dated November 3rd, 2011.[46] In the appealed Resolution CG327/2011, it was stated that no political party or coalition could include more than 60 % of proprietary candidates for deputies and senators of the same gender out of the total applications for registration of candidacies, both in the relative majority and in proportional representation. In Mexico, every nomination of a senator or deputy is joined by the nomination of a "substitute" (*suplente*): that is, the person designated to take office were the first person to resign or be unable to perform public functions (due to death or incapacity). The resolution also "recommended" that the "substitute" candidate be of the same gender.

The applicants specified that, among other arguments, the configuration of the quotas allowed a distorted interpretation of gender nominations. Therefore, the appealed resolution should not recommend having a same-gender candidate and substitute, as that would deprive women of being nominated as substitute candidates in a great number of cases. They claimed that, subsequently, such a recommendation should only be applicable in the case of female candidates (thus making it mandatory for female candidates to have female substitutes). At the same time, such a requirement should not be imposed on male candidates (which would allow male candidates to have female substitutes and thus provide women with a greater margin for accessing public office).

The Supreme Chamber of the Electoral Court resolved the appeal in the ruling JDC 12624/2011. The Supreme Chamber stated that political parties must present a minimum of 120 candidates for deputies and 26 candidates for senators who are of the same gender (for relative majority legislators), and that at least 40 % of the total number of applications for registrations should be proposed with same-gender full formulas (candidate and substitute). According to the Supreme Chamber, the appealed resolution did not meet the quota requirements as it allowed the gender of the candidates to be varied in the process of substitution by allowing mixed formulas. In its ruling, it stated that if the quotas are not reflected in the effective conformation of the body (because

46 Acuerdo CG327/2011 del Consejo General del Instituto Federal Electoral por el que se indican los criterios aplicables para. el registro de candidaturas a los distintos cargos de elección popular que presenten los partidos políticos y, en su caso, las coaliciones ante los Consejos del Instituto, para. el proceso electoral federal 2011–2012.

of possible variation due to the "substitute" taking over the primary candidate) the whole gender equality affirmative measure would be rendered senseless.

This ruling, as underlined by many authors, was one of the most important rulings in the history of Mexican electoral law: representing one of the greatest advances in terms of gender equality. It transformed the formal, theoretical understanding of the quota's system into a functional comprehension of the effective exercise of the proposed position and deprived political parties of the main weapon which had been used to avoid affirmative actions (thus ending the "Juanitas" phenomenon).[47]

As a result of this ruling, and the multiple appeals regarding this issue which were presented to the various electoral courts over many years in Mexico,[48] the Federal Electoral Court of Mexico[49] issued two important jurisprudences (binding case-laws) in the year 2015. In its binding case law, the Federal Electoral Court stated that gender parity must be respected in the federal, state and municipal popular elections under the proposed vertical and horizontal approaches, that is:

- Jurisprudence number 6/2015 "Gender parity must be observed in the application of candidatures for the integration of federal, state and municipal popular representation bodies. The systematic and functional interpretation of the right to political participation under conditions of equality, in light of the guidance drawn up by the pro persona principle, recognized in Article 1 of the Political Constitution of the United Mexican States leads to the consideration that the inclusion of the parity postulate in article 41 of the fundamental norm, in the case of candidates for federal and local legislators, is framed in the context delineated by the numerals 2, 3, 25, 26 of the International Covenant on Civil Rights and Politicians; 1, 23, 24 of the American Convention on Human Rights; 1, 2, 3 and 7 of the Convention on the Elimination of All Forms of Discrimination against Women; I, II and III, of the Convention on the Political Rights of Women; 4, subsection j);

47 L. Córdova, E. Buendía, "Artículo 41," [in:] *Constitución Política de los Estados Unidos Mexicanos Comentada*, ed. J.R. Cossío Díaz, México City 2017, p. 809.

48 The case law of the Electoral Court has evolved greatly. A résumé of its evolution may be accessed herein: J. Sánchez, "Igualdad, equidad y Paridad de Género," [in:] *Tratado de Derecho Electoral*, eds. F. de la Mata, C. Coello, Mexico City 2018, pp. 340–369.

49 It must be noted that the Federal Electoral Court (Tribunal Electoral del Poder Judicial de la Federación) is composed by five "Regional Chambers," one Specialized Chamber and the Supreme Chamber.

and 5 of the Inter-American Convention to Prevent, Punish and Eradicate Violence against Women; the regulatory scheme that conforms national legal order and shows that the nomination of candidates is aimed at effectively generating access to the exercise of public power of both genders, under true conditions of equality. In this sense, the principle of parity emerges as a validity parameter that is derived from the constitutional and conventional mandate of establishing norms to guarantee the registration of candidatures in accordance with this principle, as well as measures of all kinds for their effective compliance: so it must permeate in the nomination of candidacies for the integration of the federal, local and municipal popular representation bodies, in order to guarantee a plural and inclusive model of political participation in the different areas of government."[50]

- Jurisprudence number 7/2015 "Gender parity – dimensions of its content in the municipal order. The systematic and functional interpretation of the right to political participation under conditions of equality, in light of the guidance outlined by: articles 1, 2, 4, 41, paragraph I, of the Political Constitution of the United Mexican States; in the context of articles 2, 3, 25, 26 of the International Covenant on Civil and Political Rights; 1, 23, 24 of the American Convention on Human Rights; 1, 2, 3 and 7 of the Convention on the Elimination of All Forms of Discrimination against Women; I, II and III, of the Convention on the Political Rights of Women; 4, subsection j) and 5 of the Inter-American Convention to Prevent, Punish and Eradicate Violence against Women, allow affirmation that the parties and the electoral authorities must guarantee gender parity in the nomination of municipal candidates from a double dimension. Not only must they ensure vertical parity, for which they are called to nominate candidates from the same town hall for: president, councillors and municipal trustees, in the same proportion of genders, they must also, from a horizontal approach, ensure parity in the registration of these candidacies, among the different municipalities that are part of a specific State. Through this dual perspective, a useful and material effect of the gender parity principle is achieved, which makes it possible

50 The author's own translation of the Spanish original version. Sala Regional del Tribunal Electoral del Poder Judicial de la Federación, correspondiente a la Cuarta Circunscripción Plurinominal, con sede en el Distrito Federal (online: at https://bit.ly/39dYu5E, available: 27.02.2020).

to effectively and comprehensively ensure compliance with the obligations to promote, respect, protect and guarantee the human rights of women."[51]

The presented case law constituted an important step forward regarding gender equality and protection of the human rights of women in Mexico as it established a binding interpretation of such principles for the relevant judicial bodies that ensure their compliance.

5. Conclusions

As may be drawn from this presented analysis, the international community has been making great efforts to achieve gender equality in all spheres of human life, and, therefore, has adopted various international and regional conventions prohibiting any form of discrimination in order to achieve improvement in the social-political position of women.

It may also be concluded that the analysed country – Mexico – for many years has been undertaking a profusion of actions to prevent gender discrimination, amongst others, in the national political arena. Not only have the appropriate legal instruments been adopted prohibiting discrimination, but also the phenomenon of gender-based political violence has been widely diagnosed and targeted. Therefore, plenteous reforms (including constitutional ones) have been undertaken and the electoral courts – the guardians of political-electoral processes – have been acting accordingly in order to prevent and eradicate political violence against women.

As a result, the Organization of American States recognized Mexico as one of the countries where the greatest progress in terms of equity and parity for women and in their access to positions of popular election has been made on a worldwide scale.[52]

To conclude, the words of one of the very few female presidents – Michelle Bachelet (ex-President of Chile) – must be recalled: "When a woman enters politics, the woman changes; when many enter, the politics change." Certainly, it is only a matter of time, when a great number of women will change world politics

51 The author's own translation of the Spanish original version. Sala Regional del Tribunal Electoral del Poder Judicial de la Federación, correspondiente a la Cuarta Circunscripción Plurinominal con sede en el Distrito Federal (online at https://bit.ly/39cgHRh, available: 27.02.2020).

52 https://bit.ly/38cEKOL, available: 20.02.2020.

forever and the slogan "Votes for Women" will not, anymore, express a fight for equal treatment, but real political power.

Bibliography:

Albaine L., "Marcos normativos contra el acoso y/o violencia política en razón de género en América Latina," [in:] *Cuando hacer política te cuesta la vida. Estrategias contra la violencia política hacia las mujeres en América Latina*, eds. F. Freidenberg, G. del Valle Pérez, Mexico City 2017.

Ávila García V. R., *Análisis Comparativo de las Políticas Publicas en materia de Igualdad de Género promovidas por los Gobiernos de la Ciudad de México en los Periodos de 2000–2006, y 2006–2012*, Mexico City 2018.

Byrnes, J. Connors, *The International Bill of Rights for Women: The Impact of the CEDAW Convention*, Oxford 2018.

Castro Apreza I., "Paridad y violencia política. Los retos de las mujeres indígenas de Chiapas," [in:] *Cuando hacer política te cuesta la vida. Estrategias contra la violencia política hacia las mujeres en América Latina*, eds. F. Freidenberg, G. del Valle Pérez, Mexico City 2017.

Centro de Investigaciones para. la Equidad Política Pública y Desarrollo, *Igualdad y Justicia: La violencia política por razón de genero durante el proceso electoral 2018 en México*, Mexico City 2018.

Chandler M., *Votes for Women C. 1900–28*, Oxford 2001.

Córdova L., Buendía E., "Artículo 41," [in:] *Constitución Política de los Estados Unidos Mexicanos Comentada*, ed. J.R. Cossío Díaz, México City 2017.

de Dios V.C., "Violencia política contra las mujeres en México," *Derechos Fundamentales a Debate*, No. 3, Guadalajara 2017.

Fawcett, M.G., *Electoral Disabilities of Women*, London 1872.

Freidenberg F., "La violencia política hacia las mujeres: el problema, los debates y las propuestas para. América Latina," [in:] *Cuando hacer política te cuesta la vida. Estrategias contra la violencia política hacia las mujeres en América Latina*, eds. F. Freidenberg, G. del Valle Pérez, Mexico City 2017.

Galeana P., "Lucha de las mujeres por sus derechos políticos," [in:] *Perspectivas sobre las mujeres en México: Historia, administración pública y participación política*, eds. A. Pérez Correa, G.L. Ramírez, Mexico City 2018.

González, J.A., del Pilar Hernández M., Sánchez-Castañeda A., "La pluralidad de los grupos vulnerables: un enfoque interdisciplinario," [in:] *Derechos humanos: Memoria del IV Congreso Nacional de Derecho Constitucional*, eds. D. Valadés, R. Gutiérrez Rivas, Mexico City 2001.

Iglesias Gutiérrez E. A., "Violencia política de género," [in:] *Temas Selectos Sobre Violencia Política de Género,* eds. C. A. Vázquez Azuara, C. García Méndez, Xalapa, Veracruz, Mexico City 2019.

Iglesias M., "La acción positiva en la forma de cuotas electorales rígidas: algunas reflexiones en torno a los casos de Coahuila y Veracruz," [in:] *Tópicos electorales: un diálogo judicial entre América y Europa*, eds. L. Ríos, Madrid 2011.

Licona Vite C., *Un Siglo de Participación Política de la Mujer en México (1916–2016)*, Mexico City 2016.

Lindbolm T., "Article 1," [in:] *The Universal Declaration of Human Rights: A Common Standard of Achievement*, eds. A. Gudmundur, E. Asbjorn, The Hague 1999.

López Vences R.B., "Violencia política hacia las mujeres indígenas en los municipios de Oaxaca," [in:] *Cuando hacer política te cuesta la vida. Estrategias contra la violencia política hacia las mujeres en América Latina*, eds. F. Freidenberg, G. del Valle Pérez, Mexico City 2017.

Nava S., "Igualdad de género en las sentencias del Tribunal Electoral del Poder Judicial de la Federación. Avances progresivos para. su consolidación," [in:] *La Justicia Electoral*, eds. M. Zavala, F. Zertuche, Mexico City 2015.

Osbürne, R., "¿Son las mujeres una minoría?," *ISEGORÍA: Revista de Filosofía Moral y Política* 1996, No. 14.

Pérez Fernández Ceja Y., *La incorporación de la jurisprudencia internacional de derechos humanos por los Tribunales de Derecho Interno*, Mexico City 2017.

Rivera León M.A., "¿Abrir o desbloquear? El debate de las listas electorales en Mexico," *Revista Mexicana de Derecho Electoral* 2012, No. 2.

Sánchez J., "Igualdad, equidad y Paridad de Género," [in:] *Tratado de Derecho Electoral*, eds. F. de la Mata, C. Coello, Mexico City 2018.

Tribunal Electoral del Poder Judicial de la Federación, *Protocolo para. la Atención de la Violencia Política Contra las Mujeres en Razón de Género*, Mexico City 2017.

Małgorzata Myl
University of Silesia in Katowice
e-mail: malgorzata.myl@us.edu.pl
ORCID ID: 0000-0003-3034-7446

Increased vulnerability of women to enforced disappearances

Abstract: Enforced disappearances have been recognized as a serious and continuing violation of human rights that creates serve social, physical and psychological repercussions on direct victims and their relatives. Although statistics show that mainly men are forcibly disappeared, women are often at the forefront of the struggle against the act. The Working Group of Enforced or Involuntary Disappearances has clearly and unequivocally acknowledged in its General Comment from 2013 that women are in a situation of particular vulnerability in case of enforced disappearances. While being direct victims, they experience special type of harm often based on their gender, sexual violence and long-lasting psychological damage and social stigma. Additionally, women suffer indirectly from enforced disappearances by being socially excluded and negatively affected economically and psychologically. The paper aimed mainly to evaluate the situation of women in the context of enforced disappearance and to determine the reasons of increased vulnerability of women-victims to enforced disappearances.

Keywords: women, enforced disappearances, vulnerable groups

1. Introductory remarks

Pursuant to international law, missing person is someone whose whereabouts are unknown and/or who has been reported missing in accordance with the national law. Furthermore, one's disappearance is connected with international or non-international armed conflict, a situation of internal violence or disturbance, natural catastrophes or any situation that may require the State's intervention.[1] Different types of disappearance can be identified, one of which is an enforced disappearance. As defined in Article 2 of the International

1 *Guiding principles/model law on missing. The Domestic Implementation of International Humanitarian Law: A Manual*, International Committee of the Red

Convention for the Protection of All Persons from Enforced Disappearance (hereafter: ICPPED)[2] 'enforced disappearance' is considered to be an arrest, detention, abduction or any other form of deprivation of liberty by agents of the State or by persons or groups of persons acting with the authorization, support or acquiescence of the State. It is followed by a refusal to acknowledge the deprivation of liberty or by concealment of the fate or whereabouts of the disappeared person. Enforced disappearances have been in the center of international interest since the end of the 1960s, which is mainly due to the policies pursued by Latin Americas States. From the very beginning universal and regional human rights bodies have emphasized that the act constitutes serious violation of human rights. Therefore, international community is responsible for preventing and deterring such acts. It follows directly from the States' obligation to respect human dignity, right to live, right to liberty and security and right to be free from torture or cruel, inhuman or degrading treatment and punishment.[3]

This paper will argue that women are particularly vulnerable direct and indirect victims of enforced disappearances. It will analyze and evaluate various reasons and premises that lead to the increased vulnerability of females. Finally, conclusions make suggestions for preventive measures that should be undertaken by States in order to provide women with proper protection.

2. Women: direct and indirect victims of enforced disappearances

Enforced disappearance constitutes act which violates rights and freedoms of both direct and indirect victims. As expressed in Article 24 of the International Convention for the Protection of All Persons from Enforced Disappearances 'victim of enforced disappearance' is a disappeared person and any individual who has suffered harm as a direct result of an enforced disappearance. The definition of victims has been discussed in preparatory phase before adopting the

Cross 2007, [online:] https://www.icrc.org/en/document/guiding-principles-model-law-missing-model-law [available: 28.05.2020].

2 International Convention for the Protection of All Persons from Enforced Disappearance adopted on 20 December 2006, UN Treaty Series, Vol. 2716, p. 3, C.N.737.2008.

3 H. Keller, O. Chernishova, "Disappearance Cases before the European Court of Human Rights and the UN Human Rights Committee: Convergences and Divergences," *Human Rights Law Journal* 2012, Vol. 32, p. 237.

ICPPED and it was emphasized at the time that the concept of victim cannot be limited only to a disappeared person. It should also include relatives of a disappeared (particularly spouse, children, parents and siblings) and other persons who are negatively affected by enforced disappearances.[4] The broad definition of victim has been reflected in a practice of human rights bodies. The Working Group on Enforced or Involuntary Disappearances (hereafter: WGEID) has repeatedly noted that the act continuously and seriously violates rights of direct victims and their relatives. Moreover, WGEID pointed out that although mainly men are forcibly disappeared, women are considered as particular direct and indirect victims of the violation.[5]

Women and girls are often directly targeted because of their real or perceived resistance to repressive regimes. It should be noted here that various types of activities may be considered as the opposition: work with social justice organizations, participation in women's movements and involvement in armed resistance groups or political parties. Females may be victimized also as a form of punishment for participation in a public sphere, for work with victims or for their engagement in searching for truth about violations.[6] In a significant number of cases women are targeted also because of violation they may have witnessed, their relationships with activists or as a part of broader reprisal against communities. The disappearance of Maria Olga Flores Barraza (that has been reported to Chilean National Commission on Truth and Reconciliation) can be the example of practices mentioned above. The woman went missing after being arrested with her husband, the Communist leader, who also disappeared.[7]

---

4 Report of the intersessional open-ended working group to elaborate a draft legally binding normative instrument for the protection of all persons from enforced disappearance prepared, 12.02.2003, E/CN.4/2003/71, para. 83.

5 Report of the Working Group on Enforced or Involuntary Disappearance on promotion and protection of all human rights, civil, political, social and cultural rights, 21.12.2009, para. 655.

6 P. Dewhirst, A. Kapur, *The Disappeared and Invisible. Revealing the Enduring Impact of Enforced Disappearance on Women*, International Center for Transitional Justice, New York 2015, p. 5.

7 Report of the Chilean National Commission on Truth and Reconciliation, 1991, [online:] United State Institute of Peace, https://www.usip.org/sites/default/files/resources/ collections/truth_commissions/Chile90-Report/Chile90-Report.pdf [available: 4.03.2020], Part III, Chapter 2A, para. 5.

Women, as wives, mothers and children of someone who has disappeared, can be also indirectly victimized by enforced disappearances. They often bear the consequences and are the most affected by the violation.[8] They suffer diverse, long-lasting consequences and other human rights violations as a result of the crime. Gender inequalities steeped in tradition, race, culture, religion, and class often mean that women experience the social, economic, and psychological consequences of disappearances differently than men.[9] It is therefore appropriate to evaluate various reasons and premises that lead to increased vulnerability of women to enforced disappearances.

3. Increased vulnerability to sexual abuses

The Working Group on Enforced or Involuntary Disappearances, in its General Comment from 2013, took the view that females should be recognized as particularly vulnerable victims of enforced disappearances, especially during a time of conflict. Disappeared women, as well as men, suffer different forms of torture, ill-treatment and abuses, however, females usually face a higher risk of sexual violence and gendered forms of abuses.[10] They are often subjected to humiliation and violence around biological functions such as menstruation and childbirth.[11] Women and girls, while disappeared, live in constant fear of sexual violence including rapes which are very often committed by groups of people and repeated many times. It was confirmed *inter alia* by the Argentinian National Commission on the Disappearance of Persons (hereafter also: CONADEP). The commission included in its report *'Nunca mas'* (ang. Never again) testimonies of woman who was repeatedly raped during her disappearance and consequently suffered from a hemorrhage.[12] Increased vulnerability women to sexual violence during disappearance was confirmed also by

8 Report of the Working Group on Enforced or Involuntary Disappearance on promotion and protection of all human rights. . ., para. 655.

9 P. Dewhirst, A. Pakur, *The Disappeared and Invisible. . .*, p. 4.

10 General Comment of the Working Group on Enforced or Involuntary Disappearance on women affected by enforced disappearances, 14.02.2013, para. 7.

11 B. Goldblatt, "Evaluating the Gender Content of Reparations: Lessons from South Africa," [in:] *What happened to the women? Gender and Reparations from Human Rights Violations,* ed. R. Rubis-Marin, New York 2006, p. 54.

12 Report of the Argentinian National Commission on the Disappearance of Persons: Nunca Más: Informe Final de la Comisión Nacional sobre la Desaparición de Personas, [online:] http:// web.archive.Org/web/20031002040053/http://nuncamas.org: 80/index2.htm [available: 04.03.2020], Part. I, Case 1583.

the Inter-American Commission on Human Rights (hereafter: IACHR), e.g. in case of *Ana, Beatriz and Celia Gonzalez Perez v. Mexico.*[13] The Commission established that three sisters had been detained by military staff and multiply raped in order to extort confessions about their political activities.[14] Similar conclusions were brought by the Inter-American Court of Human Rights (hereafter: IACtHR) in case of *Maria Elena Loayza-Tamayo v. Peru*. The victim, while disappeared, was raped and tortured by State agents in order to confess her participation in communism party.[15]

Women are in a situation of particular vulnerability to sexual abuses also as indirect victims of enforced disappearances. They very often suffer poor economic situation caused by a disappearance of a family's main or even sole breadwinner. Women, while trying to find a job, are subjected to a significant risk of unsafe practices or sex services.[16] They are exposed to increased risk of violence, sexual transmitted diseases and unplanned or unwanted pregnancy.[17] Moreover, in some cultures single women, with no protection from men, are more vulnerable to sexual abuses. They are sexually exploited in return for protection or any information about fate and whereabouts of the disappeared relative.[18]

4. Particular vulnerability due to pregnancy and motherhood

International human rights bodies agree that women are very often forcibly disappeared because of their pregnancy or motherhood. Argentinian National Commission on the Disappearance of Persons estimated that at least 10 % of disappeared women were pregnant and their pregnancy could be the main reason for the disappearances.[19] It was established that females were kept alive until their babies were born and then executed. Their children were probably

13 *Ana, Beatriz and Celia González Pérez v. Mexico*, Inter-American Commission on Human Rights, Case 11.565, Report No. 53/01, 4.04.2000.

14 Ibidem, para. 28 et. seq.

15 *Loayza Tamayo v. Peru,* Inter-American Court of Human Rights, Ser. C No. 33, Merits Judgment, 17.09.1997.

16 P. Dewhirst, A. Pakur, *The Disappeared and Invisible. . .*, p. 6.

17 C. Duggan, C. P. Bailey, J. Guillerot, "Reparations for Sexual and Reproductive Violence: Prospects for Achieving Gender Justice in Guatemala and Peru," *International Journal of Transitional Justice* 2008, Vol. 2, iss. 2, p. 196.

18 P. Dewhirst, A. Pakur, *The Disappeared and Invisible. . .*, p. 9.

19 Report of the Argentinian National Commission. . ., Part II.

given to military families and raised without knowing their real identity.[20] Furthermore, CONADEP found that relationships with children and maternal instincts were used to psychologically torture women during their detention.[21] Similar conclusions were presented by Chilean Commission on Truth and Reconciliation. The body confirmed sever cases of disappearances of pregnant women but has been unable to determine if any of their babies were born, or if so, what happened to them.[22] Females are also forcibly disappeared in order to impregnate them. This practice was confirmed *inter alia* by Sierra Leone Truth and Reconciliation Commission which established that it was very common to rape disappeared women for the insemination purpose and, consequently, cause their exclusion from family and society.[23]

Women, who are mothers of disappeared persons, are also exposed to great psychological damage and emotional trauma.[24] They are very often socially stigmatized and blamed for bad upholding or for not taking proper care of their disappeared children. This results in their family and social rejection and exposed them to even greater psychological and emotional harm.[25] Women-mothers become very often victims of intimidation. Inter-American Court of Human Rights continuously emphasizes that females whose children disappeared are particularly vulnerable to psychical suffering and social persecutions. In case of *Gómez Paquiyauri Brothers v. Peru*[26] the Court established that mother of two disappeared boys were intimidated by authorities and prevented from finding a job what resulted in her deep psychological harm. The IACtHR focused its attention on mothers also in case of *Street Children v. Guatemala.*[27] The case concerned the kidnapping, torture and death of five minors committed by Guatemalan secret forces and the State's failure to provide

20 Ibidem.

21 Ibidem.

22 Report of the Chilean National Commission. . ., Part III, Chapter II, para. 5 f.

23 Final Report of the Sierra Leone Truth and Reconciliation Commission: Witness to Truth, 5.10.2004, [online:] http://www.sierraleonetrc.org/index.php/view-the-final-report/table-of-contents [available: 06.03.2020], Vol. 2, Chapter 1, para. 54.

24 General Comment of the Working Group on Enforced or Involuntary Disappearance on women. . ., para. 11.

25 Ibidem.

26 *Gómez Paquiyauri Brothers v. Peru*, Inter-American Court of Human Rights, Ser. C No. 110, Merits, Satisfactions and Costs Judgment, 8.07.2004.

27 *"Street Children" (Villagran-Morales* et al.*) v. Guatemala,* Inter-American Court of Human Rights, Ser. C No. 63, Merits Judgment, 19.11.1999.

adequate judicial protection to the victims' families. It was determined that the circumstances surrounding the death of these children (in particular the way in which their bodies were abandoned and the visible signs of torture) had caused a great deal of suffering to the relatives of victims.[28] The IACtHR also emphasized that these circumstances as well as subsequent treatment given to the remains of the victims constituted cruel and inhuman treatment for relatives, particularly for their mothers.[29]

5. Disproportionate and uneven economic and social suffering

Women, whose beloved ones went missing, are exposed not only to psychological trauma but also to great economic and social harm. The harm, due to traditional gender roles and structural inequalities, may be confront by them differently than by men.[30] Working Group on Enforced or Involuntary Disappearances continues to emphasize that disappearance of a head of household results economically in entire family but particularly in women.[31] They have to step into role of family breadwinner which in many societies is held mostly by man. This leads to situation whereby women need to get a job for the first time in their lives, even though they do not have proper education nor experience. They are therefore very often subjected to a significant risk of different types of abuse, e.g. low pays, informal employment and sex services[32] and, consequently, they are further victimized.

Relatives of direct victims commonly have to change or abandon their life plans as they are barely able to make ends meet. The issue was noted by Inter-American Court of Human Rights e.g. in case of *Gomez Palomino v. Peru.*[33] As the only breadwinner disappeared, his sisters had to drop out of education due to lack of money.[34] Similar conclusions were drawn also by Human Rights Committee[35] and Truth and Reconciliation Commission in South

28 Ibidem, para. 153 et al.

29 Ibidem, para. 174.

30 P. Dewhirst, A. Kapur, *The Disappeared and Invisible...*, p. 6.

31 E.g. General Comment of the Working Group on Enforced or Involuntary Disappearance on women..., Preamble and para. 12.

32 P. Dewhirst, A. Kapur, *The Disappeared and Invisible...*, p. 6.

33 *Gomez Palomino v. Peru*, Inter-American Court of Human Rights, Ser. C No. 136, Merits, Reparations and Costs Judgment, 22.11.2005.

34 Ibidem, para. 54 at eq.

35 E.g. *Mukunda Sedhai v. Nepal,* Human Rights Committee, Communication No. 1865/2008, 26.97.2013, para. 2.9.

Africa.[36] All these negative consequences can be even greater in societies facing traditional gender roles and structural inequalities. As there is no money for proper education of all relatives, the priority is usually given to men what, in turn, leads to further marginalization and victimization of women.[37] Females sometimes are forced to get married as it is believed in some communities that marriage can help to improve economic situation of whole family.[38] It must be noted that national law, which maintains gender inequalities, also causes the particular vulnerability of women to economic suffering. Females sometimes are not allowed to own land, houses or other goods. They cannot change an ownership as sometimes it is extremely expensive or simply impossible.[39]

Enforced disappearances are also a source of negative social effects, which may be suffered by females differently due to gender roles.[40] WGEID noted that disappeared women, even if they eventually manage to survive, are exposed to great social and familial stigma.[41] The same conclusions were reached by Sierra Leone Truth and Reconciliation Commission. The body drawn attention to the fact that women, while disappeared, are often subjected to violence resulting in humiliation not only them, but also their families and the whole community.[42] The trauma and damage can be even greater as the women's role in some societies is clearly defined. Saving virginity until marriage very often is considered as a great value of girls as well as their relatives. It contributes to preserve the family status and influences on family well-being. Loosing virginity, in turn, brings shame on the whole family and leads to their exclusion from society.[43] Commission in Sierra Leone also emphasized that women are very often force

36 Truth and Reconciliation Commission of South Africa Report, [online:] http://www.justice.gov.za/trc/report [available: 07.03.2020], Vol. 3, Chapter 4, para. 25.

37 P. Dewhirst, A. Kapur, *The Disappeared and Invisible...*, p. 6.

38 D. Mazurana, T. Atim, *Making Gender-Just Remedy and Reparations Possible: Upholding the Rights of Women and Girls in Uganda's Greater North,* Feinstein International Center and ISIS Women's International Cross Cultural Exchange, Somerville 2014, p. 53.

39 Ch. Yakinthou, *Living with the Shadows of the Past. The Impact of the Disappearance on Wives of the Missing in Lebanon,* International Center for Transitional Justice, New York 2015, p. 14.

40 General Comment of the Working Group on Enforced or Involuntary Disappearance on women..., Preamble and para. 5.

41 Ibidem.

42 Final Report of the Sierra Leone Truth and Reconciliation Commission.,.Vol. 2, Chapter 1, para. 50.

43 Ibidem, Vol. 3B, Chapter 3, para. 81.

to marry the perpetrators in order to 'repent their blame.'[44] This results in even greater damage, humiliation and further victimization of women-survivors of enforced disappearances.

Women face negative social effects also as indirect victims of enforced disappearances. In some societies females, after their husbands' or fathers' disappearances, struggle intra-familiar harassment. They are perceived as a burden for the rest of the family.[45] Single woman may need special protection or financial support which eventually results in deteriorated material situation of other relatives as well as in disturbed family hierarchy. On the other hand women who take up a job may be blamed for breaking with tradition.[46]

6. Prolonged uncertainty and unspecified legal status

Enforced disappearances are usually followed by concealment of the fate or whereabouts of a disappeared person. Prolonged period of not knowing what has happened to the missing relative may result in trauma, which can be even greater if the missing relative is a child. For the same reason, long-lasting unawareness and uncertainty has been considered as a form of torture or inhuman treatment. Human Rights Committee in case of *Maria del Carmen Almeida de Quinteros v. Uruguay* came to conclusion that State had been engaged in cruel and inhuman treatment by refusing to inform mother about fate of her disappeared child.[47] Similar opinion was expressed by the Committee also in many subsequent cases, e.g. in case of *Yamina Guezout* et al. *v. Algeria.*[48] It must be also noted that lack of information about what has happened precludes relatives from experience and close the mourning period.[49] They live in hope that their beloved ones are still alive. Chilean National Commission on Truth and Reconciliation noted that women very often refuse to change their living place fearing that their disappeared relatives would not be able to find them once they return. For the same reason, they keep houses,

44 Ibidem, Vol. 3, Chapter 3, para. 90.

45 C. M. Beristain, "The Value of Memory," *Forced Migration Review* 1998, Vol. 2, p. 24.

46 Ibidem, pp. 25–26.

47 *Maria del Carmen Almeida de Quinteros v. Uruguay*, Human Rights Committee, Communication No. 107/1981, 21.07.1983, para. 14.

48 *Yamina Guezout* et al. *v. Algeria*, Human Rights Committee, Communication No. 1753/2008, 27.07.2012, para. 10.

49 M. Blaauw, "'Denial and silence' or 'acknowledgment and disclosure'," *International Review of the Red Cross* 2002, Vol. 84, p. 768.

rooms and belongings in the unaltered state thereby deepening their trauma.[50] Psychological and emotional harm can be suffered as long as the victims are not under proper treatment. It must be remembered though that in some societies women struggle with unequal access to healthcare system what place them in situation of increased vulnerability to suffering.[51]

Social stigma and marginalization of women may also arise from their uncertain and unspecified status (especially if there live in a community with strongly divided gender roles). Wives of the disappeared may struggle with familial and societal pressure to determine their position and to conform to the traditional role of either a widow or a wife.[52] The pressure may be even greater in countries where bodily remarking and rituals are used to signify the status of marriage and widowhood. Wearing the symbols and participating in the rituals may sometimes be considered as inauspicious. Consequently, wives of the disappeared do not enjoy the same privileges as their married peers.[53] In addition, women can also face pressure about remarriage what results in greater deal of suffering.[54]

Uncertain legal and social situation of women is also caused by the lack of legal recognition of a status of disappeared. Relatives, particularly wives, are left with no provision for the administrative and legal complications resulting from an enforced disappearance. This is especially relevant in societies where men have traditionally been the family representative in legal matters. International human rights bodies agree that unresolved legal status of disappeared, as well as their relatives, results in many serious social, economic and psychological problems. The Special Rapporteur on extrajudicial, summary or arbitrary executions drew attention to the fact that a refusal or a failure to issue a document confirming a disappearance or a death is a source of further victimization.[55] The similar conclusions were reached also by the Working Group on

50 Report of the Chilean National Commission…, Part III, Chapter 4, para. C.2–3.

51 P. Dewhirst, A. Kapur, *The Disappeared and Invisible…*, p. 11.

52 Ibidem, p. 9.

53 S. Robins, "Ambiguous Loss in a Non-Western Context: Families of the Disappeared in Postconflict Nepal," *Family Relation. Interdisciplinary Journal of Applied Family Science* 2010, Vol. 59.3, p. 256; D. Somasundaram, "Individual, Familial and Social Impacts of Enforced Disappearances," [in:] *We need the truth. Enforced Disappearances in Asia*, ed. K. Lauritsch, Guatemala 2010, p. 16.

54 P. Dewhirst, A. Kapur, *The Disappeared and Invisible…*, p. 10.

55 See e.g.: the report of 1996 of the Special Rapporteur on extrajudicial, summary or arbitrary execution, 21.12.1996, E/CN.4/1997/60, paras. 46–47; The report of 2010 of

Enforced or Involuntary Disappearance. The body concluded that the absence of a death certificate, in some cases, makes impossible for relatives (particularly wives) to receive pension or other means of support.[56] Therefore, women very often have to declare relatives' death as it seems to be the only option in order to access to certain rights, including inheritance, child custody or reparations. Declaring death of beloved one, while still having a hope, is a heartbreaking and traumatic process, with legal, social and psychological implications for women. Females very often have a guilty conscience at having to accept the death of their missing ones when in reality that person's fate and whereabouts has not been clarified yet.

In case of enforced disappearances receiving the declaration of death sometimes might be very hard, if not impossible, due to lack of body as a proof of the death.[57] With regard to this the Committee on Enforced Disappearances recommended on several occasions not to make the right of reparation contingent on the existence of evidence of death of the disappeared person or statement of presumption of death.[58] It was confirmed by Human Rights Committee which emphasized that States should not make the relatives' rights to seek reparations contingent on securing a death certificate.[59] The issue was addressed also by the Chilean National Commission on Truth and Reconciliation in its report from 1991. The commission recommended to change national regulations and

---

the Special Rapporteur on extrajudicial, summary or arbitrary execution, 20.05.2010, A/HRC/14/21, paras. 56–58.

56 General Comment of the Working Group on Enforced or Involuntary Disappearance on women. . ., para. 12.

57 Ch. Yakinthou, *Living with the Shadows*. . ., p. 18.

58 Concluding observations to Argentina, Committee on Enforced Disappearances, CED/C/ARG/CO/1, 12.12.2013, para. 35; Concluding observations to Uruguay, Committee on Enforced Disappearances, CED/C/URY/CO/1, 8.05.2013, para. 32; Concluding observations to Armenia, Committee on Enforced Disappearances, 11.02.2015, para. 25; Concluding observations to Spain, Committee on Enforced Disappearances, CED/C/ESP/CO/1, 12.12.2013, para. 30; Concluding observations to France, Committee on Enforced Disappearances, CED/C/FRA/CO/1, 8.05.2013, para. 35; Concluding observations to Netherlands, Committee on Enforced Disappearances, CED/C/NLD/CO/1, 10.04.2014, para. 33; Concluding observations to Paraguay, Committee on Enforced Disappearances, CED/C/PRY/CO/1, 24.09.2014, para. 26; Concluding observations to Serbia, Committee on Enforced Disappearances, 5.02.2015, paras. 24 and 25.

59 See e.g.: *Hero v. Bosnia and Herzegovina*, Human Rights Committee, Communication No. 1966/2010, 28.10.2014, para. 11.

establish special procedures in such a way as to ensure that relatives of missing people can enjoy their rights under a special procedure. It was determined that it is not necessary to find remains of a victim in order to declare dead. Instead, enrolment on the special list prepared by the Commission was tantamount to the right to receive reparations.[60] The procedure aimed to reduce the suffering of relatives and to ensure that they receive required support and help. Similar conclusions were presented also by the Truth and Reconciliation Commission of South Africa.[61]

7. Conclusions

Although different statistics show that mainly men are forcibly disappeared, women are particularly vulnerable to the violation. They are directly and indirectly victimized, they suffer economically, socially and psychologically. Their particular situation is due to their gender roles and inequality rooted in tradition, race, culture and social class. These factors cause that women's situation (legal and factual) is different from men's.

Females are very often (disproportionately) exposed to sexual violence and to suffering and humiliation. They are commonly used as a tool to achieve specific objective due to their subordinate status and social vulnerability. Their bodies are used as part of strategy of social control. It is because of the biological attributes of women, especially ability to reproduce and maternal relationship. Moreover, women suffer economical, emotional, psychological and social harm. The suffering is even greater when the disappeared is a child and a main or an only breadwinner of the family. Situation of females are divers depending on the community their belong. In some societies, women cannot enjoy the same rights as men and, therefore, in case of the disappearance of male relative they are in particularly difficult situation. They cannot fully (if at all) exercise the right to effective remedy, right to information and right to reparation.

Given the above, States should be obliged to provide women with special protection procedures and mechanisms. Females-victims of enforced disappearances should be given the priority attention. The scale of the violation should be carefully determined as number of reported cases of disappeared women still seems to be underestimated. Preventive and reparative mechanisms, applied by States, should be based on gender-sensitive factors.

---

60 Report of the Chilean National Commission. . ., Part IV, Chapter I, para. C.2.

61 Truth and Reconciliation Commission of South Africa Report. . ., Vol. 5, Chapter 5, para. 79.

It is also necessary to evaluate reasons which lead to disappearances of women. Special attention should be given to women's right to information and right to the truth. State, while establishing the truth about violations, should take into account following aspects: gender roles in culture, tradition and religion. It will contribute to discover a special pattern of enforced disappearances of women. It will also enable women to access and receive reparations. Without determined efforts and strong actions taken by States, the issue of particular vulnerability of women to the enforced disappearances will still be undervalued and unsolved.

Bibliography:

Beristain C.M., "The Value of Memory," *Forced Migration Review* 1998, Vol. 2.

Blaauw M., "'Denial and silence' or 'acknowledgment and disclosure'," *International Review of the Red Cross* 2002, Vol. 84.

Dewhirst P., Kapur A., *The Disappeared and Invisible. Revealing the Enduring Impact of Enforced Disappearance on Women*, International Center for Transitional Justice, New York 2015.

Duggan C., Bailey C.P., Guillerot J., "Reparations for Sexual and Reproductive Violence: Prospects for Achieving Gender Justice in Guatemala and Peru," *International Journal of Transitional Justice* 2008, Vol. 2, iss. 2.

Goldblatt B., "Evaluating the Gender Content of Reparations: Lessons from South Africa," [in:] *What happened to the women? Gender and Reparations from Human Rights Violations,* ed. R. Rubis-Marin, New York 2006.

Keller H., Chernishova O., "Disappearance Cases before the European Court of Human Rights and the UN Human Rights Committee: Convergences and Divergences," *Human Rights Law Journal* 2012, Vol. 32.

Mazurana D., Atim T., *Making Gender-Just Remedy and Reparations Possible: Upholding the Rights of Women and Girls in Uganda's Greater North,* Feinstein International Center and ISIS Women's International Cross Cultural Exchange, Somerville 2014.

Robins S., "Ambiguous Loss in a Non-Western Context: Families of the Disappeared in Postconflict Nepal," *Family Relation. Interdisciplinary Journal of Applied Family Science* 2010, Vol. 59, iss. 3.

Somasundaram D., *Individual, Familial and Social Impacts of Enforced Disappearances* [in:] *We need the truth. Enforced Disappearances in Asia,* ed. K. Lauritsch, Guatemala 2010.

Yakinthou Ch., *Living with the Shadows of the Past. The Impact of the Disappearance on Wives of the Missing in Lebanon,* International Center for Transitional Justice, New York 2015.

Aleksandra Szczerba

The Jacob of Paradies University in Gorzów Wielkopolski

e-mail: szczerba.aleksandra@gmail.com

ORCID ID: 0000-0001-7857-0554

Protection of women with respect to pregnancy and maternity in European Union law: between paternalism and equality

Abstract: Pregnancy is considered a premise justifying the special treatment of women by both the EU legislator and the Court of Justice of the European Union. As a result, the normative mechanism for protection of women against discrimination based on pregnancy was introduced into the EU secondary legislation.

The purpose of this chapter is to offer a critical analysis of selected protective measures stipulated by Directives 92/85 and 2006/54 and construed by the CJEU through the gender equality glass. The EU normative standard on pregnant workers and workers who have recently given birth undoubtedly contributes to ensuring equal opportunities for women implying changes to social and legal attitude towards pregnancy. Nevertheless, the protective mechanisms at issues are based on often stereotypical assumptions about the needs of women during pregnancy and the follow-up period, assumptions which excessively interfere with women's autonomy. As a result, the provisions which are intended to protect women in connection with pregnancy and maternity and form part of the EU gender equality law do result in less favorable treatment of women as defined in terms of *substantive* equality.

Keywords: EU gender equality, the CJEU case-law, pregnancy, directive 92/85, directive 2006/54

1. Introductory remarks

The EU legislator assumed that pregnant workers, as well as workers who have recently given birth or are breastfeeding must be considered as a particularly sensitive risk group, which justifies taking appropriate measures with regard to their safety and health protection as well as protection of their legal status.[1]

---

1 See recitals of the Council Directive 92/85/EEC of October 19, 1992 on the introduction of measures to encourage improvements in the safety and health at work of

A similar approach towards pregnancy as a premise justifying the special treatment of women is shared by the Court of Justice of the European Union. It was as a result of its jurisprudence that the prohibition of discrimination based on sex was extended to cases of unequal treatment of women related to pregnancy and maternity even though this was not and still isn't explicit treaty standard.

The TEU highlights the fundamental role of the equality, including gender equality (art. 2) and declare combating discrimination and promotion of equality between women and men as a EU objective (art. 3 (3)). TFEU stipulates that the Union, in all its activities, should aim to eliminate inequalities, and to promote equality, between men and women (art. 8) and clarifies that in defining and implementing its policies and activities, the Union should aim to combat discrimination based on all protected characteristics, including sex (art. 10). It adds also that each Member State shall ensure the principle of equal pay for male and female workers for equal work or work of equal value (art. 157 (1)) and allows Member States to maintain or adopt measures providing for specific advantages in order to make it easier for the underrepresented sex to pursue a vocational activity or to prevent or compensate for disadvantages in professional careers with a view to ensuring full equality in practice between men and women in working life (art. 157 (4)).

Nevertheless, juridical standard at issue is confirmed by the provisions of equality directives. In accordance with Art. 2(2)(c) of Directive 2006/54[2] any less favorable treatment of a woman on grounds of pregnancy or maternity is a form of direct discrimination. Protection against discriminatory treatment of women due to these criteria is based, on the one hand, on maternity protection measures, including the protection of the biological condition of pregnant women and women during postpartum, on the other on solutions that help women (and men) reconcile family and professional life. Both types of measures are considered as complementary instruments for achieving real equality (recitals 24 and 11 of Directive 2006/54). As a consequence, the normative mechanism for protection of women against discrimination based on pregnancy should be reconstructed upon the provisions of the EU gender equality

---

pregnant workers and workers who have recently given birth or are breastfeeding (Official Journal of the European Union L 348/1), hereinafter: Directive 92/85.

2 Directive 2006/54/EC of the European Parliament and of the Council of July 5, 2006 on the implementation of the principle of equal opportunities and equal treatment of men and women in matters of employment and occupation (recast) (Official Journal of the European Union L 204/23), hereinafter: Directive 2006/54.

law *sensu largo*, which consists of Directive 92/85 aimed at protecting the health and life of pregnant women and women in the postpartum period, Directive 2006/54 prohibiting discrimination against women based on these premises, and Directive 2010/18, which facilitates the work-life balance of employees.[3]

The purpose of this chapter is to offer a critical analysis of selected protective measures stipulated by Directives 92/85 and 2006/54 and construed by the CJEU through the prism of their equality potential. The protective mechanisms at issue are characterized by specificities which are justified by the special position of women during pregnancy, followed by the period of maternity leave, which is not comparable either with that of a man or with that of a woman actually at work.[4] It is determined, to a great extent, by the paternalistic approach of the EU legislator and the EU judiciary towards pregnant women as a particularly sensitive risk group that must be protected against the dangers which affect them exclusively. As a result, the protective mechanisms that have been introduced are based on often stereotypical assumptions about the needs of women during pregnancy and the follow-up period, assumptions which excessively interfere with women's autonomy. The judicialization of pregnancy as a ground for objective differentiation in treatment in a situation where the equality criteria are still set from a male perspective, leads, as a consequence, to rationalization of the restrictions of rights of women (in the professional sphere) and men (in the family sphere) in the EU gender equality law. An attempt to depart from the described paradigm of women's protection in the anti-discriminatory *acquis* is visible in Directive 2010/18, behind which there is a different intention, taking into account not the differences in the situation of women and men resulting from biological differences between the sexes, but the similarity of the position of women and men in relation to their parental roles with respect to socially constructed gender. This act of EU law, which does not directly concern the premise of pregnancy but rather the sexually neutral criterion of parenthood, remains, however, outside the scope of the analysis in this study.[5]

---

3 Council Directive 2010/18/EU of March 8, 2010 implementing the revised Framework Agreement on parental leave concluded by BUSINESSEUROPE, UEAPME, CEEP and ETUC and repealing Directive 96/34/EC (Official Journal of the European Union L 68/13), hereinafter: Directive 2010/18.

4 *Gillespie*, C-342/93, EU:C: 1996: 46, para. 17.

5 For more on the EU provisions on protection with respect to parenthood, see A. Szczerba-Zawada, "Ochrona rodzicielstwa w systemie Unii Europejskiej. Uwagi de lege lata," *Studia Prawnicze i Administracyjne* 2014, No. 1, p. 26 et seq.

2. Pregnancy as a premise for protection in EU gender equality law

The introduction into EU law of solutions protecting women against the negative consequences of pregnancy and maternity is undoubtedly an important factor in achieving substantive gender equality. The normativization of the issue at stake is not only an instrument for *ad hoc* impact on the behavior of participants of legal relations falling under the scope of application of the EU equality legislation. It also implies changes in the social perception of pregnancy, a perception which, in the light of relevant EU norms, can no longer be considered as a burden, and in particular no longer as a problem exclusive to female employees. Protective mechanisms introduced in this respect, imposing specific obligations on the employer, both positive and negative ones, lead to dispersion of the "costs of pregnancy," in particular those of an economic nature,[6] and thus contribute to the eradication of bias against mothers in employment.[7] The normative mechanism at issue encompasses both protecting women's biological condition during pregnancy and maternity as well as their legal status as workers, and is established by both Directive 92/85 and Directive 2006/54.

Due to its legal basis (Art. 118(a) of ECC Treaty), Directive 92/85 cannot be classified as equality instrument *sensu stricto*, although its purpose, which is to protect the woman's biological condition during pregnancy and motherhood, is considered an important aspect of real gender equality.[8] This makes it possible to qualify Directive 92/84 as an instrument of EU gender equality law *sensu largo*. Such a classification is also justified by the reasons for its adoption – the need to counteract the decrease in the working population of professionally active women and to protect women against the negative consequences on their legal status as employees resulting from social attitudes towards pregnancy.[9]

---

6 See *Dekker*, C-177/88, EU:C:1990:383, in which the CJEU stated that the refusal of employment of a female candidate based on the possible adverse consequences for an employer of employing a pregnant woman, owing to national law which assimilates inability to work on account of pregnancy and confinement to inability to work on account of illness, constitutes direct gender discrimination.

7 For more on this issue, see C. J. Vinkenburg, M.L. Van Engen, J. Coffeng, J.S.E. Dikkers, "Bias in Employment Decisions about Mothers and Fathers: The (Dis) Advantages of Sharing Care Responsibilities," *Journal of Social Issues* 2012, Vol. 68, No. 4, pp. 725–741.

8 See recital 24 and Art. 2 (2)(c) of the Directive 2006/54.

9 As explained by R. Guerrina, *Mothering the Union. Gender politics in the EU*, Manchester – New York 2005, p. 68.

This is also confirmed in the light of the CJEU case-law, according to which it is clear that a worse treatment of women based on the characteristics typically exclusive to the female sex (pregnancy and motherhood) is a form of direct discrimination on the grounds of sex.[10] Seen in this perspective, Directive 92/85 undoubtedly marks progress in the efforts to ensure the health, safety, and working conditions of pregnant workers by introducing protective measures for women as a manifestation of the so-called "differentiated equality."[11] In explaining its relationship with the EU equality law *sensu stricto*, recital 24 and Art. 28 of Directive 2006/54 indicate that its provisions should be without prejudice to Directive 92/85. This suggests that the specific provisions concerning the protection of women, particularly as regards pregnancy, are treated as an exception to the principle of equal treatment for women and men provided for in Directive 2006/54.[12]

However, the substantive equality between women and men, which is an aim of the EU law at issue, is achieved using means that in many respects contribute to the enhancement, rather than the eradication, of existing social inequalities between the sexes.[13] This is the result, to a great extent, of a paternalistic approach towards pregnancy and maternity, resulting in addressing certain

10 CJEU judgments: *Brown*, C-394/96, EU:C:1998:331, paras: 16, 24 and 25; *McKenna*, C-191/03, EU:C:2005:513, para. 47; and *Paquay*, C-460/06, EU:C:2007:60, para. 29, in which Court held that less favorable treatment of women based on pregnancy or a reason essentially based on that condition as affecting only women constituted direct discrimination on the grounds of sex.

11 I. Boruta, *Równość kobiet i mężczyzn w pracy w świetle prawa Wspólnoty Europejskiej. Implikacje dla Polski*, Łódź 1996, p. 99.

12 Despite such a wording, which is typical to the derogation from the principle of equal treatment, the CJEU does not interpret the provisions of Directive 92/85 narrowly, as noted by S. Prechal, "Equality of treatment, non-discrimination and social policy: Achievements in three themes," *Common Market Law Review* 2004, Vol. 41, No. 2, p. 539.

13 As confirmed by positions in the doctrine, including J. Kantola, *Gender and the European Union*, Basingstoke–New York 2010, pp. 105–106; D. Schiek, "Commentary on the Article 6 of the EU Charter of Fundamental Rights," [in:] *The EU Charter of Fundamental Rights. A Commentary*, eds. S. Peers, T. Hervey, J. Kenner, A. Ward, Oxford–Portland 2014, p. 639; M. Weldon-Johns, "EU work-family policies – Challenging parental roles or reinforcing gendered stereotypes?," *European Law Journal* 2013, Vol. 19, No. 5, pp. 662–663; and R. Guerrina, *Mothering. . .*, p. 5. See also the CJEU judgment *Danfoss*, C-109/88, EU:C: 1989: 383, para. 21, in which the Court stated that women "because of household and family duties for which they are frequently responsible, are not as able as men to organize their working time flexibly."

privileges exclusively to women, including some of a compulsory nature, i.e. which women are obliged to exercise irrespectively of their will and even when the nature of the relevant rights does not exclude men from exercising them as well. In particular, this remark relates to the sharing of care responsibilities in the case of a newborn child resulting from the institution of maternity leave adopted in EU law, which leads to the marginalization of the role of a father in childcare as a consequence of giving priority to a specific family model,[14] thus hindering the attainment of substantive gender equality. The intention behind such a construction of maternity leave in EU law reflects the perception of women through the prism of the stereotypical assumption about the emotional and physical consequences of pregnancy. This kind of paternalistic approach results in the assumption of the need to "protect women," an assumption accepted by the CJEU as a justification for the specific treatment of pregnant women and women who have recently given birth, a treatment which is considered to be an exception to formal gender equality. This assumption thus replaces that of pursuing material equality between women and men on the grounds of EU gender anti-discriminatory law, an approach which should lead to the legal appreciation of parenthood as such, and not just motherhood.[15]

This specificity of the equality *acquis* is the result of its strong connection, especially at the early stage of development of the integration processes, with the requirements of the internal market. EU anti-discrimination law was supposed to be an instrument for the creation of this market, and not of its correction.[16] This subordination of women's and men's rights to the economic aspects of integration had an impact on equality law, which inevitably normalized the existing social relations based largely on the stereotypical division of social

14 As assessed by M. Weldon-Johns, *EU work-family policies*, p. 666. See also the CJEU judgment in *Hofmann*, C-184/83, EU:C:1984:273, para. 24, where the Court stated explicitly that the Council Directive 76/207/EEC of February 9, 1976 on the implementation of the principle of equal treatment for men and women as regards access to employment, vocational training and promotion, and working conditions (Official Journal of the European Union L 039/40) – the predecessor of Directive 2006/54, was not designed to settle questions concerned with the organization of the family or to modify the division of responsibility between parents.

15 Cf. C. McGlynn, "Ideologies of Motherhood in European Community Sex Equality Law," *European Law Journal* 2000, Vol. 6, No. 1, p. 35.

16 See E. Caracciolo di Torella, "Brave New Fathers for a Brave New World? Fathers as Caregivers in an Evolving European Union," *European Law Journal* 2014, Vol. 20, No. 1, p. 89.

roles ascribed to women and men, and therefore normalized existing gender stereotypes rather than eliminate them. Although the Court of Justice of the European Union has made attempts to overcome the stereotypical perception of male and female roles, it does so within the scope of and on the basis of relevant EU law, which, firstly, continues to enhance the described model of the division of professional and family responsibilities between women and men; and secondly is characterized by a lack of consistency due to differences in the scope of application of the relevant directives, i.e. Directive 2006/54, 92/85 and Directive 2010/18, resulting in the Court's sometimes incoherent and inconsistent case-law. As a consequence, the evolutionary jurisprudence of the CJEU can only partially contribute to mitigating the identified deficiencies of EU law, and then only to the extent it is not a factor for deepening or even rationalizing the gender stereotypes.[17]

The above-mentioned situation may be, in part, due to implementation of notions of sex defined primarily through the prism of biological masculine and feminine characteristics into the EU gender equality law on pregnancy.[18] This leads to a narrow interpretation of the concept at issue, which is complemented by a narrow – biological – construction of pregnancy under Directive 92/85. This is confirmed by the *Mayr* judgment, in which the CJEU stated that although it is clear that the earliest possible date in a pregnancy must be chosen to ensure the safety and protection of pregnant workers, the protection established by Art. 10 of Directive 92/85 may not be extended to a female worker who is undergoing *in vitro* fertilization treatment where, on the date she is given notice of her dismissal, her ova have already been fertilized by her partner's sperm cells, so that *in vitro*-fertilized ova exist, but they have not yet been transferred into her uterus.[19] Otherwise the protection introduced for reasons linked to the pregnancy would be granted before the pregnancy has started. By analogy, a female worker who is a commissioning mother who has had a baby through a surrogacy arrangement does not fall within the scope of Directive 92/85.[20]

17 For more on this issue, see A. Szczerba-Zawada, "Gender Stereotypes and EU Antidiscrimination Case Law – (fighting) a Hidden Threat to the EU Value of Equality?," *Studia Europejskie* 2018, No. 4, pp. 225–234.

18 The EU equality law is therefore based on the traditional binary division into two sexes.

19 Mayr, C-506/06, EU:C:2008:119, paras. 42 *et seq.*

20 As can be inferred from CJEU judgment in *D.*, C-167/12, EU:C: 2014:169.

Nevertheless, the refusal to grant protection under Directive 92/85 in the circumstances discussed above does not preclude the admissibility of a claim for protection under Directive 2006/54. In its *Mayr* judgment the CJEU decided that the latter precludes the dismissal of a female worker who is at an advanced stage of *in vitro* fertilization treatment, that is, between the follicular puncture and the immediate transfer of the *in vitro*-fertilized ova into the uterus, insofar as it is established that the dismissal was essentially based on the fact that the woman has undergone such treatment. The treatment in question directly affects only women. It follows that the dismissal of a female worker essentially because she is undergoing that important stage of *in vitro* fertilization treatment constitutes direct discrimination on the grounds of sex.[21] Such an opinion of the CJEU proves that although it extended protection against unequal treatment on the grounds of sex to a woman who underwent *in vitro* fertilization, it did so not because of the premise of pregnancy *per se*, which in accordance with the CJEU's assessment did not appear in the analyzed case, but due to the specificity of this procedure, characteristic only for one sex. This may indicate an extension of the concept of direct discrimination on account of sex to include less favorable treatment based on medical treatment affecting exclusively one sex,[22] which can enhance the protection of women against discrimination essentially based on pregnancy.

3. Protection of the health of pregnant workers as a component of the EU gender equality principle

The protection of women's work on the grounds of pregnancy is understood broadly in EU law as covering all norms aimed at safeguarding the interests of employees during pregnancy and maternity leave.[23] The starting point of the protection period varies depending on whether it is analyzed under Directive 92/85, which should be considered a *lex specialis* (granting protection only to a pregnant worker who has informed the employer of her condition in accordance with national law or practice and therefore only concerning ongoing employment relationships), or in relation to the provisions of Directive 2006/54 establishing a general prohibition of discrimination against women on

21 *Mayr*, C-506/06, paras. 50–52.

22 As noted by K. Koldinská, "Case law of the European Court of Justice on sex discrimination 2006–2011," *Common Market Law Review* 2011, Vol. 48, No. 5, pp. 1621–1622.

23 On the broad scope of protection of female employees in EU law, see: H. Szewczyk, *Równość płci w zatrudnieniu*, Warszawa 2017, p. 142.

account of pregnancy and maternity. As a consequence, only the latter applies to formally non-existent employment relationships, and in addition protection against unequal treatment under Directive 2006/54 is granted in relation to access to employment and therefore it can be invoked during the recruitment process. Having regard to the fundamental nature of the right to effective legal protection, workers should continue to enjoy protection both under Directive 92/85 and Directive 2006/54 even after the relationship giving rise to an alleged breach of the principle of equal treatment has ended.[24] The objective of EU equality with regard to both the rights of pregnant women as well as women who have given birth, which informs both Directive 92/85 and Directive 2006/54, makes this protection available regardless of the formal categorization of the employment relationship under national law or the choice made at the time of appointment between one type of contract and another.[25] The relevant EU provisions impose on the employer the obligation to provide a safe and healthy workplace environment during both pregnancy and the breastfeeding period by temporarily adjusting the working conditions and/or the working hours of the female worker, either by moving the worker concerned to another job or granting leave to her for the whole period necessary to protect her safety or health if the results of the assessment of a specific risk of exposure reveal a risk to her safety or health or an effect on the pregnancy.[26]

The above-mentioned legal solutions, introduced due to the care for the well-being of a pregnant woman and taking into account her specific needs, should be assessed positively. They enable the taking of measures that are individualized, i.e. dependent on whether, in a specific case, there is a threat to the life and health of a woman or a child, and adjusted to the needs (and will) of the pregnant worker and the employer's abilities. A similar balancing of the interests of both parties to the employment relationship is visible in the prohibition against requiring women to perform night work during pregnancy and for a period following childbirth, the length of which is determined not by the EU law but by the Member States.[27] The prohibition of night work by women during pregnancy also applies to a situation where a female worker does shift work in the context of which only part of her duties are performed at night,[28]

---

24 See recital 32 of the Directive 2006/54.

25 *Danosa*, C-232/09, EU:C:2010:674, paras. 68–69.

26 Art. 5(1)–(3) of the Directive 92/85.

27 Art. 7 of Directive 92/85.

28 *González Castro*, C-41/17, EU:C:2018:736.

but is subject to submission, in accordance with the national law, of a medical certificate stating that this is necessary for her safety or health.

A very interesting instrument for protecting employees' rights in relation to pregnancy is maternity leave, with a minimum mandatory length of 14 days and a minimum allowable length of 14 weeks.[29] This means that the exercise of a right to maternity leave by a woman for the minimum period of 14 days is mandatory. During this period, a woman is obliged to cease her working activity. As explained by the CJEU in the *Hupt-Lizer* case, the EU legislator assumed that a woman would be unable to carry out any professional activity at this time, therefore the female employee is required to refrain from performing work during this period.[30] This obligation to remain inactive for 14 days of the postpartum period, required even against the woman's will, is assessed in the settled CJEU case-law as justified by legitimate aims, which are: firstly, to ensure the protection of a woman's biological condition during pregnancy and thereafter until such time as her physiological and mental functions have returned to normal after childbirth; and secondly, to protect the special relationship between a woman and her child over the period which follows pregnancy and childbirth, by preventing that relationship from being disturbed by the multiple burdens which would result from the simultaneous pursuit of employment.[31] Suffice it to say that public authorities or employers are not allowed in any way to call the legitimacy of that ground into question.[32]

The EU legislator's and judiciary's assessment that the fundamental changes in the living conditions of the female worker during pregnancy and childbirth justifies the concern for a woman's well-being – manifestations of which constitute both the period of professional inactivity for health reasons and the necessity to ensure the physical and mental bonds between the child and mother after delivery – has led to the legal sanctioning of the traditional family model based on a stereotypical distribution of the roles of women and men, according to which the responsibility for caring for a new-born is placed on the mother and the burden of providing funds to support the family on the father, who is

29 See I. Boruta, *Równość kobiet i mężczyzn*. . ., p. 101.

30 *Haupt-Lizer*, F-86/12, para. 50.

31 This justification for maternity leave was indicated by the CJEU in *Hofmann*, C-184/83.

32 *Rosselle*, C-65/14, EU:C:2015:339, para. 30.

thus released from his childcare obligation. This legitimizes the worse treatment of men by granting specific parental rights exclusively to women, even if the nature of these rights allows them to be exercised by representatives of both sexes, which reproduces and therefore further legitimizes the dominant ideology of motherhood in the EU gender equality law.[33] As a consequence, under Directive 2006/54 it is permitted to grant to mothers a period of obligatory and additional maternity leave, which the state encourages them to take by the payment of an allowance, while denying such measures to be granted to fathers, even where the parents themselves decide differently.[34] It also grants exclusively to an adoptive mother the right to maternity leave for the first three months following the actual entry of the child into the adoptive family, which is considered justified by the legitimate concern to assimilate as far as possible the conditions of entry of the child into the adoptive family in the same way as the arrival of a newborn child in the family during this very delicate initial period.[35]

The negative consequence of the classification of maternity leave by the CJEU as a measure of social law, but of a specific – biological – justification which takes shape in the form of restriction of fathers' rights, is deepened by the narrow interpretation of pregnancy as a ground for maternity leave. According to CJEU's interpretation of Art. 8 of Directive 92/85, Member States are not required, pursuant to that provision, to provide maternity leave to a female worker who, as a commissioning mother, has delivered a baby through a surrogacy arrangement, even in circumstances where she may or does breastfeed the baby following the birth. While a commissioning mother who has had a baby through a surrogacy arrangement cannot, by definition, be the subject to less favorable treatment related to her pregnancy, given that she has not been made pregnant with that baby she cannot be regarded as having been subject to discrimination on grounds of sex for the purposes of Directive 2006/54.[36] Declaring the ability to breastfeed as an inadequate ground for protection under Directive 2006/54 is surprising in the light of the CJEU judgment in *Ramos*, in which the Court stated that the condition of a

---

33 McGlynn, *Ideologies of Motherhood...*, p. 43.

34 See *Hofmann*, C-184/83.

35 *Commission of the European Communities v. Italian Republic*, C-163/82, EU:C:1983:295, para. 16.

36 *D.*, C-167/12, para. 43, 52 and 54.

breastfeeding woman is intimately related to maternity, and in particular 'to pregnancy or maternity leave' and thus workers who are breastfeeding must be protected on the same basis as workers who are pregnant or have recently given birth.

> Accordingly, any less favorable treatment of a female worker due to her being a breastfeeding woman must be regarded as falling within the scope of Article 2(2)(c) of Directive 2006/54 and therefore constitutes direct discrimination on grounds of sex.[37]

In contrast to this case, which refers to the right of a female employee who gave birth to a child who was then breastfed, the CJEU judgment in *D.* highlights the conservatism of this EU institution, exemplified by its interpretation of the provisions of the anti-discrimination *acquis* in connection with pregnancy and maternity in such a way that it gives priority to the traditional heterosexual model of a family with biological children.[38]

On the other hand, the narrow interpretation of the premise of pregnancy by the CJEU contributes to increasing the level of protection against the unequal treatment of men. This results from its qualification of the granting of certain rights in relation to the care of child exclusively to women as discrimination against men, if such granting of rights exceeds what is required to ensure the protection of the biological condition of the woman during and after pregnancy or the protection of the special relationship between a mother and her child. Thus, the EU gender equality law precludes national measure which provide that

> female workers who are mothers and whose status is that of an employed person are entitled, in accordance with various rules, to take leave during the first nine months following the child's birth, whereas male workers who are fathers with that same status are not entitled to the same leave unless the child's mother is also an employed person. Given that such leave may be taken by the employed father or the employed mother without distinction, implying that feeding and devoting time to the child can be carried out just as well by the father as by the mother, that leave seems to be accorded to workers in their capacity as parents of the child.[39]

---

37 *Ramos*, C-531/15, EU:C:2017:789, para. 60.

38 As indicated by P. Foubert, Š. Imamović, "The pregnant workers directive: Must do better: Lessons to be learned from Strasbourg?," *Journal of Social Welfare & Family Law* 2015, Vol. 37, No. 3, p. 249.

39 As held by the CJEU in *Manuel Roca Álvarez*, C-104/09, EU:C: 2010: 561.

4. Pregnant workers vs. workers who have recently given birth: Unequal treatment on the grounds of pregnancy in the EU gender equality law?

A specific feature of the protection granted to women with respect to pregnancy is that it is gradual – its scope is the widest during pregnancy; narrower during maternity leave; and the narrowest after the elapse of this protective period.

This is exemplified by the varied impact of the exercise of women's reproductive rights on their right to financial benefits. During pregnancy, a woman has the right to full remuneration, even if she performs the work only to a limited extent or even if she ceases to perform the work at all due to fact that the employer sends home a woman who is pregnant, although not unfit for work, when he considers that he cannot provide work for her, in accordance with Art. 5 (3) of Directive 92/85.[40] The same does not apply to a woman who is inactive during maternity leave. According to the settled case-law of the CJEU, a female employee is not entitled to receive full pay while on maternity leave as though she was actually working like the other workers.[41] Under EU equality law she is entitled to an adequate allowance, i.e. allowance at least equivalent to that which the worker concerned would receive in the event of a break in her activities on grounds connected with her state of health, subject to any ceiling laid down under national legislation.[42] The consequences of the abovementioned schemes are twofold. Firstly, such a normative solution contributes to the stigmatization of a (pregnant) woman by equating her absence due to maternity leave with the situation of a male employee absent due to illness.[43] Secondly, it legitimizes a worse treatment of a woman on the grounds of pregnancy insofar as the EU gender equality law does not qualify as discrimination a reduction in the woman's pay during her maternity leave, as compared to the amount of remuneration she received before going on maternity leave. The taking by a female worker of an obligatory break in her professional activity in the form of maternity leave, justified by a significant change to the woman's

---

40 See CJEU explanation in *Handels- og Kontorfunktionaerernes*, C-66/96, EU:C:1998:549, para. 6.

41 *Ornano*, C-335/15, EU:C:2016:564, para. 31 and the CJEU judgments cited there.

42 Art. 11(3) of the Directive 92/85. Hence the income indicated in the directive 92/85 doesn't amount to pay under art. 157 TFEU, P. Craig, G. de Búrca, *EU Law. Text, cases and materials*, Oxford 2015, p. 926.

43 Although in CJEU's view pregnancy is not in any way comparable to a pathological condition. See para. C-66/96, para. 33.

living conditions connected with her pregnancy and childbirth (as assumed by the EU gender equality law), thus provides a reason for her worse treatment with respect to remuneration. It seems that this is the result of prioritizing the economic interest of the employer and the state over the economic interest of the employee on maternity leave as well as the social value of the normativization of maternity in EU law. This proves that the EU's anti-discrimination law is still subjected to the economic goals of integration.[44]

The mechanism of protection of pregnant woman in EU law also encompasses a prohibition against discrimination as regards access to employment[45] and its duration, exemplified by the qualification of a dismissal of a woman in connection with pregnancy as direct discrimination on grounds of sex, regardless of the length of the employment relationship.[46] These protective measures, undoubtedly directed at taking the burden of pregnancy off a woman, are nevertheless rooted in a paternalistic approach to the issue of pregnancy under EU law, revealing the conservative approach of the CJEU towards women's reproductive rights. In the Court's view, the EU legislature decided to provide for special protection for women by prohibiting dismissal during the period from the beginning of pregnancy to the end of maternity leave pursuant to Article 10 of Directive 92/85, because of

> the harmful effects which the risk of dismissal may have on the physical and mental state of women who are pregnant, have recently given birth or are breastfeeding, including the particularly serious risk that pregnant women may be prompted to voluntarily terminate their pregnancy.[47]

This approach treats a woman's termination of her pregnancy not as a woman's right, but a potential risk assessed by the EU legislator as undesirable, prevention of which becomes both one of the objectives as well as a justification of the above-mentioned protective measures. Notwithstanding this approach, the protection at issue may be diminished when, in accordance with Art. 10 (1) of Directive 92/85, there are specific reasons not related to the condition of

---

44 The relationship between the economic aspects of integration and equality principle in the EU law is discussed by A. Szczerba-Zawada, *Równość jako fundament Unii Europejskiej. Studium kryteriów równego traktowania w konstrukcji rynku wewnętrznego*, Warszawa 2019.

45 See *Dekker*, C-177/88, EU:C:1990:383.

46 As held by the CJEU in *Tele Denmark*, C-109/00, EU:C:2001:513.

47 See *Danosa*, C-232/09, para. 60 and the CJEU case law cited there.

pregnancy, permitted by national law and/or practice and, if appropriate, the relevant authorities have given their consent to the dismissal of such workers.

The latter can be considered as an attempt to take into account the economic interest of the employer in the process of balancing the social costs of pregnancy, which is the second characteristic feature of EU equality legislation and, in particular, its interpretation by the CJEU. Its manifestation is the limitation on the period of protection granted in connection with pregnancy until the end of the period of maternity leave. Therefore, the dismissal of a woman because of her absence from work due to a disease related to pregnancy or a confinement that occurs after the period of maternity leave is not qualified as contrary to the prohibition of discrimination against women. In such a case, the EU law does not distinguish an illness attributable to pregnancy or childbirth from any other illness. "Such a pathological condition is therefore covered by the general rules applicable in the event of illness."[48] Hence under EU gender equality law it is permissible to dismiss a female employee as a consequence of her absence due to a disease related to pregnancy or childbirth that arises after the maternity leave, and to reduce her remuneration for that reason under the same conditions as a man's absence of the same duration related to an incapacity to work, as opposed to an illness of that kind that arose during the period extending from the start of her pregnancy to the end of her maternity leave.[49] Such juridical pathologization of pregnancy after this limited period enhances the stereotypical perception of women's biological condition, and seen through that prism, the woman's professional capacity,[50] even though the aim of equality legislation should be to eliminate these kinds of stereotypes. The classification of the termination of an employment contract due to a pregnancy-related illness, if such is revealed after the period of maternity leave, although being a characteristic inherent of one sex, is not treated as contrary to the prohibition of discrimination. This treatment is inconsistent with the CJEU's characterization of less favorable treatment due to a medical procedure intended to lead to conception, also characteristic for only one sex, as direct gender discrimination. This leads to the conclusion that the CJEU is inconsistent in its normative assessment of the premise of pregnancy and essential consequences of this condition, depending on the period of the assessment, which is the third

48 *Hertz,* C-179/88, EC:1990:384, para. 16.

49 As held by the CJEU in *Brown*, C-394/96.

50 Critical of Brown judgment E. Ellis, "Case C-394/96, Brown v. Rentokil Ltd, judgment of 30 June 1998," *Common Market Law Review* 1999, Vol. 36, No. 3, pp. 625–633.

signum specificum of the EU gender equality law with respect to pregnancy and maternity.

5. Conclusions

The provisions of EU law which are intended to protect female workers in connection with pregnancy are undoubtedly part of the EU equality mechanism. These measures increase the effectiveness and comprehensiveness of EU gender equality law. They also have a great equality potential, which materializes based on the teleological interpretation employed by the Court of Justice of the European Union. The Court's case law on pregnant workers and workers who have recently given birth undoubtedly contributes to ensuring equal opportunities for women. In addition, its narrow interpretation of the criteria justifying special treatment of women in connection with pregnancy as an exception to the overall principle of gender equality may contribute to equal rights for men and lead to their stronger involvement in family life. All this, in turn, undoubtedly leads to the elimination of harmful gender stereotypes impairing real equality between women and men.

At the same time, however, the EU legislation related to pregnancy is characterized by certain equality deficiencies. Suffice to say that it justifies and rationalizes a less favorable treatment of women based on a paternalistic approach towards the premise of pregnancy *per se* and as a criterion of assessment of women's professional capacity. This premise is not only considered to be an objective criterion for differentiating the situation of working women and men (due to biological differences between the sexes), but it is also the reason for limiting the rights of women in those situations in which gender as a social construct is decoded based on criteria resulting from assumptions of the dominant (male) group about what is good for representatives of the subordinate (female) group. Considering pregnancy as a justified ground for interference with women's rights as a result of this paternalistic approach makes the mechanism of protection against discrimination on the grounds of sex similar to the prohibition of unequal treatment on the grounds of disability before embracing the social model of disability.[51] It may lead to the strengthening of gender stereotypes instead of eliminating them.

51 S. Favalli, D. Ferri, "Defining Disability in the European Union Non-discrimination Legislation: Judicial Activism and Legislative Restraints," *European Public Law* 2016, Vol. 22, No. 3, p. 546.

Against this it could be said that, in fact, the EU law protects women not against less favorable treatment based on pregnancy and maternity as such, but against the negative consequences of protective measures addressed to women (especially during pregnancy, and to a narrower extent – in the period after confinement), which are an expression of the protectionist treatment of women and which may be a cause for a deterioration of the legal status of female employees. This is confirmed by the recital of Directive 92/85, according to which "*the protection of the safety and health* of pregnant workers, workers who have recently given birth or workers who are breastfeeding *should not treat women on the labour market unfavourably* [italics added]," and by the *Dekker* judgment, in which the Court held explicitly that the employer's refusal "to enter into a contract of employment with a female candidate whom he considers to be suitable for the job where such *refusal is based on the possible adverse consequences for him of employing a pregnant woman, owing to rules on unfitness for work adopted by the public authorities, which assimilate inability to work on account of pregnancy and confinement to inability to work on account of illness* [italics added]" constitutes a direct contravention of the principle of equal treatment between men and women as well as of the criteria specified by the CJEU for determining the amount of benefit to be paid to women during maternity leave, according to which "*the amount payable could not*, however, *be so low as to undermine the purpose of maternity leave*, namely the protection of women before and after giving birth [italics added]."[52]

Thus, the provisions which are intended to protect women in connection with pregnancy and maternity do not result in less favorable treatment of women as defined in terms of *formal* equality, but do result in a lack of *substantive* equality. In this context the evolution of CJEU's jurisprudence should be noted, which more often highlights the need to ensure gender equality in practice, as in the *Roca Álvarez* judgment cited above or the judgment in *Betriu Montull*. In the light of the latter it is obvious that EU provisions on maternity leave do not preclude a national measure which provides that the father of a child, who is an employed person, is entitled, with the consent of the mother, who is also an employed person, to take maternity leave for the period following the compulsory leave of six weeks which the mother must take after childbirth, except where the mother's health would be at risk.[53] Thus the regime of maternity leave as strictly understood is being progressively loosened by EU law,

52 *Gillespie*, C-342/93, para. 20.

53 *Betriu Montull*, C-5/12, EU:C:2013:571, para. 66.

which may contribute to improving the normative status of female employees in connection with pregnancy.

Bibliography:

Boruta I., *Równość kobiet i mężczyzn w pracy w świetle prawa Wspólnoty Europejskiej. Implikacje dla Polski*, Łódź 1996.

Caracciolo di Torella E., "Brave New Fathers for a Brave New World? Fathers as Caregivers in an Evolving European Union," *European Law Journal* 2014, Vol. 20, No. 1.

Craig P., de Búrca G., *EU Law. Text, cases and materials*, Oxford 2015.

Favalli S., Ferri D., "Defining Disability in the European Union Non-discrimination Legislation: Judicial Activism and Legislative Restraints," *European Public Law* 2016, Vol. 22, No. 3.

Foubert P., Imamović Š., "The pregnant workers directive: must do better: lessons to be learned from Strasbourg?," *Journal of Social Welfare & Family Law* 2015, Vol. 37, No. 3.

Guerrina R., *Mothering the Union: Gender politics in the EU*, Manchester–New York 2005.

Kantola J., *Gender and the European Union*, Basingstoke–New York 2010.

Koldinská K., "Case law of the European Court of Justice on sex discrimination 2006–2011," *Common Market Law Review* 2011, Vol. 48, No. 5.

McGlynn C., "Ideologies of Motherhood in European Community Sex Equality Law," *European Law Journal* 2000, Vol. 6, No. 1.

Prechal S., "Equality of treatment, non-discrimination and social policy: Achievements in three themes," *Common Market Law Review* 2004, Vol. 41, No. 2.

Schiek D., "Commentary on the Article 6 of the EU Charter of Fundamental Rights," [in:] *The EU Charter of Fundamental Rights. A Commentary*, eds. S. Peers, T. Hervey, J. Kenner, A. Ward, Oxford–Portland 2014.

Szczerba-Zawada A., "Gender Stereotypes and EU Antidiscrimination Case Law – (fighting) a Hidden Threat to the EU Value of Equality?," *Studia Europejskie* 2018, No. 4.

Szczerba-Zawada A., "Ochrona rodzicielstwa w systemie Unii Europejskiej. Uwagi de lege lata," *Studia Prawnicze i Administracyjne* 2014, No. 1.

Szczerba-Zawada A., *Równość jako fundament Unii Europejskiej. Studium kryteriów równego traktowania w konstrukcji rynku wewnętrznego*, Warszawa 2019.

Szewczyk H., *Równość płci w zatrudnieniu*, Warszawa 2017.

Vinkenburg C. J., Van Engen M. L., Coffeng J., Dikkers J. S. E., "Bias in Employment Decisions about Mothers and Fathers: The (Dis)Advantages of Sharing Care Responsibilities," *Journal of Social Issues* 2012, Vol. 68, No. 4.

Weldon-Johns M., "EU work-family policies – Challenging parental roles or reinforcing gendered stereotypes," *European Law Journal* 2013, Vol. 19, No. 5.

Urszula Torbus

University of Silesia in Katowice

e-mail: urszula.torbus@us.edu.pl

ORCID ID: 0000–0002–4454–9885

Facilitating the work of mothers: How to diminish female vulnerability in the labour market?

Abstract: Rising the female labour force participation has been one of the most remarkable economic developments of the last century. Yet the employment rates of women are lower than those for men and women's global labour force participation rate is 26.5 percentage points below that of men. Among factors that trigger female underrepresentation in the labour market it is the motherhood considered as the most significant one. The workplaces have been built around the men's traditional life patterns and it inevitably leads to widespread attrition among women that have children or provide care of other family members. Therefore, measures aimed at facilitating the balance between work and family obligations should be developed. Some of them have been introduced into a relatively recent EU Directive 2019/1158 of June 2019 on work life balance that is to be implemented by the EU Member States until June 2022. The WLB directive provides five such work-life balance measures – a paternity leave, a parental leave, a carers' leave, a time off from work on grounds of *force majeure* and the flexible working arrangements.

WLB measures have a great potential to facilitate the work of women and diminish their vulnerability in the labour market, what has been particularly visible during the COVID-19 pandemic containment. However, the effective implementation of WLB directive requires the enterprises' favourable attitude and protection against the discrimination. At the same time, WLB measures are just a part of a multidimensional system required to enable the full enjoyment of two EU fundamental right – the right to work and the right to gender equality.

Keywords: work-life balance, gender equality, paternity leave, parental leave, carer's leave

1. Introductory remarks

Rising the female labour force participation has been one of the most remarkable economic developments of the last century.[1] However, in all EU Member

1 See e.g.: https://ourworldindata.org/female-labor-supply, [available: 1.03.2020].

States employment rates of women are lower than those for men, although with important variations across the EU.[2] At 48.5 per cent in 2018, women's global labour force participation rate is 26.5 percentage points below that of men.[3] There are many factors that trigger female underrepresentation in the labour market, but seemingly it is motherhood that is among the most significant ones. Maternity is often associated with woman's withdrawal from employment for at least a long period of time. Mothers therefore demonstrate lower employment rates than other prime-age women.[4] Moreover, while working, women globally are paid less than men, therefore women also face the motherhood wage penalty, which increases with the number of children born.[5] The gender pay gap in present in every European country and is estimated by Eurostat at the level of 16,2 %, although the size of the gap varies considerably in EU member states.[6] The gender pay gap leads also to gender pensions gap and to greater risk of social exclusion and poverty.

One of the important factors contributing to the underrepresentation of women in the labour market is the difficulty in balancing work and family obligations.[7] As underlined recently on the EU level, when they have children, women are likely to work fewer hours in paid employment and to spend more time fulfilling unpaid caring responsibilities. Having a sick or dependent relative has also been shown to have a negative impact on women's employment and results in some women dropping out of the labour market entirely (WLB Directive, rec. 10). Therefore, to increase the representation of women in the labour market, measures aimed at facilitating the balance between work and

2 European Commission, European semester thematic factsheet women in the labour market, 2017.

3 International Labour Organization, *World Employment and Social Outlook: Trends for Women 2018: Global Snapshot,* Geneva 2018.

4 J. Baran, A. Bartha, A. Chłoń-Domińczak, O. Fedyuk, A. Kamińska, P. Lewandowski, M. Lis, I. Magda, M. Potoczna, V. Zentai, ed. I. Magda, *Women on the European labour market,* 2014.

5 D. Grimshaw, J. Rubery, *The motherhood pay gap: A review of the issues, theory and international evidence,* International Labour Organization, Conditions of Work and Employment Series No. 57, Geneva, 2015.

6 H. Conley, G. Healy, D. Gottardi, B. Mikołajczyk, M. Peruzzi (eds.), *The gender pay gap and social partnership in Europe. Findings form "Close the Deal, Fill the Gap,"* Routledge 2019.

7 A. Ludera-Ruszel, "The situation of women in the labor market in Poland in the light of existing labor Law provisions concerning the working time," *Przegląd Politologiczny* 2016, No. 4.

family obligations should be developed. Some of them have been introduced into a relatively recent EU Directive 2019/1158 of June 2019 on work life balance (the WLB directive)[8] that is to be implemented by the EU Member States (MS) until June 2022. The WLB directive introduces five such work-life balance measures – a paternity leave, a parental leave, a carers' leave, a time off from work on grounds of *force majeure* and the flexible working arrangements.

The WLB directive is a consequence of the European Commission policy, formulated in Commission Work Programme for 2017.[9] This new approach, that took into consideration both demographic and life-style changes in societies, led to the introduction of systemic solutions.[10] The protection of parenthood was earlier provided by various EU directives – starting from the Directive 92/85/EEC[11] referring, among others, to the protection of pregnant workers and to a maternity leave, the Directive 2006/54/EC[12] introducing, among others the prohibition of discrimination on the grounds of pregnancy or maternity leave, the Directive 2010/41/EU[13] providing the maternity allowance for self-employed allowing the break in their economic activity during

8 Directive (EU) 2019/1158 of the European Parliament and of the Council of 20 June 2019 on work-life balance for parents and carers and repealing Council Directive 2010/18/EU, OJ L 188, 12.7.2019, pp. 79–93.

9 Communication from the Commission to the European Parliament, the Council, the European Economic and Social Committee and the Committee of the Regions Commission, Work Programme 2017 Delivering a Europe that protects, empowers and defends, COM/2016/0710 final.

10 M. Półtorak, "Projekt dyrektywy WLB – nowe podejście do równości płci w zatrudnieniu?," *Studia z Zakresu Prawa Pracy i Polityki Społecznej* 2019, 26, No. 4.

11 Council Directive 92/85/EEC of 19 October 1992 on the introduction of measures to encourage improvements in the safety and health at work of pregnant workers and workers who have recently given birth or are breastfeeding (tenth individual Directive within the meaning of Article 16 (1) of Directive 89/391/EEC) OJ L 348, 28.11.1992, pp. 1–7.

12 Directive 2006/54/EC of the European Parliament and of the Council of 5 July 2006 on the implementation of the principle of equal opportunities and equal treatment of men and women in matters of employment and occupation (recast), OJ L 204, 26.7.2006, pp. 23–36.

13 Directive 2010/41/EU of the European Parliament and of the Council of 7 July 2010 on the application of the principle of equal treatment between men and women engaged in an activity in a self-employed capacity and repealing Council Directive 86/613/EEC, OJ L 180, 15.7.2010, pp. 1–6.

pregnancy or due to maternity for at least 14 weeks and the Directive 2010/18/EU[14] introducing an individual right to parental leave on the grounds of the birth or adoption of a child.[15] The WLB directive can be perceived as a next step aimed at achieving the equality between men and women (art. 1) and a first regulation on the EU level addressing directly the work-life balance, understood as "reconciliation of work and family," by introducing further complementary measures supporting working parents in the period after the maternity leave and during their return to work.

Since it is women who take on a disproportionate burden of the carers duties in comparison to men, this chapter will focus at measures aimed at facilitating the work of mothers. Its objective is to present the new WLB directive and the corresponsive measures provided by the Polish legislator, as the directive itself is the EU instrument of a harmonisation, not a unification of the MS laws.[16] According to art. 288 TFEU a directive shall be binding, as to the result to be achieved, upon each MS to which it is addressed, but shall leave to the national authorities the choice of form and methods. From this perspective it is interesting to look at the solutions existing in national law, to compare and if possible – to draw the conclusions.[17] Therefore, this chapter aims to present the examples of all five WLB measures provided by the WLB directive, existing in the Polish national legislation. Most of those solutions are regulated by the Polish labour code[18] (PLC) that after wide amendments of 2009–2016 provides a relatively extensive protection of parenthood.[19] They will be presented in the order given by the WLB directive. In a summary, the effectiveness of those measures in the Polish labour market will be assessed.

14 Council Directive 2010/18/EU of 8 March 2010 implementing the revised Framework Agreement on parental leave concluded by BUSINESSEUROPE, UEAPME, CEEP and ETUC and repealing Directive 96/34/EC (Text with EEA relevance), OJ L 68, 18.3.2010, pp. 13–20.

15 M. Półtorak, "Projekt dyrektywy WLB. . .."

16 M.A. Moreau, "Règlements et directives en matière sociale," [in:] *Les norms sociales européennes*, B. Teyssié (ed.), Pantheon-Assas 2000.

17 O. Kaufmann, "L'actualité du droit social comparé," [in:] *Le droit social – le droit comparé. Etudes dédiées à la mémoire de Pierre Ortscheidt*, Presses Universitaires de Strasbourg, 2003, No. 6.

18 The Law of 26 June 1975 Labour Code, O.J. 2020, item 1320, as amended.

19 U. Torbus, "Zmiany w zakresie uprawnień rodzicielskich ułatwiających łączenie obowiązków zawodowych z opieką nad dzieckiem," [in:] *Uprawnienia pracowników związane z rodzicielstwem*, J. Czerniak-Swędzioł (ed.), Wolters Kluwer 2016.

This analysis, nevertheless, needs also a broader context. According to article 2 of TEU Union is founded, among others, on the value of equality, also between men and women, that is a common value to all MS. It means that not only the Union and its institutions, but also all MS are obliged to respect it.[20] Article 3 of the TEU provides that the Union should promote equality between women and men. The equality between men and women is also granted by the EU Charter of Fundamental Rights (art. 23), as well as the protection from dismissal for a reason connected with parental rights given to reconcile family and professional life (art. 33). In this context, the development of the work-life balance mechanism derives directly from the fundamental EU principle of equal treatment of men and women as a tool to achieve it.

Second introductory remark concerns the right to a maternity leave. To understand fully the work-life balance mechanisms such as a paternity leave or a parental leave it is important to bear in mind that they are connected to a maternity leave and are exercised after it or in parallel. The directive 92/85/EEC grants the right to a maternity leave to all female employees, regardless the length of service or any qualifying period. Similarly, in Poland, each female employee is entitled to maternity leave of twenty weeks and in the case of a multiple birth, the leave is extended to: 31 weeks (if two children are born), 33 weeks (if three children are born), 35 weeks (if four children are born) or 37 (if five and more children are born) (art. 180 § 1 PLC). The employee is also entitled to return to work after the compulsory minimum 14 weeks of the leave, provided the rest of the leave is taken by the child's father (art 180 § 4 PLC). On the other hand, six weeks of maternity leave can be taken before the expected date of birth (art. 180 § 2 PLC). During the maternity leave the employee is entitled to an allowance covered by social security in the amount of 100 % of remuneration.

2. Paternity leave

The paternity leave, according to the WLB directive, means a leave from work for fathers or, if recognised by national law, for equivalent second parents, on the occasion of the birth of a child for the purposes of providing care (art. 1 al. 1a). The WLB directive provides that fathers or, if recognised by national law, equivalent second parents, should have the right to paternity leave of 10 working days that is to be taken on the occasion of the birth of the worker's

---

20 M. Półtorak, "Projekt dyrektywy WLB. . .."

child. The MS may determine whether to allow the paternity leave to be taken partly before or only after the birth of the child and whether to allow such leave to be taken in flexible ways. To strengthen the scope of the leave, the directive stipulates that the right to paternity leave shall not be made subject to a period of work qualification or to a length of service qualification and that the right to paternity leave shall be granted irrespective of the worker's marital or family status (art. 4).

In Poland, the paternity leave was introduced into PLC in 2009.[21] Art. 182(3) PLC grants the right to paternity leave to male employees. It is granted in case of the birth or adoption of a child. The leave amounts to 2 weeks and since 2016[22] it may be divided into two parts, each of 7 days long. The leave can be taken before the child reaches the age of 24 months (before 2016 it was the age of 12 months) or up to 24 months from the moment the decision of the court on adoption becomes final, but not longer than up to the moment the child reaches the age of 7 (sometimes the age of 10). Comparing to the directive, PLC provides more flexible use of the paternity leave – not only directly on the occasion of the birth of the child, but during first two years of his life. Apparently, the prolongation of the period in which the paternity leave can be used is connected with the join period of maternity and parental leave (that amounts to 52 weeks – *see infra*) and the paternity leave can be used after to elongate the period of a childcare. However, the paternity leave cannot be used before the birth of the child (contrarily to the maternity leave – *see supra*).

Due to PLC, the paternity leave is not obligatory – it is granted upon an employee's written request, filed at least 7 days before the employee starts to use the leave. The employer is obliged to accept the employee's request. To encourage the exercise of this right, during the parental leave the employee is entitled to an allowance covered by social security, amounting to 100 % of remuneration (BSIM). Additionally, during the paternity leave the employee is protected against the dismissal (art. 182(3) § 3 PLC).

Additionally, apart from the right to parental leave, working fathers are also entitled to two days off, paid by the employer. According to the ordinance of 1996,[23] the employer is obliged to release from work an employee for a period of

21 The Law of 6 December 2008, O.J. No. 237, item 1654.

22 The Law of 24 July 2015, O.J. 2015, item 1268.

23 The Ordinance of the Ministry for Labour and Social Policy of 15 May 1996, regarding the manner of justification of absence from work and granting employees release from work, O.J. 2014, item 1632, as amended.

2 days in the case of, among others, the employee's child's birth. What's important in the context of the time off on grounds of *force majeure* (see *infra*), the days off are also granted in case of death and funeral or a wedding of his/her child or another member of a family.

3. Parental leave

The right to a parental leave, as mentioned above, is not a new solution on the EU level. An individual right to a parental leave on the grounds of the birth or adoption of a child was already granted by the directive 2010/18/EU that is repealed by the WLB directive.

The parental leave means a leave from work for parents on the grounds of the birth or adoption of a child to take care of that child (art. 1 al. 1b). Article 5 of the WLB directive grants each worker an individual right to parental leave of four months that is to be taken before the child reaches a specified age, up to the age of eight, to be specified by each MS or by a collective agreement. That age shall be determined with a view to ensuring that each parent is able to exercise their right to parental leave effectively and on an equal basis. What is important, the MS shall ensure that two months of parental leave cannot be transferred (art. 5 al. 2). Comparing to the directive 2010/18/EU, this period was prolonged from one month (clause 2), although the initial Commission proposal included four months of non-transferrable parental leave.[24] The non-transferrable character of the leave means that each parent shall exercise at least two months of the leave and if not, the right cannot be used by the second parent.

The WLB directive stipulates that the MS may make the right to parental leave subject to a period of work qualification or to a length of service qualification, which shall not exceed one year. In the case of successive fixed-term contracts with the same employer, the sum of those contracts shall be taken into account for the purpose of calculating the qualifying period (art. 5 al. 4). Due to the directive, the right to a parental leave is not of an absolute character, since the MS may establish the circumstances in which an employer is allowed to postpone the granting of parental leave for a reasonable period of time on the grounds that the taking of parental leave at the time requested would seriously disrupt the good functioning of the employer. Employers shall provide reasons

24 A. Ślęzak-Gąsiorowska, "Dyrektywa w sprawie równowagi miedzy życiem zawodowym a prywatnym rodziców i opiekunów – perspektywa polska," *Monitor Prawa Pracy* 2019, No. 4.

for such a postponement of parental leave in writing. According to the directive, the right to parental leave shall be exercised upon workers request delivered with a reasonable period of notice. This period should take into account the needs of both the employers and the workers. The request shall also specify the intended beginning and end of the period of leave.

Important regulation stems from article 5 al. 5 that obliges the MS to take the necessary measures to ensure that the workers have the right to request that they take parental leave in flexible ways. The employer shall consider and respond to such requests, taking into account the needs of both the employer and the worker. The employer shall also provide reasons for any refusal to accede to such a request in writing within a reasonable period after the request. The WLB directive also underlines the special needs of adoptive parents, parents with a disability and parents with children with a disability or a long-term illness – in this case the MS shall assess the need for the conditions of access to and the detailed arrangements for the application of parental leave to be adapted to the needs of abovementioned parents (art. 5 al. 8).

In Poland, the parental leave was introduced into PLC in 2013[25] and amended in 2016.[26] The parental leave, in contrast to the maternity leave, is not obligatory, which means that the working parents are not obliged to exercise it, although due to the right to an allowance covered by the social security in most cases they do (see *infra*). Presently, an employee (both male and female) is entitled to the parental leave in the amount up to 32 weeks (in case of a single birth) or 34 weeks (in case of multiple birth). The parental leave can be used upon using the maternity leave, not later than up to the end of the calendar year in which the child reaches the age of 6 (art 182(1a) PLC). In practise, the parental leave is used directly after the maternity leave, although last 16 weeks can be used later, in the periods not shorter than 8 weeks, for example when the child starts the kindergarten education (in the age of 3 in Poland) (art. 182(1c) PLC).

To assure the flexibility the parental leave can be divided into maximum four parts used by both working parents alternately, provided that each part covers at least 8 weeks. The flexibility is also granted by the possibility to share the care of the child between employees and workers under civil law contracts or self-employed. Moreover, both parents of the child may take the parental leave at the same time, which obviously shortens the length of the leave (art. 182(1c) PLC).

25 The Law of 28 May 2013, O.J. 2013, item 675.
26 The Law of 24 July 2015, O.J. 2015, item 1268.

The parental leave is also granted in case of adoption (art. 183 PLC). During the parental leave the employee is protected against the dismissal (art.182(1g) PLC).

The parental leave is granted upon the written request of an employee, submitted within not less than 21 days before the beginning of the leave. The employer is obliged to accept the request of the employee. Similarly, he is obliged to accept the alternate use of it by both parents. On the other hand, an employee may curtail parental leave at any time and to return to work, but it requires the consent of the employer (art. 181(1d) PLC).

Due to BSIM the parental leave is connected with the right to an allowance amounting to 100 % of employee's remuneration during first 6 weeks (or 8 weeks in case of multiple birth). During the remaining part of the parental leave the allowance amounts to 60 % of remuneration. However, a female employee may, not later than 21 days after the date of birth, submit a written request to be granted, directly after the maternity leave, the parental leave in the full length resulting from the PLC (art. 179(1) PLC). In that case the maternity allowance is paid during the joint period of maternity and parental leave in the amount of 80 % of the remuneration. When added to the maternity leave, the joint period of maternity and paternity leave allows to assure a year (52 weeks) of a paid work break to take a care of a child in the first year of his/her life. It is worth mentioning that in practise the parental leave in the prevailing cases is exercised as a one part. Despite all the flexibility provided by PLC, it is usually mothers that apply for the parental leave, directly after the birth of a child and withdraw in consequence from work for a year.

Moreover, apart from the right to the parental leave, PLC since its introduction in 1975 provides also a right to a childcare leave. Each employee who has been employed for at least 6 months has the right to take childcare leave in order to take personal care of the child. The six-month employment period includes also the previous periods of employment (art. 186 PLC). The length of childcare leave must not exceed 36 months and presently the leave is granted for not longer than up to the end of the calendar year in which the child reaches the age of 6.[27] However, if the child requires the personal care of an employee for health reasons confirmed by a medical certificate on the child's disability or the degree of the child's disability, the employee may be granted additional childcare leave up to 36 months before the child reaches the age of 18.[28] This

27 Changed from the initial three years by the Law of 24 July 2015, O.J. 2015, item 1268.
28 Added by the Law of 14 November 2003, O.J. 2003, No. 213, item 2081.

PLC provision can be regarded as the measure ensuring full enjoyment of rights by children with disabilities postulated by the WLB directive.

To assure the flexibility, presently both working parents or carers may take the childcare leave at the same time. In such case the total length of childcare leave may not exceed the length of 36 months. Similarly to the parental leave, the childcare leave can be divided between both parents, but no more than into 5 parts (art. 186 § 8 PLC). The childcare leave is granted upon the written request of an employee, submitted within not less than 21 days before starting using the leave and the number of parts of the leave is established on the basis of the number of the submitted requests. Similarly to the parental leave, the employer is obliged to accept the request of an employee. Moreover, the employee may waive childcare leave at any time, with the employer's consent or after a prior notification of an employer – at the latest 30 days before the date of the intended commencement of work. During the childcare leave, similarly to the parental leave, an employee is protected against the dismissal (art. 186(8) PLC), apart from the case of insolvency or collective redundancies.

However, the childcare leave is not very popular among the working mothers, contrarily to the parental leave that is nearly "automatically" used directly after the maternity leave. The reason lies in the lack of any financial benefits during the childcare leave,[29] therefore it becomes a period of an unpaid break in the employment and is connected with a lack of social protection (e.g. the right to a sickness benefit).

4. Carers' leave

According to the WLB directive, in order to provide men and women with caring responsibilities with greater opportunities to remain in the workforce, each worker should have the right to the carers' leave. The MS are encouraged to make the right to carers' leave available with regard to additional relatives, such as grandparents and siblings (WLB Directive, rec. 27). The carers' leave' means a leave from work for workers in order to provide personal care or support to a relative, or to a person who lives in the same household as the worker, and who is in need of significant care or support for a serious medical reason, as defined by each MS (art. 3 al. 1 point c). Article 6 grants each worker the right to carers' leave of five working days per year, although the MS may determine additional

29 Apart from benefits covered by the social assistance in case of very low household incomes provided by the Law of 28 November 2003 on the family benefits, O.J. 2020, item 111, as amended.

details regarding the scope and conditions of carers' leave in accordance with national law or practice. Moreover, the use of that right may be subject to appropriate substantiation, in accordance with national law or practice.

The Polish law does not introduce the right to the carers' leave directly. However, PLC prohibits the termination of the employment contract if the employee is absent from work due to taking care of a child while receiving allowance on this account (art. 53). It is regulated by the law of 1999 on benefits from social insurance in case of illness and maternity (BSIM). The carers' allowance is granted to an insured (a worker covered by the social security) when the need of personal taking care of a child or another sick member of a family occurs, although its length and conditions of receiving it vary. The carers' allowance is granted to take a personal care of a child up to the age of 8 in case of (1) unforeseen closure of nursery, children's club, kindergarten or school to which the child attends or in case of the illness or a daily caregiver, (2) childbirth or illness of a spouse of the insured, who permanently takes care of the child, (3) stay of the spouse, who permanently looks after the child, in a healthcare institution.

BSIM also provides a right to a carers' allowance in case of a need to personal care of a sick child up to the age of 14, a child with disabilities up to 18 years old or other sick member of family (a spouse, parents, parents-in-law, grandparents, grandchildren, siblings and children above the age of 14, provided they stay during the sickness in the same household with the insured person) for the period of maximum 60 days in a calendar year (in case of the child) or 14 days (if the care is taken of another member of a family or a child over 14). However, the allowance is granted only if there are no other members of the household who could take care of a child or an ill relative (apart from the care over a child up to two years old).

The allowance is covered by the social security and similarly to the sickness benefit, it amounts to 80 % of worker's remuneration. The right to a carer's allowance is from the first day of the sickness insurance coverage. Both the child's mother and father are entitled to a carers' allowance, however the allowance is payable only to one of them.[30]

The carers' allowance has played an important role in the COVID-19 pandemic containment. When the lockdown was announced in spring 2020 in Poland, the government also introduced a special carers' allowance for parents or carers of children up to 8 years in case of the closure of schools,

30 https://lang.zus.pl/en/benefits/care-allowances [available: 1.03.2020].

kindergartens, nurseries or other instructions attended by a child.[31] It also amounted to 80 % of a worker's salary and it was paid by the national social security institution (ZUS). This special allowance was paid from March to July and in September. Since October, the carers' can apply for the allowance on regular basis under BSIM.

5. Time off from work on grounds of *force majeure*

According to article 7 of the WLB directive, the MS shall take the necessary measures to ensure that each worker has the right to time off from work on grounds of *force majeure* for urgent family reasons in the case of illness or accident making the immediate attendance of the worker indispensable. The MS may limit the right of each worker to time off from work on grounds of *force majeure* to a certain amount of time each year or by case, or both. This measure was also already granted by the directive 2010/18/EU.

This solution is also present in PLC that since its introduction in 1975 and provides the employee raising at least one child of up to the age of 14 the right to be released from work for 2 days in a calendar year, while retaining the right to remuneration paid by the employer. However, the length of the time off is fixed and not dependant on the number of children raised, therefore it puts large families in less favourable situation in comparison with a single child family.[32] Moreover, it also disfavours working parents, because if both parents or carers are of the child are employed, this right may be exercised by one of them (art. 189(1) PLC). In practise, working parents can split those two days between them or decide that the leave will be used by one of them. Usually, it is exercised by mothers. By contrast, when only one parent or carer is working, he/she is entitled to two days off.[33] To grant the flexibility, since 2016[34] this time off, by the employee's decision, can also be used not by days, but by hours. In practise, it is used upon employee's request, without the necessity to prove the existence of *force majeure*.

---

31 The Law of 16 October 2020 on special solutions related to the prevention of COVID-19, other infectious diseases and crisis situations caused by them, O.J. 2020, item 1842, as amended.

32 U. Torbus, "Zmiany w zakresie uprawnień rodzicielskich. . .."

33 M. Włodarczyk, "Protection of parenthood," [in:] *Outline of Polish Labour Law System*, K. W. Baran (ed.), Wolters Kluwer 2016.

34 The Law of 24 July 2015, O.J. 2015, item 1268.

6. Flexible working arrangements

Flexible forms of employment are regarded as a key tool for increasing women's involvement in the labour market.[35] The WLB directive obliges the MS to take the necessary measures to ensure that workers with children up to a specified age (which shall be at least eight years) and carers have the right to request flexible working arrangements for caring purposes (art. 9 al. 1). The duration of such flexible working arrangements may be subject to a reasonable limitation, as they should take into account the needs of both the employer and the employee. However, employers shall provide reasons for any refusal of such a request or for any postponement of such arrangements (art. 9 al. 2). According to the directive, the flexible working arrangements means the possibility for workers to adjust their working patterns, including through the use of remote working arrangements, flexible working schedules, or reduced working hours.

PLC provides a number of possibilities of flexible working arrangements, both explicitly for parents or for employees in general. Parents rights include a reduction of working time. All employees, among them working parents, can apply for a part-time work, a compressed working hours, a weekend work, a staggered working hours, a task-based working time and a time off *in lieu*.

Reduction of working time is the mechanism allowing to combine the use of parental leave and the performance of work for the employer (art. 182(1e)). It was added into PLC since 2016[36] to introduce a greater flexibility in the exercise of the parental leave. Presently the employee entitled to a parental leave may fill a request with the employer to reduce the working time to the level not lower than half-time basis. The request shall be filed no later than 21 days prior to the commencement of work. Due to PLC, the employer is obliged to accept the employee's request, unless it is not possible due to the type of work performed by the employee or its organisation. The reasons for refusal shall be notified by the employer in writing. Moreover, in case of combining parental leave and work for the employer, the maternity allowance is reduced proportionately and the leave gets extended to a maximum of 64 or 68 weeks (art 182(1 f) PLC). The employee shall specify the manner in which he/she intends to take exercise the reduced working time, for example by working half-time or reducing the working time of two hours a day, by which the leave automatically is to be

---

35 I. Magda (ed.), *Women on the European labour market*. ... Similarly, A. Ludera-Ruszel, "The situation of women in the labor market. ..."

36 The Law of 24 July 2015, O.J. 2015, item 1268.

proportionally extended. Similar right to the reduction of working hours is connected with a childcare leave since 2004[37] (art. 186(7) PLC).

Part-time work, connected with lower workload in a day or a week, is available to all workers, not only for parents or workers with care responsibilities. PLC, similarly to directive 97/81/EC,[38] allows all workers to apply for part-time work and obliges the employer to accept, as far as possible, a request from an employee in relation to changing the length of working time determined in the employment contract (art. 29(2) § 2 PLC). However, the decision depends on the possibilities of the enterprise and creates no absolute duty to the employer. In Poland, this possibility is relatively rarely used by working mothers in comparison to other European countries. The obstacle lies, among others, in the relatively low level of remunerations in Poland, therefore the part-time employment often does not cover the living expenses. In 2020 the minimum wage amounts to 2600 PLN (approx. 600 €).[39]

Compressed working hours, also called a shortened working week system, were introduced into PLC in 2004,[40] altogether with the system of weekend work. The shortened working week system allows the employee to work for less than five days per week, while extending the daily working time, but not more than up to 12 hours, within a calculation period not exceeding 1 month (art 143 PLC). This system can be introduced at any time. Moreover, compressed working hours can be applied both in case of full time and part time work and the work can be performed at any days of a week. The only requirement is connected with the consent of an employee, as compressed working hours can be used only at the written request of an employee and should be introduced explicitly into the employment contract, contrarily to other systems or schedules of working time that are determined in a collective labour agreement or other internal regulations (art. 150 PLC). The introduction of the compressed working hours on the basis of employment contracts guarantees that this system is not imposed by the employer, however it requires his approval. Due to the required employee's initiative, it can be assumed that this system

---

37 The Law of 14 November 2003, O.J. 2003, No. 213, item 2081.

38 Council Directive 97/81/EC of 15 December 1997 concerning the Framework Agreement on part-time work concluded by UNICE, CEEP and the ETUC – Annex: Framework agreement on part-time work, OJ L 14, 20.1.1998, pp. 9–14.

39 The Decree of Council of Ministers of 10 September 2019 on the amount of the minimum wage for work and the amount of the minimum hourly wage in 2020, O.J. 2019, item 1778.

40 The Law of 14 November 2003, O.J. 2003, No. 213, item 2081.

meets employees' individual needs, especially connected with the carer's duties. Although it is not provided explicitly by PLC, an employee should be able to choose the working days, applying simultaneously for individual working time schedule (art. 142 PLC) or indicating preferred working days in his written request.[41] An employee is not obliged to justify his request, however nor is the employer obliged to accept it.

Those conditions apply equally to the system of weekend work, in which the work is performed only on Fridays, Saturdays, Sundays and on public holidays (art 144 PLC). Analogically, this system allows the extension of daily working time up to 12 hours within the calculation period not exceeding 1 month and can be introduced upon employee's written request in the employment contract. The weekend work can be introduced at any condition, provided that the work on Sundays and public holidays is allowed (in situations widely indicated in art. 151(10) PLC). As the weekend work can strongly interfere with worker's non-professional life, it also cannot be imposed by the employer.

Staggered working hours have been introduced into PLC in 2013,[42] implementing solutions existing in practise. Due to art. 140(1) § 2 PLC a working time schedule may provide for the period in which an employee decides on an hour of starting work on his/her working day. This solution allows the employees to adjust the start of work each day to their carers' obligations (e.g. the opening of the kindergarten or the start of schools in case of younger children). It also allows one parent or carer to start the working day early in a day, at 7 a.m. for example, leaving the care of the children to another parent, and to finish it early, at 3 p.m. in the given example, to take over the childcare responsibilities. However, the introduction of staggered working hours requires the consent of the employer and the workers' representatives.

A similar elasticity is connected with the individual working time schedule introduced into PLC since 2004[43] (art. 142 PLC). It allows the employer, upon the written request of an employee, to set out an individual schedule of his working time. It allows both – to adjust the working hours by setting individual hours of starting and finishing work for an individual employee in comparison to the working time in the enterprise (for the same reasons as given above for example) or to introduce a different working time system.[44] The individual

---

41 M. Nałęcz, *Kodeks pracy. Komentarz*, W. Muszalski (ed.), C.H. Beck 2019, [Legalis/el, art. 143].

42 The Law of 12 July 2013, O.J. 2013, item 896.

43 The Law of 14 November 2003, O.J. 2003, No. 213, item 2081.

44 U. Torbus, "Rola elastycznych form. . .."

working time schedule, as its name suggests, is regarded as a tool to adjust the organisation of a working time to the needs of an individual employee, whereas the staggered working hours may apply to all employees within the given enterprise.[45]

The individual working time schedule is introduced upon employee's request, so similarly to compressed working hours or system of weekend work, it can be assumed that this organisation of working time meets employees' individual needs, especially connected with the carer's duties. Analogically, the employee's request must not be accepted by the employer, who must not justify the refusal. However, since 2018[46] the employer is obliged to grant the request for the staggered working hours or the individual working time schedule in few cases. It concerns a case of an employee-spouse or an employee-parent of the child in the prenatal phase, in case of a complicated pregnancy or an employee-parent of disabled child (art. 142(1) PLC). In this case the employer may refuse to accept employee's request only if it is not possible due to the work organization or the type of work performed by the employee. The refusal must be presented in writing. This PLC provision can also be regarded as the measure ensuring full enjoyment of rights by children with disabilities postulated by the WLB directive.

Even greater flexibility is connected with the task based working time, introduced into PLC in 1996.[47] It can be introduced if it is justified by the type of work or its organisation, or by the place of performing work (art. 140 PLC). The employer, having consulted the employee, determines the time necessary to perform the assigned tasks, taking into consideration the general working time norms (eight hours in a 24-hour period and an average of 40 hours in an average five-day working week in a calculation period not exceeding four months, art. 129 PLC). The task based working time is regarded as one of the most flexible forms of the working time arrangements. It is connected with the resignation of the determination of formal working hours, in particular of indicating the exact time of beginning and ending work each day. It gives the employee the flexibility to organise his/her work, both on daily and weekly basis, and to adapt it to his/her carer's obligations. The employer may, however, indicate certain hours or a time interval in a working week in which the employee shall be accessible or present in the premises of the enterprise for

45 A. Sobczyk, *Kodeks pracy. Komentarz*, C.H. Beck 2020, [Legalis/el. art. 140(1)].

46 The Law of 10 May 2018, O.J. 2018, item 1076.

47 The Law of 2 February 1996, O.J. 1996, No. 24, item 110.

example.[48] This system is usually introduced where the demand of work varies within the calculation period or the control of employees presence at work is impossible or highly difficult (e.g. he/she performs work outside the enterprise's premises). It can be also used in connection with tasks that can be performed outside the normal enterprise's operating hours. The task based working time system is often used by enterprises in practise.

Time off *in lieu* is connected with the overtime work, usually performed in the afternoons or at night hours and therefore interfering with the family obligations. According to art. 151(2) PLC in exchange for the overtime work, instead of an additional remuneration, an employer, at the written request of an employee, may grant him/her the time off equal to the overtime work. In that case the time off is granted till the end of the calculation period. PLC does not stipulate when the request should be submitted, therefore it can be submitted each month or on a permanent basis. Equally, PLC does not determine whether an employee is entitled to decide when the time off will be exercised. As the employee's demand is required, he/she should have the possibility to decide upon the date of the time off that should be agreed between employee and employer.[49] Certainly, granting the time off *in lieu* cannot cause a reduction of the remuneration due to an employee for the full monthly working time, but using the time off an employee is not entitled to a bonus for overtime work (art 151(2) al. 3 PLC). Since 2003,[50] granting the time off *in lieu* may also take place without a request from an employee. In this case the employer shall grant the employee a time off, before the end of the calculation period, amounting to one and a half times the number of hours worked overtime (art. 151(2) al. 2 PLC).

7. Conclusions

The workplaces have been built around the men's traditional life patterns, with long working hours and full-time schedule. It inevitably leads to widespread attrition among women that have children or provide care of other family members. To boost women's participation in the labour market, namely to facilitate the work of women, the change of the perspective of "the outdated, masculine norm of the ideal worker of the 1950s" to "the new balanced worker

48 U. Torbus, "Rola elastycznych form. . .."

49 A. Sobczyk, *Kodeks pracy. Komentarz*, C.H. Beck 2020, [Legalis/el. art. 151(2)].

50 The Law of 14 November 2003, O.J. 2003, No. 213, item 2081.

of today"[51] seems to be fundamental. However, the enterprises in general are unlikely to reshape their workplaces themselves, therefore a reasonable social policy must be continued.

The solutions introduced by the WLB directive, presented in this chapter, may contribute importantly to reduce the gap between male and female employment ratio. Family support policies that aim to improve work–life balance, including rights to paid leave and return to equivalent work, as well as affordable childcare services for working parents, are known to have made a substantial contribution to lifting the participation rates of women, and especially those of mothers.[52] However, the work-life balance remains one of the biggest challenges for the contemporary labour law.[53]

In a summary it is important to express that nonetheless of the best legal measures, as those introduced by the WLB directive given as an example, the employers' favourable attitude and their "good will" are crucial it achieve the work-life balance. The research proves that the availability and the real use of WLB solutions largely depend on the employers.[54] Indeed, despite the flexibility given in PLC, according to national social security institution (ZUS) in the first half of 2020 less than 2 % of working fathers exercised the right to parental leave. The usage of the paternity leave was higher, reaching approximately 30 % of all male workers.[55]

Therefore, to facilitate the work of mothers and diminish their vulnerability in the labour market further actions are required. According to G20 members and stakeholders those actions shall include, among others, further strengthening of long-term care and care leave provision, as well as changing the stereotypes and norms around caregiving and housework. To strengthen male participation in childcare and carer's leaves, also actions such as awareness campaigns are required, aimed at reducing bias against male caregiving and highlighting

51 J.C. Williams, S. Bornstein, *The Evolution of "FReD:" Family Responsibilities Discrimination and Developments in the Law of Stereotyping and Implicit Bias*, 59 Hastings L.J. 1311 (2008).

52 *Women at Work: Trends 2016*, International Labour Office – Geneva: ILO, 2016.

53 U. Torbus, "Zmiany w zakresie uprawnień. . .."

54 A. Andysz, A. Najder, D. Merecz-Kot, "Organizacyjne i indywidualne uwarunkowania korzystania z rozwiązań sprzyjających równoważeniu życia zawodowego i prywatnego," *Medycyna Pracy* 2014, No. 65(1).

55 https://www.wnp.pl/parlamentarny/spoleczenstwo/zus-wielu-mezczyzn-korzysta-z-urlopu-ojcowskiego-rzadziej-biora-urlop-rodzicielski,82162.html [available: 1.07.2020].

women workers' significant contribution to family income and national GDP, thereby promoting gender-equitable sharing of unpaid work.[56]

Aforementioned postulates are in line with the priorities of the European Commission chaired by Ursula von der Leyen from December 2019. Political guidelines for the European Commission for 2019–2024 highlight the need for equality for all, especially gender equality, as a one of the major priorities for EU and a critical component of its economic growth. The support for parents and carers in better reconciling work and family life is one of the elements of declared the European Gender Strategy that will give women and men equal legal rights across all of life decisions including starting a job, running a business, getting paid, getting married, having children, managing assets and drawing a pension.[57] Full implementation of the WLB directive, which encourages better sharing of responsibilities between women and men is one of the steps in this process. Further actions concern the introduction of pay transparency measures, setting the quotas for gender balance on company boards and measures to prevent domestic violence against women, protect victims and punish offenders (e.g. by the EU accession to the Istanbul Convention on fighting domestic violence).

It shows that the multidimensional actions are still required to diminish the female vulnerability in the labour market. Despite positive changes, women continue to take on a disproportionate burden of long-term care work and this may importantly influence their ability of paid work. It has been strongly noticeable during the COVID-19 pandemic, especially in relation to unpaid care work and educational support of the children. The national lockdowns introduced by many countries in spring 2020, including Poland, highlighted already existing inequalities.[58] Therefore, measures enhancing the share of care responsibilities between working parents, such as those introduced by the WLB directive, should be effectively implemented. If not, any future crisis will strengthen women withdrawal from the labour market or at best strongly

---

56 *Women at Work in G20 countries: Progress and policy action*. Paper prepared under Japan's G20 Presidency (2019), https://www.oecd.org/g20/summits/osaka/G20-Women-at-Work.pdf (accessed on 1st March 2020).

57 *A Union that strives for more: My agenda for Europe*. Ursula von der Leyen. Political guidelines for the next European Commission 2019–2024, https://ec.europa.eu/info/sites/info/files/political-guidelines-next-commission_en_0.pdf [available: 1.03.2020].

58 T. Alon, M. Doepke, J. Olmstead-Rumsey, M. Tertilt, *The impact of COVID-19 on gender equality*, NBER Working Paper No. 26947, April 2020.

weaken the female position in it. The COVID-19 crisis showed the importance of paid family leave to all workers.[59] However, since it concerns mostly women, the exercise of paid family leaves influences directly or indirectly female availability, productivity and the number of working hours. It has the immediate impact on female wages and may induce redundancies in some cases. The COVID-19 crisis, in contrast to previous economic recessions, has hit mostly women – the unemployment rises faster among women that among men all around the world.[60] Therefore, all non-standard forms of employment that can provide labour market opportunities for women and better work-life balance should not be used to circumvent anti-discrimination requirements.

The presentation given in this chapter showed that WLB mechanisms determined in Polish legislation are rather generous in comparison to other countries.[61] It is a year of paid leave that is of a great importance for work-life balance. Also flexible working time arrangements, in particular the staggered working hours or the task-based working time facilitate the work of mothers, along with widely exercised the carers' leave or time off on grounds of *force majeure*. However, the widespread of precarious forms employment among younger people (thus young mothers) and relatively low salaries, along with not fully coherent social policy do not support the working women. Contrarily, certain recent incentives, such as the reversal of retirement reforms in 2016[62] and lowering of the retirement age back to 60 years for women and 65 years for men or introduced in 2016 "the 500+ allowance,"[63] granting the right to a benefit to all parents, regardless their economic activity, result in the female withdrawal from the labour market.[64]

Moreover, despite the widening of parental rights presented in this chapter, the demographic situation in Poland remains very difficult. The birth rate has been negative since 2012 and the fertility ratio stays on a level of 1.435 (2018). The successive development of the rights of working parents in 2009–2016 did

---

59 ILO 2020 Monitor 5, ILO Monitor: COVID-19 and the world of work. 5th edition, 30 June 2020.

60 ILO 2020 Monitor 6, ILO Monitor: COVID-19 and the world of work. 6th edition, 23 September 2020.

61 R. Ray, J.C. Gornick, J. Schmitt, *Parental Leave Policies in 21 Countries. Assessing Generosity and Gender Equality*, September 2008.

62 The Law of 16 November 2016, O.J. 2017, No. 38, item 1452 that entered into force on 1st October 2017.

63 The Law of 11 February 2016, O.J. 2019, item 2407, as amended.

64 I. Magda, A. Kiełczewska, N. Brandt, *The "Family 500+" child allowance and female labour supply in Poland*, March 2018.

not reverse this negative tendency. Therefore, a wide system supporting working mothers must be further developed, including actions mentioned above. It allows the conclusion that the work-life balance mechanisms, although very important, are just a part of a multidimensional system required to facilitate the work of mothers and to diminish their vulnerability in the labour market, simply – to enable the full enjoyment of two EU fundamental right – the right to work and the right to gender equality.

Bibliography:

Alon T., Doepke M., Olmstead-Rumsey J., Tertilt M., "The impact of COVID-19 on gender equality," *NBER Working Paper* No. 26947, April 2020.

Andysz A., Najder A, Merecz-Kot D., "Organizacyjne i indywidualne uwarunkowania korzystania z rozwiązań sprzyjających równoważeniu życia zawodowego i prywatnego," *Medycyna Pracy* 2014, No. 65 (1).

Baran J., Bartha A., Chłoń-Domińczak A., Fedyuk O., Kamińska A., Lewandowski P., Lis M, Magda I., Potoczna M. Zentai V., ed. I. Magda, *Women on the European labour market*, 2014.

Conley H., Healy G., Gottardi D., Mikołajczyk B., Peruzzi M. (eds.), *The gender pay gap and social partnership in Europe. Findings form "Close the Deal, Fill the Gap,"* Routledge 2019.

Grimshaw D., Rubery J., *The motherhood pay gap: A review of the issues, theory and international evidence*, International Labour Organization, Conditions of Work and Employment Series No. 57, Geneva, 2015.

Kaufmann O., "L'actualité du droit social comparé," [in:] *Le droit social – le droit comparé. Etudes dédiées à la mémoire de Pierre Ortscheidt*, Presses Universitaires de Strasbourg, 2003, No. 6.

Ludera-Ruszel A., "The situation of women in the labor market in Poland in the light of existing labor law provisions concerning the working time," *Przegląd Politologiczny* 2016, No. 4.

Magda I., Kiełczewska A., Brandt N., *The "Family 500+" child allowance and female labour supply in Poland*, March 2018.

Moreau M.A., "Règlements et directives en matière sociale," [in:] *Les norms sociales européennes*, B. Teyssié (ed.), Pantheon-Assas 2000.

Nałęcz M., *Kodeks pracy. Komentarz*, W. Muszalski (ed.), C.H. Beck 2019, [Legalis/el, art. 143].

Półtorak M., "Projekt dyrektywy WLB – nowe podejście do równości płci w zatrudnieniu?," *Studia z Zakresu Prawa Pracy i Polityki Społecznej* 2019, 26, No. 4.

Ray R., Gornick J.C., Schmitt J., *Parental Leave Policies in 21 Countries. Assessing Generosity and Gender Equality*, September 2008.

Sobczyk A., *Kodeks pracy. Komentarz*, Sobczyk A (ed.) C.H. Beck 2020.

Ślęzak-Gąsiorowska A., "Dyrektywa w sprawie równowagi między życiem zawodowym a prywatnym rodziców i opiekunów – perspektywa polska," *Monitor Prawa Pracy* 2019, No. 4.

Torbus U., "Rola elastycznych form zatrudnienia w godzeniu nauki z pracą zawodową," [in:] Elastyczne formy zatrudnienia i organizacji czasu pracy, A. Bieliński, A. Giedrewicz-Niewińska, M. Szabłowska-Juckiewicz (eds.), Diffin 2015.

Torbus U., "Zmiany w zakresie uprawnień rodzicielskich ułatwiających łączenie obowiązków zawodowych z opieką nad dzieckiem," [in:] *Uprawnienia pracowników związane z rodzicielstwem*, J. Czerniak-Swędzioł (ed.), Wolters Kluwer 2016.

Włodarczyk M., "Protection of parenthood," [in:] *Outline of Polish Labour Law System*, K. W. Baran (ed.), Wolters Kluwer 2016.

Anna Jaworska-Wieloch
University of Silesia in Katowice
e-mail: anna.jaworska-wieloch@us.edu.pl
ORCID ID: 0000-0002-1209-4433

Pregnant women and those serving a prison sentence with a child under international law

Abstract: Serving a sentence of imprisonment is a difficult issue for every human being. Prison is a total institution so it limits the normal course of life. The severity of this punishment is not the same for everyone. Prisons are designed for men. The isolation is much more difficult for women. Women are more exposed to the deprivation of their needs and rights. Children are also vulnerable but sometimes they have to stay in prisons with their mothers. They have long been of intense interest for both domestic legislators and those responsible for international law. A question should be whether this protection is sufficient.

Keywords: prison, women, child, a prison sentence, European prison rules

1. Introductory remarks

Each individual can fall victim to unequal treatment, but certain persons are more exposed to the deprivation of their needs and rights than the general public due to their specific predispositions, characteristics or properties. The natural consequence is that such persons require special support from the State and international organizations.

Particularly vulnerable groups have long been of intense interest for both domestic legislators and those responsible for international law. The awareness that States should take care of individuals most exposed to exclusion gave rise to the identification of so-called vulnerable persons, i.e. persons most susceptible to harm, disadvantaged persons, those in unfavorable circumstances, with special needs, or alternatively, persons in an unprotected situation.[1] Alongside

1 B. Mikołajczyk, "Obowiązki państw w zakresie identyfikacji poszczególnych potrzeb cudzoziemców ubiegających się o status uchodźcy," [in:] *Uchodźcy w Polsce i w Europie. Stan prawny i rzeczywistość*, eds. T. Gardocka, J. Sobczak, Toruń 2010, p. 71.

the elderly, disabled and immigrants,[2] the group particularly vulnerable to deprivation includes women and children.

The recognition of the exceptional susceptibility of women and children to violations and discrimination resulted in the establishment of guarantees of their rights within many legal acts, both domestic[3] and international,[4] intended to counteract any violations. Setting aside the correct functioning of the mechanisms contained therein, it should be noted that some women are even more vulnerable to the deprivation of rights in a situation where they are simultaneously assigned to another group exposed to discrimination, i.e. prisoners.

Prison is a total institution that limits the normal course of life: it is clearly symbolized by the physical barriers preventing contact with the outside world: closed doors, high walls or barbed wire fences.[5] It is an oppressive institution:[6] apart from the obvious distress related to the deprivation of liberty, as soon as the prison walls are crossed, access to material and service facilities, sexual contacts or family as well as the possibility of self-determination are lost, whilst the sense of security is shattered by a threat posed by fellow inmates,

---

2 Cf. S. Golinowska, *O polskiej biedzie w latach 1990–2015. Definicje, miary i wyniki*, Warsaw 2018, p. 85.

3 Such guarantees are provided for, inter alia, in the Constitution (Journal of Laws of 1997, No. 78, item 483), The Labor Code (i.e. of 2019, item 1040), the Act of 3 December 2010 on the implementation of some European Union provisions regarding equal treatment (i.e. of 2016, item. 1219).

4 Convention on the Elimination of All Forms of Discrimination against Women adopted by UN General Assembly on 18 December 1979 (Journal of Laws of 1982, No. 10, item 71); Recommendation Rec. (2002)5 of the Committee of Ministers on the Protection of Women against Violence of 30 April 2002 (http://niebieskalinia.info/pliki/dokumenty/Wa%C5 %BCne%20dokumenty/Rekomendacja%20Komitetu%20Ministr%C3%B3w%20Rec.%282002%295%20w%20sprawie%20ochrony%20kobiet%20przed%20przemoc%C4 %85 %20z%20dnia%2030 %20kwietnia%202002 %20roku.pdf – viewed 23.03.2020; European Convention on the Exercise of Children's Rights prepared in Strasbourg on 25 January 1996 (Journal of Laws. 2000.107.1128); Convention on Preventing and Combating Violence against Women and Domestic Violence (Journal of Laws. 2015.961).

5 E. Goffman, "Charakterystyka instytucji totalnych," [in:] *Współczesne teorie socjologiczne*, eds. A. Jasińska-Kania, L.M. Nijakowski, J. Szacki, M. Ziółkowski, Warsaw 2006, p. 316.

6 M. Leśniak, M. Szaszkiewicz, "Więzienie jako instytucja opresyjna i sytuacja depresyjna," *Państwo i Społeczeństwo* 2015 (XV), No. 2, pp. 11–12.

penal institution and prison officers.[7] In such a difficult life situation, the probability of deprivation of prisoners' rights is very high – both during incarceration due to their dependence on the prison administration and inmates, as well as on release as a consequence of social stigma. The literature review shows that ex-prisoners are publicly perceived as the group most vulnerable to discrimination.[8]

Belonging to both these groups simultaneously significantly increases the vulnerability to violations of rights. The situation of women detained in penal institutions is extremely difficult. Prisons are ill-suited for female inmates in so far as women constitute a tiny minority of the prison population, penal institutions are designed predominantly for male inmates and prison regimes fail to meet women's specific needs.[9] Suffice it to note that as at 31 December 2019, there were only 3,202 women in the overall number of 74,564 inmates,[10] i.e. 4.29 %. That disproportion results in the scarceness of prisons dedicated to female inmates, thus leading to a situation where women have to serve a sentence far away from their place of residence. Moreover, numerous rules and regulations in force during incarceration were designed specifically for men, creating only unnecessary restrictions in the case of women.

For the reasons set out above, incarcerated women are exposed to deprivation of rights. This should in turn reinforce the need for the State and international institutions to properly guarantee the rights granted to women. Deprivation of liberty is in itself a penalty and prison is a place where that penalty is served – the offender goes there as a result of being punished, but not to be punished, therefore penalties should be shaped in such a manner that

7 G.M. Sykes, *The Society of Captives: A Study of a Maximum Security Prison*, 1958; qtd. after: M. Kosewski, *Agresywni przestępcy*, Warsaw 1977, pp. 228–237; Cf. also I. Wesołowska – Krzysztofek, "Wpływ kontaktów z dziećmi na deprywację niektórych potrzeb u osadzonych kobiet," [in:] *Problemy więziennictwa u progu XXI wieku*, eds. B, Hołyst, Sł. Redo, Warsaw – Wiedeń – Kalisz 1996, pp. 476–477; M. Badowska-Hodyr, "Percepcja orzeczonej kary pozbawienia wolności w żeńskiej populacji więźniów," [in:] *Optymalizacja oddziaływań resocjalizacyjnych w Polsce i w niektórych krajach europejskich*, ed. F. Kozaczuk, Rzeszów 2006, p. 199; A. Matysiak – Błaszczyk, *Sytuacja życiowa kobiet pozbawionych wolności*, Krakow 2010, p. 102.

8 Cf. Report of the Month – Poles on the treatment in the place of work, https://zielonalinia.gov.pl/upload/raporty/Wersja%20PDF/Raport%20miesi%C4 %85ca-relacje%20(2).pdf, viewed 23.03.2020.

9 Cf. Resolution 1663 (2009) Women in Prison, PWP 2011, No. 72–73, p. 153 et seq.

10 https://www.sw.gov.pl/assets/95/70/75/c1cee7d03200820a03cdaa2c6afe897c482422ca.pdf; viewed 21.03.2020.

the suffering endured on that account is not exacerbated.[11] The question thus arises whether, even at the level of international law containing declarations of rights at a more general level and referring primarily to axiology, the rights of female inmates are ensured in such a way as to take into account the principle of proportionality[12] and necessity,[13] and appropriate recommendations are made for national legislators. A further question is to what extent the Polish legislator managed to adapt the national penitentiary law to the requirements and recommendations formulated at the international level.

2. The rights of prisoners under international law

The basic documents in international law guaranteeing the rights of prisoners are The Standard Minimum Rules for the Treatment of Prisoners[14] and The European Prison Rules.[15] These documents are valid within the structures of the Council of Europe and are only recommendations, or so-called soft law.[16] The countries that decided to sign the above resolutions assumed the obligation to comply with their guidelines and regularly inform the Council of Europe

11 D. Gajdus, B. Gronowska, *Europejskie standardy traktowania więźniów*, Toruń 1998, pp. 20–21, Cf. also H. Machel, "Czym jest dzisiejsze polskie więzienie?," [in:] *Wykonywanie kary pozbawienia wolności w Polsce – w poszukiwaniu skuteczności*, ed. H. Machel, Gdańsk 2006, p. 11.

12 J. Zakolska, *Zasada proporcjonalności w orzecznictwie Trybunału Konstytucyjnego*, Warsaw 2008, p. 20.

13 J. Zakolska, *Zasada proporcjonalności w orzecznictwie Trybunału Konstytucyjnego*, Warsaw 2008, p. 25; Cf. also M. Królikowski, "Dwa paradygmaty zasady proporcjonalności w prawie karnym," [in:] *Zasada proporcjonalności w prawie karnym*, ed. T. Dukiet-Nagórska, Warsaw 2010, p. 45.

14 Adopted in Geneva in 1955 by the First United Nations Congress on the Prevention of Crime and the Treatment of Offenders and approved by the Economic and Social Council in Resolution 663C (XXIV) of 31 July 1957 and 2076 (LXII) of 13 May 1977.

15 Adopted on 11 January 2006 by the Committee of Ministers for Council of Europe member states as Recommendation Rec (2006)2 at the 952nd meeting – The European Prison Rules replaced the previous versions of the Rules, i.e. Recommendation R (87)3 of the Committee of Ministers to Member States on the European Prison Rules adopted by the Committee of Ministers on 12 February 1987 at the 404th meeting of the Ministers' Deputies.

16 J. Migdał, G. Skrobotowicz, "Możliwość realizacji europejskich reguł więziennych z 2006 r. w zakresie reintegrowanego modelu wykonywania kary pozbawienia wolności a przeludnienie polskich jednostek penitencjarnych," *Roczniki Nauk Prawnych*, Vol. XXIV, No. 1–2014, p. 110.

of the state of compliance of their own system of enforcement of custodial sentences with the standards contained in the rules.[17] These documents have immense significance for the lawful, rational and humanitarian treatment of perpetrators of crimes, in particular of persons deprived of liberty.[18] They surely cannot replace the detailed provisions of the penal enforcement code, they are after all addressed to countries in the form of recommendations because they do not specify all the enforcement procedures or determine many competent institutions of particular countries.[19] However, they provide national legislators with a clear guideline on how to shape their prison policies.

The Standard Minimum Rules for the Treatment of Prisoners give an indication already in the first general rule that discrimination on grounds of race, color, sex, language, religion, political or other opinion, national or social origin, property, birth or other status is prohibited.[20] In a similar vein, the European Prison Rules provide in Rule 13[21] that the rules shall be applied impartially, without discrimination on any ground such as sex, race, color, language, religion, political or other opinion, national or social origin, association with a national minority, property, birth or other status.[22] Resolution 45/111 adopted by the UN General Assembly on 14 December 1990 regarding the basic principles of treatment of prisoners also drew attention to the prohibition of discrimination,[23] providing in Principle 2 that there shall be no discrimination on the grounds of race, color, sex, language, religion, political or other opinion,

17 J. Nikołajew, "Reguły Minimalne i Europejskie Reguły Więzienne a prawo więźniów do wolności sumienia i religii w Polsce," *Studia z Prawa Wyznaniowego* 2013, Vol. 16, p. 112.

18 T. Szymanowski, "Wstęp. Międzynarodowe standardy wykonywania kar," *Przegląd Więziennictwa Polskiego* 2011/72–73, pp. 9–10.

19 T. Szymanowski, "Rekomendacja Rec (2006) 2 Komitetu Ministrów dla państw członkowskich Europejskie Reguły Więzienne. Komentarz," *Przegląd Więziennictwa Polskiego* No. 72–73, Warsaw 2011, p. 75.

20 https://www.sw.gov.pl/assets/38/60/34/fd6222b4fd9a2310766f25582c667ae39f1831ba.pdf, viewed 23.03.2020.

21 https://bip.sw.gov.pl/SiteCollectionDocuments/CZSW/prawaczl/document.pdf, viewed 23.03.2020.

22 Cf. B. Myrna, "Wykonywanie kary pozbawienia wolności w świetle Europejskich Reguł Więziennych z 2006r. Podstawowe zasady, zakres i zastosowanie przedmiotowych reguł," *Nowa Kodyfikacja Prawa Karnego*, Vol. XXIV, (ed.) L. Bogunia, Wrocław 2009, p. 230.

23 https://www.arch-bip.ms.gov.pl/Data/Files/_public/bip/prawa_czl_onz/prawa_czlow_26_2.doc, viewed 23.03.2020.

national or social origin, property, birth or other status. This demand was reiterated by the resolution adopted in 2015 by the UN General Assembly: UN Standard Minimum Rules for the Treatment of Prisoners (Nelson Mandela Rules),[24] being in fact an amended version of the Standard Minimum Rules for the Treatment of Prisoners of 1955.

Thus, it appears that the basic sources of guarantees of prisoners' rights on the international arena emphasize the principle of non-discrimination indicating, inter alia, that the sex of the prisoner cannot constitute a criterion of differentiation. Women's special needs are addressed in Resolution 1663 (2009) *Women in Prison*.[25] It is observed in its introduction that even though the number of women incarcerated in European prisons is on the increase, they still constitute a minority of the prison population. As given above, prisons were designed primarily for men. For this reason, as well as due the fact that female prisoners frequently originate from lower social backgrounds and tend to be less educated in comparison with the male inmates, penal institutions, the prison regime as well as rehabilitation and educational programs fail to meet their specific needs.[26] This is not simply a matter of biological differences between men and women. As indicated by research, it is clear that the specific needs of women deprived of liberty are not limited only to hygiene needs or those related to pregnancy and feeding, but have a much broader psychological and social dimension.[27] The question thus arises to what extent the Polish Penal Enforcement Code (hereinafter abbreviated as PEC) seeks to meet those needs through the implementation of the demands and guarantees of rights provided for in international law, and above all in the Resolution.

Resolution *Women in Prison* points out, first of all, that custodial penalties should be avoided as far as possible for women under the age of 18, or alternatively, consideration be given to the establishment of weekend prisons dedicated specifically for women. A more general rule is included in Polish criminal law: pursuant to Art. 58 § 1 of the Criminal Code, where a statute provides for various types of penalties for a crime which is punishable by a penalty involving deprivation of liberty for a term no longer than 5 years, the court shall impose

24 https://www.rpo.gov.pl/sites/default/files/Reguly_Mandeli.pdf, viewed 23.03.2020.

25 "Rezolucja 1663 (2009) Kobiety w więzieniu, Międzynarodowe standardy wykonywania kar," *Przegląd Więziennictwa Polskiego* 2011/72–73, p. 153 et seq.

26 Section 1 of the Resolution indicated above.

27 B. Stańdo-Kawecka, "Rezolucja 1663 (2009) Kobiety w więzieniu. Komentarz, Międzynarodowe standardy wykonywania kar," *Przegląd Więziennictwa Polskiego* 2011/72–73, p. 162.

a penalty of deprivation of liberty only if no other penalty or penal measure can meet the aims of punishment. This means that the penalty of deprivation of liberty should be imposed only in exceptional cases and refraining from the imposition of custodial penalties, even at the stage of enforcement proceedings, promotes the *ultima ratio* principle of the penalty of deprivation of liberty.[28] It must nonetheless be recalled that many offenses punishable by a penalty of deprivation of liberty for a term exceeding five years do not have to be associated with high culpability. In such situations, there is no special provision indicating a preference for non-custodial penalties, in particular in relation to women who in general find it harder to serve a penalty of imprisonment. In fact, apart from the electronic supervision system, the Polish Penal Enforcement Code does not envisage any other form of serving a prison sentence, and the possibility of the application of a probation measure in the form of conditional suspension of the enforcement of penalty was severely limited in 2015.[29] Weekend prisons proposed in the Resolution were contemplated in Poland,[30] but ultimately, due to organizational problems, the project was not implemented.

3. The scope of protection of women and children in the Polish law

This does not mean that Polish penitentiary law did not seek to provide female prisoners with more freedom during incarceration. Art. 87 § 2 PEC lays down the principle that women shall serve a custodial sentence in semi-open prisons, unless the degree of their depravity or security reasons give grounds for serving a sentence in another type of prison. By contrast, men can benefit from a similar presumption only if they are serving a sentence in the system of programmed rehabilitation (Art. 88 § 1 PEC). This stems from a belief that women do not pose the same risk and danger to the penal institution as men and that

28 J. Lachowski, *Kodeks karny. Część ogólna. Komentarz*, eds. M. Królikowski, R. Zawłocki, Vol. II, Warsaw 2011, p. 589; Cf. also in the Decision of the Court of Appeals in Krakow of 8 April 2003, case file II AKz 125/03, Decision of the Prosecutor's Office: Orz. Prok. i Pr. 2003/10/10, p. 9.

29 Act of 20 February 2015, Journal of Laws of 2015, item 396.

30 https://wiadomosci.wp.pl/weekendowe-wiezienia-6031575588398209a, viewed 23.03.2020.

female inmates find it more difficult to put up with serving a custodial sentence than men.[31]

Resolution *Women in Prison* emphasized that due to the relatively low percentage of female prisoners and women detained on remand, there are generally few women's prisons and even a smaller number of penal institutions intended for women detained on remand. This in turn means that women are placed in facilities far away from their place of residence, which cuts family ties. Meanwhile, ensuring closeness to the loved ones is to ensure maintenance of family ties by the convict.[32] Polish penal enforcement law does not contain a guarantee of incarceration in a penal institution located as close to home as possible. As of 1 January 2012, even the demand that, to the extent possible, prisoners should serve a custodial sentence in a place as near as possible to their place of residence was abandoned.[33] Such declaration is still derived in legal writings from other norms, mainly from Art. 67 § 1 PEC, which relates to the aims of serving a prison sentence.[34] All in all, as from 1 January 2012, there is in essence no provision that would explicitly require or, at least, call for the incarceration as close to home as possible in spite of its relevance for maintaining family ties. Women are doubly disadvantaged by that legal status: first, their small proportion in the total prison population means that the number of prisons for women is limited, which consequently implies that numerous detained and convicted women are placed in prisons far away from their place of residence and they experience acute difficulties in maintaining contact with the family in the form of visits or temporary releases.[35] Second, separation from

---

31 Cf. K. Sitnik, "Wykonywanie kary pozbawienia wolności wobec kobiet," [in:] *Postępowanie z wybranymi grupami skazanych w polskim systemie penitencjarnym. Aspekty prawne*, ed. A. Kwieciński, Warsaw 2013, p. 309.

32 D. Gajdus, B. Gronowska, *Europejskie standardy traktowania więźniów*, Toruń 1998, p. 79.

33 Art. 100 PEC had the following wording until 1 January 2012: "A convicted person shall serve a sentence in an appropriate prison located, where possible, closest to his place of residence. Transfer of a convict may take place only for justified reasons." Cf. also K. Postulski, *Kodeks karny wykonawczy. Komentarz*, Warsaw 2012, pp. 456–457.

34 K. Dąbkiewicz, "W sprawie "miejsca" odbywania kary pozbawienia wolności przez skazanego," *Probacja* 2015/1, p. 23 et seq.

35 B. Stańdo-Kawecka, "Rezolucja 1663 (2009) Kobiety w więzieniu. Komentarz, Międzynarodowe standardy wykonywania kar," *Przegląd Więziennictwa Polskiego* 2011/72–73, p. 163.

family members and sporadic contacts with them are typically a more painful experience for women than men.[36]

Resolution *Women in Prison* also draws attention to the manner of incarceration of women in penal institutions. It calls for providing an assurance that female juveniles are imprisoned separately from adult females. As noted in the Resolution, if this would lead to fewer opportunities for education, safeguards should be put in place so that juveniles do not mix with women with serious long-term criminal histories (Rule 11.3).

Polish penal enforcement law lays down several rules regarding the incarceration of convicts: the criteria for the classification include, inter alia, sex (Art. 82 § 2 point 1 and Art. 87 § 1 PEC), age (Art. 82 § 2 point 2 PEC), or prior imprisonment record (Art. 82 § 2 point 3 PEC). It also indicates that the degree of depravity and social threat should be taken into account (Art. 82 § 2 point 7 PEC). In other words, following the recommendations set out in the Resolution, the Penal Enforcement Code seeks to separate prisoners depending on their prison experience, introducing various types of prison facilities: for juveniles (Art. 84), for those serving a first sentence (Art. 85) and for repeat offenders (Art. 86).

Incarceration cannot deprive prisoners of their dignity, and women are particularly sensitive as regards the need to undergo personal checks. For this reason, Resolution *Women in Prison* calls on the member states to ensure that male prison guards do not hold positions requiring direct physical contact with female prisoners and do not supervise them in situations where they are likely to be in a situation of undress. This demand ties in closely with the prohibition of degrading treatment indicated in many international acts.[37] In turn, the Nelson Mandela Rules highlight the prohibition of cruel, inhuman and degrading treatment (Rule 1) and prescribe that intrusive searches (strip and body cavity searches) should be undertaken only if absolutely necessary (Rule 52). The Penal Enforcement Code fulfils these demands: pursuant to Art. 116 § 3

---

36 P. Wierzbicki, "Wykonywanie kary pozbawienia wolności wobec kobiet," [in:] *Przestępczość kobiet. Aspekty kryminologiczne i penitencjarne*, eds. T. Kolarczyk, J. R. Kubiak, P. Wierzbicki, Warsaw 1984, pp. 194–195; G. Lewandowski, "Kobieta i jej macierzyństwo w warunkach zakładu karnego," *Universitas Gedanensis* 1995/12, p. 19.

37 Indeed, e.g. the European Convention for the Protection of Human Rights and Fundamental Freedoms drawn up in Rome on 4 November 1950; European Parliament Resolution of 15 December 2011 on detention conditions in the EU CE 168/82 (CE 168/82).

PEC, body searches and the checking of clothing and footwear shall be carried out indoors, in the absence of bystanders and persons of the opposite sex, and undertaken by a person of the same sex.[38] This norm should be regarded as an important guarantee of the rights of female prisoners in view of the case law of the European Court of Human Rights which held that body searches carried out by prison officers of a different sex may show a clear lack of respect for detainees and in effect diminish their human dignity.[39]

Resolution *Women in Prison* also raises the issue of the level of education of prisoners. It is clear that uneducated women do worse in the labor market[40] mainly due to the narrower scope of physical work available to women, and it should be borne in mind that work constitutes a fundamental part of the correctional program.[41] Therefore, as regards the educational needs of female

38 Cf. E. Dawidziuk, "Kontrole osobiste osób pozbawionych wolności – rozważania na temat potrzeby wprowadzenia zmian," *Przegląd Więziennictwa Polskiego* 2013, No. 78, p. 36.

39 *Case Valasinas v. Lithuania*, judgment delivered on 24 July 2001, Application No. 44558/98.

40 https://tvn24bis.pl/ze-swiata,75/niewyksztalcone-kobiety-radza-sobie-gorzej-od-mezczyzn-na-rynku-pracy,742485.html, viewed 22.03.2020.

41 St. Walczak, *Prawo penitencjarne. Zarys systemu*, Warsaw 1972, p. 349; S. Lelental, *Prawo karne wykonawcze*, Warszawa 1990, p. 88; T. Kalisz, "Teoretyczne i prawne aspekty zatrudnienia skazanych," *Nowa Kodyfikacja Prawa Karnego* Vol. VIII, (ed.) L. Bogunia, Wrocław 2001, p. 331; B. Hołyst, "Oddziaływania penitencjarne jako sposób zapobiegania przestępczości," [in:] *Misja Służby Więziennej a jej zadania wobec aktualnej polityki karnej i oczekiwań społecznych, IV Polski Kongres Penitencjarny*, eds. W. Ambrozik, H, Machel, P. Stępniak, Poznań – Gdańsk – Warszawa – Poznań 2008, p. 135; J. Galicki, "Zatrudnienie osadzonych w zakładach karnych jako czynnik resocjalizacji," [in:] *Misja Służby Więziennej a jej zadania wobec aktualnej polityki karnej i oczekiwań społecznych, IV Polski Kongres Penitencjarny*, eds. W. Ambrozik, H, Machel, P. Stępniak, Poznań – Gdańsk – Warszawa – Poznań 2008, p. 637; R. Słowiński, "Zatrudnienie skazanych – szanse i bariery," [in:] *Misja Służby Więziennej a jej zadania wobec aktualnej polityki karnej i oczekiwań społecznych, IV Polski Kongres Penitencjarny*, eds. W. Ambrozik, H, Machel, P. Stępniak, Poznań – Gdańsk – Warszawa – Poznań 2008, p. 655; H. Machel, "Polska praktyka penitencjarna a oczekiwania społeczne," [in:] *Węzłowe problemy prawa karnego, kryminologii i polityki kryminalnej. Księga pamiątkowa ofiarowana Profesorowi Andrzejowi Markowi*, eds. V. Konarska-Wrzosek, J. Lachowski, J. Wójcik, Warsaw 2010, p. 883; E. Dawidziuk, *Traktowanie osób pozbawionych wolności we współczesnej Polsce na tle standardów międzynarodowych*, Warsaw 2013, p. 158; T. Szymanowski, *Prawo karne wykonawcze i polityka penitencjarna*, T. Szymanowski, J. Migdał, Warsaw 2014, p. 317; M. Bramska, *Realizacja prawa skazanego do kształcenia, Stan i*

prisoners, the Resolution calls on the member states to recognize the problem of very low levels of literacy and numeracy among prisoners, including women, and to provide all women with a minimum of twenty hours of education and training classes per week. A similar problem was noted by the European Prison Rules. As indicated in Rule 28.1, every prison shall seek to provide all prisoners with access to educational programs which are as comprehensive as possible and which meet their individual needs and aspirations, and that priority shall be given to prisoners with literacy and numeracy needs and those who lack basic or vocational education (Rule 28.2). In the same spirit, it follows from Recommendation 914 (1981) on the social situation of prisoners[42] that education and vocational training are an essential element of the process of preparing prisoners to resume their normal lives. It appears that the importance of education during incarceration is recognized in many international legal acts.

Instruction which raises educational attainment and vocational courses are also provided in Poland, although the provisions of the applicable Act do not guarantee a minimum number of educational hours offered in penal institutions. Meanwhile, the provision of training and educational courses for convicts is of crucial importance not only to increase their earning potential, but also to shape their attitudes by imbuing them with ethical and humanistic values.[43] It would surely be useful to introduce a minimum number of hours of educational offer for uneducated or unskilled women, given that prisons are oriented to the enforcement of penalties and custodial measures in relation to men, and consequently, they do not provide women with individualized treatment in terms of adjustment of the degree of security in prison and the offer of educational and rehabilitation classes to women's properties and needs.[44] At present, the legislator does not specify such a minimum number.

It also seems appropriate to explore the issue of healthcare of female prisoners. The European Prison Rules point out in Rule 34 that prison authorities shall safeguard the health of all prisoners in their care, and that prisoners shall have access to the health services available in the country without discrimination

węzłowe problemy polskiego więziennictwa, Część IV, Biuletyn RPO No. 42, Warsaw 2000, p. 259.

42 *Przegląd Więziennictwa Polskiego* 2011/72–73, p. 205 et seq.

43 Cf. T. Szymanowski, *Przemiany systemu penitencjarnego w Polsce*, Warsaw 1996, pp. 53–54.

44 B. Stańdo-Kawecka, "Rezolucja 1663 (2009) Kobiety w więzieniu. Komentarz, Międzynarodowe standardy wykonywania kar," *Przegląd Więziennictwa Polskiego* 2011/72–73, p. 163.

on the grounds of their legal situation (Rule 40 (3)). The Penal Enforcement Code contains general provisions providing the convict with free health services, medicines and sanitary articles (Art. 115 § 1), stipulating at the same time, that a convicted person serving a prison sentence shall not be free to choose: a doctor and a nurse of the outpatient clinic with a sick room, primary health care doctor, nurse and midwife, as well as an outpatient healthcare provider, dentist and hospital (Art. 115 §1a). It is thus evident that apart from depriving prisoners of the freedom of choice of doctors and healthcare establishments, Polish penitentiary law declares that all the necessary medical services are appropriately provided.

It is not uncommon for a woman who is to be put in prison to be pregnant. This leads to increased difficulties, since the situation of a female prisoner exposed to deprivation of rights due to the very fact of being a woman is aggravated by the issue of her fetus, and later of her child, that is another group of vulnerable persons incapable of taking proper care of their own interests and thus requiring systemic support. For this reason, Resolution *Woman in Prison* calls for ensuring that pregnant prisoners are transferred, at an appropriate time, to outside hospitals so that their children are not born in prison. The resolution prescribes that, in particular, pregnant women should not be shackled or otherwise attached to beds or other items of furniture during gynecological examinations or during and immediately after childbirth – other means of meeting security needs can and should be found. In turn, the European Prison Rules state that prisoners shall be allowed to give birth outside prison, and where a child is born in prison, the authorities shall provide all necessary support and facilities (Rule 34.3). Along the same line, the Nelson Mandela's Rules emphasize that women's prisons shall have special accommodation for all necessary prenatal and postnatal care and treatment. In cases where it is possible, arrangements shall be made for children to be born in a hospital outside the prison. If a child is born in prison, this fact shall not be mentioned in the birth certificate (Rule 28).

The Polish Penal Enforcement Code seeks to provide adequate care to pregnant prisoners. Pursuant to Art. 87 § 3 PEC, pregnant or lactating women shall be provided with specialist care. Moreover, such prisoners shall have the right to enjoy longer walks (Art. 112 § 1 PEC) and make additional food purchases (Art. 113a § 1 PEC). Disciplinary penalties such as removal of the opportunity to receive food parcels for a period of up to three months, removal or restriction of the opportunity to purchase food products or tobacco products for a period of up to three months and placement in an isolation cell for a period of up to 28 days shall not apply to them (Art. 143 § 2 PEC).

Contrary to the recommendations set out in the Resolution, the placement of pregnant women in penal institutions has not thus far been limited. The Regulation on the administrative activities related to the execution of detention on remand and penalties and coercive measures resulting in deprivation of liberty as well as documentation of such activities[45] does not envisage a prohibition on admission of pregnant women. Notably, the legislator indicated that in the event of admission to prison of a person requiring immediate hospital treatment due to an immediate threat to life or health or of a woman from the 28th week of pregnancy, that person shall immediately be provided with appropriate medical care (§ 35 item 1). Failing to take into account the recommendations of the Resolution, these provisions appear to be very severe, especially in view of the fact that the preceding Regulations in force[46] prohibited the admission of women from the 28th week of pregnancy to remand centers. At the same time, it is laid down in § 34 item 2 that the admission of women reporting or brought with their child to a penal institution at which a prison mother-and-child unit operates is governed by the provisions on the procedure for the admission of children of mothers deprived of liberty to prison mother-and-child units in the indicated prisons and the detailed rules for the organization and operation of such institutions.

It should be noted that the Polish legislator strives to provide pregnant incarcerated women with specialist care, as pursuant to § 28 item 2 of the regulation indicated above, convicted pregnant women shall be transferred two months prior to the expected date of birth to a gynecology and obstetrics hospital ward in a prison or remand center. Yet contrary to the provisions contained in the international acts, the legislator did not guarantee the right, or at least include a demand, allowing pregnant prisoners to give birth outside penal institutions.

The aim of the statutory guarantee of non-use of coercive measures against pregnant women is to protect a conceived but unborn child. For this reason, the Nelson Mandela Rules prescribe that instruments of restraint shall never

45 Regulation of 23 June 2015, (Journal of Laws of 2015, item. 927).

46 Yes § 34 item 2 point 2 of the Regulation of the Minister of Justice of 2 October 2012 on the administrative activities related to the execution of detention on remand and penalties and coercive measures resulting in deprivation of liberty as well as documentation of such activities (Journal of Laws of 2012, item 1153). That prohibition did not apply to a person reporting or brought after interruption in the enforcement of a penalty, after absconding, person who did not return to prison at a set time from a furlough, as well as to a person reporting or brought to a pre-trial detention which has a hospital where specialist medical care may be provided to that person.

be used on women during labor, during childbirth and immediately after childbirth (Rule 48).

The Polish legislator made some endeavors to comply with that recommendation, though with only partial success. Pursuant to the contents of Art. 19 item 3 of the Act of 9 April 2010 on the Prison Service,[47] the use and application of instruments of restraint and firearms as well as documentation of that use and application takes place in accordance with the principles set out in the Act of 24 May 2013 on instruments of restraint and firearms. Art. 9 item 1 of that legal act[48] allows authorized persons to apply physical force only in the form of incapacitation techniques against women whose pregnancy is showing. Only where it is necessary to repel a direct, unlawful attempt on the life or health of the authorized person or another person, and the use of physical force against such person is insufficient or impossible, the authorized person may use other instruments of restraint, or firearms, taking into account its properties and the condition of the person against whom it is to be used (Art. 9 (2) and (3)). Where a straitjacket or a restraining belt is used on a woman whose pregnancy is showing, that person shall immediately be provided with medical assistance, and further use of those means shall depend on the opinion of the person providing the assistance (Art. 16 (5) of the aforementioned Act). This means that the Act does not prohibit the use of instruments of restraint against pregnant women, but it only introduces additional restrictions and conditions for the use of such instruments.

Hygienic care is also important for women prisoners. The Nelson Mandela's Rules state that prisoners shall be required to keep their persons clean, and to this end they shall be provided with water and with such toilet articles as are necessary for health and cleanliness, and that in order that prisoners may maintain a good appearance compatible with their self-respect, facilities shall be provided for the proper care of the hair and beard (Rule 18 (1) and (2)). By contrast, the European Prison Rules state that prisoners shall have ready access to sanitary facilities that are hygienic and respect privacy. Moreover, adequate facilities shall be provided so that every prisoner can have a bath or shower, at a temperature suitable to the climate, if possible daily but at least twice a week (or more frequently if necessary) in the interest of general hygiene (Rule 19). It is also noted that special provisions shall be made for the sanitary needs of women. It is very important insofar as women are typically deeply

47 Journal of Laws of 2019, item 1427.
48 Journal of Laws of 2019, item 2418.

affected by restrictions on the freedom of dress and discomfort associated with maintaining personal hygiene.[49]

Polish penitentiary law seeks to comply with these requirements. Pursuant to Art. 102 point 1 PEC, a convicted person shall have the right, in particular, to food, clothing, living conditions, premises as well as health services and appropriate hygiene conditions. Furthermore, pursuant to § 31 item 4 of the Rules and Conditions of Serving a Penalty of Deprivation of Liberty, a convicted woman shall have the right to use warm water at least once a day and be allowed to have a bath twice a week. Thus, the living conditions provided for women correspond in this respect to those laid down in international law (whereas the same is not true for men, as pursuant to item 3 of the Rules and Conditions indicated above, male prisoners do not have the right of daily access to warm water and have the right to a bath only once a week).[50]

Placement in a penal institution must naturally cut family ties. The literature review shows[51] that the only and unlimited form of impact on female convicts in prison are contacts with the family and the outside world. Women's response to being placed in prison is primarily related to the fact that their family ties are abruptly severed at the moment of imprisonment.[52] As a consequence, Resolution *Women in Prison* calls on the member states to ensure that female convicts serve a penalty of deprivation of liberty in prisons within a reasonable distance and travelling time of their families.[53] Further, the Nelson Mandela Rules indicate that prisoners shall be allowed, under necessary supervision, to communicate with their family and friends at regular intervals by corresponding in writing and using, where available, telecommunication, electronic,

---

49 J. Mazurkiewicz, J. Niedworok, "Ochrona macierzyństwa w polskim prawie karnym," *Państwo i Prawo* 1975, Vol. 10, pp. 75–76.

50 K. Więckiewicz, "Wybrane zagadnienia wykonywania kary pozbawienia wolności wobec kobiet ze szczególnym uwzględnieniem prawa do przebywania w izolacji penitencjarnej wraz z dzieckiem," [in:] *Pozbawienie wolności – funkcje i koszty. Księga jubileuszowa Profesora Teodora Szymanowskiego*, eds. A. Rzepliński, I. Rzepliński, M. Niełaczna, P. Wiktorska, Warsaw 2013, p. 662.

51 S. Milik, "Praca wychowawcza ze skazanym w świetle aktualnej polityki karnej państwa," [in:] *Misja Służby Więziennej a jej zadania wobec aktualnej polityki karnej i oczekiwań społecznych, IV Polski Kongres Penitencjarny*, eds. W. Ambrozik, H, Machel, P. Stępniak, Poznań – Gdańsk – Warszawa – Poznań 2008, p. 204.

52 J. Mazurkiewicz, J. Niedworok, "Ochrona macierzyństwa w polskim prawie karnym," *Państwo i Prawo* 1975, Vol. 10, pp. 75–76.

53 Rule 9.7.

digital and other means and to receive visits.[54] The Mandela Rules also reiterate the demand that prisoners shall be allocated, to the extent possible, to prisons close to their homes or their places of social rehabilitation.[55]

The Resolution also calls for providing all prisoners with the opportunity to have intimate visits and access to contraceptives. The Nelson Mandela's Rules also refer to that demand, indicating that where conjugate visits are allowed, this right shall be applied without discrimination, and women prisoners shall be able to exercise this right on an equal basis with men.[56] In turn, Recommendation 914 (1981) on the social situation of prisoners indicates that regulations regarding visits, including "intimate visits," shall be designed in the least restrictive and most favorable manner possible to prisoners, which will allow them to maintain contact with families and the outside world and will positively affect their emotional stability and sense of duty.[57]

It is clear that such form of visit is much welcomed by many inmates. The Penal Enforcement Code envisages a possibility of giving convicts awards (Art. 137), both in the form of visit without the presence of a supervising person (Art. 138 § 1 point 2) and in the form of a permission for visit in a separate room without the presence of a supervising person (Art. 138 § 1 point 3). The provisions do not apply different conditions of access to that award depending on the sex of the convict. There are no official data available on how many penal institutions set aside special cells for that purpose (including whether that was the case in women's prisons) and on the frequency of their use. Notably, that form of award is available only for convicts in a marital relationship or in a non-marital partnership,[58] which limits the availability of those visits for many inmates. Polish penal institutions do not provide access to contraceptives, hardly surprising given that in general the access to contraceptives in Poland is one of the lowest in Europe.[59] Consequently, partners of convicts are forced

54 Rule 58.
55 Rule 59.
56 Rule 58.
57 Rule II.1.
58 https://www.fakt.pl/kobieta/seks-i-emocje/seks-w-wiezieniu-czy-mozna-uprawiac-seks-w-wiezieniu/05fx9b1#slajd-3, viewed 22.03.2020.
59 https://www.polityka.pl/tygodnikpolityka/spoleczenstwo/1782538,1,polska-z-najgorszym-dostepem-do-antykoncepcji-w-europie.read, viewed 22.03.2020.

to secure contraceptives, if any, on their own and hope for a permission from custodial staff to bring them into the penitentiary facility.[60]

The weakening of family ties between the female inmates and their offspring is particularly painful for both sides. It is indeed a highly sensitive issue given that children are another group vulnerable to deprivation of rights. The maintenance of family ties serves to address the needs of convicts' minor children and contributes to the process of social reintegration of prisoners.[61]

Apart from highlighting the need for maintaining family ties by the convicts, international law devotes a great deal of space to safeguarding the rights of children of the inmates. The United Nations Convention on the Rights of the Child (CRC) of 20 November 1989 ratified, among others, by Poland[62] is one of such legal acts. Pursuant to Art. 2 item 1 and 2 CRC, States Parties shall respect and ensure the rights set forth in the Convention to each child within their jurisdiction without discrimination of any kind, and shall take all appropriate measures to ensure that the child is protected against all forms of discrimination. Moreover, pursuant to Art. 9 item 1 CRC, States Parties shall ensure that a child shall not be separated from his or her parents, against their will, except when competent authorities subject to judicial review determine, in accordance with applicable law and provisions, that such separation is necessary for the best interests of the child. Further, CRC specifies that States Parties shall respect the right of the child who is separated from one or both parents to maintain personal relations and direct contact with both parents on a regular basis, except if it is contrary to the child's best interests.

In a similar vein, Resolution *Women in Prison* underlines the necessity to protect the relations of the inmates with their children. Rule 8.4 calls on the member states to ensure that women who are sole carers of young children are not imprisoned while awaiting trial, except in circumstances where there is a real risk of re-offending, of absconding or of interfering with witnesses. Moreover, the member states are also called on to ensure that, where mothers are imprisoned, the state authorities are obliged to inform them of the whereabouts of their children and reassure them that their children are receiving

---

60 https://www.magazyndetektyw.pl/mokre-widzenia-to-legalny-seks-za-kratkami-w-wiezieniu-musi-byc-specjalne-miejsce-w-ktorym-moze-dojsc-do-upragnionego-sam-na-sam-z-ukochana-osoba/, viewed 23.03.2020.

61 A. Kwieciński, "Skazani-rodzice. Sytuacja prawna osadzonych sprawujących opiekę nad dziećmi," *Nowa Kodyfikacja Prawa Karnego* 2012, Vol. 28, ed. T. Kalisz, Wrocław, p. 188.

62 Journal of Laws of 1991, No. 120, item 526.

suitable care and that they will be able to be reunited with them on release (Rule 9.2). Further, Rule 9.4 stipulates that where babies and young children in prison with their mother have to be separated from her, this is done gradually, so that the process is as painless and non-threatening as possible. Finally, Resolution *Women in Prison* demands in Rule 12.5 that women prisoners, wherever possible, be permitted to see their children aged under 18 outside prison on special occasions such as birthdays or important religious festivals.

Many provisions of the Penal Enforcement Code introduce certain privileges for incarcerated parents to help them maintain their family relationships. Art. 87a § 1 PEC requires that account be taken with respect to convicts who have permanent custody of a child under 15 years of age of their need to initiate, maintain and strengthen their emotional ties with their children, fulfill their maintenance obligations and provide material assistance to the children, as well as cooperate with care and educational institutions in which those children are staying. Further, Art. 87a § 2 indicates that convicts who have permanent custody of children placed in an educational care institution shall, where possible, be detained in appropriate penitentiaries as close as possible to their children's place of stay. Art. 105a § 3 gives such convicts the right to additional visits with children. For this reason, it is evident that the Polish legislator strives to ease the stringency associated with the imprisonment of parents so as to enable them to maintain family ties with their children during incarceration.

In line with the demands put forward in international law, penal enforcement law also provides for greater opportunities for pregnant women and mothers to leave prison on a temporary basis. Pursuant to Art. 151 § 1 PEC, the court – in relation to a convicted pregnant woman and a convicted person having sole custody of a child – may postpone the enforcement of a sentence for up to 3 years after the child's birth. Pregnancy or the need to take care of a child may also justify an interruption in the enforcement of penalty of imprisonment, where family or personal reasons support it (Art. 153 § 2 PEC), or where the prisoner's state of health prevents them from serving a penalty of imprisonment (Art. 153 § 1 PEC in conjunction with Art. 150 § 1 PEC). This means that the legislator acknowledges the wider needs of pregnant women and those caring for children under 3 years of age related to interruption in the enforcement or postponement of a penalty of imprisonment.

It is extremely difficult to resolve a moral dilemma regarding the placement of a child with his or her mother in prison. On the one hand, it seems reasonable to allow a child to spend at least the first years of life with his or her mother, on the other hand, there are doubts regarding the moral assessment of the actual incarceration of children. Therefore, the imprisonment of a mother with a child is a frequent object of declarations and guarantees of rights in international acts. The Recommendation on the social situation of prisoners[63] specifies that, in accordance with the principle that children may not bear the consequences of parental offenses, special measures shall be taken to meet the needs of female prisoners incarcerated with newborn children. An age limit shall be set for children who may be in prisons [with mothers]; children shall also have access to social services outside the prison (e.g. nurseries, kindergartens, etc.). By way of comparison, The European Prison Rules provide that infants may stay in prison with a parent only when it is in the best interest of the infants concerned, and they shall not be treated as prisoners. It is stressed that where such infants are allowed to stay in prison with a parent, special provision shall be made for a nursery staffed by qualified persons, where the infants shall be placed when the parent is involved in activities where the infant cannot be present. Moreover, special accommodation shall be set aside to protect the welfare of such infants (Rule 36). That issue is also addressed by the Mandela Rules which determine that a decision to allow a child to stay in prison with his or her parent shall be based on the best interests of the child concerned. Where children are allowed to remain in prison with a parent, provision shall be made for internal or external childcare facilities staffed by qualified persons, where the children shall be placed when they are not in the care of their parent; as well as for child-specific health-care services, including health screenings upon admission and ongoing monitoring of their development by specialists. Moreover, it is stressed that children in prison with a parent shall never be treated as prisoners (Rule 29. 1).

Given the importance of the problem and the need to recognize both the interests and rights of mothers and children, separate Recommendation 1469 (2000) *Mothers and Babies in Prison*[64]was issued. It points out that, despite the calls for limiting the use of penalty of deprivation of liberty, the number of women in relation to whom courts apply the penalty of imprisonment or pre-trial detention is on the increase. It is noted that there is no data available on the number of babies and young children separated from their mothers sent to prison. For this reason and because of the importance of the mother's personal relationship with the child, the resolution calls on member States to recognize that the penalty of imprisonment should be used as a last resort in the case of

63 Rule VII in: Recommendation 914 (1981) on the social situation of prisoners, PWP 2011/72–73, p. 205.

64 *Przegląd Więziennictwa Polskiego* 2011/72–73, p. 167 et seq.

pregnant women and mothers of babies/young children and be imposed on such women as a result of conviction of the most serious crimes that pose a threat to society. The resolution also calls on member States to make provision for closed and semi-open facilities offering social assistance services for a small number of mothers who require such supervision; with priority of such facilities being the interests of the children and provision of care for the children concerned in an environment appropriate for them whilst maintaining public safety. It is also requested that fathers be provided with better visiting conditions so as to enable the children concerned to spend time with both parents.

It is pointed out in the international arena that the right of mothers to stay with their children may not be limited only to women sentenced to serve short-term penalties. The Recommendation of the Committee of Ministers to member states on the management by prison administrations of life sentence and other long-term prisoners[65] prescribes that women sentenced to long-term imprisonment or life imprisonment shall not be deprived of right to be with a small child solely because of the length of their penalty.[66]

It is apparent from the demands presented in the aforementioned acts of international law that attention is drawn to two vital aspects: the validity of maintaining the relationship between mother and child and safeguarding the interests of the child who is not to be treated as a prisoner. The question is whether these two trends can always be reconciled with each other. As has been reported in the literature, children are in prison not so much because it is in their interest, but because it is the lesser evil.[67] On the one hand, it is argued that children removed from their mother may be wrongfully punished with the harshest penalty, as there is nothing more difficult for a child than the lack of a mother. Prison bars, morning roll-calls, or the fact that the world is limited to small space behind the prison wall do not have any meaning for a child under three years of age. On the other hand, children brought up behind the prison walls have a very limited set of stimuli, their life is reduced to the prison routine, they are brought up mainly among women without a male role model, and

65 Recommendation Rec (2003) 23 of the Committee of Ministers to member states on the management by prison administrations of life sentence and other long-term prisoners, *Przegląd Więziennictwa Polskiego* 2011/72–73, p. 111 et seq.

66 Rule 30.c.

67 https://www.polityka.pl/tygodnikpolityka/klasykipolityki/1789716,1,co-sie-dzieje-kiedy-do-wiezienia-trafia-matka-z-dzieckiem.read.

the mothers may put their own interest before that of their children, treating them more as a ticket to better conditions of imprisonment.[68]

Given the above, it is necessary to consider whether the Polish implementing rules allow mothers to reside in prison with their children, and if so, whether the rules secure both the child's right to spend the first years of life with the mother and the control of its proper development where the mother is not inclined or is unable to provide the child with proper care. It must be noted that it is not possible to admit a mother with a child to a penal institution.[69] Any potential stay of a mother with a child in prison takes place in the mode specified in Art. 87 § 4 PEC, pursuant to which, in order to enable mothers deprived of liberty to exercise permanent and direct childcare, prison mother-and-child units are organized at designated penitentiaries in which a child may stay upon mother's request until the child attains the age of three, as long as educational reasons or health considerations confirmed by a doctor's or psychologist's opinion do not support the separation of the child from the mother or the extension or shortening of that period. Decisions in this regard require the consent of the guardianship court.

It is thus evident that the placement of a mother and child in a prison mother-and-child unit must necessarily be preceded by an examination by the guardianship court of the grounds for their joint stay. Pursuant to the Regulation of the Minister of Justice[70] which sets out detailed rules for such imprisonment, potential consent of the guardianship court must be preceded by obtaining the consent of the father, where he is entitled to parental responsibility, in the

---

68 https://www.rp.pl/artykul/880709-Spacerniak-z-hustawkami.html; https://www.polityka.pl/tygodnikpolityka/klasykipolityki/1789716,1,co-sie-dzieje-kiedy-do-wiezienia-trafia-matka-z-dzieckiem.read; https://www.newsweek.pl/polska/ludzie/matki-wychowujace-dzieci-w-wiezieniach-jak-sie-wychowuje-w-wiezieniu/vsrz3pn. (viewed 21.03.2020); https://www.polityka.pl/tygodnikpolityka/spoleczenstwo/1568661,1,na-przepustkach-wszystko-sie-burzy-opowiesci-wieziennych-matek.read, viewed 21.03.2020.

69 Indeed, § 34 Regulation of the Minister of Justice of 23 June 2015 on the administrative activities related to the execution of detention on remand and penalties and coercive measures resulting in deprivation of liberty as well as documentation of such activities (Journal of Laws of 2015, item 927).

70 Regulation of the Minister of Justice of 17 September 2003 on the procedure for the admission of children of mothers deprived of liberty to prison mother-and-child units in the indicated prisons and the detailed rules for the organization and operation of such institutions (Journal of Laws of 8 October 2003).

absence of such consent or inability to obtain it, the decision of the guardianship court resolves the issue (§ 3 sect. 5).

The provisions of Art. 69 shall not apply to mothers deprived of liberty who exercise permanent and direct childcare. This implies that prison mother-and-child units are not divided into separate units for juveniles, inmates serving their first prison sentence, repeat offenders, or those in military custody. Women incarcerated with a child enjoy a number of privileges, including longer walks (Art. 112 § 1 PEC), the possibility of making additional purchases of food products (Art. 113a § 1 PEC) and a limited list of applicable disciplinary penalties (Art. 143 § 2 PEC).

The provisions of international law indicated above have shown that care for the interests of children staying in prison with their mothers remains a matter of serious concern, mainly due to the limited number of stimuli that children encounter in the penitentiary unit. For this reason, Resolution *Women in Prison* recommends providing children who are in prison with their mothers with access to outside nursery or kindergarten facilities. The recommendation raises the issue of the children's opportunity to interact with peers and the influence of such interactions on their development. However, the applicable Polish regulations do not provide for the possibility of accompanying a child on a regular basis to a nursery located outside the prison. In any case, prisons have kindergartens for children whose mothers found employment while serving a prison sentence.[71] This does not mean that the children are completely deprived of contact with the outside world. A mother who benefits from a permit for a temporary stay outside the penal institution leaves the prison with her child,[72] so the child will be in contact with his or her local community during the furlough. Moreover, after obtaining the consent of the mother, custodial staff may take the children for walks outside the prison.[73]

---

71 Marta Krzyżanowska-Sołtysiak, "W tym więzieniu siedzą dzieci," https://fakty.interia.pl/wielkopolskie/news-w-tym-wiezieniu-siedza-dzieci,nId,1272684.

72 Indeed, § 6 of the Regulation of the Minister of Justice on the procedure for the admission of children of mothers deprived of liberty to prison mother-and-child units in the indicated prisons and the detailed rules for the organization and operation of such institutions.

73 Such practices are indicated, *inter alia*, in: https://www.polityka.pl/tygodnikpolityka/klasykipolityki/1789716,1,co-sie-dzieje-kiedy-do-wiezienia-trafia-matka-z-dzieckiem.read; A. Rychlewicz, Matki za murami więzienia, http://wiadomosci.onet.pl/na-tropie/matki-za-muramiwiezienia/q8p8v.

The role of the father is also significant. Therefore, in line with the recommendations of the Resolution on the special situation of women in prisons, efforts should be made to facilitate the possibility for the other parent to exercise parental responsibility when a minor child is in prison with his or her mother. For this reason, the regulations do not limit the children's contact with their fathers who can in fact visit them every day.[74]

Prior research has shown that the provisions regarding the enforcement of custodial sentences for pregnant women and mothers with small children effective in Poland fully respect all the recommendations.[75] It is reasonable to agree with this view given that making the possibility of serving a sentence with a child subject to the consent of the guardianship court offers the possibility of verification whether the joint incarceration is in the best interests of the child. However, the mechanism of accompanying the children to nurseries and kindergartens located outside the prison in order to ensure contact with the outside world recommended by the Resolution has not been implemented. Notwithstanding the efforts to ensure that the conditions in the prison mother-and-child units in which convicted women and their children stay resemble a home environment to the maximum extent possible, and regardless of the efforts to ensure that the physical and mental development of the children is normal and that the mothers adopt correct parental attitudes during childcare, previous studies have emphasized that prison is not a place where children should be brought up.[76] Therefore, it seems reasonable to agree with the opinions voiced in academic writings which call for supporting the recommendations of the Assembly to ensure that cases where mothers with small children are sentenced to imprisonment occur only in exceptional cases.[77]

4. Conclusions

In conclusion, the literature on the subject emphasizes the considerable distress that women suffer in connection with the process of adapting to the conditions

74 M. Krzyżanowska-Sołtysiak, "W tym więzieniu siedzą dzieci," https://fakty.interia.pl/wielkopolskie/news-w-tym-wiezieniu-siedza-dzieci,nId,1272684.

75 A. Szymanowska, "Rekomendacja 1469 (2000) Matki i dzieci w więzieniu Komentarz," *Przegląd Więziennictwa Polskiego* 2011/72–73, p. 169.

76 A. Szymanowska, "Rekomendacja 1469 (2000) ...," p. 173.

77 A. Szymanowska, "Rekomendacja 1469 (2000) ...," p. 173.

of prison isolation.[78] Women are more prone to the deprivation of rights merely because of the fact of belonging to the female sex and the situation becomes even more difficult once women are imprisoned. Due to their biological distinctness, they require less harsh, more "feminine" conditions of serving a custodial sentence,[79] it therefore seems necessary to ease prison regime and discipline.[80] The provisions of international law, which recognize in many acts the difficult situation of women incarcerated in penal institutions, call for similar conclusions. The demands put forward in the international law largely amount to calling for the widest possible use of non-custodian penalties, easing prison regimes and support for the maintenance of family ties, in particular those with children. The Polish penitentiary regulations seek to implement the above declarations providing for many concessions and privileges for women which do not always result solely from the biological differences between men and women.[81] The degree to which women experience discomfort associated with incarceration is of a wave-like nature and it never goes away completely,[82] women serving a custodial sentence are affected by that fact differently than men.[83] For this reason, they deserve special protection and care during that period.

---

78 T. Kalisz, "Populacja kobiet osadzonych w polskich jednostkach penitencjarnych," *Nowa Kodyfikacja Prawa Karnego*, Vol. XX, ed. L. Bogunia, Wrocław 2006, p. 263; M. Ciosek, *Psychologia sądowa i penitencjarna*, Warsaw 2001, p. 195 et seq.

79 K. Sitnik, "Odmienności w wykonywaniu kary pozbawienia wolności wobec kobiet w obowiązującym ustawodawstwie polskim," [in:] *Acta Erasmiana. Prace z zakresu integracji europejskiej i nauk penalnych*, eds. I. Dembowska, M. Szostak, Wrocław 2011, p. 294.

80 H. Machel, *Więzienie jako instytucja karna i resocjalizacyjna*, Gdańsk 2003, p. 269.

81 Cf. A. Jaworska-Wieloch, "Znaczenie płci za kratami więzienia," *Probacja* 2015/IV, p. 69 et seq.

82 M. Rudnik, "Warunki reedukacji młodocianych skazanych na krótkie kary pozbawienia wolności," Biuletyn RPO. *Materiały. Stan i węzłowe problemy polskiego więziennictwa*, Warsaw 1997, No. 32, p. 19; M. Marczak, K. Mirosław, "Funkcjonowanie kobiet w warunkach izolacji więziennej," [in:] *Skuteczność oddziaływań penitencjarnych w kontekście zjawiska podkultury więziennej oraz instytucji warunkowego przedterminowego zwolnienia skazanych*, (ed.) M. Kuć, Lublin 2009, p. 120.

83 P. Wierzbicki, "Wykonywanie kary pozbawienia wolności wobec kobiet," [in:] *Przestępczość kobiet. Aspekty kryminologiczne i penitencjarne*, T. Kolarczyk, J. R. Kubiak, P. Wierzbicki, Warsaw 1984, pp. 194–195.

Bibliography:

Ambrozik W., Machel H., Stępniak P., *Misja Służby Więziennej a jej zadania wobec aktualnej polityki karnej i oczekiwań społecznych, IV Polski Kongres Penitencjarny*, Poznań – Gdańsk – Warszawa – Poznań 2008.

Bramska M., *Realizacja prawa skazanego do kształcenia, Stan i węzłowe problemy polskiego więziennictwa, Część IV*, Biuletyn RPO No. 42, Warsaw 2000.

Ciosek M., *Psychologia sądowa i penitencjarna*, Warsaw 2001.

Dawidziuk E., "Kontrole osobiste osób pozbawionych wolności – rozważania na temat potrzeby wprowadzenia zmian," *Przegląd Więziennictwa Polskiego* 2013, No. 78.

Dawidziuk E., *Traktowanie osób pozbawionych wolności we współczesnej Polsce na tle standardów międzynarodowych*, Warsaw 2013.

Dąbkiewicz K., "W sprawie "miejsca" odbywania kary pozbawienia wolności przez skazanego," *Probacja* 2015/1.

Dembowska I., Szostak M., *Acta Erasmiana. Prace z zakresu integracji europejskiej i nauk penalnych*, Wrocław 2011.

Dukiet-Nagórska T., *Zasada proporcjonalności w prawie karnym*, Warsaw 2010.

Gajdus D., Gronowska B., *Europejskie standardy traktowania więźniów*, Toruń 1998.

Gardocka T., Sobczak J., *Uchodźcy w Polsce i w Europie. Stan prawny i rzeczywistość*, Toruń 2010.

Golinowska C. S., *O polskiej biedzie w latach 1990–2015. Definicje, miary i wyniki*, Warsaw 2018.

Hołyst B., Redo S., *Problemy więziennictwa u progu XXI wieku*, Warsaw – Wiedeń – Kalisz 1996.

Jasińska-Kania A., Nijakowski L.M., Szacki J., Ziółkowski M., *Współczesne teorie socjologiczne*, Warsaw 2006.

Jaworska-Wieloch A., "Znaczenie płci za kratami więzienia," *Probacja* 2015/IV.

Kalisz T., "Populacja kobiet osadzonych w polskich jednostkach penitencjarnych," *Nowa Kodyfikacja Prawa Karnego*, Vol. XX, L. Bogunia, Wrocław 2006.

Kalisz T., "Teoretyczne i prawne aspekty zatrudnienia skazanych," *Nowa Kodyfikacja Prawa Karnego*, Vol. VIII, L. Bogunia, Wrocław 2001.

Kolarczyk T., Kubiak J.R., Wierzbicki P., *Przestępczość kobiet. Aspekty kryminologiczne i penitencjarne*, Warsaw 1984.

Konarska-Wrzosek V., Lachowski J., Wójcik J., *Węzłowe problemy prawa karnego, kryminologii i polityki kryminalnej. Księga pamiątkowa ofiarowana Profesorowi Andrzejowi Markowi*, Warsaw 2010.

Kosewski M., *Agresywni przestępcy*, Warsaw 1977.

Kozaczuk F., *Optymalizacja oddziaływań resocjalizacyjnych w Polsce i w niektórych krajach europejskich*, Rzeszów 2006.

Królikowski M., Zawłocki R., *Kodeks karny. Część ogólna. Komentarz*, Vol. II, Warsaw 2011.

Kwieciński A., *Postępowanie z wybranymi grupami skazanych w polskim systemie penitencjarnym. Aspekty prawne*, Warsaw 2013.

Kwieciński A., "Skazani-rodzice. Sytuacja prawna osadzonych sprawujących opiekę nad dziećmi," *Nowa Kodyfikacja Prawa Karnego* 2012, Vol. 28, T. Kalisz, Wrocław.

Kuć M., *Skuteczność oddziaływań penitencjarnych w kontekście zjawiska podkultury więziennej oraz instytucji warunkowego przedterminowego zwolnienia skazanych*, Lublin 2009.

Lelental S., *Prawo karne wykonawcze*, Warszawa 1990.

Leśniak M., Szaszkiewicz M., "Więzienie jako instytucja opresyjna i sytuacja depresyjna," *Państwo i Społeczeństwo* 2015 (XV), No. 2.

Lewandowski G., "Kobieta i jej macierzyństwo w warunkach zakładu karnego," *Universitas Gedanensis* 1995/12.

Machel H., *Więzienie jako instytucja karna i resocjalizacyjna*, Gdańsk 2003.

Machel H., *Wykonywanie kary pozbawienia wolności w Polsce – w poszukiwaniu skuteczności*, Gdańsk 2006.

Matysiak – Błaszczyk A., *Sytuacja życiowa kobiet pozbawionych wolności*, Krakow 2010.

Mazurkiewicz J., Niedworok J., "Ochrona macierzyństwa w polskim prawie karnym," *Państwo i Prawo* 1975, Vol. 10.

Migdał J., Skrobotowicz G., "Możliwość realizacji europejskich reguł więziennych z 2006 r. w zakresie reintegrowanego modelu wykonywania kary pozbawienia wolności a przeludnienie polskich jednostek penitencjarnych," *Roczniki nauk prawnych*, Vol. XXIV, No. 1, 2014.

Myrna B., Wykonywanie kary pozbawienia wolności w świetle Europejskich Reguł Więziennych z 2006r. Podstawowe zasady, zakres i zastosowanie przedmiotowych reguł," *Nowa Kodyfikacja Prawa Karnego*, Vol. XXIV, L. Bogunia, Wrocław 2009.

Nikołajew J., "Reguły Minimalne i Europejskie Reguły Więzienne a prawo więźniów do wolności sumienia i religii w Polsce," *Studia z Prawa Wyznaniowego* 2013, Vol. 16.

Rudnik M., "Warunki reedukacji młodocianych skazanych na krótkie kary pozbawienia wolności," Biuletyn RPO. *Materiały. Stan i węzłowe problemy polskiego więziennictwa*, Warsaw 1997.

Rzepliński A., Rzeplińska I., Niełaczna M., Wiktorska P., *Pozbawienie wolności – funkcje i koszty. Księga jubileuszowa Profesora Teodora Szymanowskiego*, Warsaw 2013.

Stańdo-Kawecka B., "Rezolucja 1663 (2009) Kobiety w więzieniu. Komentarz, Międzynarodowe standardy wykonywania kar," *Przegląd Więziennictwa Polskiego* 2011/72–73.

Szymanowska A., "Rekomendacja 1469 (2000) Matki i dzieci w więzieniu Komentarz," *Przegląd Więziennictwa Polskiego* 2011/72–73.

Szymanowski T., Migdał J., *Prawo karne wykonawcze i polityka penitencjarna*, Warszawa 2014.

Szymanowski T., *Przemiany systemu penitencjarnego w Polsce,* Warsaw 1996.

Szymanowski T., "Rekomendacja Rec (2006) 2 Komitetu Ministrów dla państw członkowskich Europejskie Reguły Więzienne. Komentarz," *Przegląd Więziennictwa Polskiego* 2011/72–73

Szymanowski T., "Wstęp, Międzynarodowe standardy wykonywania kar," *Przegląd Więziennictwa Polskiego* 2011/72–73.

Walczak St., *Prawo penitencjarne. Zarys systemu*, Warsaw 1972.

Zakolska J., *Zasada proporcjonalności w orzecznictwie Trybunału Konstytucyjnego*, Warsaw 2008.

Katarzyna Jędrzejczyk-Kuliniak

University of Wrocław

e-mail: katarzyna.jedrzejczyk-kuliniak@uwr.edu.pl

ORCID ID: 0000-0003-1972-911X

Double discrimination of immigrant women in Poland in the context of world migration trends. Ukrainian case

Abstract: Migration movements are increasing, and there are various reasons for making a decision about leaving the place of residence which is associated with the need to function in a culturally different environment. Women already make up nearly half of the world's migrants. For many years, Poland was mainly an emigrant country, but in recent years more and more foreigners have settled in the country. The subject of this article are immigrant women who, because of their gender, and origin, may experience double discrimination. The issues of tolerance of otherness, coexistence model, as well as observance of the rights of particularly vulnerable groups become more important.

Keywords: migration, women, double discrimination, vulnerable groups, Ukrainians, Poland

1. Introductory remarks

The decision to leave one's place of residence is not easy, especially if a long stay abroad is planned. Although the phenomenon of migration has been known to mankind for centuries and people have always travelled to change their location voluntarily or forced in search of a better and safer place to live, the twent first century will be the century of massive global migrations. Thanks to the latest technology achievements, people move faster and more often, and also decide more easily to change their current location not only within their own country, but also abroad.

The reasons and consequences of migration can be complex and complicated. Migrations, especially to culturally distant places, mean abandonment of the current environment, detachment from the roots, overcoming technical, administrative and economic barriers as well as the necessity to function in a new surrounding which sometimes means a completely different culture. The choice of place of residence and work depends on many factors such as the legal system of the host country, the country's economic condition, presence of the diaspora or funds at one's disposal. Other factors include also culture, knowledge of the language, similarity of customs, and openness of the society to foreigners. Moreover, emigration is one of the main mechanisms that shapes relationships between human communities. It is one of the main forms of cultural contact, becoming in the modern world, also in Europe, the main way of formation of pluralistic societies.[1] Foreigners, including immigrants, are people particularly vulnerable to experience discrimination. Discrimination is understood as "deprivation of equality, disability, harassment of a certain group due to their origin or class, national or racial affiliation."[2]

Poland is still in the context of ethnically and religiously homogeneous countries,[3] it is also a country with a predominance of emigration over immigration, while nowadays Ukraine is sometimes pejoratively described as Europe's Mexico[4] as it has become a supplier of cheap labour for the EU countries. Poland is not a country of a typical settlement destination. Its geopolitical location (including, to some extent, historical conditions) and economic situation make it a short-term goal. Despite the influx of immigrants to Poland that has been observed for years, the presence of foreigners in the social space is still not a topic of public discourse. The importance of the issue concerning the migration of Ukrainian citizens to Poland is primarily determined by the unstable and dynamic political and economic situation in Ukraine.

---

1 T. Paleczny, *Socjologia stosunków międzynarodowych*, Kraków 2001, p. 12.

2 W. Kopaliński, *Słownik wyrazów obcych i zwrotów obcojęzycznych*, Warszawa 1994, p. 135.

3 According to the National Census from 2011, foreigners are 0,2 % of the 38 million population. As many as 91,6 % of respondents declared homogeneous Polish national identity, while only 2,17 % of people hold Polish and simultaneously other than Polish national or ethnic identity. Those who declare solely non-Polish national or ethnic identity are 1,46 % of the population. Narodowy Spis Powszechny, Główny Urząd Statystyczny. Warszawa 2012, [online:], http://stat.gov.pl/cps/rde/xbcr/gus/lud_raport_z_wynikow_NSP2011.pdf [available: 24.01.2019].

4 F. Düvell, *Ukraine – Europe's Mexico?* Research Resource Report 1. Oxford: COMPAS, [online:] https://www.compas.ox.ac.uk/fileadmin/files/Publications/Research_projects/Flows_dynamics/Transit_migration_Ukraine/Ukraine_Country%20Report_1of3.pdf [available: 27 June 2019].

The aim of the paper is to present the theoretical approach to the problem of immigrant women from Ukraine in Poland against the embedded in global migration trends, the feminization of migration in particularly. It took into account the presence of Ukrainian women on the labor market, stereotypes about their origin and gender, as well as their invisibility in public space.

The paper is in two parts. The first part presents global migration trends, including the phenomenon of feminization of migration. The second part analyzes the case of immigrant women in Poland, Ukrainians as the chosen example, the challenges and problems they face when taking up a job, discrimination on the basis of gender and the status of a foreigner in the host country, according to the theory of intersectional discrimination.

Two important assumptions were made to limit the scale of scientific research. Firstly, the phenomenon of migration to Poland fits in the trend of feminization of migration, secondly, the analysis focuses on the assumption that women, migrants in Polish society, regardless of whether it concerns permanent or temporary migration, face a number of barriers resulting from both their gender and status newcomer.

2. Phenomena of global migrations

Change is a feature of the modern times sometimes referred to as the era of migration, and it is accompanied by two types of increased mobility of people.[5] The main human types of global reality facilitating movement are a cosmopolitan, a citizen of the world, but also an emigrant. While the former is the beneficiary of the globalization process, the latter is its victim.[6]

The fact is that around 3 % of the world's population currently migrates, which means that over 200 million people stay in a foreign country for over a year.[7] The most common type of migration are economic migrations aimed at taking up work, however, trying to capture the complexity of this phenomenon, the typology of migration divides them into: voluntary and forced, economic and political, external and intra-state migrations, regulated and unregulated

5 S. Castles, M.J. Miller, *The Age of Migration*, London 2014, p. 5.

6 *Poza barierą czasu i przestrzeni. Księga jubileuszowa dla Jerzego Chłopeckiego*, ed. by A. Rozmus, Rzeszów 2007, p. 285.

7 *Global Migration Trends. Factsheet* (2016). International Organization for Migration. Retrieved, [online:] https://www.iom-nederland.nl/images/Nieuws/2016/april/Global-Migration-Trends-2015-Factsheet.pdf [available: 20.08.2020]; Castles, Miller, *The Age of Migration*, p. 8.

(also called illegal), and there are also chain migrations that imply settlement of specific immigrant groups in one place, or individual migrations. There are also settling, temporary (including shuttle) and fluid migrations. No matter what division will be used, it only indicates certain aspects of the process of human movement and does not exhaust the description of this phenomenon.[8]

It is difficult to predict in which direction the international population flows will be shaped globally as there are many factors that push people to migrate, such as political (wars, armed conflicts, coups, political persecution, violation of human rights), economic (crises, pauperization of society, low wage levels, collapse of the social protection and education system), social (discrimination on the grounds of ethnic, religious, persecution of specific social groups) and environmental ones (natural disasters such as drought, tsunami, etc.).[9] A good example illustrating the spontaneity of migration is the 2015–2016 migration crisis, which affected both European host countries and countries from which residents emigrate en masse, as well as the entire international community. The consequences, though fundamentally different, are experienced by both migrant host countries and those whose residents are emigrating.

When examine the flows of Ukrainian migration to Poland, as another example of changing trends, we may observe interdependence of migration processes on internal factors in Ukraine and those related to the conditions of the host country, in this case Poland.[10] Following the example of push-pull factors, it can be observed that in both cases, economic factors are of significant importance, although after the annexation of the Crimean Peninsula in 2014, also those of a political nature were taken into account when deciding to emigrate.

Migrations imply leaving one's permanent residence temporarily or permanently and moving to another place. This general definition of migration does not take into account the complexity and dynamism of this phenomenon.

---

8 K. Pędziwiatr, "Migracje globalne i lokalne z perspektywy Polski," [in:] *Globalna układanka* Warszawa 2015, p. 90; Eurostat (2016). *Migration and migrant population statistics*, [online:] http://ec.europa.eu/eurostat/statistics-explained/index.php/Migration_and_migrant_ population_ statistics/pl [available: 20.08.2020].

9 A. Potyrała, "Pozamilitarne aspekty bezpieczeństwa międzynarodowego – kryzys migracyjny 2015–2016," *Przegląd Strategiczny* 2016, Vol. 9, pp. 296–299.

10 O. Gulina, O. Pozniak, *Migration flows from Ukraine: changing trends*, ZOiS Spotlight 13/2013, [online:] https://en.zois-berlin.de/publications/zois-spotlight/migration-flows-from-ukraine-changing-trends/ [available: 20.09.2020].

Chart 1. *Migration motives*

	Push factors	Pull factors
Economic and demographic	Poverty, unemployment, low wages, high fertility rates, lack of basic health and education	Prospects of higher wages, potential for improved standard of living, personal or professional development
Political	Conflict, insecurity, violence, poor governance, corruption, human rights abuses	Safety and security, political freedom
Social and cultural	Discrimination based on ethnicity, gender, religion, and the like	Family reunification, ethnic (diaspora migration) homeland, freedom from discrimination

Source: *Migration and Remittances. Eastern Europe and the Former Soviet Union*, (Eds.) A. Mansoor, B. Quillin, World Bank, 2006.

Most often, the word immigrant defines a person who does not have citizenship of the country to which one comes for a long stay or to settle.[11]

In this paper, the terms of foreigner and newcomer are also used and understood as any person arriving in a given country, regardless of their legal status and the length of the intended stay (e.g. tourist, immigrant, student, businessperson). Forced migrants include asylum seekers and those who have already obtained refugee status. Of all international migrants, refugees represent only 8 %. The term refugee means a person

> who is unable or unwilling to return to their country of origin owing to a well-founded fear of being persecuted for reasons of race, religion, nationality, membership of a particular social group, or political opinion,

which corresponds to the definition of a refugee from the Geneva Convention of 28 July 1951, which concerned refugee status and the attached New York Protocol of 31 January 1967. People leaving their habitual residence for other reasons are referred to as migrants.[12]

11 *Key Migration Terms*, International Organization of Immigration, [online:] https://www.iom.int/key-migration-terms [available: 10.04.2020].

12 The Geneva Convention Relating to the Status of Refugees from 28 July 1951 (Dz. U. 1991 No. 119, items 515 and 517). Office of the United Nations High Commissioner for Refugees, [online:] http://www.unhcrcentraleurope.org/_assets/files/content/resources/pdf_pl/refugee_covention/konwencja_genewska.pdf [available: 20.03.2020].

Sometimes in the mass media or in statements of decision-makers, the term "migrant" includes both people who voluntarily or forced leave their place of residence for fear of their lives. This approach blurs the differences between people who require special legal protection, such as protection against expulsion or return (refoulement) and being punished for crossing the border without permission in search of security, and people who decide to migrate to improve living conditions. Such a dichotomy affects the social perception and prejudices against economic migrants. As those who deserve less sympathy than people forced to flee their homes due to ongoing military conflict or natural disasters. Poverty, in the media discourse, to a lesser extent justifies a positive perception of an immigrant.[13] However, it is important to note that a risk to life does not necessarily occur due to the political situation in the country of origin. The question arises whether economic coercion and extreme living conditions that prevent meeting basic needs of a person and their families are sufficient for the host country to consider such migration to be forced? Usually, European countries use provisions related to the Geneva Convention and interpret coercion strictly, therefore obtaining refugee status is extremely difficult and rare. For example, in Poland, out of 4.1 thousand decisions on refugee status filed in 2018, only 406 people received a positive decision.[14] According to Anna Potyra, migration movements that include refugees are forced movements, while those affecting economic immigrants, are considered a forced displacement only when the decision of leaving results not from socio-economic reasons but from legitimate fear of life.[15]

The multitude of typologies of migration, trying to capture the essence of the phenomenon, divides them into voluntary and forced, external, international of various scope and internal (within one state), regulated and unregulated (also referred to as illegal), periodic (short-term), permanent and shuttle; also chain migrations involve the settlement of specific groups in one place.[16]

13 K. Andrejuk, "Entrepreneurial strategies as a response to discrimination: Experience of Ukrainian women in Poland from the intersectional perspective," *Anthropological Notebooks* 2018, Vol. 24, No 2, p. 34.

14 Office for Foreigners, Summary: international protection in 2018, [online:] https://udsc.gov.pl/podsumowanie-ochrona-miedzynarodowa-w-2018-r/ [available: 20.03.2020].

15 A. Potyrała, "Pozamilitarne aspekty. . .," p. 299.

16 P. Kraszewski, "Typologia migracji," [in:] *Migracje Europa-Polska*, ed. W.J. Burszta, J. Serwański, Poznań 2003, pp. 11–15; M. Kubiak, K. Slany, "Migracje," [in:] *Encyklopedia socjologii,* Warszawa 1999, Vol. 2, pp. 243–249; M. Okólski, "Współczesne europejskie migracje międzynarodowe a dynamika procesów

Contemporary migration trends indicate four main migration directions. The most important line runs between the global North and the global South.[17] The highest intensity of migration is noted from countries of the South to rich countries of the North. The other important direction is North–North, for the example of migration of Poles to the West. The other two directions are South–South, North–North, however, the intensity of migration in these two cases is lower. Regardless of their form and causes, migrations are always associated with leaving the current place of residence and starting functioning in a different environment.

3. Feminisation of migration

Migrations as a social, political and economic phenomenon have always accompanied human activities. As Stephen Castles and Mark J. Miller point out:

> population movements in response to demographic growth, climatic change and the development of production and trade have always been part of human history. ... Warfare, conquest, formation of nations and the emergence of states and empires have all led to migrations, both voluntary and forced.[18]

In modern migration movements according to Castles and Miller, certain trends can be distinguished. The first of these refers to the phenomenon of globalization of migration. The intensity of flows and their diversity increases. More and more countries are experiencing migratory movements at the same time. Immigrants come from a growing number of places with various economic, social and cultural conditions (they have different education and social status, and are in different age groups). Migration flows are increasing, more and more people are migrating, and host countries are facing challenges in shaping migration policies. This trend is referred to as migration acceleration. Another feature is the diversity of migration in respect to the reasons for leaving the current place of residence, so host countries are experiencing many categories of migrants simultaneously. The fourth trend is the feminisation of the migration process, which results into the visibility of women in all types

---

integracyjnych," *Studia Socjologiczne* 2001, Vol.1, pp. 11–16; A. Sakson, "Migracje – fenomen XX i XXI wieku," *Przegląd Zachodni* 2008 Vol. 2, pp. 11–19.

17 The Brandt Line is an imaginary line that divides North and South on the basis on economical, and social development. It was marked in 1980 as an effect of work of Independent Comission on International Development Issues chaired by Willy Brandt, the former chancellor of West Germany.

18 S. Castles, M.J. Miller, *The Age of Migration*, p. 84.

of international migration, especially in employee flows. The mass nature of contemporary migration contributes to a significant politicization of the phenomenon of migration, both in the field of internal policies of states, international agreements, as well as linking migration with internal and international security.[19]

Gender and migration are mutually conditioned. These links can be analyzed from many points of view: from the assessment of traditional gender roles in the family, community, country of origin and host country; cultural conditions of masculinity and femininity,[20] changes in gender roles, access to education or emancipation and equality on the labor market. Migration can facilitate the development of women who enter the labor market (ensure economic independence, better social status), but can also make them more likely to be victims of domestic violence, as well as too often they encounter the division of labor resulting from stereotypical perception of gender or ethnicity. Gender dynamics plays a key role in the question of who emigrates and why and how this decision is made.

Women may want to leave their country for economic, social, political or climate change reasons, and all of these factors are often linked. A person may want to emigrate to study or work (to support family or become financially independent). Another reason for migration could be getting married and/or joining family. Initially, women's migrations consisted in following their husband or father, which gave them social status resulting primarily from the role of wife or daughter. Until the 1980s, men dominated in international migrations.[21] As the family model changed, more and more women participated in economic emigration.[22] In addition, structural discrimination based on gender affects patterns of emigration from countries of origin, as well as migration route and patterns in host countries. Migration of women can be mentioned here to avoid gender-based social pressure, such as lack of education, employment, divorce or difficult access to property rights.

---

19 S. Castles, "The Forces Driving Global Migration," *Journal of Intercultural Studies* 2013, Vol. 34/2, pp. 122–140.

20 More in: G. Hosftede, G. Jan Hofstede and M. Minkov, *Cultures and Organizations: Software of the Mind*, New York 2010.

21 K. Slany, M. Ślusarczyk, "Genderowa specyfika rynku pracy-na przykładzie imigrantek w Polsce," *Studia Migracyjne – Przegląd Polonijny* 2012, Vol. 38/1, p. 9.

22 H. Kulu, N. Milewski, "Family change and migration in the life course: An introduction," *Demographic Research*, Vol. 17, [online:] http://www.demographic-research.org/Volumes/Vol17/19/ [available: 15.03.2020].

A separate issue is the issue of gender-based violence against women (sexual and physical violence, forced marriages, lack of access to reproductive and sexual rights and care, female genital mutilation) and feminization of poverty (due to the availability of the female workforce to unskilled and informal places work in the country). Gender-based violence is multiple and can accumulate it: can be individual or collective, it can take place in the public or private sphere, during peace and during armed conflicts. This multi-faceted violence is based on gender stereotypes and the roles attributed to men and women. Other factors, such as skin color, ethnicity, and sexual orientation increase vulnerability to violence.[23] Gender does not function in isolation from ethnicity, race and religion. Women can decide to leave their place, considering many of these reasons at the same time. When characterizing the issue of women's migration, Krystyna Slany and Magdalena Ślusarczyk point out the increasing presence of women in formal and informal economics (prostitution, housework, care, tourism, entertainment). There are still stereotypes about the masculinization of migration and the perception of women as following and dependent on men, which results in deficiencies in migration and integration policies, which would take into account the gender dimension.[24]

Among the effects of the feminization of international migrations, the emancipatory processes of women are noted. Women becoming the main breadwinners, strengthen their position in families, are more visible on the labour market. Nevertheless, many negative phenomena are also noticed, and this is related to the deficit of care in families in the country of origin, the issue of migrant orphans,[25] the emergence of a group of "new servants" working in the gray/ black market below their qualifications, discrimination, violation of human rights. There are also social pathologies resulting from separation from relatives, as well as sexual crime and human trafficking.

---

23 K. Lohmann and C. Thallmayer, *The Europe we want? Feminist approaches to gender, migration, and democracy*, Wiedeń 2018, p. 8.

24 K. Slany, "Co to znaczy być migrantką?," [in:] *Migracje kobiet. Perspektywa wielowymiarowa*, ed. K. Slany, Kraków 2008, p. 12; K. Slany, M. Ślusarczyk, "Genderowa specyfika rynku pracy-na przykładzie imigrantek w Polsce," *Studia Migracyjne – Przegląd Polonijny* 2012, Vol. 38/1, pp. 10–12.

25 A. Grzymała-Kazłowska, A. Brzozowska, "From Drifting to Anchoring. Capturing the Experience of Ukrainian Migrants in Poland," *Central and Eastern European Migration Review* 2017, Vol. 6, No. 2, p. 117.

4. Multiple discrimination

There are different types of discrimination depending on different spheres of life: social, institutional, professional, economic, political, legal and symbolic.[26] The result of discrimination is an impediment or action that excludes people who experience discrimination from the application of equality with the same rights, freedoms and goods as other members of society. Discrimination can be manifested in many ways: from physical violence, direct harm, to unfavorable approach and non-verbal behavior. The 1966 International Convention on the Elimination of All Forms of Racial Discrimination defines discrimination as:

> any distinction, exclusion, restriction or preference based on race, colour, descent, or national or ethnic origin which has the purpose or effect of nullifying or impairing the recognition, enjoyment or exercise, on an equal footing, of human rights and fundamental freedoms in the political, economic, social, cultural or any other field of public life.[27]

The features considered to be grounds for discrimination, e.g. according to the law, are the original elements of identity, i.e. those which a person does not choose himself, with which one most often comes into the world and which are much more difficult to change, if they can be changed at all.

Research on discrimination based on more than one factor began in the multicultural environment of the United States in the 1980s. Scholar Kimberlé W. Crenshaw formulated the concept of *intersectionality* then used to describe the overlaping of the categories of race and gender, and defined multiple discrimination. The intersectionality theory emphasizes the interpenetration of social and cultural categories.[28] Relationships between gender, race, ethnicity, disability, sexuality, class, nationality, and immigration status are examined, which lead to social systems. This applies to a situation in which persons belonging to more than one minority group experiences multiple forms of unequal and inferior treatment at the same time, i.e. multiple discrimination. In the case of immigrant women, two premises: gender and migration status

---

26 More: M. Reisigl, "Dyskryminacja w dyskursach," *Tekst i dyskurs – Text und Diskurs* 2010, Vol.3.

27 International Convention on Elimination of All Forms of Racial Discrimination (Dz.U. 1969 No. 25, item 187).

28 S. V. Knudsen, "Intersectionality – A Theoretical Inspiration in the Analysis of Minority Cultures and Identities in Textbooks," [in:] *Caught in the Web or Lost in the Textbook?* ed. E. Bruillard Caen 2006, p. 61.

intersect and create the "simultaneous, multiple and overlapping oppression" of women.[29]

In the academic discourse, the concept of multiple discrimination is widely used, in which three types are distinguished: narrowly understood multiple discrimination, meaning one person is discriminated due to belonging to different minority groups, but experiences this discrimination separately, at different times; compound discrimination, in which various grounds of discrimination appear in one specific situation and intersectional discrimination. The grounds for intersectional discrimination are related to different identity features of one person and affect the person at the same time. It is not a simple sum of prejudices and discriminatory attitudes because of belonging to different groups, but new, characteristic system of exclusion is created, as pointed out by Timo Makkonen.[30] Therefore, a key feature of current research on gender and migration is the increased awareness of the internal diversity of the categories of immigrant women and the consideration of intersectionality as a factor shaping migration processes.[31]

Immigrant women may also experience violence from the environment in which they operate, employers, officers of administration bodies and law enforcement (institutional racism), in public space. This is violence resulting from stereotypes. They are also exposed to sexual harassment and become victims of forced labor, as functioning in a closed environment affects the low level of manifestation of gender-based violence. Therefore, violence against immigrant women can be divided into two groups, taking into account their causes: gender-based violence (GBV) and violence resulting from prejudices and stereotypes related to their national, ethnic and cultural origin.[32]

Women immigrants do other jobs than immigrant men, gender segregation is visible on the immigrant labor market. Emphasizing the phenomenon of feminisation of migration, it should be noted that it is associated, among others, with the growing development of the care services sector. According to Bridget Anderson, women migrants perform jobs referred to as 3C which stands for

29 S. Mann & M. Grimes, "Common and contested ground: Marxism and race, gender and class analysis," *Race, Gender & Class* 2001, Vol. 8, No. 2, p. 8.

30 T. Makkonen, *Multiple, Compound and Intersectional Discrimination: Bringing the Experience of the Most Marginalized to the Fore, Institute for Human Rights*, Turku 2002, pp. 9–10.

31 S. Bilge & A. Denis, "Introduction: Women, Intersectionality and Diasporas," *Journal of Intercultural Studies* 2010, Vol. 31, No. 1, p. 3.

32 W. Klaus, *Forced female migrants as victims of violence in Poland*, Warszawa 2014, p. 2.

cleaning, cooking and caring,[33] often in the grey area exposed to discrimination and violation of rights. They may experience double discrimination as women and as foreigners. Additional factors making immigrant women a particularly sensitive group are poor knowledge of the language and law of the country they live in, pressure from a traditional patriarchal family, a sense of loneliness, lack of support from the environment, cultural barriers, and previous traumatic experiences related to violence. Immigrant women are also more vulnerable to domestic violence, which can be an instrument of oppression on the part of a partner unable to reconcile with the work of a woman. In the case of immigrant families, there is often a change in the temporal roles in the relationship, women become the main breadwinners, and they are also easier to adapt to new conditions. The issue here is about gender-related violence, mainly domestic violence and violence rooted in the culture of migrants' origin.

5. Poland as a destination country

Poland has great historical experience with emigration because for centuries Poles have been leaving their homeland for ideological, political and economic reasons. However, Poland has relatively less experience receiving newcomers. It is rather a transit country, despite the fact that in the 1990s the state received over 80,000 refugees, mainly Muslims, from war-torn Chechnya.[34] For many years Poland has been a country of emigration; the key date is joining the European Union in 2004. In the first years after accession, the phenomenon of both temporary and permanent emigration from Poland to the countries of Western and Northern Europe was of particular importance. Over the years, the migration movement has slightly weakened, still though 2.5 million Poles emigrate, of which 90 % remains in Europe according to the report of the Central Statistical Office.[35] Currently, Poland is classified as an emigration country transforming into an emigration and immigration one,[36] but the

---

33 More: B. Anderson, *Doing the Dirty Work? The Global Politics of Domestic Labour,* New York 2000.

34 *Integracja uchodźców w Polsce w liczbach*, ed. A. Kosowicz, A. Maciejko, Warszawa 2007.

35 Central Statistical Office, *Information on the size and directions of temporary emigration from Poland in 2004–2017,* [online:] https://stat.gov.pl/obszary-tematyczne/ludnosc/migracje-zagraniczne-ludnosci/informacja-o-rozmiarach-i-kierunkach-czasowej-emigracji-z-polski-w-latach-2004-2017,2,11.html [available: 11.02.2020].

36 M. Szylko-Skoczny, M. Duszczyk, "Trzy koncepcje polskiej polityki imigracyjnej," *Polityka Społeczna* 2010, Vol. 7, pp. 2–5.

advantage of emigration over immigration is still noticeable. At the same time, Poland remains a country with a homogeneous nationality structure, despite the national and ethnic minorities living in the country. Comparing to other countries, there are relatively few immigrants in Poland, but trends from 2014 indicate that more and more immigrants are settling in the country. It is influenced by several factors, which include: liberalization of regulations legalizing the stay of foreigners in the Republic of Poland (Act on foreigners, which entered into force on May 1, 2014), introduction of simplified employment procedures, deterioration of the economic condition of some countries neighboring Poland (Belarus, Ukraine) and ongoing conflicts (Ukraine). In addition, Poland is becoming an increasingly attractive country in terms of study opportunities and professional prospects. The International Migration Outlook 2019 report, published annually by the OECD, reports that in 2017 Poland, ahead of the United States, became a leader when it comes to the influx of foreign, short-term, seasonal labor force with 1.1 million arriving for less than 12 months.[37] In the old countries of the European Union, migrants constitute even a dozen or so percent of the population (Luxembourg was the country with the highest percentage of foreigners in 2017, where they constituted 48 % of the total population). A high percentage of foreigners (at least 10 % of the resident population) was also recorded in Cyprus, Austria, Estonia, Latvia, Belgium, Ireland, Malta and Germany, while in Poland it is less than 1 %.[38]

In comparison with other European countries, the scale of immigration to Poland is small: in Poland foreigners constitute about 0.3 % of the population, which is one of the lowest rates in Europe.[39] From 423 thousand foreigners who on 1 January 2020 had valid residence permits, the largest groups were citizens of: Ukraine (214.7 thousand), Belarus (25.6 thousand), Germany (21.3 thousand), Russia (12.5 thousand), Vietnam (12.1 thousand), India (9.9 thousand), Italy (8.5 thousand), China (8.5 thousand), the United Kingdom (6.3 thousand) and Spain (5.9 thousand).[40] According to the Social Insurance Institution (ZUS)

37 International Migration Outlook 2019 OECD,[online:] https://www.oecd-ilibrary.org/sites/c3e35eec-en/index.html?itemId=/content/publication/c3e35eec-en [available: 11.02.2020].

38 Statistics on migration and population of migrants, Eurostat,[online:] https://ec.europa.eu/eurostat/statistics-explained/index.php?title=Migration_and_migrant_population_statistics/pl&oldid=174838 [available: 20.03. 2020].

39 Eurostat data, [online:] http://ec.europa.eu/eurostat/statistics-explained/index.php/Migration_and_migrant_population_statistics [available: 11.03.2020].

40 Office for Foreigners, Legalization of stay in 2019, [online:] https://udsc.gov.pl/legalizacja-pobytu-w-2019-r-podsumowanie/ [available: 13.03.2020].

data, the number of foreigners paying monthly insurance reached 665.6 thousand at the end of the third quarter of 2019. The largest group of foreigners insured in ZUS are Ukrainians. Citizens of Ukraine excel in the statistics of entry, settlement, applying for visas, undertaking studies and work, but also applying for Polish citizenship.

Their number at the end of the third quarter of 2019 reached 499.6 thousand against 425.7 thous. in the third quarter of 2018. Next were Belarusians (32.6 thousand), Vietnamese (8.1 thousand), Moldovans (7.3 thousand) and Russians (7.3 thousand).[41] It is problematic to clearly define the comprehensive indication of the number of foreigners residing in Poland due to the diversity of statistics, different formal grounds for staying in the country, or different legal statuses of foreigners. It can therefore be assumed that, taking into account also illegal migration, there are many more foreigners staying in Poland than those registered by the Office for Foreigners.

6. Ukrainian women in Poland

Poland as a destination country is attractive to migrants from Ukraine due to its geographical and cultural proximity. Although when coming to Poland, they do not have major problems with communication with Poles and adaptation to Polish living conditions, they are not always positively perceived by Polish society. Over one million Ukrainian citizens are already working in Poland. Most of them decided to emigrate after the outbreak of the armed conflict in eastern Ukraine in 2014, when the value of the hryvnia fell sharply and prices increased. Initially, immigrants of this wave were mainly located in the agricultural sector and the Warsaw agglomeration. Over time, Ukrainian citizens also lived in other agglomerations and smaller towns, working in other sectors.[42]

There are two very different types of migration trends represented by Ukrainians in Poland. The first is short-term labor migration, subject to the liberal rules of short-term access to the Polish labor market. The majority of Ukrainian migrants who come to Poland belong to this group and usually do not intend to stay in Poland. The second group, smaller but steadily growing,

41 *Cudzoziemcy w polskim systemie ubezpieczeń społecznych*, ed. R. Adamowicz P. Nasiński, Warszawa 2019.

42 M. Lubicz-Miszewski, "Nowi imigranci z Ukrainy w Polsce 5 lat po "rewolucji godności" – wprowadzenie," [in:] *Imigranci z Ukrainy w Polsce. Potrzeby i oczekiwania, reakcje społeczne, wyzwania dla bezpieczeństwa*, ed. M. Lubicz-Miszewski, Wrocław 2018, pp. 7–8.

are long-term immigrants who look for permanent jobs in Poland, study there or are married to Polish citizens. Settlement migration from Ukraine to Poland has a relatively high feminization rate of around 60 %. However, in the case of labor migration, women constitute less than half of the population.[43]

The Polish labor market of foreigners over the last several years has been divided into two segments. On the one hand people with high qualifications, specialists working in their profession legally, and the one existing in the gray zone, where there is a need for cheap, unskilled labor. Taking the example of employees from Ukraine, who dominate in the second sector, it is clear that belonging to a given segment of the labor market is to a large extent related to the country of origin of the immigrant. Additionally, the Polish labor market has created niches (mainly in construction, trade, agriculture and the domestic help sector), where there is a need for cheap labor and taking up jobs without high professional qualifications. Due to the lack of interest on the part of Poles, these niches are partially filled by foreigners, mainly Ukrainians.[44] In the case of undeclared work, foreigners, regardless of their education, undertake similar jobs: women clean, take care of the housekeepers' house or look after the elderly or children, they are also present in the agricultural sector, with occasional work, men work in agriculture or construction sites.

The labor market for immigrants in Poland is characterized by processes in which immigrant women are placed in low-paying market sectors that generate uncertainty, instability, short contracts, and often employment contrary to applicable labor law. These elements contribute to the syndrome of discrimination against immigrant women. Initially, Ukrainian women coming to Poland worked mostly in the care services sector. As is clear from the research conducted by the Institute of Public Affairs,[45] the majority of women worked illegally, without any contract, managing the employer's home, and in many

43 *Monitoring of Migration Data and Policy Changes Conducted in Ukraine, Poland, Czechia and Slovakia*, ed. D. Drbohlav, M. Jaroszewicz, M. Seidlová, D. Čermáková, [online:] https://ec.europa.eu/migrant-integration/librarydoc/monitoring-of-migration-data-and-policy-changes-conducted-in-ukraine-poland-czechia-and-slovakia [available: 11.03.2020].

44 J. Frelak, M. Bieniecki, "Praktyka funkcjonowania migrantów ekonomicznych w Polsce," [in:] *Migranci na polskim rynku pracy. Rzeczywistość, problemy, wyzwania* ed. W. Klaus, Warszawa 2007, pp. 46–47.

45 A. Kondrasiewicz, *Etniczny wymiar funkcjonowania rynku usług domowych w Warszawie*, [online:] https://www.isp.org.pl/uploads/drive/oldfiles/Kordasiewicz.pdf [available: 20.03.2020].

cases also their own one – from far. Many immigrant women worked not only below their qualifications, but also below their expectations. It was caused among others by the necessity of nostrification of the diploma and taking supplementary courses, but also insufficient language skills.

The most typical reasons for taking illegal forms of employment are: inability to find a legal job, difficult financial situation, amount of social security contributions due for legal employment, employers offering higher wages when employment is not legalized, unwillingness to make commitments on the part of the employer.

In recent years, however, more and more specialists have been coming: IT specialists, doctors, engineers and numerous students. According to the estimates of the National Bank of Poland, only 9 % of Ukrainian migrants in Poland do not have secondary or higher education, but as much as 70.7 % perform manual work.[46] A relatively new group of migrants are highly qualified women who are moving to Poland with their husbands and children. More and more independent migrant women come to Poland and they will meet their life partner in the place where they live.[47] Even before getting to know their husband or getting married, these foreigners have a stable residence and professional situation. According to data published by the Ministry of Family, Labor and Social Policy in 2018, 36 % of declarations of intention to entrust work to Ukrainian citizens concern women. Personnel Service experts indicate that the greatest interest in employing women can be seen in the light and food industries. Increasingly, Ukrainian women also work in professions for the future, including nursing or caring for the elderly.[48] However, the stereotype of a Ukrainian woman illegally looking after a Polish family's home or working in sex services is still strong. The stereotype of the "girl from the East" is harmful because it reduces women to the role of an object – a sexual object and a cleaner. This does not change the fact that in Poland the problem is the phenomenon of illegal employment of workers from Ukraine, without providing them with

46 I. Chmielewska, G. Dobroczek, A. Panuciak, *Obywatele Ukrainy pracujący w Polsce – raport z badania,* [online:] https://www.nbp.pl/publikacje/migracyjne/obywatele-Ukrainy-pracujacy-w-Polsce-raport-2017.pdf [available: 17.02.2020].

47 I. Koryś, *Kobiety-imigrantki: warunki udanej integracji*, Warszawa 2009, p. 5; K. Iglicka, K. Gmaj, I. Bąbiak, *Cudzoziemscy małżonkowie obywateli polskich – wymiar genderowy. Przegląd literatury*, Warszawa 2011.

48 I. Chmielewska, G. Dobroczek, A. Panuciak, *Obywatele Ukrainy pracujący w Polsce – raport z badania,* [online:] https://www.nbp.pl/publikacje/migracyjne/obywatele-Ukrainy-pracujacy-w-Polsce-raport-2017.pdf [available: 17.02.2020].

minimum safety standards when performing hazardous work, healthcare or sometimes even first aid to employees who suffered, e.g. stroke, while working.

7. Ukrainian stereotypes

The issue of immigrants can be considered from the perspective of cultural distance which means treating them as strangers in public space. Newcomers, although more numerous, are disadvantaged because of cultural differences. Proximity and distance are also used to categorize migrants themselves – there are more familiar migrants and those who are perceived as strangers/distinctively others. Research of Public Opinion Research Center (CBOS) "The attitude of Poles to other nations" from early 2019 indicates that the ranking of the most-liked nations is opened by Czechs, Italians, Slovaks, Hungarians and Americans, who are liked by more than half of the respondents (from 51 % to 56 %). 46 % to 50 % of Poles have a positive attitude towards English, Croatian and Irish people. Approximately one-third of respondents are favorable towards Bulgarians (34 %), Belarusians (31 %), Chinese (31 %), Ukrainians (31 %) and Jews (31 %). In relation to other groups included in the survey, mostly negative rather than positive attitude prevailed. This also applies to Ukrainians, the largest group in Poland. 41 % of respondents declared in the survey their reluctance. Over half of the respondents are cautious about Roma (57 %) and Arabs (65 %), and relatively few (17 % and 13 %, respectively) declare their positive approach.[49]

According to Krzysztof Jurek, the most common stereotypes about Ukrainian citizens are negative, and they present a picture of a poor, civilization and ideologically retarded nation, while its representatives are aggressive, lazy, backward, alcohol-abusing and uncultured people.[50] Stereotypes functioning in Poland are characterized by clearly defined bipolarity. On the one hand, we are dealing with an idealized, glorified West, and on the other hand, with a negatively portrayed East.[51]

49 Attitudes Towards Other Nations. Research report of CBOS No. 17/2019, [online:], https://cbos.pl/SPISKOM.POL/2019/K_017_19.PDF [available: 25.03.2020].

50 K. Jurek, "Stereotypy na temat Ukraińców funkcjonujące w Polsce," [in:] *Imigranci z Ukrainy w Polsce. Potrzeby i oczekiwania, reakcje społeczne, wyzwania dla bezpieczeństwa*, ed. M. Lubicz-Miszewski, Wrocław 2018, p. 36.

51 J. Błuszkowski, "Przemiany stereotypów narodowych w procesie transformacji systemowej w Polsce," *Studia Politologiczne* 2007, Vol. 11, p. 98.

Stereotypes often turn into prejudices and discriminatory behavior against immigrants, which, what was stressed in the report "Ukrainian minority and migrants from Ukraine in Poland" after 2016, are becoming more and more numerous due to the influx of more Ukrainians, taking the form of symbolic and physical violence against migrants and the Ukrainian minority.[52]

The Ombudsman's research on legal awareness in the field of equal treatment, pointed out that the most common perceived reason for discrimination in Poland is ethnicity and nationality – this condition was indicated by as much as 49 % of respondents in 2018 and this indicator has recently increased significantly: in 2016 44 % gave this reason, while in 2015–35 % of respondents. In Poland, the the most common phenomena related to the discrimination of people and groups distinguished from the majority by their origin and culture include physical violence, threats and hate speech against ethnic, national or racial differences as well as iconic expression of hostility towards groups in public space, or online. Therefore, the Internet as a communication channel and medium has significant responsibility for perpetuating negative views on immigrants. Apparent anonymity on the web also facilitates the so-called "hate," insults and offensive opinions, propagating stereotypes and unverified information.[53] As shown by research carried out by the Ombudsman in cooperation with the Office of Democratic Institutions and Human Rights of the Organization for Security and Cooperation in Europe, in 2016–2017, as much as 43 % of people from Sub-Saharan Africa, 18.5 % of Ukrainian citizens and 8 % living in Poland Islam followers may have experienced hate crime. Migrants are particularly vulnerable to hate crimes that reveal the main types of bias motivations. Ukrainians are the target of attacks because of their nationality, which is revealed by their language, Muslims because of their religion, and people from Sub-Saharan Africa because of their skin color.

Ukrainian stereotypes should be sought in the common history of both nations, complex relations, as well as the general negative image of Russia, to which Ukraine was subject for a long time, national conflicts at the beginning of the 20th century and during World War II, especially the Volyn slaughter. Many of these negative images translate into disadvantageous attitudes among immigrants. Discrimination can be permanent and systemic (structural). The

---

52 *Raport. Mniejszość ukraińska i migranci z Ukrainy w Polsce Analiza dyskursu,* ed. P. Tyma, Warszawa 2018, pp. 17, 28–29.

53 *Raport 2. Mniejszość ukraińska i migranci z Ukrainy w Polsce Analiza dyskursu,* ed. P. Tyma, Warszawa 2019, pp. 58–73.

most expressive one is that of employment. There is a common belief that there are only certain sectors on the labor market that are "intended" for newcomers. Well-paid jobs account for a small percentage of all working immigrants, and the vast majority of newcomers are laborers and simple workers. In the opinion of immigrants themselves, employers are reluctant to hire immigrants for higher positions.[54]

Public opinion polls indicate that Poles have a reluctant attitude towards Ukrainians, however, as Joanna Bielecka-Prus emphasizes, these stereotypes do not show a division of negative traits by gender. Only the data on mixed marriages shows that Polish men choose Ukrainian women more often, which gives rise to the supposition that the gender of immigrants influences the attitude towards foreigners. Fewer data concerns the image presented in the media, which shows that the image of Ukrainian migrant women is sometimes negative and is based on sexualization (illegal prostitution) or criminal attitudes (fraud, petty crime, illegal trade). Ukrainian women are also sometimes presented as defenders of the traditional family model, candidates for wives who put their husband's ambitions ahead of their own aspirations. In case of women, discriminating factors should be supplemented with different attire indicating ethnicity and stereotypical perception of women from Ukraine as an unskilled labor force or employees of sexual services. Only 5 % of such acts were reported to the police.[55] Foreigners are treated as a threat to social order and competition on the labor market, they cause fear of the increase in crime.

8. Conclusions

A certain paradox can be seen in attitude of Poles towards foreigners. On the one hand, they glorify the tradition of multiculturalism, invoking the traditions of the First and Second Polish Republic, common customs and traditions shared with national and ethnic minorities, while on the other, there is so-called transplanted discourse consisting in building a society closed to the flood of strangers, the idea of "Europe fortress" defending its borders against

54 *Obywatele Ukrainy pracujący w Polsce – raport z badania*, NBP Report, [online:] https://www.nbp.pl/aktualnosci/wiadomosci_2016/20161212_obywatele_ukrainy_pracujacy_w_polsce_-_raport_z_badania.pdf [available: 25.03.2020].

55 Survey on the nature and scale of unreported hate crimes against members of selected communities in Poland, Survey report, [online:] https://www.rpo.gov.pl/sites/default/files/Badanie%20charakteru%20i%20skali%20niezgłaszanych%20przestępstw%20z%20nienawiści.pdf [available: 25.03.2020].

newcomers. In addition, a dual approach to migration is visible in Poland, depending on the direction from which migrants come to the country. Policy towards foreigners from the Middle East and North Africa is restrictive and is part of the anti-immigration discourse of several European Union countries, immigration from Ukraine is necessary for the functioning of the economy, and immigration from Asian countries such as Vietnam, China, India and Bangladesh is bypassed. In turn, immigrants from the Caucasus-Chechen or Crimean Peninsula are considered primarily through the prism of their religious affiliation.

In Poland, foreigners are a group that is the most invisible in the political, social and symbolic sense, although they are physically visible especially in large cities. The state does not conduct a coherent migration policy, and the issue of migration to Poland itself has become strongly politicized in recent years, one can speak of the politicization of this phenomenon and its simultaneous mediatization.

However, Europe, including Poland, cannot cope without immigrants – mainly illegal, hidden in the grey economy, working at the lowest rates, often discriminated against, but still driving the economic development of EU countries. An attempt was made to capture phenomena related to the broadly understood migration of women, also from the perspective of Poland as a country that mainly experienced emigration and is becoming a host country. In the case of immigrants, the phenomenon of distance and closeness, sharing public space, face-to-face meetings for Polish society ceases to be an abstract concept, and takes the shape of actual multiculturalism. Reactions to this range from real indifference, tolerance, acceptance, to hostility and hate crimes. In this aspect, it is particularly important to draw attention to a group that is particularly sensitive and vulnerable to discrimination – immigrant women who are subject to double discrimination – on grounds of ethnicity, nationality, religion and gender. When characterizing immigrant women in Poland, it should be noted that:

1. The community of immigrant women in Poland is diverse. Currently, it is dominated by Ukrainian citizenship, but other women who were refugees, such as Chechen women, or migrants from Asian countries such as Vietnam should be remembered.
2. Women are perceived in very different ways, in many cases perception is burdened with stereotypes related to gender and country of origin.
3. The reasons for migration to Poland are mainly of economic nature.

4. The problems of immigrant women, including the violence they face, remain in the grey area and its real scale cannot be indicated.

The image of Ukrainian women reduces them to sexual objects and the role of home caregivers (often not their own), which influences the intersectionality of discrimination against immigrant women. Most studies on national stereotypes do not include gender-based analyzes. Migrant women from Ukraine have to compete with Polish women on the labor market and often, to get a job, they agree to employment without insurance, for lower wages and below their qualifications. They also take short-term work more often, which does not give them the possibility of professional stabilization in Poland, and also makes it difficult to gain a solid position in the host society.

The information collected in the presented paper indicates the need of dissemination of knowledge about the phenomenon of discrimination against foreigners, and especially women, who experience double discrimination due to their origin and gender. Foreigners, although increasingly noticeable in Polish cities, are invisible in public discourse, and therefore are symbolically excluded. As Turner comments:

> as members of society, most of us see only what we expect to see, and what we expect to see is what we are conditioned to see when we have learned the definitions and classifications of our cultures.

Outsiders must therefore remain 'hidden, since it is a paradox, a scandal, to see what ought not to be there.'[56] This invisibility is maintained through employment practices and the working conditions in which they experience abuse. Physically and symbolically, immigrant women are located on the periphery of society.

Bibliography:

Anderson B., *Doing the Dirty Work? The Global Politics of Domestic Labour*, New York 2000.

Andrejuk K., "Entrepreneurial strategies as a response to discrimination: Experience of Ukrainian women in Poland from the intersectional perspective," *Anthropological Notebooks* 2018.

56 V. Turner, "Betwixt and between: The liminal period in rites de passage," [in:] *Reader in Comparative Religion: An Anthropological Approach*, ed. A.W. Lessa, E.Z. Vogt, New York 1972, pp. 235, 237.

Bilge S. & Denis A., "Introduction: Women, Intersectionality and Diasporas," *Journal of Intercultural Studies* 2010, Vol. 31, No. 1.

Błuszkowski J., "Przemiany stereotypów narodowych w procesie transformacji systemowej w Polsce," *Studia Politologiczne* 2007, Vol. 11.

Castles S., Miller M.J., *The Age of Migration*, London 2014.

Castles S., "The Forces Driving Global Migration," *Journal of Intercultural Studies* 2013, Vol. 34: 2.

Chmielewska I., Dobroczek G., Panuciak A., *Obywatele Ukrainy pracujący w Polsce – raport z badania,* [online:] https://www.nbp.pl/publikacje/migracyjne/obywatele-Ukrainy-pracujacy-w-Polsce-raport-2017.pdf [available: 17.02.2020].

Cudzoziemcy w polskim systemie ubezpieczeń społecznych, ed. R. Adamowicz P. Nasiński, Warszawa 2019.

Düvell F., *Ukraine – Europe's Mexico?* Research Resource Report 1. Oxford: COMPAS, [online:] https://www.compas.ox.ac.uk/fileadmin/files/Publications/Research_projects/Flows_dynamics/Transit_migration_Ukraine/Ukraine_Country%20Report_1of3.pdf [available: 27 June 2019].

Frelak J., Bieniecki M., "Praktyka funkcjonowania migrantów ekonomicznych w Polsce," [in:] *Migranci na polskim rynku pracy. Rzeczywistość, problemy, wyzwania* ed. W. Klaus, Warszawa 2007.

Grzymała-Kazłowska A., Brzozowska A., "From Drifting to Anchoring. Capturing the Experience of Ukrainian Migrants in Poland," *Central and Eastern European Migration Review* 2017, Vol. 6, No. 2.

Gulina O., Pozniak O., *Migration flows from Ukraine: changing trends*, ZOiS Spotlight 13/2013, [online:] https://en.zois-berlin.de/publications/zois-spotlight/migration-flows-from-ukraine-changing-trends/ [available: 20.09.2020].

Hosftede G., Hofstede G.J. and Minkov M., *Cultures and Organizations: Software of the Mind*, New York 2010.

Iglicka K., Gmaj K., Bąbiak I., *Cudzoziemscy małżonkowie obywateli polskich – wymiar genderowy. Przegląd literatury*, Warszawa 2011.

Integracja uchodźców w Polsce w liczbach, ed. A. Kosowicz, A. Maciejko, Warszawa 2007.

Jurek K., "Stereotypy na temat Ukraińców funkcjonujące w Polsce," [in:] *Imigranci z Ukrainy w Polsce. Potrzeby i oczekiwania, reakcje społeczne, wyzwania dla bezpieczeństwa*, ed. M. Lubicz-Miszewski, Wrocław 2018.

Klaus W., *Forced female migrants as victims of violence in Poland*, Warszawa 2014.

Knudsen S. V., "Intersectionality – A Theoretical Inspiration in the Analysis of Minority Cultures and Identities in Textbooks," [in:] *Caught in the Web or Lost in the Textbook?* ed. E. Bruillard Caen 2006.

Kondrasiewicz A., *Etniczny wymiar funkcjonowania rynku usług domowych w Warszawie*, [online:] https://www.isp.org.pl/uploads/drive/oldfiles/Kordasiewicz.pdf [available: 20.03.2020].

Kopaliński W., *Słownik wyrazów obcych i zwrotów obcojęzycznych*, Warszawa 1994.

Koryś I., *Kobiety-imigrantki: warunki udanej integracji*, Warszawa 2009.

Kraszewski P., "Typologia migracji," [in:] *Migracje Europa-Polska*, ed. W.J. Burszta, J. Serwański, Poznań 2003.

Kubiak M., Slany K., "Migracje," [in:] *Encyklopedia socjologii*, Warszawa 1999.

Kulu H., Milewski N., "Family change and migration in the life course: An introduction," *Demographic Research*, Vol. 17, [online:] http://www.demographic-research.org/Volumes/Vol17/19/ [available: 15.03.2020].

Lohmann K. and Thallmayer C., *The Europe we want? Feminist approaches to gender, migration, and democracy*, Wiedeń 2018.

Lubicz-Miszewski M., "Nowi imigranci z Ukrainy w Polsce 5 lat po "rewolucji godności" – wprowadzenie," [in:] *Imigranci z Ukrainy w Polsce. Potrzeby i oczekiwania, reakcje społeczne, wyzwania dla bezpieczeństwa*, ed. M. Lubicz-Miszewski, Wrocław 2018.

Makkonen T., *Multiple, Compound and Intersectional Discrimination: Bringing the Experience of the Most Marginalized to the Fore, Institute for Human Rights*, Turku 2002.

Mann S., Grimes M., "Common and contested ground: Marxism and race, gender and class analysis," *Race, Gender & Class* 2001, Vol. 8, No.2.

Okólski M., "Współczesne europejskie migracje międzynarodowe a dynamika procesów integracyjnych," *Studia Socjologiczne* 2001.

Paleczny T., *Socjologia stosunków międzynarodowych*, Kraków 2001.

Pędziwiatr K., "Migracje globalne i lokalne z perspektywy Polski," [in:] *Globalna układanka*, Warszawa 2015.

Potyrała A., "Pozamilitarne aspekty bezpieczeństwa międzynarodowego-kryzys migracyjny 2015–2016," *Przegląd Strategiczny* 2016, Vol. 9.

Poza barierą czasu i przestrzeni. Księga jubileuszowa dla Jerzego Chłopeckiego, ed. by A. Rozmus, Rzeszów 2007.

Raport 2. Mniejszość ukraińska i migranci z Ukrainy w Polsce Analiza dyskursu, ed. P. Tyma, Warszawa 2019.

Raport. Mniejszość ukraińska i migranci z Ukrainy w Polsce Analiza dyskursu, ed. P. Tyma, Warszawa 2018.

Reisigl M., "Dyskryminacja w dyskursach," *Tekst i dyskurs - Text und Diskurs* 2010, Vol. 3.

Sakson A., "Migracje- fenomen XX i XXI wieku," *Przegląd Zachodni* 2008.

Slany K., "Co to znaczy być migrantką?," [in:] *Migracje kobiet. Perspektywa wielowymiarowa*, ed. K. Slany, Kraków 2008.

Slany K., Ślusarczyk M., "Genderowa specyfika rynku pracy-na przykładzie imigrantek w Polsce," *Studia Migracyjne–Przegląd Polonijny* 2012, Vol. 38/1.

Szylko-Skoczny M., Duszczyk M., "Trzy koncepcje polskiej polityki imigracyjnej," *Polityka Społeczna* 2010, Vol. 7.

Turner V., "Betwixt and between: The liminal period in rites de passage," [in:] *Reader in Comparative Religion: An Anthropological Approach*, ed. A.W. Lessa, E.Z. Vogt, New York 1972.

Part III Children's (and motherhood) vulnerability

Agnieszka Wedeł-Domaradzka
Kazimierz Wielki University in Bydgoszcz
e-mail: awedel@ukw.edu.pl
ORCID ID: 0000-0001-8128-9536

Between need and desire: the vulnerability of woman and child in surrogacy proceedings

Abstract: Legal systems are increasingly beginning to regulate the issue of surrogacy. Unfortunately, it does not mean that a uniform standard relating to this phenomenon has developed. It is quite the opposite. The variety of legal solutions adopted and the lack of coherent international regulations are conducive to abuses. This study aims to look at the phenomenon of surrogacy from the perspective of possible violations of women's and children's rights.

Keywords: judicial interpretation, women, best interests of the child, surrogacy, vulnerability determinants

1. Introductory remarks

The issue of surrogacy is currently one of the most interesting challenges in respect of children's and women's rights. However, in both cases (a child and a woman) it carries several threats to their legal situation, status and possibilities of implementing the law provided for in international documents. In most publication dedicated to surrogacy, it is possible to find a motive of the ancient situation of Sarah and her husband, Abraham. This element is mostly commented as proof; the phenomenon is not new, but rarely show as the first sign of human rights violations. In many studies, the fact that the surrogate was a slave, a woman forced to do so by her social and perhaps economic situation, is not particularly evident. The main tone of the narrative focuses rather on the first case of handing over a child to a woman other than the parent.[1]

---

1 T. Peters, *For the Love of Children: Genetic Technology and the Future of the Family*, Westminster John Knox Press, 1996, pp. 59–62; E. Brodeala, "The Legal Status of

According to the commonly accepted approach in the doctrine, surrogate motherhood is treated as a practice whose goals are carrying and giving birth to a child or children by a woman who ultimately does not plan to raise this child or children and wants to transfer it to another person or persons.[2] The purpose of her proceedings is to hand over a child to the intended parents. A woman's behaviour can be the result of two types of practice. She will give birth to a child genetically derived from her, in this case, this practice is referred to traditional surrogacy, or she will give birth to a child who does not genetically come from her. Then we are dealing with gestational surrogacy. In the latter case, the child's origin may be from the intended mother or from a completely different person who is the donor of the ovum then fertilised in an in vitro procedure.

The aim of this paper is to describe and analyse, from a legal standpoint, two aspects related to the protection of vulnerability groups regarding children and women. The first issue will be the diagnosis of the legal status of women and children in the case of surrogacy. In particular, this will be an attempt to answer which of the rights of these groups and to what extent they may be violated through the surrogacy procedure. A fundamental matter will also be the possibility of crossing in vulnerability systems of vulnerability determinants such as disability and minority, poverty and the situation of a woman in the indicated country. This aspect will concern the diagnosis of the occurrence of regulations in the sphere of international law that may contribute to the protection of women and children. In this context, special attention will be required by legal acts adopted at the level of international organisations and an analysis of the case-law of international courts. The second aspect is the need to determine what scopes of protection should be regulated at the national level and which solutions will need to be developed at the international level. Issues related to the assessment of sufficient scopes of protection and, possibly, actions necessary to limit the scale of human rights violations in relation to children and women will also be addressed. Especially that the protection of women

---

Assisted Human Reproduction in Romania. A Brief Discussion on Surrogacy," *Revista Română de Drept Comparat* 2016, No. 1, p. 56.

2 *Principles set out in the report of the ad hoc committee of experts on progress in the biomedical sciences* (CAHBI, published in 1989), Texts of the Council of Europe on bioethical matters, Volume II, Directorate General I – Human Rights Directorate Bioethics Department, Strasbourg, March 2012, p. 71.

and children is considered one of the fundamental objectives of international human rights law.[3]

In addition to current and even case-law issues related to surrogacy, several fields can still be diagnosed where knowledge and identification of potential violations may exist, but these are often overlooked. Because they may directly or indirectly hit vulnerable groups such as women and children, and to a fairly wide extent, the analysis will also cover these "unnoticed" but likely violations.

2. Status of women in the surrogacy procedure

2.1 General remarks

Generally speaking, surrogation procedures would not have been possible without the participation of a woman. The level of commitment foreseen for a woman can be twofold. It can be like in a traditional surrogation, the birth of a child genetically derived also from a surrogate, or as in a gestational surrogation, "only" birth of a child derived from other genetically people. Although, as F. Fines points out, women are not treated as such as belonging to vulnerable groups, and because of the far-reaching demand for gender equality,[4] there may be situations in which women find themselves in a situation requiring protection as a member of a vulnerable group. In the Council of Europe's opinion, such persons include:

> pregnant women and women with young children, persons with disabilities, including those with mental or cognitive impairments, persons living in rural or remote areas, substance abusers, prostitutes, persons of national or ethnic minority background, migrants – including undocumented migrants and refugees, gay men, lesbian, bisexual and transgender persons as well as HIV-positive persons, homeless persons, children and the elderly.[5]

Thus, surrogates, as pregnant women or women in difficult social situations will certainly be included in the vulnerable groups.

3 M. Wells-Greco, *The status of children arising from inter-country surrogacy agreements: The Past the present the future*, The Hague 2016, pp. 271–272.

4 F. Fines, "European Protection for woman," [in:] *Protecting Vulnerable Groups: The European Human Rights Framework*, ed. F. Ippolito, S. Iglesias Sánchez, London 2015, p. 95.

5 Explanatory Report to the Council of Europe Convention on preventing and combating violence against women and domestic violence Istanbul, 11 May 2011, p. 87, Council of Europe Treaty Series – No. 210.

2.2 Legal regulations

The legal status of women in the case of surrogation is not subject of dedicated regulations at the level of international law. Therefore, any legal considerations can only be made based on general provisions on the protection of human rights. The starting point for reflection should be the issue of human dignity.[6] Human dignity is the starting point for all major documents regarding the protection of human rights.[7] It is also referred to by the Convention on Human Rights and Biomedicine,[8] additionally indicating that "the human body and its parts shall not, as such, give rise to financial gain."[9] Although preparatory works[10] rather indicate solutions for organ transplantation and blood collection, it does not seem justified to exclude from this regulation reproductive material and the woman's body as the subject of the "carrying a child" service.

Surrogacy practices are also a violation of the Convention on the Elimination of All Forms of Discrimination against Women.[11] This convention provides for

---

6 A. Czubik, "Ochrona praw kobiet i zdrowia w prawie międzynarodowym publicznym versus surrogacy business," [in:] *Fundamentalne prawne problemy surrogate motherhood. Perspektywa krajowa*, ed. P. Mostowik, Warszawa 2019, p. 348.

7 UN General Assembly, Universal Declaration of Human Rights, preamble; International Covenant on Civil and Political Rights, preamble; International Covenant on Economic, Social and Cultural Rights, preamble, adopted and opened for signature, ratification and accession by General Assembly resolution 2200A (XXI) of 16 December 1966 entry into force 3 January 1976, in accordance with article 27, [online:] https://www.ohchr.org/en/professionalinterest/pages/cescr.aspx [available: 17.04.2020].

8 Preamble, art 1, Convention for the protection of Human Rights and Dignity of the Human Being with regard to the Application of Biology and Medicine: Convention on Human Rights and Biomedicine, Oviedo 4 April 1997, European Treaty Series No. 164.

9 Art 21, Convention for the protection of Human Rights and Dignity of the Human Being with regard to the Application of Biology and Medicine.

10 Steering Committee on Bioethics (CDBI) Convention for the protection of Human Rights and Dignity of the Human Being with regard to the Application of Biology and Medicine, Preparatory work on the Convention, [online:] www.coe.int/t/dg3/healthbioethic/texts_and_documents/CDBI-INF%282000%291PrepConv.pdf [available: 17.04.2020].

11 Convention on the Elimination of All Forms of Discrimination against Women, New York, 18 December 1979, [online:] https://www.ohchr.org/en/professionalinterest/pages/cedaw.aspx [available: 17.04.2020].

> a proper understanding of maternity as a social function and the recognition of the common responsibility of men and women in the upbringing and development of their children, it being understood that the interest of the children is the primordial consideration in all cases.

This means looking at motherhood from a social function perspective rather than introducing any aspect of the commercial function.[12] However, one could not conclude that surrogation meets the criteria provided for in the UN Slavery Convention.[13] Yes, we may be dealing with certain use of a woman, but it is not the property and total power over her. However, one cannot forget that we are dealing here with a far-reaching impact on the situation of a woman and what will happen to her body and with the possibility of influencing her behaviour.

2.3 Women's motives to become surrogate mother

Women who decide to become a surrogate may have different motives. In the case of those countries that allow altruistic surrogacy and is still made for the benefit of family members, these motives can be considered determined by the desire to help people who cannot have their offspring. In the case of legal systems that allow commercial surrogacy, the motivation may be different, although many surrogates at least officially declare that I want to help others also influenced their decision.[14] However, it should not be forgotten that even if it were so, the financial means received certainly constitute the main motive for such conduct. What is more, even in cases of altruistic surrogation, there is the question of the need to reimburse the expenses and expenses incurred by the surrogate in connection with being pregnant, giving birth and giving birth. It cannot be overlooked that the intended parents' relationship with the surrogate mother is maintained throughout the pregnancy, which can ultimately promote informal financial flows. As a consequence, there is a

---

12 M. Wells-Greco, *The Status of Children Arising from Inter-Country Surrogacy Arrangements: The Past, the Present, the Future,* The Hague 2016, p. 301.

13 Slavery Convention signed at Geneva on 25 September 1926, entry into force: 9 March 1927, in accordance with article 12, [online:] https://www.ohchr.org/en/professionalinterest/pages/slaveryconvention.aspx [available: 17.04.2020].

14 However, this is quite skeptical: Judge Dedov: "As regards solidarity, I do not believe in surrogate motherhood as a voluntary and freely-provided form of assistance for those who cannot have children; I do not believe that this is a sincere and honest statement. Solidarity is intended to help those whose life is at stake, but not those who merely desire to enjoy a full private or family life," Concurring opinion in *Paradiso and Campanelli v. Italy* [GC].

situation of financial benefits obtained from certain properties and specific use of a woman's body, which is part of the prohibition already provided for by the Convention on Human Rights and Biomedicine. The fact of the existence of benefits is, therefore, a special violation of human dignity. This interpretation was also supported by ECHR judges: De Gaetano, Pinto de Albuquerque, Wojtyczek and Dedov, indicating that the degrading treatment of a mother is degrading her mother by completely breaking her relationship with the child she gave birth to. In their opinion, this is of particular importance due to the bonds formed in the prenatal period and the brutality and unconditionality of breaking them. Moreover, as they indicate: "Both the child and the surrogate mother are treated not as ends in themselves, but as means to satisfy the desires of other persons."[15] It should be agreed that the sacrifice and possible risk of a surrogate woman are far too widely required in the case of surrogacy. Moreover, one cannot forget that there are specific obligations arising from the surrogation agreement. They even concern the obligation to undergo specific examinations or even medical interventions. These agreements also include specific prohibitions such as a ban on sexual intercourse during in vitro therapy to ensure that fertilization occurs with the intended father semen.[16] As well as the need to change the way of life or even where you live during pregnancy. All this also interferes with her dignity and family and private life.

2.4 Possible violations of women's rights

One should also remember that the determinant qualifying a woman to become a surrogate is often the fact that she has her own children. The fact of having these children, the number of births carried out, abortions performed, correct menstruation, the use of contraceptives, age as well as the medical history of the woman herself and her family as well as information on addictions are the elements that are required to be passed in the qualification procedure. All this information constitutes a very deep interference in the privacy and data of women, including data referred to as "sensitive." In addition to overviews

---

15 Join concurring opinion of judges De Gaetano, Pinto de Albuquerque, Wojtyczek and Dedov in *Paradiso and Campanelli v. Italy* [GC].

16 Juridical practice knows the case of refraining from sexual intercourse of a surrogate with her partner, which resulted in the birth of a child genetically not from the intended father. – more: J. Stelmach, B. Brożek, M. Soniewicka, W. Załuski, *Paradoksy bioetyki prawniczej*, Warszawa 2010, p. 106, and the court case cited there [in:] *Stiver v. Parker*, 975 F.2d 261 (6th Cir. 1992).

of even if a woman agrees to provide these data, their scope and impact on the "qualification" mechanism bears some objectification.

One cannot ignore the health aspect and the impact on the further health of the woman undergoing therapy and pregnancy. In addition to the factors already mentioned that may have a negative impact on emotional health, physical health threats are also identified. These include hormonal interventions, multiple pregnancies and caesarean sections. The lack of legal regulations regarding the scope or obligation to insurance for a woman whose health would suffer in a particular way after surrogation should also be identified as an important threat.

In essence, all these activities, their scope, intensity and significant emotional aspect because that surrogate women are exposed to violation of their rights, the scale of which in many cases (such as women in India, for whom surrogation was extremely important from a financial point of view) may be unaware.

3. Status of children in the surrogacy procedure

3.1 General remarks

Regarding the issue of children's rights, it should be recognised that it is much more complex than in the case of women. This conclusion is due to two reasons. Firstly, surrogacy procedures interfere more with the child's situation and his or her whole future life. They determine, among others, the position as a citizen, as a family member or sense of identity. Secondly, children because of their immaturity tend to be not only incapable of claiming violations of their rights, but are often unaware that these violations occur. It does not mean, however, that it is impossible to take actions that would secure the best interests resulting from the regulations concerning the best interests of the child.

3.2 Legal regulations

Any international legal document does not directly regulate the standard of treatment of children regarding surrogacy procedures. Such attempts were considered[17] or made.[18]

---

17 S. Mohapatra, "Adopting an International Convention on Surrogacy – A Lesson from Intercountry Adoption," *Loyola University Chicago International Law Review*, Vol. 13, 2015.

18 Committee on Social Affairs, Health and Sustainable Development, Draft Recommendation: Children's rights related to surrogacy, Doc. 14140,

Two initiatives deserve attention. The first of these was the work of the Bioethics Committee, or rather its predecessors already started in 1989. A report was then presented regarding the principles of progress in biomedical sciences. Rule No. 15[19] included in the document, recommended not to consider surrogacy as medically assisted procreation. At the same time, it was emphasized that any contracts concluded between the surrogate mother and the person or couple for whom the woman would give birth are not considered valid. Intermediation in such activities is also expressly prohibited. However, the work of the Committee allowed for a solution based on the admissibility under the national legislation of a situation in which surrogacy procedures would be altruistic (without remuneration) and provide the ability to maintain a child by the surrogate.

The second initiative is an attempt to adopt a short recommendation at Council of Europe level. Only two issues were to be included in this recommendation. First, a recommendation to the Committee of Ministers to consider the advisability and possibilities of developing European guidelines to protect children's rights in connection with arrangements for surrogacy. Second, collaboration with the Hague Conference on Private International Law (HCCH) in ensuring that the instruments developed under HCCH would take into account the opinions of the Council of Europe bodies and the jurisprudence of the European Court of Human Rights. In the opinion of rapporteur Petra De Sutter, the determinants of the need to accept the recommendation and to undertake further work on the regulation of surrogacy were the risk of violating children's rights resulting from the lack of legal regulations. The optimal model that has emerged from the justification is, on the one hand, the diversification of regulations based on national mechanisms and their specificity, and on the other hand, actions to reduce the cross-border element in surrogacy procedures. In both cases, care for the principle of the best interest of the child would be the primary determinant of activities. As indicated, this can only be "closed" to surrogacy in the national order and to its citizens, and a general ban on surrogacy with a cross-border element. Despite the failure of the recommendation,

---

23 September 2016, [online:] https://assembly.coe.int/nw/xml/XRef/Xref-XML2HTML-en.asp?fileid=23015&lang=en [available: 17.04.2020].

19 Report on Human Artificial Procreation, Principles set out in the report of the Ad Hoc Committee of Experts on Progress in the Biomedical Sciences (CAHBI), 1989, available at https://rm.coe.int/16803113e4 [available: 17.04.2020].

it cannot be considered that the rights provided for, in both universal and regional documents regarding the rights of the individual, cannot relate to the problems of the child's situation in the surrogacy procedure. It is necessary to identify potential threats that may occur towards children as part of surrogacy procedures in order to analyse these rights.

3.3 Possible violations of children's rights

3.3.1 Legal subjectivity and citizenship

First of all, attention should be paid to the child's right to respect for his legal subjectivity and citizenship. These issues are reflected in the instruments of universal international law having the status of declarations or international agreements that generally relate to the sphere of protection of human rights or are dedicated to the protection of individual groups. The Universal Declaration of Human Rights (UDHR) already refers to the issue of legal subjectivity and citizenship. Despite its formally non-binding character, it is sometimes considered a basic document from the sphere of human rights. According to some,[20] the nature of the Declaration is even binding, because its provisions reflect the rights accepted and applied by the international community, i.e. having custom status. The rights indicated in the UDHR include the right to recognise legal personality[21] and the right to have citizenship.[22] A similar solution was adopted in the document that already has the status of an international agreement, which is the International Covenant on Civil and Political Rights. This document identifies the right to recognition everywhere as a person before the law.[23] Recognition of legal personality is a key right which determines the fact of

20 H. Hannum, "The Status of the Universal Declaration of Human Rights in National and International Law," *Georgia Journal of International and Comparative Law* 1996, Vol. 25 (287), pp. 316–351.

21 Art. 6, UN General Assembly, Universal Declaration of Human Rights, 10 December 1948, 217 A (III), [online:] https://www.refworld.org/docid/3ae6b3712c.html [available: 17.04.2020].

22 Art. 15, Universal Declaration of Human Rights.

23 Art. 16, International Covenant on Civil and Political Rights, adopted and opened for signature, ratification and accession by General Assembly resolution 2200A (XXI) of 16 December 1966, entry into force 23 March 1976, in accordance with Article 49, [online:] https://www.ohchr.org/en/professionalinterest/pages/ccpr.aspx [available: 17.04.2020].

"perceiving" and subsequently including the protection of the individual. This right is considered not to be derogated.[24] M. Nowak[25] presents quite interesting considerations in this context. He points out that *travaux préparatoires* to the ICCR assume that the recognition of legal personality may, in some cases also include the foetus. Although an unborn child does not have the right to exercise all the rights provided for in the Convention, however, with an individual approach to analysing the scope of use, it can be considered that he or she has the right to enjoy specific rights such as a prohibition of inhumane treatment[26] or a prohibition of discrimination.[27] The prohibition of inhumane treatment, in this case, would rather refer to possible physical harm and, as a detrimental consequences, could be considered only in a situation in which the intended parents would express the will to terminate the pregnancy. The opening of the foetus position to the prohibition of discrimination makes consideration of his position and possible damages current in virtually every case of surrogacy. First of all, there is the issue of discrimination in terms of the possibility of ultimately meeting natural parents (especially mothers), who somehow "disappear" after the child's status as the foetus. Secondly, discrimination may concern knowledge of one's genetic origin, including the possible burden of hereditary diseases. Thirdly, there is the question of responsibility for what happened before birth and possible investigation of damages from that period, which, if the fact of origin from surrogacy procedures is unknown, maybe significantly impeded.

3.3.2 Registration after birth

The issue of legal subjectivity also involves the right of every child provided for by Covenant to be registered immediately after birth, and the right to have their own name undergoing the registration procedure. The term "own name" does not, however, clearly indicate whether the name must be the name of one or both parents, or whether any name may be given so that the child can be identified.

---

24 S. Joseph, M. Castan, *The International Covenant on Civil and Political Rights Cases, Materials, and Commentary*, Oxford 2013, p. 336.

25 M. Nowak, *U.N. Covenant on Civil and Political Rights: CCPR Commentary*, Kehl 2005, pp. 371–372.

26 Art. 7, International Covenant on Civil and Political Rights.

27 Art. 26, International Covenant on Civil and Political Rights.

Nevertheless, when it comes to the right of every child to acquire citizenship, it is treated as a determinant of child protection by a particular state. Consequently, single signatory countries to the Covenant will be obliged to ensure that every child born on the territory of such a state of citizenship is acquired. Adopted as the dominant model of acquiring citizenship (*ius soli* or *ius sanguinis*) does not matter. In the case of surrogacy practices with a cross-border element, a child may be deprived of access to citizenship. This may be the case if the child is born on the territory of a state that recognises surrogacy practices as legal, but its parents come from a state that does not allow surrogacy. When the intended parents transferred the child to the territory of their state of citizenship, the issue of recognition of the parent-child relationship may arise; thus, the inability to assign citizenship to that child follows. This will apply to both countries that opt for the law of blood and those who prefer the law of the land. In both cases, there will be a lack of citizenship connector. In the case of blood law, both parents may not be recognised as parents if the child is not genetically derived from them, whereas in the case of the law of land states it is evident that since it was born abroad and there is no supplementary link to the parent's citizenship, the child will also be deprived of access to citizenship. The state is faced with a dilemma. On the one hand, there is the need for the Pact to recognise the child's right to citizenship and to actually grant this citizenship. On the other hand, the basis for granting citizenship is the relationship with parents of intent, which is treated as contrary to applicable law.

As regards general regional standards, it should be pointed out that the issue of children's rights relating to respect for their legal subjectivity and citizenship is not regulated in the European Convention for the Protection of Human Rights and Fundamental Freedoms (ECHR). This does not mean, however, that this Convention cannot apply to children and their situations in surrogacy practices. Contrastingly, unlike universal mechanisms, regional human rights standards usually have more effective mechanisms to verify compliance with individual rights. The Convention itself, or rather its creators, however, assume not to diversify rights and not to emphasise their special group of addressees. Thus, all situations concerning just the parent-child relationship as well as the child's situation are most often the matter of consideration of the Act of the Court of Human Rights (ECHR) based on art. 8 (protection of private and family life). Legal subjectivity and citizenship should also be considered in this regard.[28]

---

28 See *Karassev v. Finlane*, Application No. 31414/96, 12 January 1999; *Slivenko v. Latvia* [GC], application No. 48321/99, 9 October 2003, § 77; *Genovese v. Malta*, Application No. 53124/09, 11 October 2011, § 30.

3.3.3 Convention on the Rights of the Child and the impact of the rights of the child

As specific standards at the universal level are concerned, there is an obvious need to pay attention to the basic document regulating children's rights issues, namely the Convention on the Rights of the Child. This document contains several rights that may be violated in the context of surrogacy practices. First of all, attention should be drawn to two articles having a special status in the Convention, namely to Articles 2 and 3. As regards Article 2 of the Convention, it provides for a prohibition of discrimination in exercising the rights contained in the Convention on the Rights of the Child. Rights that could also be violated when considering the situation of children include rights protected under Article 7. This article is complex in its scope and concerns, in fact, already mentioned and impressed in universal documents of a general nature of rights. It provides for the registration of a child and the right to receive a name, as well as the right to obtain citizenship. Importantly, the Convention mentions immediate registration. In the case of surrogate procedures, such immediate registration may take place in the country where this practice is carried out and, if it is considered legal, it should not cause major problems. However, difficulties may arise in the case of cross-border surrogacy and the need to register the child again in their parents' country of origin. In the case (and this is usually the case), when this country does not provide for the possibility of recognising surrogacy practices, the issue of registration may be problematic. In such a situation, the understanding of the term "immediately" will have to be extended to include time spent on proceedings regarding the determination of the legal grounds for such registration, in particular determining whether there is a biological relationship between the child and at least one parent. In the absence of such a biological relationship, there is a need and possibility to establish such a relationship; in this case, the main determinant will unquestionably be the child's best interest.

3.3.4 ECtHR practice in surrogacy cases

This is how the European Court of Human Rights (ECtHR) argued in one of its cases.[29] This case concerned an Italian couple who had benefited from surrogacy procedures in Russia through the intervention of one of the agencies for cross-border surrogacy. As a result of the agreement, a child was born. The

29 *Paradiso and Campanelli v. Italy* [GC], Application No. 25358/12, 24 January 2017.

document issued in Russia stated that the child's parents are intended parents and did not indicate the child's origin from the surrogacy procedure. Based on this document, the parents obtained a travel document for the child from the Italian consulate and came with him Italian territory. In Italy, they tried to register a child. They were denied this, arguing that the files on that child contained false information. Then they were accused of using documentation containing invalid data, and a lack of genetic relationship between the child and intended parents was established.

As a consequence, the child they brought to Italy was taken away from them and placed in institutional care. Until 2013, the child had no legal status or identity in Italy. After obtaining it, the child was transferred to an adoption procedure, from which intended parents were excluded. The complaint to the Tribunal alleged violation of Art. 8 of the Convention due to the withdrawal of the intended parents of the child and the refusal to recognise their parenthood established abroad as well as registration of the Russian birth certificate of the child. In examining this case, Iza found a violation of art. 8; however, it was forwarded to the Grand Chamber for further proceedings. The Grand Chamber focused primarily on determining whether there had been a violation of the right to protection of private and family life. The government claimed that

> in view of the applicants' unlawful conduct, no tie protected by Article 8 of the Convention could exist between them and the child. They also argued that the applicants had lived with the child for only eight months.[30]

However, the applicants argued that their legal parental relationship "was recognised in Russian law and that they had formed close emotional ties with the child during the first eight months of his life." Referring to its previous judgments, the Court pointed out that the existence of family life is a matter of fact and depends on the existence of close personal ties.[31] At the same time, under the Convention, there is neither the right to found a family nor the right to adopt a child.[32] Possible protection could exist if, at the very least, the potential relationship existed. In considering this aspect, the Court found that it would be inappropriate to define a minimum duration of shared life, but its duration and what was happening at that time must be reviewed. Referring to previous rulings, the ECtHR identified, however, longer periods of contact with

30 *Paradiso and Campanelli v. Italy* [GC], § 137.

31 *Marckx v. Belgium*, Application No. 6833/74, 13 June 1979, § 31, *K and T v. Finland*, Application No. 25702/94, 12 July 2001, § 150.

32 *EB v. France* [GC], Application No. 43546/02, 22 January 2008, § 41.

the child than six months,[33] and if they were shorter than they were accompanied by biological origin from at least one parent.[34] In the considered case, the contact period was eight months, and the biological relationship did not exist, including thus the short duration of the relationship with the child and the uncertainty of the ties from a legal perspective.

In consequence, the Court considered that the conditions enabling it to conclude that there existed a de facto family life have not been met. Referring to the lawfulness of the interference of the national authorities, its admissibility was recognised on the grounds of the need to provide care to a child who was in a state of abandonment under Italian law. At the same time, it was emphasised that the interference was legitimate and necessary in democratic society due to the total incompatibility with Italian law of the activities of intended parents and the danger of sanctioning the state of unlawfulness which arose as a result of the activities of intended parents. Consequently, no violation of art. 8 ECHR was found.

Importantly, the ECtHR always applies to the Convention on the Rights of the Child (CRC) and interprets when the case concerns children and refers to its provisions under several documents that have been issued in relation to the provisions of the Convention. In particular, it includes interpretative documents such as General Comments. In this particular case, reference is made to article 3 and indicated that "the principle that the best interests of the child are a primary consideration in all actions concerning children."[35] In this context, it is quite puzzling and distressing that the Italian authorities were not held accountable for the child's remaining without any identity for such a long time. It seems that such conduct was contrary to the basic principles of interpretation of the CRC regulations, and as a consequence, can impact negatively on a child's sense of personal identity social welfare. Only after obtaining the registration status the child could be transferred to further adoption procedures.[36] The mere fact of the need for state interference and verification of

---

33 *Wagner and J.M.W.L. v. Luxembourg*, Application No. 76240/01, § 117, 28 June 2007; *Nazarenko v. Russia*, Application No. 39438/13, § 58.

34 *D. and Others v. Belgium* (dec.) No. 29176/13, § 49, 8 July 2014.

35 Art 3, Convention on the Rights of the Child, New York, 20 November 1989 United Nations, Treaty Series, Vol. 1577, p. 3.

36 UN Committee on the Rights of the Child (CRC), *General Comment No. 7 (2005): Implementing Child Rights in Early Childhood*, 20 September 2006, CRC/C/GC/7/Rev.1, [online:] https://www.refworld.org/docid/460bc5a62.html [available: 18 May 2020].

the origin and manner and reasons for the child's appearance on the territory of the state, of course, take place. As ECtHR has indicated, dismissing a case against Belgium,[37] states have the right to interfere in private life for legitimate purposes. These include the prevention of trafficking in human beings, the protection of the rights of others like the surrogate mother and also a child who is an "effect" of surrogacy agreement. Contrary to appearances, such behavior should be considered to serve the best interests of the child. It does not affect the possibility of establishing a parent-child relationship, but it guarantees that the rights of the child itself are respected. In the Belgian case, proceedings to determine whether a child born as a result of surrogacy procedures should or should not receive Belgian travel documents resulted in the separation of intended parents from the child. However, it was conducted as a matter of necessity, the child received the entry document as soon as it was possible to establish that there had been no violation of the vulnerable group's rights. Additionally, ECtHR rightly pointed out "the applicants could reasonably have foreseen that the procedure to have the family relationship recognised and to take the child to Belgium would necessarily take a certain time."[38]

In the area of child registration, several problems were identified based on French cases.[39] In their case, there was a situation where children from surrogacy procedures born abroad were brought to France.[40] In both cases, the mother of the child who is a third-country national concluded a contract with the parents of intent, which resulted in the birth of the child. After birth, the children were issued, they were following the legal system of the mother (American), documents in which the content in both cases, as mother, identified women who were intentional mothers. Then the intentional parents returned to their

---

37 *D. and Others v. Belgium* (dec.) 29176/13, Information Note on the Court's case-law No. 177.

38 *D. and Others v. Belgium* (dec.) – 29176/13.

39 *Mennesson v. France*, Application No. 65192/11, 26 June 2014, *Labassee v. France*, Application No. 65941/11, 26 June 2014. The ECtHR came to similar conclusions in the Foulon and Bouvet case, *Foulon and Bouvet v. France*, Application Nos. 9063/14 and 10410/14, 21 July 2016.

40 The French Civil Code expressly indicates that all surrogacy agreements are invalid – Art 16.7: "Toute convention portant sur la procréation ou la gestation pour le compte d'autrui est nulle," Code civil Version consolidée au 14 février 2020, https://www.legifrance.gouv.fr/affichCode.do;jsessionid=6E3B610257A28F8C7F2047C113A589C5.tplgfr35s_2?cidTexte=LEGITEXT000006070721&dateTexte=20200523 [available: 30 April 2020].

country of origin and applied for the regulation of their child's status by registering a foreign birth certificate. In the case of France, this was difficult because it is a country which, like most European countries,[41] does not recognize surrogacy practices as legal. Consequently, the domestic courts decided that the refusal to register a birth certificate issued in the USA did not infringe upon the right to respect for family and private life[42] or upon the interests of the child.[43]

When considering these cases, the ECtHR took into account the previously mentioned acts of both the ECHR and CRC, mainly focusing on those considered regarding Article 8. The Court also emphasized that the use of surrogacy arrangements raises delicate ethical questions. It also confirms that countries should in principle be given a wide margin of appreciation,[44] not only as to whether to allow surrogation, but also whether and how to recognize a legal parent-child relationship between children resulting from a surrogate motherhood agreement abroad. In this last aspect, ECtHR recognized at the same time need for special protection of the vulnerable group, which are children, indicating that in a situation where we are dealing with an important aspect of the identity of natural persons in the case of a legal parent-child relationship, the consequence of this should be to reduce the margin of appreciation granted to the defendant.

The issue of registering a child can also very highly determine his or her citizenship. In both French cases, the question of the possibility of recognizing a parent-child relationship also determined the de facto possibility of acquiring citizenship, since under French law, for a child to obtain citizenship, it is necessary for at least one of his or her parents to be a French citizen. Therefore, the lack of recognition of the parent-child relationship could negatively affect the possibility of obtaining French citizenship,[45] as well as have a significant and still negative impact on the possibility of these children exercising their inheritance rights.

In both cases, the inconformity of the lack of recognition with the better interest of the child,[46] noticed by the national court, was also highlighted,

---

41 *Mennesson v. France*, § 78. For some states, this is not explicitly prohibited but is not tolerate, also.

42 Art. 8 ECHR.

43 Art. 3, Convention on the Rights of the Child.

44 This interpretation existed already recognized from the case *S. H. and Others v. Austria*, Application No. 57813/00.

45 *Mennesson v. France*, § 96–97, *Labassee v. France*, § 75–76.

46 *Mennesson v. France*, § 99, *Labassee v. France*, § 78.

and that France had exceeded its margin of appreciation.[47] Consequently, the ECtHR made it very clear the need to protect children and that this protection takes precedence over legal regulations that would seek to eliminate surrogacy practices.[48] In issuing its advisory opinion on this subject, the ECHR added that the right to respect for the private life of a child born abroad as a result of surrogacy procedures requires that national law contain mechanisms allowing recognition of a legal parent-child relationship with a mother of intent which was indicated in the foreign birth certificate as a "legal mother." Moreover, the uncertainty situation should be ended as soon as possible.[49]

3.3.5 The problem of stateless

These considerations perfectly fit into the postulated universal standard. United Nations High Commissioner for Refugees (UNHCR) in one of his interventions to the Committee on Legal Affairs and Human Right just pointed out that children born by surrogate mothers are at risk of child statelessness. The fact that this threat has its source in the absence of procedures guaranteeing the child's citizenship in a situation where the legal regime of the surrogate mother does not grant him citizenship and the state of intentional parents does not provide for the legality of surrogation procedures. UNHCR assumes that the basic determinant of subcontracted activities should be regulations assuming respect for the best interests of the child. The Dakar Conclusions[50] states that the Convention and Preventing Statelessness must be interpreted in the light of subsequent human rights treaties including the CRC. The CRC provides for the right to acquire citizenship. Consequently, it is necessary for national legal mechanisms to operate so as to enable stateless children to automatically acquire citizenship as soon as they are born. This is to be determined by being born on the territory of a given country. In a situation where a child (or rather his or her

---

47 *Mennesson v. France*, § 100, *Labassee v. France*, § 79.

48 R.F. Storrow, "International Surrogacy in the European Court of Human Rights," *North Carolina Journal of International Law and Commercial Regulation*, Vol. 43, 2018, p. 53.

49 Advisory Opinion concerning the recognition in domestic law of a legal parent-child relationship between a child born through a gestational surrogacy arrangement abroad and the intended mother, requested by the French Court of Cassation, 10 April 2019, request No. P16-2018-001, § 46 and § 49.

50 Interpreting the 1961 Statelessness Convention and Preventing Statelessness among Children: ("Dakar Conclusions") September 2011, [online:] http://www.refworld.org/docid/4e8423a72.html [available: 30 April 2020].

legal representatives) would apply for citizenship, the states are obliged to limit formal requirements to enable these children to obtain citizenship as soon as possible.[51] The citizenship gap is also filled by the principle contained in the recommendation of the Committee of Ministers,[52] which stipulates that states should:

> apply to children their provisions on acquisition of nationality by right of blood if, as a result of a birth conceived through medically assisted reproductive techniques, a child – parent family relationship is established or recognized by law.

More importantly, however, it should be recognized that the right to citizenship should not be interpreted in such a way as to refer to the right to acquire every possible citizenship. Such a situation will be the subject of an ECtHR decision in the Schlittner-Hay v. Poland[53] case communicated to the Polish government. In this case, the homosexual marriage of a man with Israeli citizenship and a man with Polish and Israeli citizenship complained about the inability of their children to acquire Polish citizenship. It should be mentioned that the children were born from a surrogacy agreement in the United States, acquired American citizenship, and his parents indicated on the American birth certificate reside in Israel. It should be recognized that this case should be considered based on of the concept of "effective citizenship."[54] Otherwise, this would open up the possibility of applying for citizenship hypothetically to all those who do not have real relations with a given country, moreover, they do not want to have them, but their legal situation implies the possibility of applying for citizenship. It is obvious that if the facts were different and the child actually needed to exercise the rights arising from citizenship in the territory of the Polish State, there would be a premise for granting him citizenship under a simplified procedure based on the blood ties of a child with one of the parents having Polish citizenship.

---

51 Parliamentary Assembly of the Council of Europe, UNHCR intervention at the Committee on Legal Affairs and Human Rights, Paris, 12 November 2012.

52 Recommendation CM/Rec(2009)13 of the Committee of Ministers to member states on the nationality of children, adopted by the Committee of Ministers on 9 December 2009 at the 1073rd meeting of the Ministers' Deputies.

53 *Schlittner-Hay v. Poland*, Applications Nos. 56846/15 and 56849/15.

54 *Nottebohm Case (second phase)*, Judgment of April 6th, 1955, I.C.J. Reports 1955, p. 4: "In order to appraise its international effect, it is impossible to disregard the circumstances in which it was conferred, the serious character which attaches to it, the real and effective, and not merely the verbal preference of the individual seeking it for the country which grants it to him."

3.3.6 *The right to know and be raised by one's parents*

The second aspect relating to identity is the right to know and be raised by one's parents. This right in the Convention on the Rights of the Child is included collectively in the aforementioned right to the recognition of legal personality and citizenship.[55] In accordance with CRC, this right is a third, somehow complementary element. From the perspective of surrogacy, identity will refer to a sense of individuality, but also belonging and awareness of one's origin. Therefore, it will also cover the parental aspect. In the case of surrogacy, this issue is more complicated than in the case of origin from natural parents. This is because in this procedure we are dealing with at least one other person, separate from the intended parents, which significantly affects the genetic identity of the child.[56] The sense of identity, therefore, includes the right to meet a natural parent, but also the right to meet a genetic parent, or a person who has actually (and thus classically identifies motherhood) gave birth to a child. A child certainly has a personal interest in knowing who his parent is. Therefore, there is a situation similar to artificial insemination or adoption practices. The issue of artificial insemination and the right to meet their parents was the subject of German court case law. In the ruling from 2013,[57] when deciding on the disclosure of donor data, the national court concluded that the interest of a child who was brought to life through artificial insemination speaks to know his genetic origin. Moreover, this interest should be placed higher than the interests of the doctor or the semen donor in the confidentiality of donation. Consequently, the child has the right to ask the doctor for disclosure of these data. The German national court also stated that any contracts between the parents and the doctor conducting the insemination procedure regarding the anonymity of donation are inadmissible as being concluded concerning a third party, which is an unborn child. In another judgment, the German Supreme Court[58] went step further and declared that the child's right to meet his parents does not require

55 Art 7 CRC, ICCPR also contains a similar solution in art. 24 "1. Every child shall have, without any discrimination as to race, colour, sex, language, religion, national or social origin, property or birth, the right to such measures of protection as are required by his status as a minor, on the part of his family, society and the State. 2. Every child shall be registered immediately after birth and shall have a name. 3. Every child has the right to acquire a nationality."

56 D. Kuźnicka, "Prawo do tożsamości jako prawo dziecka – wybrane zagadnienia," *Folia Iuridica Universitatis Wratislaviensis* 2016, Vol. 5 (2), p. 190.

57 Oberlandesgericht (OLG) in Hamm, 6 February 2013, 2013 NJW 1167.

58 BGH of 28 January 2015 – XII ZR 201/13, openJur 2015, 5945.

a minimum of many requests for information. Moreover, that court pointed out the parents' right to have access to the donor's data to guarantee that they would be able to inform the child even shortly after the child was born. Similar solutions can also be found in ECtHR practice concerning adoptive children and the possibility for these children to obtain information about their natural parents.[59] Besides, the tendency is to allow, even if there is a mechanism for anonymous adoption, to obtain the consent of a parent (mainly mother) to provide her child with natural information about her personal data.[60]

3.3.7 Genetic and biological identity

Therefore, the importance of this knowledge and its importance for children or even later adults should be recognized. The need to know genetic identity in the context of one's origin is particularly important for at least three reasons. First of all, it results from the child's personal need to get to know his parents, from natural curiosity about his origin and the effects that such behaviour will have on the sense of identity. Secondly, it is important from a child's health perspective. In the case of a surrogation involving the use of genetic material other than the genetic material of at least one of the intended parents, the issue of hereditary diseases may arise. It cannot be ruled out that some people will be interested in knowing whether and for which diseases they may have genetic conditions, especially in situations where appropriate prophylaxis can be used to avoid or delay the effects of these diseases. Finally, and thirdly, there may also be threats to the possibility of marrying and begetting offspring between relatives. Even if we accept, that there are still few people who have the option of using a commercial surrogation and this problem may not be a large-scale problem, we need to be aware it cannot be excluded that in small communities, whose inhabitants would use the same surrogacy clinic, such a situation could take place.

Nevertheless, the existence of regulations relating to the protection of the understanding of parenthood based solely on biological fact in this case is insufficient. First of all, because there is a difference in legal regimes. In the country of origin of parents, biological kinship is a determinant of parenthood, but often in the country of surrogacy such regulation already exists. As a consequence, the government of the parents' country of origin will not ensure equality in the child's exercise of the rights contained in the CRC, since there is

59 *Godelli v. Italy*, Application No. 33783/09, 25 September 2012.

60 *Odièvre v. France*, Application No. 42326/98, 13 February 2003.

no real possibility to influence the knowledge of natural parents, in particular of a surrogate mother. It should be emphasized that children's rights arising from the CRC and in particular the right to identity should be understood broadly.[61] After all, the Convention mentions not only the right to know your own identity, but also implies the state's obligation to concept actions to "to respect the right of the child to preserve his or her identity, including nationality, name and family relations as recognized by law without unlawful interference."[62] In this aspect, the cultural element and the right to preserve a sense of cultural and sometimes ethnic separation is also important. This right covers two aspects: facilitating the child's access to information about his or her identity including its historical elements and the obligation to ensure that the child will be able to express and to enjoy his or her identity.[63] As in the case of anonymous births, surrogacy practices will not serve the purpose of exercising this right. However, elements of non-disclosure of identity that could check that a child would be more vulnerable to discrimination caused by his or her identity are considered acceptable.[64]

3.3.8 Separation from parents and child trafficking

The last of the aspects that may affect a child's situation as a sensitive subject are their rights related to parents. Nevertheless, it is not only about their identification, but about art. 9 CRC prohibition on separating a child from parents, except for circumstances justifying such separation and provided for in art. 18 CRC the responsibility of parents and guardians for bringing up children. The regulations contained in both articles exhaust the features of art. 8 ECHR.[65] Although in most cases these provisions are considered in the context of the legitimate the best interests of the child separation of the child from the parents and procedural guarantees associated with it,[66] in the absence of the surrogate's

61 M. Freeman, "The New Birth Right? Identity and the Child of the Reproduction Revolution," *International Journal of Children's Rights*, 1996, No. 273, p. 291.

62 Art 8, CRC.

63 *The UN Convention on the Rights of the Child: A Commentary*, ed. J. Tobin, Oxford 2019, p. 295.

64 Ibidem, p. 289.

65 To some extent also apply art. 5 Protocol No. 7 to the Convention for the Protection of Human Rights and Fundamental Freedoms.

66 J.E. Doek, *A Commentary on the United Nations Convention on the Rights of the Child, Articles 8–9: The Right to Preservation of Identity and The Right Not to Be Separated from His or Her Parents*, Leiden; Boston 2006, pp. 24–27.

will to surrender the child, these provisions could apply. The issue of the scope of enforceability of a surrogation agreement and possible options for leaving a child are in most cases outside the legal regulation.

In the scope of violating children's rights, one can also pay attention to the regulations contained in art. 35 CRC and in the option protocol to this document. According to the content of art. 35 it is necessary to underline that "States Parties shall take all appropriate national, bilateral and multilateral measures to prevent the abduction of, the sale of or traffic in children for any purpose or in any form." In option protocol 2, a general ban on child trafficking, child prostitution and child pornography is expressed and defines the concept of child trafficking, child prostitution and child pornography.[67] According to the provided definition, "sale of children means any act or transaction whereby a child is transferred by any person or group of persons to another for remuneration or any other consideration." There is no consensus in the doctrine as to whether surrogacy practices should be considered child trafficking. In the opinion of J. Tobin, surrogation mechanisms can be qualified as meeting the conditions of understanding such terms as 'transfer,' 'remuneration' and 'consideration' indicates that a commercial surrogacy will fall within the definition of the sale of a child.[68] On the other hand, there are voices about the necessity of interpreting on purpose, indicating that surrogation agreements are not aimed at exploitation and that the intended parents themselves do not have the right to property for children and do not have unlimited control over children.[69] Irrespective of which point of view would be adopted, it should be recognized, in the context of the considerations made above, that a surrogation situation may have a negative impact on a child. As a consequence, her unconsciousness and lack of self-protection makes children particularly vulnerable to violations of fundamental rights.

---

67 Art. 1 and art. 2, Optional Protocol to the Convention on the Rights of the Child on the sale of children, child prostitution and child pornography, adopted and opened for signature, ratification and accession by General Assembly resolution A/RES/54/263 of 25 May 2000, entered into force on 18 January 2002, United Nations, Treaty Series, Vol. 2171, p. 227.

68 J. Tobin, "To prohibit or permit: what is the (human) rights responses to the practice of international commercial surrogacy?," *International and Comparative Law Quarterly*, Vol. 63, No. 2, 2014, p. 335.

69 K. Wade, "The regulation of surrogacy: a children's rights perspective," *Child and family law quarterly*, Vol. 29, 2017, and the literature quoted there, available https://www.ncbi.nlm.nih.gov/pmc/articles/PMC5540169/# [available: 17.04.2020].

4. Conclusions

Analyzing the situation of women and children from the perspective of identifying them as vulnerable groups, it seems that we are only at the beginning of the road, which may lead, if not to eliminate, at least to limit the violations. However, before the goal is achieved, the issue of protecting women and children from infringements will require a considerable amount of work.

The first aspect that is necessary to concentrate on language issues. Naming certain phenomenon or their participants in a way that serves the intentions of those practices is not the optimal solution. For example, the concept of "gestational carrier" may be of a reducing nature, and the consequence of its use is bypassing the emotional relationships between mother and foetus. Some terminological order is introduced by the work of the Hague Conference on Private International Law, which has developed a glossary of terms related to surrogation and has undertaken the first harmonization work. Despite this, there are still many problems in terms of terminology, even in relation to the term "mother" for an age taken for granted. Currently, many terms are added to this term "biological," "genetic," "natural," "surrogate" or "intended."

The second aspect is the issue of the standards of operation of intermediary institutions in those legal systems in which surrogation is legal. Experience to date shows that there are medical clinics, at least those legally operating, are very well equipped with medical equipment and use legal offices as part of registration procedures in their countries. However, it can be assumed – although there are no examples from case-law – the safeguards under the law relate to the service of the clinic and clients, i.e. intended parents. Surrogate women can count on their salary, but not on full protection as to whether their rights are respected or what to do if surrogacy has had negative consequences for their lives and health.

The possibility of intersection of factors affecting the qualification for vulnerable groups is also considered a serious danger. Surrogate women may, in extreme cases, suffer health damage resulting in disability. Even more far-reaching consequences may occur in the case of births of children with disabilities. Such situations can generate both identity problems and those that can result from the unwillingness of the parents to take their child away. This then makes this child a "defective product," which from the perspective of the parents of intentions is not an adequate performance of the service of bringing a child into the world. In such a situation, the issues of violating the dignity and the need to protect children with disabilities as a cross-sensitive group are revealed even more.

Lack of willingness to take care of the child may also be the result of the breakdown of the intended parents' relationship. In this case, they or one of them may no longer be interested in providing surrogacy services and ultimately looking after the child. The legal system may not provide for the surrogate to be included as the mother of the child, or she may not be interested in it. Then, except that the child will be treated as abandoned or abandoned. American jurisprudence practice[70] then indicates the need to analyze the aspect of the "intention" of a child's calling and indicates as persons responsible for his fate intended parents, regardless of whether they are still in marital or partner relationships or not.

Freeman brings to the attention the other important aspects of the commercialization of reproduction. That it can affect children in two ways: by commercializing their further lives – somehow the "investment"[71] should, after all, bring a certain "rate of return" to meet expectations and balance the effort made for their vocation. Secondly, commercial practice in a commercially functioning world can also pose the risk of repetitive transactions. The child's sense of security, aware that his birth was the result of payment to his mother for births, may also include the fear that his further life, at some point, may also become the subject of a transaction and transfer to another family. This last aspect may also affect children who were earlier surrogate children. Interestingly, these children and their best interests in surrogation considerations are completely forgotten. It should be remembered that in this context two groups of children are at risk. Those who are current surrogate children (it is recommended that the surrogate candidate be a mother before) and those children who are intended parents and will only become siblings of a child coming from surrogacy (in this case these children can also be the result of such practices). As for the former, the fact that their mother's next child will be transferred to others certainly affects their sense of security, in the latter case it may aggravate identity problems.

The sense of relationship that can arise between a child and his siblings about to be born is completely ignored. Depending on the age of the child, their awareness of the fact that siblings are born from surrogacy procedures may, of course, vary. However, one cannot forget that immediate family members, including siblings, build a sense of identity. In the context of a broad understanding of the

---

70 *In re Marriage of Buzzanca*, 61 Cal. App. 4th 1410, 72 Cal. Rptr. 2d 280, 1998 Cal. App. LEXIS 180, 98 Cal. Daily Op. Service 1782, 77 A.L.R.5th 775, 98 Daily Journal DAR 2436 (Cal. App. 4th Dist. Mar. 10, 1998).

71 M. Freeman, "The New Birth Right?," p. 297.

concept of the best interests of the child, there is no justification for ignoring the good of those children who are the siblings of a child coming from surrogacy. This may be particularly important if there is genetic co-existence between these children (i.e. the egg was derived from a surrogate). One can imagine the situation when in adult life a need arises and siblings are sought to support medical therapies or, as is the case with seeking siblings, fulfilling the existing sense of lost bond going beyond the legal framework. On the other hand, the existence of a surrogacy practice involving the birth and surrender of a child may affect earlier surrogate children as some intimidation. If this child is to be born and is to be given away, then whether such a child may be in doubt, whether this practise of "giving back" will not include either him or his siblings growing up together with him. It seems that the complexity of surrogacy practices, including medical interference regarding the birth of a child, far exceeds the possibilities of surrogate children analyzing and understanding this. Even in a different situation, i.e. if a woman deciding to surrogate disconnected from her current children during the visible pregnancy and childbirth, this practice – at least a few months – may also have the most negative impact on the functioning of these children.

As the above examples and potential problems point out, there are still many issues to be investigated and regulated in depth. It seems that without taking initiative at the international level it will not be possible to guarantee adequate protection of vulnerable groups, which include women and children. These initiatives are necessary because of the increasingly frequent cases of cross-border surrogation. In this sphere, sometimes completely unexpected problems may arise, complicating the status of surrogate children, which is already more difficult and vulnerable. An example of such violations may be events in Ukraine that took place in connection with the COVID-19 epidemic. Due to the closing of state borders and the inability to enter the territory of Ukraine just in one clinic,[72] over fifty babies were waiting for intended parents. In addition to the already identified identity problems and the negative consequences of the lack of care of relatives after birth, there was however a difficulty. These children did not acquire Ukrainian citizenship, because under Ukrainian law as parents, the intended parents are entered in the birth certificate so that they can register the child and acquire their citizenship.

72 *Surrogacy: babies are waiting for their parents*, [online:] https://biotexcom.com [available: 17.04.2020].

The anticipated legal regulations should include, first, a reference to the assessment of surrogacy practices, both voluntary and commercial – in most legal systems it is attempted to prohibit them. Secondly, to ensure the effectiveness of the ban, recognition should be denied to foreign judgments or to regulate the status of a child only based on a surrogate motherhood agreement. Of course, in the case of a genetic or actual relationship between a child and one parent, it should be possible to regulate this relationship, but with a focus on the child's best interests. Perhaps in such cases solutions similar to those adopted should be adopted. The requirements should cover the period of contact, examination of parents' qualifications, training in which the parent or parents who led to the unlawful facts should participate. This would prevent the feeling of easy settlement of the state incompatible with applicable law and guarantee that the child's needs and his best interests are being effectively guided. To ensure the effectiveness of state regulation, they should also be obliged to introduce a system of sanctions against intermediaries, recruiters or other entities benefiting from illegal activities.

Bibliography:

Brodeala E., "The Legal Status of Assisted Human Reproduction in Romania. A Brief Discussion on Surrogacy," *Revista Română de Drept Comparat*, No. 1(56), 2016.

Czubik A., "Ochrona praw kobiet i zdrowia w prawie międzynarodowym publicznym versus *surrogacy business*," [in:] *Fundamentalne prawne problemy surrogate motherhood. Perspektywa krajowa*, ed. P. Mostowik, Warszawa 2019.

Doek J. E., *A Commentary on the United Nations Convention on the Rights of the Child, Articles 8–9: The Right to Preservation of Identity and The Right Not to Be Separated from His or Her Parents*, Leiden; Boston 2006.

Fines F., "European Protection for Women," [in:] *Protecting Vulnerable Groups: The European Human Rights Framework*, ed. F. Ippolito, S. Iglesias Sánchez, London 2015.

Freeman M., "The New Birth Right? Identity and the Child of the Reproduction Revolution," *International Journal of Children's Rights*, No. 273, 1996.

Hannum H., "The Status of the Universal Declaration of Human Rights in National and International Law," *Georgia Journal of International and Comparative Law*, 1996, Vol. 25(287).

Joseph S., Castan M., *The International Covenant on Civil and Political Rights Cases, Materials, and Commentary*, Oxford 2013.

Kuźnicka D., "Prawo do tożsamości jako prawo dziecka – wybrane zagadnienia," *Folia Iuridica Universitatis Wratislaviensis*, 2016, Vol. 5 (2).

Mohapatra S., "Adopting an International Convention on Surrogacy – A Lesson from Intercountry Adoption," *Loyola University Chicago International Law Review*, Vol. 13, 2015.

Nowak M., *U.N. Covenant on Civil and Political Rights: CCPR Commentary*, Kehl 2005.

Peters T., *For the Love of Children: Genetic Technology and the Future of the Family*, Westminster John Knox Press, 1996.

Stelmach J., Brożek B., Soniewicka M., Załuski W., *Paradoksy bioetyki prawniczej*, Warszawa 2010.

Storrow R. F., "International Surrogacy in the European Court of Human Rights," *North Carolina Journal of International Law and Commercial Regulation*, Vol. 43, 2018.

The UN Convention on the Rights of the Child: A Commentary, ed. J. Tobin, Oxford 2019.

Tobin J., "To prohibit or permit: what is the (human) rights responses to the practice of international commercial surrogacy?," *International and Comparative Law Quarterly*, Vol. 63, No. 2, 2014.

Wade K., "The regulation of surrogacy: a children's rights perspective," *Child and family law quarterly*, Vol. 29, 2017, available https://www.ncbi.nlm.nih.gov/pmc/articles/PMC5540169/# [available: 17.04.2020].

Wells-Greco M., *The status of children arising from inter-country surrogacy agreements: The Past the present the future*, The Hague 2016.

Olga Sitarz

University of Silesia in Katowice

e-mail: olga.sitarz@us.edu.pl

ORCID ID: 0000-0002-2075-3507

International law and national law of selected countries on the issue of infanticide

Abstract: This publication addresses the issue of the normative approach to the crime of infanticide in the light of each child's right to life. The question is whether the states – within the scope of their legislative duties – duly guarantee the right to life of the youngest members of society. In many countries (including Poland), in addition to the crime of murder, there is a special character – infanticide with a very mild punishment. The dogmatic and criminological analysis carried out justify the radical thesis that the concept of infanticide as a privileged type is a systemic, even normative discrimination against the weaker. It should be added that the essence of the problem is noticed by the Implementation Handbook for the Convention on the Rights of the Child, noting:

Many legal systems recognize the particular crime of infanticide as a distinctly defined form of homicide with reduced penalties. The ostensible intention is to provide a special defense for mothers suffering psychological trauma as a result of the process of birth. But by denoting a special and lesser crime, such laws appear to discriminate against children as victims of homicide.

Keywords: infanticide, postnatal abortion, the right to life, neonaticide

This publication addresses the issue of the normative approach to the crime of infanticide in the light of the right of every child to life. The question is whether the States – within the scope of their legislative duties – provide an adequate guarantee of the right to life of the youngest members of society.

1. Regulations of international law relating to the right to life of a child

The basic act of international law relating to children – Convention on the Rights of the Child[1] – in Art. 6 item 1 provides that "States Parties recognize that every child has the inherent right to life." In that regard, the regulations of the said Convention do not represent a significant breakthrough given that it reaffirms the right to life previously guaranteed in numerous other international treaties on fundamental rights.[2] By way of illustration, it should be pointed out that, under international law, the right to life is proclaimed, among others, by Art. 3 of the Universal Declaration of Human Rights, which States that everyone has the right to life, liberty and security of person. Moreover, the Convention for the Protection of Human Rights and Fundamental Freedoms of 4 November 1950 provides in Art. 2 that:

1. Everyone's right to life shall be protected by law. No one shall be deprived of his life intentionally save in the execution of a sentence of a court following his conviction of a crime for which this penalty is provided by law.
2. Deprivation of life shall not be regarded as inflicted in contravention of this article when it results from the use of force which is no more than absolutely necessary:
   a) in defence of any person from unlawful violence;
   b) in order to effect a lawful arrest or to prevent the escape of a person lawfully detained;
   c) in action lawfully taken for the purpose of quelling a riot or insurrection.[3]

---

1 Adopted and opened for signature, ratification and accession by General Assembly resolution 44/25 of 20 November 1989 entry into force 2 September 1990, in accordance with article 49, [online:] https://www.ohchr.org/EN/ProfessionalInterest/Pages/CRC.aspx [available: 25.10.2020].

2 Cf. E. E. Sutherland, "The Child's Right to Life, Survival and Development: Evolution and Progress," *STELL* LR 2015 2, [online:] https://www.researchgate.net/publication/304784603_The_Child's_Right_to_Life_Survival_and_Development_Evolution_and_Progress [available: 25.10.2020].

3 Convention for the Protection of Human Rights and Fundamental Freedoms, Rome, 04/11/1950 – Treaty open for signature by the member States of the Council of Europe and for accession by the European Union, [online:] https://www.coe.int/en/web/conventions/full-list/-/conventions/rms/0900001680063765 [available: 25.10.2020].

The acceptance by the State of commitments regarding respect for the child's right to life arising from ratified international agreements means that the State is to refrain from violating that right and take measures – including legislative – to effectively protect that right against violations by third persons.

2. The role of national law in protecting the child's life

Given that life is the most precious value and primary in relation to others, every legal system has provisions protecting that interest. At the level of criminal law, such protection is granted through the criminalization of behavior that undermines the legal interest in the form of human life. The criminal law protection of human life is typically very profound and extensive – not only intentional acts of deprivation of life are punishable, but also unintentional behavior resulting in death, actions that expose others to danger of loss of life, and even failure to provide help in a life-threatening situation. Euthanasia and assisted suicide are penalized in numerous countries. No legal system provides for an evaluation of human life; the intensity of criminal law protection does not depend on legal and social status or financial standing. The only exception is the age of the victim. Paradoxically, it seems that in many countries the (very young) age of the victim will in fact predispose the legislator to ease criminal liability. In addition to the standard crimes of homicide, murder and unintentional causing of death, such legal systems also include the offense of infanticide punishable by a substantially lower penalty as compared to the penalty provided for homicide. The matter is somewhat more complicated in view of the fact that, as a rule, it concerns not only the age of the victim.

3. Models of national legal systems relating to the problem of infanticide

Based on the monographic work prepared by Agnieszka Księżopolska-Breś,[4] it is crucial to indicate that there are a number of basic patterns/models of treating infanticide on the basis of European legislation:

Model I is characterized by a lack of separate article providing for penalty for infanticide; infanticide should be thus qualified as manslaughter (with exceptional articles which define a type of an aggravated form of manslaughter) or homicide treated less severely than the corresponding standard homicide.

---

4 A. Księżopolska-Breś, *Odpowiedzialność karna za dzieciobójstwo w prawie polskim*, Warsaw 2010, pp. 28–50.

Such solutions exist within criminal justice of Germany, France, Turkey and Hungary.

Model II provides for a separate article concerning infanticide, according to which extenuations include extra-labour causes (e.g. moral and material desertion by a mother of a newborn baby). An example of such regulation is article 578 of the Italian Penal Code.

Model III which utterly omits the influence of any factors on a parturient, either perinatal or bearing no relation to labour. The sole additional attribute of the act is time (most often the confinement period) which determines a mitigated penalty. Such model was applied in the penal codices of Bulgaria, Ukraine, Estonia, Norway, Albania and the Federation of Bosnia and Herzegovina.

Model IV which provides a separate article concerning infanticide, according to which the mitigating circumstances are time as well as the mental state of the mother. It is of utmost importance that the aforementioned circumstances constitute an alternative – thus, an infanticide may take the advantage of a more lenient provision if she performed the act during the period of confinement or under the influence of specified circumstances. Such solution was accepted in Switzerland, Sweden, Macedonia, Lithuania, Moldova and Russia.

Model V in which the article concerning infanticide bears the attributes of time and influence of perinatal circumstances, where both of the aforementioned attributes must appear jointly for it to be treated less severely than the corresponding standard homicide.

Model VI which completely omits time as one of the attributes of an offence, thus creating the type of homicide treated less severely than the corresponding standard homicide solely on the basis of mental or physical state of the mother (caused by confinement or occasionally also lactation). Regulations of this kind can be found in the penal codices of Malta, Finland or the British Infanticide Act 1938.

4. Legal regulations related to infanticide in selected countries

Katarzyna K. Borkowska prepared an interesting list of regulations applicable in the event of infanticide in selected 58 countries.[5] Having regard to the subject

5 K. K. Borkowska, *Przestępstwo dzieciobójstwa w ujęciu komparatystycznym*, Białystok 2018, unpublished doctoral thesis, pp. 465–482, [online:], https://repozytorium.uwb.edu.pl/jspui/bitstream/11320/7799/1/K_Borkowska_%20Przestepstwo_dzieciobojstwa_w_ujeciu_komparatystycznym.pdf [available: 25.10.2020].

of this publication and its basic research question, special attention should be paid to legislative solutions and their evolution in selected countries, which will provide a more wide-ranging view on the issue of criminal liability for infanticide.

4.1 France

With the entry into force of the Criminal Code of 1 March 1994, infanticide, which was considered one of the most controversial laws in French legislation over the past two centuries, lost the status of a *sui generis* crime. The elimination of the regulations on the crime of infanticide from the French Criminal Code was justified by its near disappearance in statistics. As regards intentional crimes against life, the following categories of homicide can currently be distinguished in the French Criminal Code: 1) homicide of the basic type; 2) aggravated homicide in the following categories: a) premeditated homicide (murder) – Art. 221–3, b) a concurrence of offenses, provided that the homicide precedes, accompanies or follows another crime – Art. 221–2, c) homicide aggravated by reason of the special status of the victim – Art. 221–4. One of the six prerequisites determining the exceptional status of the victim, on which the aggravation of criminal liability of the perpetrator rests, is the victim's age. Its upper limit set at 15 years of age of the child is not narrowed solely to the newborn, although currently the criminalization of infanticide occurs precisely on the basis of the aggravated homicide under analysis here. By repealing the previous regulations typifying infanticide as an independent crime, the French legislator drew attention to the fact that the bonds related to the child's origins do not constitute a specific context for the existence of the said prohibited act. Homicide under Art. 221–4 is punishable by a penalty of life imprisonment.[6]

4.2 Germany

In the second half of the eighteenth century, the analysis of the structure of the crime of infanticide became the focus of numerous German doctrinal studies. In 1780, Dalberg and Michaelis issued a call for a thesis on how to prevent that crime. The reasons why mothers committed such acts identified in the submitted dissertations included: the surroundings of the child-murderess (in particular her parents), social beliefs, and above all, the behavior of the child's

6 J. Brzezińska, "Regulacja przestępstwa dzieciobójstwa w wybranych państwach Europy Zachodniej," *Ius Novum* 59–3/2012, pp. 58–59.

father who left the single woman subjecting her to widespread harassment in her community. Notably, a specific aspect of the construction of the crime of infanticide in the considerations of German researchers concerns the motive of the loss of reputation by the pregnant woman. Gans recognized the existence of infanticide only where the perpetrator first concealed her condition, then the fact of childbirth and, as a consequence, her crime. That view was not fully accepted in the doctrine. Although it was widely seen that the concealment of pregnancy and childbirth may form the elements of the child-murderess' intention, in no way do they constitute the existence of infanticide. The term 'infanticide' appeared relatively early in German science, yet it was not until 1824 that the draft of the Bavarian Criminal Code drew attention in the structure of its relevant provision to the motive of disgrace and the woman's particular mental state caused by the delivery process resulting in her diminished sanity. That aspect was subsequently taken into account in the particular German regulations: Brunswick, Baden and Hamburg. The mother's anomalous behavior (resulting in the death of a newly born child) was justified above all by her insufficiently developed feeling of maternal love. In terms of the nature of criminalization, two separate groups of laws can be distinguished. The former included the Austrian regulation and the Brunswick Code. They introduced a differentiation in the level of penalties depending on the child's origins. Namely, paragraph 122 of the Austrian Code provided that a mother who kills her legitimate child shall be sentenced to life imprisonment in the harshest prison, the killing of an illegitimate child shall be punishable by a term of imprisonment between ten and 20 years; whereas in the case of the offense of abandonment, she shall be liable to a penalty of deprivation of liberty for a term between 5 and 10 years. In contrast, the Brunswick Code was definitely less casuistic in its regulation, it provided for a higher penalty of imprisonment for killing a legitimate child, while in the case of killing an illegitimate child, the penalty ranged between two and ten years of imprisonment.[7]

Another landmark codification of criminal law was the draft of the Prussian Criminal Code of 1851. The legislative act was prepared by the Ministry of Justice of Prussia, adopted by Parliament and finally approved by the king. The Act entered into force on 1 July 1851. Section 180 of the Act stated that

---

7 J. Brzezińska "Dzieciobójstwo w regulacjach wybranych państw Europy Zachodniej od starożytności do 1914 r.," *Wrocławskie Studia Erazmiańskie. Zeszyty Studenckie – Studia Erasmiana Wratislaviensia. Acta Studentium* 2009, Vol. 2, pp. 280–286, [online:] https://www.bibliotekacyfrowa.pl/Content/32207/0018.pdf [available: 25.10.2020].

a mother who intentionally kills her illegitimate child during or immediately after delivery shall be punishable by a penalty of imprisonment from 5 to 20 years. The legislation of 1851 was largely reproduced in the law of the German Empire and formed the core of the criminal law of 1871. The original intention of the legislator was to adopt the constituent elements of the crime of infanticide essentially unchanged, while at the same time modify the severity of the penalty. In the first draft of the Act of 1869, the offense of infanticide of the basic type was punishable by a penalty of imprisonment from two to ten years, while in less serious cases – from two to five years. The legislator substantiated the need to ease criminal repression for infanticide by referring to the special nature of that criminal act and various reasons reducing the level of the perpetrator's culpability. The initial proposal submitted by the legislators was commented critically by the legal community. The objections concerned above all the inability to predict the impact of the delivery on the woman immediately after its completion, and in particular the lack of a direct causal relationship between the completed childbirth and the decision to kill the newly born child, as well as the insufficient determination of the constituent elements of the offense leading to the unnecessary distinction between infanticide and murder or homicide.[8]

Section 217 of the German Criminal Code (StGB) which typified the crime of infanticide underwent final amendment in 1953 to be worded as follows:

> A mother who kills her illegitimate child during or immediately after delivery incurs a penalty of imprisonment for a term not shorter than 3 years. In less serious cases, a penalty of between 6 months and 5 years of imprisonment is imposed.

It was widely argued in the doctrine of German criminal law that the prerequisites justifying more lenient treatment of mothers killing their illegitimate children became anachronistic and fictitious. The substantial increase in the number of children born outside marriage resulting from a growing number of informal relationships called into question the very motive of women seeking to save their own reputation, given the equal social status enjoyed by married and unmarried mothers alike. Moreover, in the 1990s, it was a widely held view that the provision of section 217 StGB was not properly structured since it allowed unlawful differential treatment of children on grounds of their origins and mothers as regards their marital situation, which was untenable in the light of the provisions of the German Constitution which prohibits treating

8 K.K. Borkowska, "Przestępstwo dzieciobójstwa. . .."

comparable situations differently. Despite all the objections to the shape of the German regulations on infanticide (§ 217 StGB), attempts were made to retain them in the criminal code but in a heavily revised version. However, the proposed legislative amendments failed to win strong endorsement and ultimately, in the face of growing criticism, the German legislator chose to eliminate the regulation of the crime of infanticide altogether.[9]

On 26 January 1998, the German Parliament adopted the so-called Sixth Reform of the Criminal Law Act (*das Sechste Gesetz zur Reform des Strafrechts*), which abolished the crime of infanticide after 127 years of its presence. Since then, the killing of a newborn by his mother is qualified as a homicide (§ 212 DStGB – *Totschlag*) or as a murder (§ 211 DStGB – *Mord*).[10] It is accepted in the doctrine that the special psychological situation of the mother accompanying the killing of her child justifies the application to her of the provision of § 213 StGB ("less serious case of homicide").[11] The proponents of the reform of criminal law indicated the following objectives of the new law: harmonization of the penalty system, the need to amend, complement or modernize the provisions, which was intended to ensure better protection of legal rights, facilitate the application of law and eliminate outdated and unnecessary provisions. Further, the proponents of the reform relied on the fact that the crime of infanticide played a marginal role in judicial practice. In support of that view, reference was made to the figures from 1986 to 1994 indicating that annually from one to 12 preparatory proceedings regarding infanticide were conducted, leading to convictions in one to ten cases a year.[12]

4.3 Italy

Pursuant to Art. 578 of the Italian Criminal Code,

> the mother causing the death of her newborn immediately after childbirth, or of the fetus during childbirth, when the fact is determined by conditions of material and moral abandonment directly related to childbirth, is punished with imprisonment from 4 to 10 years.[13]

It should be noted that Art. 2 of the Act of 5 August 1981 (Act No. 442) previously in force stated that

---

9 J. Brzezińska, "Dzieciobójstwo w regulacjach...," pp. 60–64.
10 K.K. Borkowska, "Przestępstwo dzieciobójstwa...," pp. 320–321.
11 J. Brzezińska, "Dzieciobójstwo w regulacjach...," pp. 60–64.
12 K.K. Borkowska, "Przestępstwo dzieciobójstwa...," pp. 327–328.
13 J. Brzezińska, "Dzieciobójstwo w regulacjach...," p. 65.

> Whoever causes the death of a newborn immediately after childbirth, or of the fetus during childbirth, to save their own honour or that of their closest relative, is punished with imprisonment from 3 to 10 years.

It is emphasized in modern doctrine that the conditions of moral and material abandonment occur when the woman giving birth finds herself at the time of childbirth or immediately after it in a state of complete isolation (of a social nature), which consists in her abandonment and lack of intervention and any help (physical and moral) from third parties and lack of material or moral support.[14]

4.4 The United Kingdom[15]

Katarzyna K. Borkowska points to the absence of a single consistent trend in the history of legal policy towards infanticide in the United Kingdom. The period of state acquiescence to infanticide drew to a close with the Stuart Bastardy Act of 1623, in particular, An Act to Prevent the Destroying and Murthering of Bastard Children. The introduction to the Act states that

> whereas many lewd Women that have been delivered of Bastard Children, to avoid their Shame, and to escape Punishment, do secretly bury or conceal the Death of their Children, and after, if the Child be found dead, the said Woman do alledge, that the said Child was born dead.

The 1623 Act came under heavy criticism in the seventeenth century. As a consequence, it was repealed by the Act of 1803, which equated infanticide with murder. In 1922, the Parliament adopted the Infanticide Act, which concerned the mother killing her newly born child in a state of mental disturbance – a woman causes the death of her newborn child, but

> at the time of the act or omission the balance of her mind was disturbed by reason of her not having fully recovered from the effect of giving birth to the child.

It was the first English law that directly linked the killing of a child with disorders in the mother's psyche ("the balance of her mind was disturbed"). In 1938, Lord Dawson, President of the Royal College of Physicians, presented

---

14 Ibidem, pp. 65–67.

15 For a detailed historical review of the British regulation on infanticide Cf. M. Oberman, "Mothers Who Kill: Coming to Terms with Modern American Infanticide," *DePaul Journal of Health Care Law*, Vol. 8, No. 1, Fall 2004. Cf. also A. Малешина, *Преступления против жизни в странах общего права*, Moscow 2017, p. 323 et seq.

a bill that proposed extending the definition of infanticide to the killing of a child under 1 year of age. The argument advanced in support of that solution was the fact that the balance of the mother's mind may be disturbed by delivery and its consequences, among others, lactation process.[16] The bill was adopted by Parliament, the Infanticide Act 1938 repealed the previous regulation of 1922. It has the following wording:

> At the time of the act or omission the balance of her mind was disturbed by reason of her not having fully recovered from the effect of giving birth to the child or by reason of the effect of lactation consequent upon the birth of the child.

The act is valid until today in England and Wales, and in 1939 it was adopted in the same wording in Northern Ireland.[17] As indicated in the literature, that regulation is based on an outdated concept of lactational insanity,[18] but the social need for a more lenient punishment of infanticide resulted in the archaic provision not being removed. In practice, women are convicted of infanticide, although no mental disorders are demonstrated.[19]

4.5 Polish criminal law solutions regarding the murder of a newborn child by own mother

In this context, reference should also be made to the Polish solutions. All the last three Polish codes (1932, 1969 and 1997) provided for a separate, privileged type of crime – infanticide. The provision currently in force bears the following wording:

> A mother who kills an infant during the period of delivery under the influence of its course, is subject to the penalty of deprivation of liberty for between three months and five years.

Notably, doubts are expressed among some Polish academics who call this provision obscurantist.[20] There have been calls for its detypification – its removal

16 It was assumed that childbirth and lactation cause women high stress. It was thought that in certain circumstances stress leads to madness during which attempted infanticides and suicides are quite common: S.E. Pitt, E.M. Bale, "Neonaticide, Infanticide, and Filicide: A Review of the Literature," *Bull Am Acad Psychiatry Law*, Vol. 23, No. 3, 1995, p. 376.

17 K.K. Borkowska, "Przestępstwo dzieciobójstwa...," pp. 386–389.

18 S.E. Pitt, E. M. Bale, "Neonaticide, Infanticide, and Filicide...," p. 376.

19 S. H. Fiedman, P. J. Resnick, "Child murder by mothers: patterns and prevention," *World Psychiatry*, 6(3)/2007, pp. 137–141.

20 K. Daszkiewicz, "O dzieciobójstwie (w świetle kodeksu karnego z 6 czerwca 1997 r.)," *Palestra*, Vol. 5–6, 1998, p. 38.

from the criminal justice system.[21] There is no doubt that the provision refers only to the influence of delivery, which should be understood as biological and physiological. Nonetheless, the case-law includes views broadening the notion of "influence" to cover difficult life situations that the legislator chose not to make reference to. For instance, the Court of Appeals in Krakow stated that

> The intention to commit infanticide under the influence of delivery (Art. 149 of the Criminal Code) is the result of a set of psychophysical, psychological, physiological and social factors related to both delivery and the mother's life situation. There are no cases of the release of aggression caused only by the course of delivery unaccompanied by other factors, and if they occur, they should be evaluated according to sanity criteria as pathological cases.[22]

The correct interpretation of the provision was made by the Court of Appeals in Wrocław which stated that

> Recognition that the defendant's behavior satisfies the constituent elements of the subjective and objective sides of the offense under Art. 149 of the Criminal Code requires determining that the influence of delivery disturbed the mental functions of the defendant and "triggered" the intention to cause the death of the newborn. The lack of symptoms of disturbance of the mental processes of the woman giving birth excludes the possibility of applying the provision of Art. 149 of the Criminal Code as the basis of liability for the death of a newly born child ... The current structure of the crime of infanticide excludes any influence of exogenic (social and environmental) factors on the mother giving birth. The provision of Art. 149 of the Criminal Code clearly indicates the influence of only endogenic factors. Social (exogenic) factors may only affect the level of penalty.[23]

4.6 Ways of defining infanticide in the provisions of criminal law: Summary

On the whole, it should be stated that in various systems providing for a separate type of infanticide, the privileged type of that crime is underpinned by, among others, such circumstances as the influence or effect of the course of

---

21 O. Sitarz, *Ochrona praw dziecka w polskim prawie karnym na tle postanowień Konwencji o prawach dziecka*, Katowice 2002, pp. 71–72. Cf. also: D. Lorek, O. Sitarz, "Children's Right to Life in Polish Penal Law," *Children's European Citizenship*, Vol.1, No. 1, May 2011, [online:] http://www.csmcd.eu/downloads/lorek_full_paper.pdf [available: 25.10.2020].

22 Ruling of the Court of Appeals in Krakow of 24 October 2002, II AKa 256/02, KZS 2002, No. 12, item 34.

23 Judgment of the Court of Appeals of 16 September 2015 (II AKa 212/15).

delivery on the woman giving birth, as well as the related changes occurring in her psyche (e.g. lactation). This means that the legislators in those countries provide for the possibility of mental disturbances caused by childbirth. Thus, the legislation typically identifies as the constituent element of the prohibited act the agitated state of mind (*der aufgewühlte Gemütszustand*), state of exhaustion (*der Zustand der Erschöpfung*), weakness, confusion or helplessness (*die Schwachung, die Verwirrung, die Ratlosigkeit*), failure to recover from childbirth (by reason of her not having fully recovered from the effect of giving birth). Sometimes the legislator simply requires that the delivery exerts influence on the woman (*der Einfluss*) or results in her confusion (*die Verwirrung*). Another reason for the existence of infanticide as a *sui generis* crime is the whole life situation of the woman giving birth, in particular her material and family situation. The legislator is aware of the role of public pressure on the woman giving birth. In that case, the delivery itself is not a criminogenic factor – the perpetrator's motivational process is located in her life situation. The mother either finds herself in an emergency situation (*eine Notsituation*) or her general life situation is difficult (*die Bedrängnis*). The legislator may indicate explicitly the economic reasons (*inter alia* Italy) or refer to the whole life situation of the woman giving birth. Some systems identify shame (*die Schande*), defending the honor of the woman (*la deshonra matare*), intention to hide the childbirth (*para. ocultar*) or saving one's own honor or that of one's family (*para. salvar el propio honor o el honor del cónyuge, o de un pariente próximo*) as the explicit condition.[24]

5. The criminological picture of infanticide

The assessment of the adequacy and correctness of the presented regulations cannot be carried out separately without the identification of the criminological aspects of infanticide around the world. First of all, a clear downward trend in the number of infanticides may be observed in Poland. Whereas in the 1920, more than a thousand infanticides were reported annually in Poland, there are several or a dozen such cases per year in the twenty-first century. A. Gałęska-Śliwka identifies the amendments introduced into Polish law by the legislator as one of the possible reasons for this state of affairs. Namely, the adopted regulations allow the newborn to be left in the hospital after birth without any

24 K.K. Borkowska, "Przestępstwo dzieciobójstwa w ujęciu komparatystycznym. . .," p. 390.

consequences.[25] A similar role is played by so-called baby hatches which ensure the anonymity of persons abandoning their child.[26] It is difficult to agree with those arguments given the small number of children abandoned in hospitals or baby hatches. Those numbers are certainly not comparable with the pre-war statistics on infanticide. The observed decline must therefore result from cultural and social changes.

5.1 Typology of infanticide in criminological terms

In the light of criminological studies, the killing of a child reveals all the complexity of that social phenomenon occurring all over the world in all periods of history.[27] The concept of 'infanticide' used in the Polish science of criminal law is grossly misleading and simplifying. In the English-language literature, criminologists use three different terms in order to convey the scope of the concept of killing a child. The killing of a child by the mother during childbirth is called *neonaticide*, while the killing of an older child by a parent is known by the term *filicide*. In contrast, the term infanticide is a general term used to define the killing of a child, sometimes used to describe a particular form of the crime of killing a child of a certain age (typically up to the age of one).[28]

From the perspective of this work, it is particularly important to distinguish between killing a child as *neonaticide* and *filicide*. These are essentially different types of behavior in terms of the circle of perpetrators, as well as the motivations driving the perpetrators to kill a child.

The killings of a child in its first day of life are generally carried out in two forms – typically handicapped or unwanted children are killed,[29] with the latter type prevailing in Poland. The perpetrators are mostly young, unmarried women having an unwanted pregnancy who have not received prenatal care.

25 A. Gałęska-Śliwka, *Dzieciobójstwo. Analiza karno-medyczna*, Toruń 2011, p. 14.

26 M. Prusik, "Dzieciobójstwo w aspekcie historycznym, prawnokarnym, społecznym oraz kryminologicznym," *Kortowski Przegląd Prawniczy* 2013, Vol. 1, p. 48, [online:] http://wpia.uwm.edu.pl/czasopisma/sites/default/files/uploads/KPP/2013/1/48-57.pdf [available: 25.10.2020].

27 Its diversity and variability over the years is shown in K.L. Moseley, "The History of Infanticide in Western Society," *Issues in Law and Medicine* 1/1986, pp. 345–361.

28 S.E. Pitt, E.M. Bale, "Neonaticide, Infanticide, and Filicide: A Review of the Literature...;" S.H. Fiedman, P.J. Resnick, "Child murder by mothers: patterns and prevention...," pp. 137–141.

29 K.L. Moseley, "The History of Infanticide...," p. 345.

They tend to be poorly educated, live in poverty and are often unemployed.[30] American studies established that those women conceal their pregnancy and isolate themselves from their surroundings.[31] Notably, they do not have any plans for the childbirth or the period after the childbirth.[32] Other studies revealed that the cause of murder of newly born children is shame and guilt about the conception of an illegitimate child.[33] That category also includes killings in developing countries (e.g. Asia) because of the child's sex, with homicide as a form of selection.[34]

The perpetrators of the killings referred to as *filicide* are most often people suffering from depression, with psychotic disorders, who previously benefited from psychological assistance, with suicidal ideation. Criminologists differentiate five types of motivation in that group of crimes:[35] 1) *altruistic filicide* – a child is killed for love or out of a sense of responsibility; the perpetrator is convinced that insurmountable difficulties do not allow the child to live, or alternatively, the killing of a child is part of so-called extended suicide not allowing the parent to leave the child alone; euthanasia is regarded as a special variation of that type; 2) *acutely psychotic filicide* – the perpetrator suffers from a mental illness, hallucination, epilepsy or delirium; it seems that this category may include deep postpartum depression (which usually occurs around 2–3 weeks after delivery),[36] mention is also made in the literature of *postpartum psychosis* which occurs most often within three months after delivery in one in 1,000 women giving birth;[37] 3) *unwanted filicide* – a born child is an obstacle in life; such a perception of the role of the child does not have to develop before or just after delivery, but at a later stage of life; 4) *accidental filicide* (*fatal maltreatment filicide*) – in this case the death of a child is the result of the abuse of

30 S.H. Fiedman, P.J. Resnick, "Child murder…," pp. 137–141.

31 M. Oberman, "Mothers Who Kill: Coming to Terms with Modern American Infanticide," *DePaul Journal of Health Care Law* 2004, Vol. 8, No. 1, p. 29.

32 S.E. Pitt, E.M. Bale, "Neonaticide…."

33 S.E. Pitt, E.M. Bale, "Neonaticide…," p. 380.

34 S.H. Fiedman, P.J. Resnick, "Child murder…," pp. 137–141. Cf. also "Women and Children: The Double Dividend of Gender Equality: The State of the World's Children 2007," The United Nations Children's Fund (UNICEF), 2006, [online:]. https://www.unicef.org/publications/files/The_State_of_the_Worlds__Children__2007_e.pdf [available: 25.10.2020].

35 S.H. Fiedman, P.J. Resnick, "Child murder…," pp. 137–141.

36 A. Gałęska-Śliwka, "Dzieciobójstwo. Analiza karno-medyczna …," p. 116.

37 M. Oberman, "Mothers…," pp. 39–42.

the child by the perpetrator, without the intention of homicide;[38] and 5) *spouse revenge filicide* – the killing of a child is a way of causing pain to a partner by whom the perpetrator was betrayed (it is an extremely rare case, and as an illustration, the Greek myth of Medea, who killed two sons after discovering her husband's betrayal, is recalled).[39] It should be mentioned that men may also be the perpetrators in that group,[40] which nonetheless happens relatively infrequently.

5.2 Postnatal abortion

Moreover, the concept of "after-birth abortion" as a synonym for infanticide emerged in the ethical and moral discussion referring to the phenomenon in question. In the opinion of the proponents of that concept, such a type of abortion should be as legal as "proper" abortion. Alberto Giubilini and Francesca Minerva[41] argue that there is no moral difference between abortion and the killing of children: "Both a fetus and a newborn certainly are human beings and potential persons, but neither is a 'person' in the sense of 'subject of a moral right to life." They are of the opinion that parents should be given a possibility of killing a child if it turns out that he is disabled, which they did not know before the birth of the child, and cite the statistics showing that "only 64 % of Down syndrome cases in Europe are diagnosed based on prenatal tests." The authors concluded: "what we call 'after-birth abortion' (killing a newborn) should be permissible in all the cases where abortion is, including cases where the newborn is not disabled."

---

38 In that regard, for a thorough analysis of killing a child in the family as a result of violence in the light of various theories Cf. A. Latoś, *Matki zabójczynie. Teoretyczno-metodologiczny model badań nad zjawiskiem oraz możliwości oddziaływań resocjalizacyjnych*, Bydgoszcz 2017, pp. 61–99.

39 Cf. Trzaska N., "Kto zabił dzieci Medei," paper presented at a conference titled: "The Image of an Ideal Woman in Greek and Roman Literature," the University of Gdańsk 2–3.12.2016, [online:] https://www.researchgate.net/publication/311572468_Kto_zabil_dzieci_Medei [available: 25.10.2020].

40 S.E. Pitt, E.M. Bale, "Neonaticide. . .."

41 A. Giubilini, F. Minerva, "After-birth abortion: why should the baby live?," *Journal of Medical Ethics* 2013, Vol. 39, pp. 261–263. Besides, it should be noted that an interesting answer was prepared by Bertha Alvarez Manninen, "Yes, the baby should live: a pro-choice response to Giubilini and Minerva," *Journal of Medical Ethics*, Vol. 39, No. 5, [online:] https://www.academia.edu/10163793/Yes_the_baby_should_live [available: 25.10.2020].

6. Conclusions

The above observations allow for the formulation of two basic conclusions. First, the criminal law regulations creating a privileged type of homicide based on the influence of the process of delivery or lactation on the mother's psyche certainly do not correspond in any way to the scientific findings regarding the real causes of killing one's own child. This is shown by a big fall in the number of killings of newly born children (neonaticides) over the years, while the process of childbirth and lactation has not changed. In addition, a more lenient penalty applies only to the mother's behavior consisting solely of killing her own child. Should the legislators indeed recognize that the woman's psyche is in a weaker condition during that period, all her acts would by law be punishable by a lighter penalty. Secondly, in the case of regulations that do not indicate any causes of infanticide or take into account real causes (poverty, helplessness, a sense of shame or disgrace), the question arises whether these are sufficient factors for such a drastic reduction of the applicable penalties, all the more so given that the mitigation of penalty applies only to mothers and their youngest children.

Michelle Oberman could conceivably be right in her assertion that

> At a visceral level, the horror of infanticide seems to grow as the victim's age increases. Thus, there is a strong temptation to regard the killings of infants after the first twenty-four hours of life as ordinary murders and to distinguish neonaticide alone as uniquely problematic.[42]

It should be emphasized that the real reasons for infanticide revealed in criminological studies also do not justify the perpetration of ordinary homicide or any other crime – they do not constitute statutory mitigating circumstances. The question thus remains why they drastically reduce the level of penalty in the situation where a mother kills her child in the first day of its life. Michelle Oberman makes her point in no uncertain terms when she writes that

> only since the Second World War has the contraceptive pill, the intrauterine device, and the legalization of abortion removed all valid excuses for unwanted pregnancy or infanticide. To the extent that these problems still exist, at least in western society, they are due primarily to carelessness, ignorance, or indifference.[43]

The above reflections justify the radical thesis that the concept of infanticide as a privileged type is a systemic, even normative discrimination against the

42 M. Oberman, "Mothers Who Kill. . .," p. 36.
43 M. Oberman, "Mothers Who Kill. . .," p. 24.

weaker. By the same token, the aforementioned after-birth abortion appears to be an extreme form of that discrimination.

The essence of the problem is recognized in the Implementation Handbook for the Convention on the Rights of the Child[44] which takes notice of the fact that

> Many legal systems recognize the particular crime of infanticide as a distinctly defined form of homicide with reduced penalties. The ostensible intention is to provide a special defence for mothers suffering psychological trauma as a result of the process of birth. But by denoting a special and lesser crime, such laws appear to discriminate against children as victims of homicide.[45]

This view should be fully shared. Mention must also be made of the provision of Art. 3 of the Convention on the Rights of the Child:

> In all actions concerning children, whether undertaken by public or private social welfare institutions, courts of law, administrative authorities or legislative bodies, the best interests of the child shall be a primary consideration.

This rule is particularly important in the case of very young, immature children, completely dependent on adults.[46] The Committee on the Rights of the Child has highlighted in article 3(1), that the best interests of the child shall be

44 [online:] http://www.unicef.org.tr/files/bilgimerkezi/doc/Implementation_Handbook_for_the_Convention_on_the_Rights_of_the_Child.pdf [available: 25.10.2020].

45 *Implementation Handbook for the Convention on the Rights of the Child*, prepared for UNICEF by Rachel Hodgkin & Peter Newell, UNICEF 1998, p. 92. The following excerpt of the document may well serve as an illustration of the extreme form of that type of legislation: "The Committee told the Islamic Republic of Iran: "The Committee reiterates its serious concern at article 220 of the Penal Code, which provides that fathers who kill their child, or their son's child, are only required to pay one third of the blood money to the mother, and are subjected to a discretionary punishment, in the event that the mother makes a formal complaint." The Committee recommends that the State Party take the necessary measures, including the amendment of the offending article of the Penal Code, to ensure that there is no discriminatory treatment for such crimes and that prompt and thorough investigations and prosecutions are carried out (Islamic Republic of Iran CR/C/15/Add.254, paras. 31 and 32)."

46 "Because of their relative immaturity young children are often reliant on parents and the authorities to uphold their best interests. Where legal decisions relating to individual children are concerned, States are urged to arrange for independent representation of the child's best interests. In addition, all laws, policies, administration and service provision that directly or indirectly impact on young children must take account of their best interests." *Implementation Handbook for the Convention on*

a primary consideration in all actions concerning children, as one of the general principles of the Convention on the Rights of the Child, alongside article 6.[47] The Committee on the Rights of the Child has very frequently referred to circumstances in which the State is failing to adequately provide for particular groups of vulnerable children. The contents of the Handbook lead to the conclusion that children in the period of early childhood belong to that range.[48] This means that in the event of a conflict of interest between parents and the child in the period of early childhood, it is the child's interest that should prevail. It should be stressed that the balancing takes place between the child's life and – if the real reasons for infanticide are accepted – the helplessness, loneliness, economic situation, fear and shame of the mother. Therefore, the question whether the legislative solutions providing for the privileged type of infanticide constitute an adequate instrument that allows to fully integrate the principle of the best interests of the child into the legal system is of a rhetorical nature. It is certainly not the case.

Bibliography:

Borkowska K.K., *Przestępstwo dzieciobójstwa w ujęciu komparatystycznym*, Białystok 2018, unpublished doctoral thesis, pp. 465–482, [online:] https://repozytorium.uwb.edu.pl/jspui/bitstream/11320/7799/1/K_Borkowska_%20Przestepstwo_dzieciobojstwa_w_ujeciu_komparatystycznym.pdf.

Brzezińska J., "Dzieciobójstwo w regulacjach wybranych państw Europy Zachodniej od starożytności do 1914 r.," *Wrocławskie Studia Erazmiańskie. Zeszyty Studenckie – Studia Erasmiana Wratislaviensia. Acta Studentium* 2009, Vol. 2, pp. 280–286, [online:] https://www.bibliotekacyfrowa.pl/Content/32207/0018.pdf [available: 25.10.2020]

Brzezińska J., "Regulacja przestępstwa dzieciobójstwa w wybranych państwach Europy Zachodniej," *Ius Novum* 2012, Vol. 59, No. 3.

Daszkiewicz K., "O dzieciobójstwie (w świetle kodeksu karnego z 6 czerwca 1997 r.)," *Palestra* 1998, Vol. 5–6.

Fiedman S. H., Resnick P. J., "Child murder by mothers: patterns and prevention," *World Psychiatry* 2007, Vol. 6(3).

---

the Rights of the Child, prepared for UNICEF by Rachel Hodgkin & Peter Newell, UNICEF 1998, p. 242.

47 *Implementation Handbook for the Convention on the Rights of the Child*, prepared for UNICEF by Rachel Hodgkin & Peter Newell, UNICEF 1998, p. 35.

48 Ibidem, p. 41.

Gałęska-Śliwka A., *Dzieciobójstwo. Analiza karno-medyczna*, Toruń 2011.

A. Giubilini, F. Minerva, "After-birth abortion: why should the baby live?," *Journal of Medical Ethics* 2013, Vol. 39.

Księżopolska-Breś A., *Odpowiedzialność karna za dzieciobójstwo w prawie polskim*, Warsaw 2010.

Sutherland C. E. E., "The Child's Right to Life, Survival and Development: Evolution and Progress," *STELL* 2015, Vol. 2, [online:] https://www.researchgate.net/publication/304784603_The_Child's_Right_to_Life_Survival_and_Development_Evolution_and_Progress.

Latoś A., *Matki zabójczynie. Teoretyczno-metodologiczny model badań nad zjawiskiem oraz możliwości oddziaływań resocjalizacyjnych*, Bydgoszcz 2017.

Lorek D., Sitarz O., "Children's Right to Life in Polish Penal Law," *Children's European Citizenship* 2011, Vol.1, No. 1.

Малешина А, *Преступления против жизни в странах общего права*, Moscow 2017.

Manninen B.A., "Yes, the baby should live: A pro-choice response to Giubilini and Minerva," *Journal of Medical Ethics*, Vol. 39, No.5, [online:] https://www.academia.edu/10163793/Yes_the_baby_should_live.

Moseley K.L., "The History of Infanticide in Western Society," *Issues in Law and Medicine* 1986, Vol. 1.

Oberman M., "Mothers Who Kill: Coming to Terms with Modern American Infanticide," *DePaul Journal of Health Care Law* 2004, Vol. 8, No. 1.

Pitt S.E., Bale E.M., "Neonaticide, Infanticide, and Filicide: A Review of the Literature," *Bull Am Acad Psychiatry Law* 1995, Vol. 23, No. 3.

Prusik M., "Dzieciobójstwo w aspekcie historycznym, prawnokarnym, społecznym oraz kryminologicznym," *Kortowski Przegląd Prawniczy* 2013, Vol. 1, p. 48, [online:] http://wpia.uwm.edu.pl/czasopisma/sites/default/files/uploads/KPP/2013/1/48-57.pdf.

Sitarz O., *Ochrona praw dziecka w polskim prawie karnym na tle postanowień Konwencji o prawach dziecka*, Katowice 2002.

Joanna Markiewicz - Stanny

University of Zielona Góra

e-mail: j.markiewicz-stanny@wpa.uz.zgora.pl

ORCID ID: 0000-0002-1842-7243

Age assessment procedures and the protection of children's rights: an analysis of international standards

Abstract: The subject of this paper is a relationship between the procedures for assessing the age of foreigners and enjoying by children of their rights guaranteed in international documents. On the one hand the recognition of a person as being a child has fundamental significance for benefitting of this status and necessity to draw special attention to the particularly vulnerable situation of unaccompanied and separated children. On the other hand, age assessment requires the use of measures that involve interference with the privacy and autonomy of individuals. In the case of medical examination, this is not only invasive, but also very often connected at risk of error. Bearing this in mind it is necessary to establish under what circumstances age assessments should be carried out in the light of provisions of the Convention of the Rights of the Child and other human rights treaties.

Keywords: age assessment, rights of the child, vulnerability

1. Introductory remarks

This research paper is dedicated to the subject matter of an admissibility of applying an age assessment procedure in respect of the foreigners from a point of view of the international law standards, with a particular reference to a protection of the children's rights. The addressed issue is complex since, on the one hand, estimating how old an individual is can play an important role as a guarantee in respecting and protecting the rights of the minors; in some cases, this is not only legally substantiated, but even necessary. On the other hand, the incorrect actions of the states in this respect can be and are an area of infringements of the children's rights, and more broadly of the human rights.

The need for age assessment is closely related not only to an irregular migration, but also to a global increase in a quantity of children whose identity – including age – is not properly documented. It is indicated that a number of the unregistered[1] or stateless children is constantly increasing due to, inter alia, an exclusion[2] or administrative barriers, as well as due to the provisions preventing the acquisition of a citizenship through mother.[3]

The subject matter of considerations are those actions of the public authorities that are aimed at estimating a chronological age of a given individual.[4] From the point of view of the legal standards, an age limit specified in years is a key manner of determining whether a person is a child which is based in Art. 1 of the Convention on the Rights of the Child. However, sometimes other criteria are also adopted for determining a maturity of an individual by indicating their biological, social or psychological age.[5]

---

1 Cf. L. Keith, "Risks of statelessness for children of undocumented parents in Europe," [in:] *The Worlds Stateless Children*, Institute of Statelessness and Inclusion 2017, pp. 267–274.

2 In case of Europe, the problem of children of Roma origin deserves attention; cf. E. Rozzi, "Out of limbo: Promoting the right of undocumented and stateless Roma people to a legal status in Italy through community-based paralegals," [in:] *The Worlds...*, pp. 427–429.

3 See UN High Commissioner for Refugees (UNHCR), *Background Note on Gender Equality, Nationality Laws and Statelessness 2018*, 8 March 2018, [online:] https://www.refworld.org/docid/5aa10fd94.html [available: 23.05.2020]; UNHCR, *I'm here, I belong: The Urgent Need to End Childhood Statelessness – UNHCR*, Statelessness Report, 2015, p. 6.

4 It should be noted already here that it is not appropriate to use the term: "determination of age" because of the margin of error inscribed in the use of all currently used researches. Cf. inter alia *UNHCR observations on the use of age assessments in the identification of separated or unaccompanied children seeking asylum*, Geneva 2015, par.9 (i); cf. V. Feltz, *Unaccompanied Minors: When European countries deny children their childhood*, Doctors of the World – Médecins du Monde International Network, August 2015, pp. 5–8.

5 Cf. T. Smith, L. Brownlees, *Age assessment practices: a literature review & annotated bibliography*, Discussion Paper, UNICEF 2011, pp. 7–8; By way of example: the level of moral and psychological development and discernment are indicated as elements that should affect an assessment of the ability to incur criminal liability – Cf. Commentary to par. 4.1 United Nations Standard Minimum Rules for the Administration of Juvenile Justice (The Beijing Rules, 1985), Adopted by General Assembly Resolution 40/33 of 29 November 1985.

As a preliminary remark, it should be mentioned that there are no treaty standards at international law level which in explicit terms refer to the rules of age assessment. The standards in this respect arise as a result of the interpretation of the provisions of the Convention on the Rights of the Child,[6] the Convention relating to the Status of Refugees,[7] as well as general standards in the field area of human rights protection.

However, this matter was directly regulated in EU law in Article 25 par. 5 Directive on common procedures for granting and withdrawing international protection.[8] In the migration context, the *soft law* documents should also be considered, i.e. primarily *the UNHCR Guidelines on Policies and Procedures in dealing with Unaccompanied Children Seeking Asylum*[9] and *the UNHCR Guidelines on International Protection no 8* from 2009.[10]

The subject of the article refers to age assessment "procedures" to emphasize that in the perspective of children's rights, it is appropriate to perceive this issue in terms of the entire sequence of decisions and actions of the authorities. In essence – as it will be further elaborated – the protection of children's rights requires, firstly, consideration of the decision itself to carry out actions aimed at estimating an age, secondly, a choice of appropriate research methods carried out in the right conditions and safeguarding the rights of the individual concerned, and thirdly, a proper interpretation the results obtained and a determination of the resulting legal effects.

---

6 Convention on the Rights of the Child, 20 November 1989, United Nations, Treaty Series, Vol. 1577, p. 3. It came into force for Poland on 7 July 1991 (Dz. U. 1991, No. 120, item 526).

7 Convention relating to the Status of Refugees, 28 July 1951, United Nations, Treaty Series, Vol. 189, p. 137 and Protocol relating to the Status of Refugees New York, 31 January 1967, United Nations, Treaty Series, Vol. 606, p. 267. It came into force for Poland on 26 December 1991 (Dz. U. 1991, No. 119, item 515, 517).

8 Directive 2013/32/EU of the European Parliament and of the Council of June 26, 2013 on common procedures for granting and withdrawing international protection (recast), (Official Journal of the European Union L 180/60)- hereinafter as Directive 2013/32/EU.

9 UN High Commissioner for Refugees (UNHCR), *Guidelines on Policies and Procedures in dealing with Unaccompanied Children Seeking Asylum*, February 1997.

10 UNHCR, *Guidelines on International Protection No. 8: Child Asylum Claims under Articles 1(A)2 and 1(F) of the 1951 Convention and/or 1967 Protocol relating to the Status of Refugees*, 22 December 2009, HCR/GIP/09/08, [online:] https://www.refworld.org/docid/4b2f4f6d2.html [available: 25.05.2020], hereinafter as Child Asylum Claims.

In practical terms, various age assessment methods are used, which can be divided into medical and non-medical ones. The actions that fail to require a medical intervention include, inter alia, searching for documents, verifying specific circumstances in the country of origin, interviewing a foreigner and psychological examinations.[11] In case of the assessment by medical means, general examinations and those that require X-ray examination are distinguished. The first ones are aimed at estimating a degree of the physiological development of a person by analysing anthropometric data of the physical appearance of the foreigner. In turn, the X-ray examinations seek to estimate a degree of development of the skeletal system or to assess the phases of a development of tooth mineralization.[12]

An important determining factor of the legal assessment of these actions is a circumstance that it refers to the actions taken against subjects often in a particularly vulnerable situation also for reasons other than their age. You can mention here even a separated or unaccompanied child,[13] an irregular migration status,[14] seeking international protection,[15] disability, being a victim of torture, human trafficking or sexual exploitation.[16] It is worthy of note in this context that in the UNHCR documents it is postulated that the standards

---

11 A detailed description of these methods together with an indication of the bibliography inter alia see: T. Smith, L. Brownlees, *Age assessment practices...*, pp. 13–18.

12 Review of the practice of EU Member-States in this regard see: *EASO practical guide on age assessment: Second edition*, European Asylum Support Office 2018, pp. 47–60.

13 All steps aiming at a proper identification of unaccompanied children should assume, that they are vulnerable persons – cf. UNHCR, Conclusion on Children at Risk No. 107 (LVIII) – 2007, Executive Commitee 56th session. Contained in United Nations General Assembly document A/AC.96/1048. In case of this group, ECtHR indicates that their vulnerability is extreme – cf. *Mubilanzila Mayeka and Kaniki Mitunga v. Belgium*, Application No. 13178/03, ECtHR Judgment of 12.10.2006, at par. 55.

14 Preamble to the UN General Assembly Resolution on Protection of Migrants of 24/2/2000, A/RES/54/166; on vulnerability in the undocumented situation see J. Ryngaert, W. Vandenhole, "Undocumented migration: Integrating the children's rights concept, of nuanced vulnerability in human rights law," [in:] *Children's rights law in the Global human rights Landscape: Isolation, inspiration, integration*, eds. E. Brems, E. Desmet, W. Vandenhole, Roudledge 2017, pp. 220–222; cf. *Chowdury et al. vs. Greece*, Application No. 21884/15, ECHR Judgment of 30/3/2017, par. 97.

15 Cf. *M.S.S. v. Belgium and Greece*, Application No. 30696/09, ECtHR Judgment (Grand Chamber) of 21.11.2011, par. 251.

16 Cf. an enumeration of vulnerable persons set out in Art. 21 Directive 2011/95/EU of the European Parliament and of the Council of December 13, 2011 on standards for the qualification of third-country nationals or stateless persons as beneficiaries of international protection, for a uniform status for refugees or for persons eligible for

developed for the child asylum claims submitted by children should also be applied to the young adults who are at least 18 year-old, but due to immaturity and vulnerability should, however, be treated in a special manner.[17] It is also rightly argued that a vulnerability situation is not a permanent phenomenon and evolves along with changes occurring in a life of the given individual.[18]

2. Legal justification for age assessment procedures

When analysing an issue of age assessment legitimate purposes, priority should be given to an insight that knowledge of whether a foreigner is a child or an adult is of fundamental significance. On the current basis, both in international and national law, an entire range of regulations detailing the standards for a treatment of children is applicable. Nevertheless, the indispensable and essential condition for their use is an awareness that the person is a minor. In the case of migration matters, this is also of importance as an overall legal status of the underage foreigners should be formalised on the basis of the rule of treating them firstly as the children, and only further as the migrants.[19] Consequently, a priority should be given to those actions of the state that aim at the protection and assistance (Article 22 of the Convention on the Rights of the Child) and considerations related to a migration policy should remain a further issue.[20]

---

subsidiary protection, and for the content of the protection granted (Official Journal of the European Union L 337) 20.12.2011, hereinafter: Directive 2011/95/EU.

17 Cf. Child Asylum Claims, p. 5.

18 Cf. "Vulnerability and resilience criteria developed for separated Somali and South Sudanese children," [in:] *Toolkit on Unaccompanied and Separated Children*, published by the Alliance for Child Protection in Humanitarian Action, [online:] https://resourcecentre.savethechildren.net/node/12197/pdf/tools-web-2017-0322.pdf., [available: 20.05.2020], p. 141.

19 Cf. M.B. Dembour, *When Human Become Migrant. Study of the European Court of Human Rights with an American Counter-Point*, Oxford 2015, pp. 387–388; Council of Europe Parliamentary Assembly, Unaccompanied Children in Europe: Issues of arrival, stay and return, Resolution 1810(2011), 15 April 2011, par. 5.1, hereinafter as Resolution 1810 (2011); Cf. *Mubilanzila Mayeka and Kaniki Mitunga v. Belgium*, par. 55.

20 *Considerations such as those relating to general migration control cannot override best interests considerations*, UN Committee on the Protection of the Rights of All Migrant Workers and Members of Their Families (CMW), Joint General Comment No. 3 (2017) of the Committee on the Protection of the Rights of All Migrant Workers and Members of Their Families and No. 22 (2017) of the Committee on the Rights of the Child on the general principles regarding the human rights of children in the

It appears to be important that the age assessment is justified both in the public interest and in the interest of the child himself/herself. Age is part of the child's identity referred to in Article 8 of the Convention on the Rights of the Child. This means that estimating how old a concerned individual is can be qualified as an action that respects the child's right to preserve his or her identity or restores that identity.[21] At the same time, the aforementioned enables to document properly an age and a registration of birth according to the regulations included in Article 7 of the Convention on the Rights of the Child, as well as Article 24 of the International Covenant on Civil and Political Rights. The Committee on the Rights of the Child stated that "a child without a provable date of birth is extremely vulnerable to all kinds of abuse and injustice regarding the family, work, education and labour, particularly within the juvenile justice system."[22] Therefore, if there is no proof of the child's age, he or she has the right to have the state implement appropriate procedures to formally estimate and document this issue.[23]

An accurate and effective documentation concerning a child to a large extent determines the protection of all other rights. First and foremost, it is the proper implementation of Art. 6 of the Convention on the Rights of the Child, and thus an obligation of the state to ensure maximum living conditions and child development. In a migration context, it had better be mentioned that the proper identification of children enables them to exercise the right to international protection[24] and the right to protection and humanitarian assistance (Art.22 par.2 of the Convention on the Rights of the Child). Furthermore, an obligation to identify a child that is unaccompanied or separated from his or her parents as soon as possible when the latter only finds himself/herself in the territory of

---

context of international migration, 16 November 2017, CMW/C/GC/3-CRC/C/GC/22, par.33.

21 UN Committee on the Rights of the Child (CRC), CRC General Comment No. 6 (2005): *Treatment of Unaccompanied and Separated Children Outside their Country of Origin*, 1 September 2005, CRC/GC/2005/6, para. 31(i).

22 CRC General Comment No. 10 (2007): *Children's Rights in Juvenile Justice*, 25 April 2007, CRC/C/GC/10, [online:] https://www.refworld.org/docid/4670fca12.html [available: 25.05. 2020], par. 39.

23 Ibidem.

24 Age is one of the constituents of the application for international protection according to Art. 4 paras. 1 and 2 of Directive 2013/33/EU of the European Parliament and of the Council of June 26, 2013 laying down standards for the reception of applicants for international protection (recast), (Official Journal of the European Union L 180), hereinafter: Directive 2013/33/EU.

a state incumbent on this state.[25] The children deprived of their family environment should be ensured a proper care (Art. 20 par. 2 of the Convention on the Rights of the Child), as well as an obligation to trace the parents and take efforts to reunify with his or her family (Art.22 par. 2 of the Convention on the Rights of the Child).[26]

Frequently, however, the mere statement that a foreigner is a child turns out to be insufficient due to a legally conditioned necessity of making more precise findings. Pursuant to many of the law provisions the child is required to be treated 'according to their age.' Therefore, firstly, the younger the child, the more vulnerable he or she is and the greater the needs for care and assistance. Then, the rule arising from Art. 12 of the Convention on the Rights of the Child requires that the state should take into account the right to express views freely in all matters affecting the child according to his or her age and maturity.[27] The aforementioned requirement is also formulated in the case of the child interview rules in procedures for granting international protection and an initial interview, which aims at a correct identification and a registration of the unaccompanied children.[28]

There are also numerous provisions of law, an application of which is associated with a strictly defined age limit set out in the national and often international law. It may be mentioned here an ability to enter into matrimony,[29] an issue of the possible penalisation of the sexual activities with a minor,[30] an ability to enter into employment relationships or employment in general,[31] a

25 Cf. CRC, General Comment No. 6, par. 31(i).

26 The European Court of Human Rights incorporates the standards contained in the Convention on the Rights of the Child into the assessment of the legality of States'actions – the Parties to the European Convention – cf. *Mubilanzila Mayeka and Kaniki Mitunga*, par. 82.

27 Cf. also, *inter alia*, Article 31 (1) of the CRC mentions the right to rest, including participation in games and recreational activities appropriate for the child's age.

28 Cf. CRC, General Comment No. 6, par. 31 (ii).

29 For example, the Polish law provides for an exception to the principle of enter into matrimony at the age of 18 for women who are at least 16 years old – Art. 10 par. 2 of the Family and Guardianship Code of 25 February 1964 (consolidated text: Dz.U. 2019, item 2086).

30 Cf. Art. 200 of the Penal Code, penalising a sexual intercourse with minors under 15 years of age.

31 Cf. Art. 32 par. 2 item 1 of the Convention on the Rights of the Child imposing an obligation on the state to set a minimum age for applying for work. In accordance with Art. 2 par. 3 ILO Convention concerning Minimum Age for Admission to Employment (so called Minimum Age Convention) No. 138, this age should not be

capacity for criminal liability according to such rules as adults,[32] and finally an issue of a direct participation in the armed conflicts and the rules of conscription set out in Art. 38 par. 2 and par. 3 the Convention on the Rights of the Child.[33] As mentioned above, this may constitute a ground for an admissibility of placing a minor in detention.[34]

Then, the age-related findings have a direct impact on the assessment of whether and at what level a person should benefit from education (Art. 28 (1) of the Convention on the Rights of the Child) and facilitate making proper decisions about subjecting the child to vaccination, as well as determining a scope of the child's discretionary powers concerning undergoing specific interventions or medical procedures

3. Legal compliance and procedural guarantees

The age assessment procedures constitute, without any doubt, an interference with the right to respect for the private life of the individual. Moreover, in practice, the need for identification sometimes substantiates a immigration detention,[35] while at the same time is a decisive element for a continued

---

less than 15 years. Convention came into force for Poland on 22 March 1979 (Dz. U. 1978, No. 12, item 53). Critical notes regarding these convention regulations see R. Mavunga, "A Critical Assessment of the Minimum Age Convention 138 of 1973 and the Worst Forms of Child Labour Convention 182 of 1999," *PER/PELJ* 2013, Vol. 16, No. 5, pp. 129–132.

32 Cf. Art. 40 par. 3 item 1 of the Convention on the Rights of the Child, establishing a minimum age limit below which children will benefit from the presumption of the inability to violate criminal law – see more broadly D. Cipriani, *Children's Rights and the Minimum Age of Criminal Responsibility: A Global Perspective*, Ashgate Publishing Limited England 2009.

33 According to this provision, States – Parties are obliged to refrain from recruiting any person under 15 years of age, and in the case of persons between 15 and 18 years of age, States should firstly try to choose older people.

34 According to the Polish law, unaccompanied children under 15 years of age are not placed in the detention centres as part of a forced return procedure, Art. 397 par. 3 of the Act of 12 December 2013 on foreigners (consolidated text: Dz.U. 2020, item 35).

35 See for example Belgium: Article 41 § 2, Law of 12 January 2007 regarding the Reception of Asylum Seekers and other categories of Aliens, available in French http://www.ejustice.just.fgov.be/cgi_loi/change_lg.pl?language=fr&la=F&cn=2007011252&table_name=loi; Netherlands, Article 3.109b(7) of Vreemdelingenbesluit 2000 (Aliens Decree) (Staatsblad, 2000-12-07, No. 497, pp. 1–71).

admissibility of this type of deprivation of liberty. At the same time, a duration of such procedures, the conditions and the manner they are carried out may lead to a violation of the prohibition on freedom from torture and degrading or inhuman treatment.[36]

A certain general standard that can be derived from the human rights standards is lawfulness and a prohibition of arbitrariness of such actions.[37] An indispensable condition is an existence of a legal basis for an age assessment for the legitimate purposes – this interference must be prescribed by law and legitimate.[38] In case of children, apart from legality understood as applicability of the proper standard in the provisions of the national law, the key is to respond to the question whether the child's best interests are effectively secured in this manner according to Art. 3 of the Convention on the Rights of the Child.

An implementation of *the best interest of the child* must take place on two levels. First of all, this must be the primary purpose of the age assessment procedure.[39] It is highlighted in this context that an interest of the state in terms of migration management is not a ground in itself sufficient for undertaking such actions.[40] The protection of the child's interest must consider a circumstance that children perceive these procedures in the best case as "daunting and confusing and in some instances, they find it frightening and traumatising."[41]

The second level is to ensure that the rule expressed in Art. 3 of the Convention on the Rights of the Child was a model for assessing all constituents of the legal and factual situation of the child that had undergone such a procedure.[42] The whole process of estimating chronological age should be based on

---

36 Cf. *Abdullahi Elmi and Aweys Abubakar v. Malta*, Application No. 25794/13 and 28151/13 22, European Court of Human Rights Judgment of 22.11.2016; *Mahamed Jama v. Malta*, Application No. 10290/13, ECtHR Judgment of 26.11.2015.

37 In case of the right to privacy, it is determined by the wording of limitation clauses in Art. 17 par. 2 ICCPR, Art. 8 par. 2 ECHR.

38 What is understood as the internal quality of law and its compliance with the *rule of law*.

39 UN Convention on the Rights of the Child, Article 3; Charter of Fundamental Rights and Freedoms, Article 24 par. 2. Directive 2013/32/EU, Article 25 par. 6; Directive 2013/33/EU, Article 23. par. 1.2.

40 Cf. D. Wenke, *Age assessment: Council of Europe member states' policies, procedures and practices respectful of children's rights in the context of migration*, Strasbourg 2017, p. 13.

41 UN Children's Fund (UNICEF), *Age Assessment: A Technical Note*, January 2013, p. 12.

42 Cf. Convention of the Rights of the Child Art. 3, Directive 2013/32/EU, Art. 25 par. 6.

a presumption that the person is a child. In addition to the Convention on the Rights of the Child, there are two international treaties in Europe which contain an almost identical wording of a presumption of minority in respect of the victims of exploitation, sexual violence[43] or trafficking where an age of the person is uncertain and there are reasons to believe that he or she is a child.[44] This last constituent is of great practical significance since there are situations when children are taught by traffickers and smugglers to pose as adults. The purpose of such actions is to leave such a child outside the mechanisms of care and relatively easy to hide its exploitation.[45]

Legal compliance should also be identified with procedural fairness, and thus safeguarding an individual against arbitrariness of the authority through information obligations and an existence of the effective appeal procedures. A constituent that guarantees effectiveness of exercising these rights consists in informing the foreigner about an existence of the age assessment procedures and the possibilities of conducting them.[46] For instance, in the Polish law, the age assessment is carried out in case of the foreigners who *claim to be minors*.[47] This means that if the foreigner does not refer to his or her child status, he or she will not be subject to the examination.

43 Cf. Council of Europe Convention on the Protection of Children against Sexual Exploitation and Sexual Abuse, 25 October 2007, (Lanzarote Convention), Art. 11. 2: "Each Party shall take the necessary legislative or other measures to ensure that when the age of the victim is uncertain and there are reasons to believe that the victim is a child, the protection and assistance measures provided for children shall be accorded to him or her pending verification of his or her age." This convention came into force for Poland on 1 June 2015 (Dz.U. 2015, item 608).

44 Europe Convention on Action against Trafficking in Human Beings (2005), Art. 10. 3: "when the age of the victim is uncertain and there are reasons to believe that the victim is a child, he or she shall be presumed to be a child and shall be accorded special protection measures pending verification of his/her age." This convention came into force for Poland on 1 March 2009 (Dz. U. 2009, No. 20, item 107); Cf. also Art. 13.2. Directive 2011/36/EU of the European Parliament and of the Council of April 5, 2011 on preventing and combating trafficking in human beings and protecting its victims, and replacing Council Framework Decision 2002/629/JHA (Official Journal of the European Union L 101).

45 Cf. *EASO*. . ., p. 17; Separated Children in Europe Programme, Position Paper on Age Assessment in the Context of Separated Children in Europe, 2012, [online:] https://www.refworld.org/docid/4ff535f52.html [available: 05.06.2020], p. 7.

46 Cf. Human Rights Watch, *Boat Ride to Detention Adult and Child Migrants in Malta* 2012, p. 45; *Mahamed Jama v. Malta*, par. 42.

47 Cf. Art. 397 par. 4 of the Act on Foreigners.

It should be noted in this context that in case of a person approaching the age of majority, the European Court of Human Rights ruled that if the applicant himself or herself, who was 17 years and 10 months old when arrested, had not applied for a registration as a minor, the state he or she had only given the year of birth did not have to consider this possibility on its own initiative.[48] The presumption that we are dealing with an unaccompanied or separated child requires an appointment of a representative or legal guardian for such a person and the latter should fulfil a condition of independence. Such a person should be appointed prior to any action is taken to estimate an age.[49] Simultaneously, "the child shall be assisted by legal representation throughout the asylum procedure."[50]

Information obligations should include the entire process of assessing an age of a foreigner and refer to all actions carried out as a part of it.[51] In case of the EU law, they have been limited to information on a possibility of conducting the medical examinations. The person under examination and his or her legal representative are to be informed about a manner of conducting the examination, the rules for conducting it, as well as about the possibilities of appealing against their results and the possible consequences of the result of a medical examination, for instance with regard to processing an application for international protection, as well as the consequences when an unaccompanied minor refuses to undergo such medical examination.[52] It is pointed out that the foreigner concerned should be informed why his or her age statement was not believed, as well as what are the reservations concerning the documents, he or she presents.[53]

As a standard, it is required to notify the foreigner, or his or her guardian about a result in the written form, as well as about a possibility of appealing.

48 *Aarabi v. Greece*, Application No. 39766/09, ECHR Judgment, 02.04.2015, par. 43–45.

49 Directive 2013/32/EU, Article 25 par. 1(a), supra, note 8. See also, UNHCR, Child Asylum Claims Guidelines, supra note 15, par. 69; cf. par. 75, p. 27.

50 Guidelines on the role and actions of the guardian in this situation Cf. Fundamental Rights Agency, *Guardianship for children deprived of parental care handbook: A handbook to reinforce guardianship systems to cater for the specific needs of child victims of trafficking*, European Union Agency for Fundamental Rights 2014, p. 101.

51 European Network of Ombudspersons for Children, 2006.

52 H. Crawley, *When is a Child not a Child? Asylum, Age Disputes and the Process of Age Assessment*, Immigration Law Practitioners' Association London 2007, p. 35.

53 UNICEF, *Age Assessment*, p. 9.

A circumstance that the child understands information about the procedures to which he or she would give his or her consent must be determined prior to commencing them.[54] A language and a manner of conveying information to the person concerned should be understandable, child friendly, free from any complications. The aforementioned also applies to a method of communicating the assessment result.[55] In this context, a possibility of informing the child not only in a language that he or she understands but also in a language that can reasonably be assumed as being understood by a child included in the EU law should be critically assessed.[56]

It appears that an issue of informing about purpose and importance of the actions taken should be put outside the brackets. There is an essential difference between understanding of words and being aware of tremendous significance of such examination and its result for the person concerned. The persons who come to the countries of the circle of the Western civilization are frequently from the countries where age and even more documenting it are not an important element of the functioning of individuals in the social life.[57]

Similarly, as in case of the information obligations, a consent to the age assessment in the EU law only applies to the medical examinations,[58] while in many countries this requirement applies to the non-medical age assessment methods, too.

In the literature, attention is drawn to a circumstance that a perception of the minors immediately upon an arrival to the territory of the state is limited due to stress, fatigue or disorientation. In this context, it is difficult to assume that if the age assessment procedures are already undertaken at this point in time, a consent to specific actions is indeed informed and given with full discernment.[59] It is also argued that, in general, persons concerned, in spite of being informed of the possibility of refusing, rather feel obliged to undergo certain examinations.[60] These are noteworthy issues, but from a normative

54 Cf. *EASO...*, p. 27.

55 Cf. UNHCR, Child Asylum Claims, p. 28, par. 77.

56 Cf. Directive 2013/32/EU, Art. 25 par. 5.

57 See more broadly A. Hjern, H. Asher, M. Vervliet, I. Derluyn, "Identification: age and identity assessment," [in:] *Research Handbook on Child Migration*, ed. J. Bhabha, J. Kanics, D. Senovilla Hernández, Cheltenham, Northampton 2018, p. 286.

58 Cf. *Yazgül Yilmaz v. Turkey*, Application No. 36369/06, ECtHR Judgment of 01.02.2011, at par. 47.

59 Cf. T. Smith, L. Brownless, *Age assessment practices...*, p. 34.

60 Cf. A. Parsons, *The best interests of the child in asylum and refugee procedures in Finland*, Helsinki 2010, p. 52.

point of view it should rather asked if the authorities have some instruments of an administrative and legal nature, the use of which can be considered as ailment for a refusal. It seems that such limitations with regard to the freedom of decision-making of the foreigners remain the legal regulations in force at least in some countries according to which the refusal to undergo the medical examinations results in a waiver of the privilege of doubt and treating a given person as an adult.[61]

4. Methodology and method of conducting: The rule of proportionality

The essence of the international law standards is to protect the individual not only against an unlawful, but also arbitrary action. Undoubtedly, this last criterion includes both a constituent of arbitrariness and discretion, as well as a lack of proportionality between a legitimate purpose and the measures adopted to achieve it. The age assessment as an interference with the privacy of an individual should fulfil a criterion of necessity and the constituent elements of arbitrariness features the use of the age assessment procedures on the routine basis. By the aforementioned is meant that they are admissible when the age of the person is in doubt. However, it fails to result directly from the provisions, it is highlighted that should be about reasonable doubts,[62] so:

> a) the person's physical appearance and the mental impression of the person do not allow any clear conclusions whether the person is under or above 18 years old; b) the individual is not in possession of any identity documents or the documents are considered unreliable or when there are obvious inconsistencies between the age declared by the person and the age stated by the document; and c) the person is not in a position to state his or her own age.[63]

The states should resort to the least interfering methods in the circumstances of the case from the point of view of legitimate purpose. Firstly, therefore, if a person does not have identity documents such as a passport or a birth certificate, it is propounded that an essential verification instrument should

---

61 See reasoning of ECtHR in the case *Ahmade v. Greece*, Application No. 50520/09, ECtHR Judgment of 25.09.2012, at par. 78; see for example The Act of 12 December 2013 on foreigners, consolidated text: Dz.U. 2018, item 2094 as amended, Art. 397 (5): "A foreigner who claims to be a minor and refuses to undergo a medical examination shall be considered an adult."

62 Cf. Resolution 1810 (2011), par. 5.10.

63 UNICEF, *Age Assessment...*, p. 13. See also: Resolution 1810(2011), par. 5.10.

be to believe the statements of the person concerned, his or her parents or guardians.[64] A confirmation of age acquired during an interview with the foreigner is directly connected with the right of the child to express his or her own views in any administrative procedure pursuant to Art. 12 of the Convention on the Rights of the Child. UNHCR even recommends that this should be a primary and essential method of the age assessment in respect of the unaccompanied children.[65] It should also be taken into account that the children whose age statement is considered insufficient feel that their truthfulness is being questioned.[66]

Thereafter, apart from the interview itself, it is important taking into account the available documents, such as for example of a school certificate, as well as about taking steps to determine specific factual circumstances, e.g. by talking to the relatives, searching for the documents in the country of origin.[67] It is worth noting at this point that there are no standards that clearly indicate which specific documents should be considered. Only when the described actions fail to produce an expected result is it correct and appropriate to perform the medical and psychological examinations.[68]

The Committee on the Rights of the Child indicates that the age assessment should fulfil the standards of science, security and fairness. It is also propounded that a method of conducting the examination itself should be consistent with the rules of objectivity, independence and professionalism, respect for dignity and intimacy of the child.[69]

---

64 Cf. wording of Art. 4 par. 5 of the Directive 2011/95/EU, which states that proof of age is not necessary under certain conditions.

65 UNHCR, *Guidelines on Policies....* At the same time, it should be noted that the Court of Justice of the European Union considered that the child's right to be heard must be fully applicable to the rules adopted under the common asylum system Cf. *M.M. v. Minister for Justice, Equality and Law Reform, Ireland, Attorney General*, C-277/11, Court of Justice of the European Union, 22 November 2012, par. 89.

66 Cf. L. Hjern et al., "Identification: age and identity assessment," p. 286.

67 EASO, *Age assessment practice in Europe*, December 2013, pp. 25–27. With exclusion of contacting with country of origin of the children seeking international protection Cf. United Nations Children's Fund, *Age Assessment: A technical note*, 2013, p. 16.

68 Cf. Art. 25 par. 5 Directive 2013/32/EU which specifies that medical examinations can be carried out only if, based on general statements or other statements used, there are doubts as to the age of the applicant. See also: Separated Children in Europe Programme, p. 8.

69 Cf. European Parliament resolution of 12 September 2013 on the situation of unaccompanied minors in the EU (2012/2263(INI)).

The aforementioned examinations are required to be carried out with due respect for the child's personal dignity, with particular regard to his or her sex in such a manner as to avoid any breach of his or her physical integrity. In view of the above, the methods that involve a total bareness of the person subject to the examination, an assessment of the development of genitals and other intimate parts of the body should be considered unacceptable.[70] A gynaecological examination, which always requires touching the genitals can be an additional trauma for the persons concerned.[71]

All medical examinations should be as little as possible invasive. It is generally accepted that an exposure to X-rays is the most invasive. An important issue is also the negative impact of the examinations performed by means of the medical equipment on the psyche of the foreigners concerned. An awareness that their fate depends on the mechanical devices that additionally often produce erroneous results evokes feelings of harm and helplessness. A long period of waiting for the result of the examinations is equally destructive to the psyche.[72] However, it must be expressively stated that there is no objective single ground to assess which of the methods is the least interfering. It is a complex issue due to the fact that it is necessary to consider not only the issue of the degree of interference in physicality, but also tan impact of the certain situations on the mental health. This means that in the circumstances of the given case, due to the migrant's individual history, the medical methodology may prove to be a less severe form of interference than an interview.[73]

Apparently, a statement that medical examinations must strictly fulfil a criterion of scientific character and credibility seems to be an unnecessary truism. Meanwhile, in case of at least some of the examinations customarily used in the

---

70 The practice of gynecological evaluation of sexual maturity can be qualified as an inhuman and degrading treatment and contrary to 3 and 37 CRC and Articles 1, 3 and 5 CFR. Cf. UN Committee on the Rights of the Child, *Concluding observations on the combined third and fourth periodic reports of Germany*, 25 February 2014, CRC/C/DEU/CO/3–4, par. 68 b.

71 Nevertheless, it should be highlighted that this statement by the ECtHR concerned not the situation of the age assessment. The examination was performed in respect of a girl aged 16 who, during her imprisonment for two days in the police custody, was subjected to several examinations, including a gynecological examination, without her consent. These examinations were performed on the routine basis to protect the members of the security forces against allegations of subjecting the prisoners to sexual violence.

72 Cf. L. Hjern et al., "Identification: age and identity assessment," p. 286.

73 Cf. EASO, *Practical Guide...*, p. 31.

European countries doubts about their compliance with the current state of the medical knowledge were reported.[74] A fact that the examinations related to a degree of the bone development or tooth mineralisation were not developed at all to indicate a probable date of birth of a given person deserves a special attention.[75] Another problem is crediblity of medical procedures in cases of the lack of reliable civil registration in asylum seekers' countries of origin.[76] It should also be highlighted that the medical examinations lead to an indication of an approximate age of a given person in a biological sense, but there is no scientific evidence of its full coincidence with the chronological age. Furthermore, representatives of the medical science emphasise that the "chronological age, dental age and skeletal (bone) age are not necessarily the same in a given individual."[77]

A reliability of the general medical examination is also questioned since it fails to consider the factors such as differences between races, social background and nutrition.[78] The same objection is made in respect of the methodology of the X-ray scans according to Greulich and Pyle,[79] whereby it is scientifically confirmed that there is a high percentage of errors in the assessments taken exclusively on the basis of x-ray examinations. This methodology includes a margin of error, which in the case of the X-ray scan of a wrist is approx. 3–4 years, while teeth examinations is of 2–3 years.[80] It should also be noted that subjecting

74 See for example case of Sweden – AIDA, Country Report: Sweden, 2018 Update, [online:] file:///D:/Pobrane/aida_se_2018update.pdf [available: 23.05.2020], pp. 42–43; P. Mostad, F. Tamsen, "Error rates for unvalidated medical age assessment procedures," *International Journal of Legal Medicine* 2019, Vol. 133, pp. 613–623.

75 Cf. arguments of the applicants in *Darboe and Camarra v. the Italy*, Application No. 5797/17, Case communicated on 14 February 2017.

76 See more specifically G. Noll, "Junk Science? Four Arguments against the Radiological Age Assessment of Unaccompanied Minors Seeking Asylum," *International Journal of Refugee Law* 2016, Vol. 28, No. 2, pp. 234–250.

77 Statement by Dr. Nalton F. Ferraro, M.D., INS Public Comment in Physicians for Human Rights et al, 2003, p. 131 cited in: T. Smith, L. Brownlees, *Age assessment practices...*, p. 19.

78 T. Smith, L. Brownlees, *Age assessment practices...*, p. 20.

79 See B. Tsehay, M. Afework, M. Mesifin, "Assessment of Reliability of Greulich and Pyle (GP) Method for Determination of Age of Children at Debre Markos Referral Hospital, East Gojjam Zone," *Ethiopian Journal of Health Science* 2017, Vol. 27(6), pp. 631–640; R.T. Loder et al., "Applicability of the Greulich and Pyle skeletal age standards to black and white children of today," *American Journal of Diseases of Children* 1993, Vol. 147, No. 12, pp. 1329–1333.

80 CoE ad hoc Committee on Rights of the Child, *Child-friendly age assessment for unaccompanied migrant Children*, Rapporteur D. Fiala, 2017, [online:]

foreigners to the examinations which lack of precision for the administrative and not medical purposes raises serious ethical doubts, provoking questions as to whether such situations should be legally permitted at all.[81] With regard to the above, it seems that a certain minimum of reliability is not only specifying a margin of the possible error in a particular case, but also imposing an obligation on the assessment bodies to take this constituent into account.[82]

An incorrectness of the obtained medical examination results also means that while relying only on one their type is increasingly identified in international[83] and national case law as the arbitrary action.[84] It should be considered as appropriate to use a combination of several methods with an indication of the medical intervention as the last resort. The Committee on the Rights of the Child indicates that a multidimensional nature of the age assessment based on a holistic approach should be a standard – while taking into account a physical appearance or traits and psychological maturity of a concerned individual,[85] at the same time considering their ethnic and cultural origin. Nevertheless, these are some generalities whose implementation in practice would require more precise guidelines, for example: is the presence of a physician and a psychologist sufficient or should another specialist be present?[86]

---

https://reliefweb.int/sites/reliefweb.int/files/resources/20170920-Rapport%20Fiala-EN.pdf [available 16.05.2020], p. 11.

81 Cf. A. Aynsley-Green et al., "Medical, statistical, ethical and human rights considerations in the assessment of age in children and young people subject to immigration control," *British Medical Bulletin* 2012, Volume 102, No. 1, pp. 17–42.

82 Cf. Resolution 1810 (2011) par. 5.10.

83 See notes of the Human Rights Committee regarding the excessive use of carpal bones as the main method of the age assessment: Human Rights Committee, Concluding observations on the fifth periodic report of France, CRC/C/FRA/CO/5, 23.2. 2016, at par. 74 b; *European Committee for Home Based Priority Action for the Child and the Family (EUROCEF) v. France*, Complaint No. 114/2015, European Committee of Social Rights Decision of 24.1. 2018, at par. 113. The Revised European Social Charter, European Treaty Series No. 163, Strasbourg 03.05.1996.

84 Administrative Court Berlin, Decision 18 L 81.16, 19 April 2016, [online:] http://bit.ly/2mJm85c [available 20.05.2020]. High Administrative Court Bavaria, Decision 12 CS 16.1550, 16 August 2016, [online:] http://bit.ly/2m2hP0 [available 20.05.2020]; Cf. also case-law of the British courts *A v. LB of Croydon & Secretary of State for Home Department (Interested Party)*; *WK v. Secretary of State for Home Department & Kent CC* [2009] EWHC 939 (Admin). B v. Merton LBC.

85 See, CRC General Comment No. 6, par. 31(i); UNHCR, Child Asylum Claims, par. 75.

86 For example, some authors suggest, that the presence of a cultural-linguistic mediator is very important. Cf. V. De Sanctis et al., "Pros and cons for the medical age

The examinations should be performed by the persons that guarantee independence and professionalism, and trained in the aforementioned accordingly.[87] The literature points out that the age assessment is entrusted to the employees of migration, social and police services who fail to have sufficient knowledge in this field area The medical personnel also should be properly trained and have knowledge related even to that how traumatic experiences affect a dynamics of child's psychophysical development. To put it briefly, simply a specialisation in paediatrics is not a sufficient ground to conclude that a physician is competent in the field area of the age assessment.[88]

A great quantity of children is erroneously recognised as adults on the basis of their general appearance, which is assessed within minutes at the border or in the port. The physical features are a decisive factor, and what is of greater importance, whether they match the ideas of migration services about what a child should look like.[89] The fate of foreigners depends on the subjective assessment of the interviewers who, without any training, can misinterpret certain behaviours, such as for example a fact that foreigners avoid looking into their eyes.[90] Simultaneously, it is difficult to ensure sufficient independence and objectivity, since the assessment is carried out by the bodies and personnel concerned as a result of it.

An important constituent is a choice of the moment when the age assessment should be conducted. On the one hand, it is recommended that it does not take place directly or promptly after an arrival of the foreigners on the border or territory of the state. The primary argument is the aforementioned disorientation and fatigue, and the need to devote adequate time to gaining the child's trust, as well as collecting and verifying information.[91] At the ports or stations of entry, it is also difficult to achieve recommendations, that the age assessment is to be carried out in a child-friendly environment.[92] On the other

assessments in unaccompanied minors: a mini-review," *Acta Biomed* 2016, Vol. 87, No. 2, p. 124.

87 Cf. European Parliament Resolution of 12 September 2013 on the situation of unaccompanied minors in the EU (2012/2263(INI)).

88 Cf. T. Smith, L. Brownless, *Age assessment practices...*, p. 34 -35; CoE ad Hoc Committee on the Rights of The Child, *Child Friendly...*, p. 10.

89 Cf. H. Parsons, *The best interest...*, p. 190.

90 See H. Crawley, *When Is a Child not a Child?*, pp. 54, 115–116.

91 Separated Children in Europe Programme, supra, note 21, p. 15.

92 Cf. D. Wenke, p. 15; European Asylum Support Office, *Age Assessment* Practice in Europe, 2014, p. 16.

hand, the aforementioned guidelines may potentially conflict with a postulate of identifying the unaccompanied children as soon as possible, i.e. *immediately upon arrival at ports of entry or as soon as their presence in the country becomes known to the authorities*[93]

A duration of the age assessment should be adequate. It seems that specifying the specific time intervals is not appropriate here. On the one hand, these procedures cannot last for a long time, as they are associated with a situation of the fate uncertainty of a person, and frequently result in a prolongation of detention.[94] On the other hand, undue haste develops a risk of a lack of reliability and an incorrect estimation of a child as an adult. The assessment of whether state actions with regard to the aforementioned are not arbitrary should be based on the *due diligence* and good faith criterion.[95]

The last problem that appears to be of the extreme importance is the practical implementation of the privilege of doubt and an interpretation of the results of the examinations. Both the interpretation of the provisions of the Convention on the Rights of the Child, regulations of the EU law and national law require that if the performed examinations fail to give an unambiguous result, the individual should be considered a minor.[96] However, the problem seems to be a lack of the actual use of the privilege of doubt in practice. In the atmosphere of disbelief towards the migrants, when in the public perception they are primarily persons intending to obtain under false grounds a privileged treatment from the state authorities, a question whether it was proven that a given person is a child undoubtedly is closer to the rule, instead of a question if it was proven in a manner raising doubts that a person is an adult. At the same time, the postulate formulated in the context of the individuals seeking the international protection deserves that focusing not on the age itself, but

93 Cf. CRC General Comment No. 6, CRC/GC/2005/6, par. 31 (i).

94 Cf. *Mahamed Jama v. Malta*, par. 144.

95 See more detailed considerations of ECtHR in the case *Abdullahi Elmi and Aweys Abubakar v. Malta*, par. 146: "It follows that, even accepting that the detention was closely connected to the ground of detention relied on, namely to prevent an unauthorised entry, and in practice to allow for the applicants' asylum claim to be processed with the required prior age assessment, the delays in the present case, particularly those subsequent to the determination of the applicants' age, raise serious doubts as to the authorities' good faith."

96 Cf. CRC General Comment No. 6, par. 31 (i): "Age assessment should be safe, child and gender sensitive and the individual should be given the benefit of the doubt." Cf. CRC, General Comment No. 10, par. 39.

whether the individual requires sensitive treatment due to its immaturity or vulnerability, and legal effects or the importance of the age criterion are limited will constitute an essential rule.[97]

These standards specified hereunder should be maintained even in a situation of a large influx or disembarkation. Even if the countries struggle with the administrative difficulties in such situations, a possibility of dividing the age assessment procedures into two stages is pointed out. The first stage can be conducted in the form of the preliminary screening upon arrival. The second one may take place when the conditions enable to carry out the age according to rules of reliability and fairness. The privilege of doubt should be applicable within this period.[98]

5. Conclusions

The conducted deliberations evidence that the correct, reliable verification of age for the purpose of the proper documentation of an identity of the foreigners is a legitimate action of the state when there are reasonable doubts whether a given individual is a child or an adult. It seems that this is a *sine qua non* condition for ensuring that the basic obligation of the state take care of the child in the proper manner is met, as well as related to all other rights arising from the Convention on the Rights of the Child. The necessity of making findings regarding the age of the individual outlined hereunder must, however, be perceived in the context of the entirety, which is the functioning of the foreign children in terms of the migration. Here, however, care and protection materialising primarily in Article 3 of the Convention on the Rights of the Child are the basis. The rule of safeguarding the child's best interests determines looking at the age assessment procedures in terms of a certain updating *ad casum* standard seeking the answer to the question of how old is the individual while using all methods and actions that are reliable.

Therefore, in the first place, the age assessment procedures should be applicable only to the foreigners whose age is doubtful, and secondly such individuals should be treated as the children until it is estimated that they are the adults. It also seems that due to a fact that inaccuracy and a wide margin of error related to the medical assessment is the subject of objection of the medical environments, it should be propounded that a possibility of using exclusively

97 UNHCR, *Guidelines on Policies…*, p. 8.
98 Cf. *EASO Practical Guide*, p. 22.

and solely one such method as a prejudging factor of the final result of the assessment should be limited.

Bibliography:

Aynsley-Green A. et al., "Medical, statistical, ethical and human rights considerations in the assessment ofage in children and young people subject to immigration control," *British Medical Bulletin* 2012, Vol. 102, No. 1.

Cipriani D., *Children's Rights and the Minimum Age of Criminal Responsibility: A Global Perspective*, Ashgate Publishing Limited, England 2009.

Crawley H., *When is a Child not a Child? Asylum, Age Disputes and the Process of Age Assessment*, Immigration Law Practitioners' Association London 2007.

Dembour M.B., *When Human Become Migrant. Study of the European Court of Human Rights with an American Counter-Point*, Oxford 2015.

De Sanctis V. et al., "Pros and cons for the medical age assessments in unaccompanied minors: A mini-review," *Acta Biomed* 2016, Vol. 87, No. 2.

Feltz V., *Unaccompanied Minors. When European countries deny children their childhood*, Doctors of the World – Médecins du monde International Network, August 2015.

Hjern A., Asher H., Vervliet M., Derluyn I., "Identification: age and identity assessment," [in:] *Research Handbook on Child Migration*, ed. Bhabha J., Kanics J., Senovilla Hernández D., Cheltenham – Northampton 2018.

Keith L., "Risks of statelessness for children of undocumented parents in Europe," [in:] *The Worlds Stateless Children*, Institute of Statelessness and Inclusion 2017.

Loder R.T. et al., "Applicability of the Greulich and Pyle skeletal age standards to black and white children of today," *American Journal of Diseases of Children* 1993, Vol. 147, No. 12.

Mavunga R., "A Critical Assessment of the Minimum Age Convention 138 of 1973 and the Worst Forms of Child Labour Convention 182 of 1999," *PER/PELJ* 2013, Vol. 16, No. 5.

Mostad P., Tamsen F., "Error rates for unvalidated medical age assessment procedures," *International Journal of Legal Medicine* 2019, Vol. 13, No. 3.

Noll G., "Junk Science? Four Arguments against the Radiological Age Assessment of Unaccompanied Minors Seeking Asylum," *International Journal of Refugee Law* 2016, Vol. 28 No. 2.

Parsons A., *The best interests of the child in asylum and refugee procedures in Finland*, Helsinki 2010.

Rozzi E., "Out of limbo: Promoting the right of undocumented and stateless Roma people to a legal status in Italy through community-based paralegals," [in:] *The Worlds Stateless Children*, Institute of Statelessness and Inclusion 2017.

Ryngaert J., Vandenhole W., "Undocumented migration: integrating the children's rights concept of nuanced vulnerability in human rights law," [in:] *Children's rights law in the Global human rights Landscape. Isolation, inspiration, integration*, eds. Brems E., Desmet E., Vandenhole W., Roudledge 2017.

Smith T., Brownlees L., *Age assessment practices: a literature review & annotated bibliography*, Discussion Paper, UNICEF 2011.

Tsehay B., Afework M., Mesifin M., "Assessment of Reliability of Greulich and Pyle (GP) Method for Determination of Age of Children at Debre Markos Referral Hospital, East Gojjam Zone," *Ethiopian Journal of Health Science* 2017, Vol. 27, No. 6.

Wenke D., *Age assessment: Council of Europe member states' policies, procedures and practices respectful of children's rights in the context of migration*, Strasbourg 2017.

Justyna Gumuła-Kędracka
University of Silesia in Katowice
e-mail: justyna-gumula@wp.pl
ORCID ID: 0000-0003-4071-9960

Protection of children's rights in cases of international parental abduction

Abstract: The need to strengthen the protection of children's rights was the fundamental premise for creating an international instrument applicable to international parental child abductions. However, the 1980 Hague Convention adopted a specific understanding of the best interest of a child. The mechanism of the child's return to the state of their habitual residence works with the general assumption that each return of a child is in the child's best interests. However, the 1980 Hague Convention refers to the best interest of a child only in the preamble. It is not desirable to examine the child's interest in individual parental abduction cases. The 1980 Hague Convention assumes that a detailed substantive examination of the case, including consideration of the child's best interest, should occur only before the court of the child's of habitual residence, where the custody case will be heard. The Hague proceeding has a simplified character, and its purpose is to restore the *status quo ante*. This causes the need to seek an interpretation of the child's interests outside the 1980 Hague Convention. Consequently, it put the most vulnerable actors of the Hague proceedings – children – at risk of their rights to be breached.

Keywords: international child abductions, the vulnerability of children in court proceedings, hearing of the child, children's representation in court

1. Introductory remarks

International parental child abduction[1] is a situation when a parent removes a child from his or her state of habitual residence or retains a child in another

1 The usage of notion abduction is questioned in the literature because the 1980 Hague Convention uses this term only in its title. In the merits the 1980 Hague Convention uses the term wrongful removal or retention. See: E. Pérez-Vera, *Explanatory Report on the 1980 Hague Child Abduction Convention, Acts and Documents of the Fourteenth Session*, 1980, Vol. III, Child abduction, p. 442. However, *the Brussels II bis* use the

state without the other parent's permission. This situation creates not only a conflict between parents but also the conflict of laws and jurisdictions. In the international parental child abduction situation, it is easy to forget about the most vulnerable actors – children. The need to strengthen children's protection was the fundamental premise for creating an international instrument applicable in these cases – the Hague Convention of 25 October 1980 on the Civil Aspects of International Child Abduction[2] hereafter *the 1980 Hague Convention*. However, these Convention adopted a specific understanding of the best interest of a child. The mechanism of the child's return to the state of their habitual residence works with the general assumption that each return of a child is in the child's best interests. However, the 1980 Hague Convention refers to the best interest of a child only in the preamble.

Moreover, it is not desirable to examine the child's interest in individual parental abduction cases. The 1980 Hague Convention assumes that a detailed substantive examination of the case, including consideration of the child's best interest, should occur only before the court of the child's of habitual residence, where the custody case will be heard. The Hague proceeding has a simplified character, and its purpose is to restore the *status quo ante*. This causes the need to seek an interpretation of the child's interests outside of the 1980 Hague Convention.

The subject of this paper attempts to analyse how the UN Convention on the Rights of the Child hereafter, *the CRC*, finds its application in matters of international parental child abduction. In the first part, the article discusses if children should be considered vulnerable members of society. If the answer is affirmative, why should they be considered vulnerable in the Hague proceedings. The second part discusses the specific understanding of the procedural protections of the children's rights in the 1980 Hague Convention in the light of the jurisprudence of the European Court of Human Rights hereafter *ECtHR*. Next, the article analyses possible modes to strengthen the child's position in Hague matters. Firstly, in the lights of possible solutions for hearing a child in the proceedings about the new instruments introduced in the reformed Council Regulation (EC) No 2201/2003 of 27 November 2003 concerning jurisdiction

term *abduction* in the headline of its Article 9 that states "[j]urisdiction in cases of child abduction" and by that very act includes the term into the legal language of the Regulation.

2 Convention On The Civil Aspects Of International Child Abduction concluded 25 October 1980 entry into force 01.10.1983, [online:] https://www.hcch.net/en/instruments/conventions/full-text/?cid=24 [available: 01.04.2020].

and the recognition and enforcement of judgments in matrimonial matters and the matters of parental responsibility, repealing Regulation (EC) No 1347/2000, commonly known as *the Brussel II bis Regulation*. Secondly, the article examines if the individual representation of a child in the Hague proceedings can be considered a method to strengthen the protection of children's rights through individual representation.

2. Children as the vulnerable actors of the Hague proceedings

When discussing certain groups' legal vulnerability, it is challenging to escape the question of why this specific group is considered inherently vulnerable in a law. Generally, the concept of legal vulnerability has been connected to criminal law and regarded as indicating to protect individuals or groups affected explicitly by the risk of exploitation.[3] The question must be asked whether the concept of legal vulnerability applies to private law cases and whether in private law, certain individuals or groups are at the risk of exploitation. It is commonly accepted that in private law, legal vulnerability revolves around the subject of the capacity of legal persons and the party's autonomy. The question is whether this concept can be applied to legal institutions but also to certain groups of people.

When discussing persons' legal vulnerability, one can find two possible ways of defining who is legally vulnerable. The first approach assumes that a legally vulnerable person is a person who belongs to a particular group that meets previously described criteria of legal vulnerability. This approach is a popular solution chosen by law-makers to protect certain groups from the risk of exploitation. In this way, in private law, as legally vulnerable are defined, e.g., consumers,[4] older people,[5] or surrogate mothers.[6] This approach was adopted by the authors of the 1980 Hague Convention when they determined that the

3 H. Bigss, C. Jones, "Legally Vulnerable: What is vulnerability and who is vulnerable," [in:] *Law and Global Health, Current Legal Issues*, eds. M. Freeman, S. Hawkes, B. Bennett; Oxford 2014, p. 134

4 *Recognising and responding to consumer vulnerability: A guide for legal services regulators*, 2014, [online:] https://www.legalservicesconsumerpanel.org.uk/ourwork/vulnerableconsumers/Guide%20to%20consumer%20vulnerability%202014%20final.pdf [available: 22.1.2020].

5 N. A. Kohn, "Vulnerability Theory and the Role of Government," *Yale Journal of Law & Feminism* 2014, Vol. 26, p. 11.

6 H. Bigss, C. Jones, *Legally Vulnerable....*, p. 135.

Convention is to protect a defined group of people – children under age 16[7] – from exploitation understood as wrongful removal or retention.[8]

The other approach assumes that a legally vulnerable person is a person who needs protection from the risk of exploitation due to the situation or environment he or she finds himself in and not because of his inherent characteristics. This approach was developed by Martha Fineman, who said that *vulnerable* is a term "describing a universal, inevitable, enduring aspect of the human condition that must be at the heart of our concept of social and state responsibility[9]". In Fineman's conception, vulnerability is a powerful conceptual tool with the potential to define an obligation for the state to ensure a more productive and more robust guarantee of equality. She observed that qualifying people as legally vulnerable based on top-down characteristics neglect the ever-present possibility that human needs and circumstances will change during a *normal* lifespan.[10] Fineman's theory of the vulnerable subject is praised for noticing that legal vulnerability cannot be limited to special populations for two reasons. Firstly, not all persons within the protected populations are disadvantaged. Secondly, people are mistakenly treated as invulnerable because there are not members of groups that are recognized as deserving special protection,[11] e.g., in consumer law, the professional contracting parties acting for purposes not related to their trade, business, or profession.[12]

The vulnerability of children as a group is widely accepted in the literature.[13] Within the Council of Europe, the ECtHR jurisprudence has developed a conceptualization of children's vulnerability as comprising both economic and emotional family dependency.[14] However, according to Fineman's theory

---

7 Article 4 of the 1980 Hague Convention, second sentence.

8 Article 3 of the 1980 Hague Convention.

9 M.A. Fineman, "The Vulnerable Subject: Anchoring Equality in the Human Condition," *Yale Journal of Law and Feminism*, 2008, Vol. 20, No. 1, p. 8, [online:] https://digitalcommons.law.yale.edu/yjlf/vol20/iss1/2 [available: 15.03.2020].

10 Ibidem, p. 12.

11 N.A. Kohn, *Vulnerability Theory*. . ., p. 15.

12 Tarcău, C-74/15, paragraph 27, Dumitraş, C-534/15 paragraph 29.

13 See: B. B. Woodhouse, "A World Fit for Children is a World Fit for Everyone: Ecogenerism, Feminism, and Vulnerability," *Houston Law Review* 2009, Vol. 46; *Protecting Vulnerable Groups: The European Human Rights Framework*, eds. F. Ippolito, S. Iglesias Sánchez, Hart Publishing 2015.

14 F. Ippolito, "(De)Constructing Children's Vulnerability under European Law," [in:] *Protecting Vulnerable Groups: The European Human Rights Framework*, eds. F. Ippolito, S. Iglesias Sánchez, Hart Publishing 2015, p. 28.

of the vulnerable subject, one cannot treat all children as legally vulnerable just because there are children. That's why at the normative level, the notion of gradated autonomy should apply. The gradated autonomy is another element of the conceptualizations of children's vulnerability,[15] which reflects the distinction between ownership of rights and the capacity to act and, at the same time, recognises that children have the progressive capacity to exercise their rights in response to their state of people in the development.[16] The interpretation of the CRC provided with a similar interpretation. The vulnerability is not assigned to all children as a group, but only to children in the situation of vulnerability, such as disability, belonging to a minority group, being a refugee or asylum seeker, a victim of abuse, living in a street situation, etc. Therefore, when deciding on a child, different kinds and degrees of each child's vulnerability should be considered, "as each child is unique and each situation must be assessed according to the child's uniqueness."[17] Therefore, when discussing a legal vulnerability of children, it should be noted that children are subject to an inherited gradated vulnerability that changes during the child's lifespan. Successive progression in child autonomy should reflect on giving children graduate capacity. That often finds reflection in substantive regulations granting children the limited capacity for legal acts.[18] Simultaneously, the progression in child autonomy is not reflected in legal procedures, which leads to frequent violations of the child's rights, mostly to express his or her opinion and participate in legal proceedings that concern them. The same appears to be the issue in the 1980 Hague Convention, which in no way reflects the graduated capacity of minors and is often seen as paternalistic, not empowering.

Indeed, the 1980 Hague Convention states in the preamble that "the interests of children are of paramount importance in matters relating to their custody." However, it forbids an in-depth examination of a child's interest in the individual Hague abduction cases. This can be seen as violating the rights of children. Therefore, the group classified as legally vulnerable and in need of protection may be put at risk of even bigger legal insecurity.

15 Ibidem, p. 31.

16 F. Ippolito, "(De)Constructing Children's Vulnerability. . .," p. 35.

17 General Comment No. 14 (2013) on the right of the child to have his or her best interests taken as a primary consideration (art. 3, para. 1), 29 May 2013, para. 76.

18 Article 15 of the Polish Civil Code states: Minors who have attained thirteen years of age and persons partially legally incapacitated have limited capacity for legal acts.

3. The 1980 Hague Convention as an instrument protecting the legal vulnerability of minors

The strengthening of the youngest children's safety was the primary assumption that guided the authors of the 1980 Hague Convention. From its beginning, the drafters were aware that they were balancing between

> the desire to protect the factual situation altered by the wrongful removal or retention of a child and that of guaranteeing, in particular, respect for the legal relationships which may underlie such situations.[19]

The 1980 Hague Convention's drafters accepted the rebuttable presumption that it is in the child's best interests to return to the state of habitual residence as soon as possible. The reason for this is that the courts in the state of habitual residence are best placed to hold custody proceedings due to the complexities of custody issues, such as the difficulties in obtaining evidence away from the child's place of habitual residence. The rebuttable presumption establishes the limited scope of exceptions for a child's nonreturn, which must be proved by the party claiming them, usually the adducting parent. However, from the *travaux préparatoires* of the 1980 Hague Convention, one can learn that children were not considered the most vulnerable subjects of the international parental abduction cases, but the left-behind parents.[20] The abducting parent was seen as holding the advantage since it is he or she who had chosen the forum for the case, which he or she usually regards as more favourable to his or her claims.[21] Whereas the aim of the 1980 Hague Convention was "to deprive his [the abducting parent] actions of any practical or juridical consequences."[22] The 1980 Hague Convention "places at the head of its objectives the restoration of the status quo, by means of the prompt return of children wrongfully removed to or retained in any Contracting State."[23] Thus, the legal vulnerability of children as a group or the single abducted child was not necessarily the main subject of the 1980 Hague Convention. Furthermore, sometimes a child may be perceived "as a legal object so that it becomes invisible inside the

---

19 E. Pérez-Vera, *Explanatory Report...*, p. 428.

20 Report of the Special Commission, Nos 3 and 7 to 15, Acts and Documents of the Fourteenth Session (1980), tome III, Child abduction, see also: J. Caldwell, "Child welfare defences in child abduction cases – some recent developments," *Child and Family Law Quarterly* 2001, Vol. 13, No. 2, p. 121.

21 E. Pérez-Vera, *Explanatory Report...*, p. 429.

22 Ibidem.

23 Ibidem.

mechanism of the Hague Convention."[24] Therefore, the legal subjectivity of minors is emphasized in the 1980 Hague Convention only with a limited scope. That could arouse from the fact that in the late 1970s, when the 1980 Hague Convention was drafted, the principle of *the best interests of a child* was used only in a narrow area of custody law. The CRC was yet to be adopted. Over time it became an essential principle shaping children's rights within the human rights law.[25]

Moreover, the Hague procedure does not include comprehensive analyses of the child's situation in the individual international abduction case as the main aim of the 1980 Hague Convention was to cause the prompt return to the state of her or his habitual residence. In the individual international abduction case, the court's role is to examine whether the prerequisites for refusal of return have been met. These prerequisites are laid down in details in the 1980 Hague Convention and are as follows: the child has no habitual residence in the applicant's state or the applicant is not entitled to custody,[26] a period of more than one year has elapsed from the date of the wrongful removal or retention to the date of the commencement of the proceedings before the judicial or administrative authority,[27] the left-behind parent was not actually exercising the custody rights at the time of removal or retention,[28] the left-behind parent consented to or subsequently acquiesced in the removal or retention,[29] there is a grave risk that the return of the child would expose the child to physical or psychological harm or otherwise place the child in an intolerable situation,[30] the child objects to being returned and has attained an age and degree of maturity at which it is appropriate to take account of its views,[31] which is the only one exception where the 1980 Hague Convention where the legal subjectivity of a minor comes to the force. The last prerequisite is that the child's return under the provisions of

---

24 Z. Ponjavic, V. Vlaskovic, "Space for the Child's Best Interests inside the Hague Convention on the Civil Aspects of International Child Abduction," *Revija za evropsko pravo: XVI* 2014, p. 49.

25 Ibidem, p. 50.

26 See more on the custody rights in: R. Schuz, "The Hague Child Abduction Convention and Children's Rights," *Transnational Law & Contemporary Problems* 2002, No. 12, p. 409.

27 Article 12 of the 1980 Hague Convention.

28 Article 13(a) of the 1980 Hague Convention.

29 Ibidem.

30 Article 13(b) of the 1980 Hague Convention.

31 Article 13, second sentence of the 1980 Hague Convention.

Article 20 may be refused if this would not be permitted by the fundamental principles of the requested State relating to the protection of human rights and fundamental freedoms. These prerequisites are to be interpreted strictly. The burden of proof lies with the person who opposes the child's return. This brief overview of the premises shows that in the 1980 Hague Convention, there is no space for the application of the best interest of child principle. That was complying with the law in 1980, yet, nowadays, it may be contrary to Article 3 of the CRC, which states that the child's best interests shall be a primary consideration in all actions concerning children.[32] Some authors think that 45 states that have ratified both the ECHR and the 1980 Hague Convention are bound by two conflicting interpretations of the best interests of the child principle.[33] It is not surprising that the 1980 Hague Convention has been challenged in front of the ECtHR on this ground.

The international parental abduction cases often are decided by the ECtHR because the Court is seen by both the abducting or the left-behind parents as a last resort in the abduction proceedings. According to ECtHR jurisprudence in the cases of international child abduction, the child rights approach applies. Moreover, Article 8 of the European Convention on Human Rights hereinafter ECHR needs to be interpreted in connection to the 1980 Hague Convention[34] and the CRC.[35] However, the ECHR does not expressly refer to *the best interests of the child*. The question of correspondence between the 1980 Hague Convention and CRC was strongly raised for the first time in *Maumousseau and Washington v. France*.[36] In this case, a French national married a United States national in New York. After a marital crisis, a French national went to stay with her parents

---

32 In 2013 the Committee on the Rights of the Child issued its General Comment No. 14 on the rights of the child to have his or her best interest taken as a primary consideration in all actions or decisions concerning children, both in the public and private sphere. Identifying Article 3, paragraph 1 of the CRC as one of the four general principles for interpreting and implementing all the rights of the child, the Committee defined *the best interests of the child* as a dynamic threefold concept requiring context-specific assessment.

33 H. Keller, C. Heri, "Protecting the Best Interests of the Child: International Child Abduction and the European Court of Human Rights," *Nordic Journal of International Law Journal* 2015, Vol. 84, p. 274.

34 *Ignaccolo-Zenide v. Romania*, No. 31679/96, 25 January 2000.

35 Handbook on European law relating to the rights of the child, European Union Agency for Fundamental Rights and Council of Europe, 2015, p. 86; *Maire v. Portugal*, No. 48206/99, 26 June 2003.

36 *Maumousseau and Washington v. France*, No. 39388/05, 6 December 2007.

in France for the holidays with her husband's consent. She finally decided to remain there and did not return to the USA, despite her husband's repeated requests. The American court awarded temporary custody to the United States national. As a result, the father applied to the United States Central Authority to secure his child's return under the 1980 Hague Convention. The French national refused to return the child to the father. The court of the first instance dismissed the application. The public prosecutor appealed against this decision. The applet court set aside the judgment of the first instance court and ordered the prompt return of a child to the place of her habitual residence. The French national appealed against this judgment to the Court of Cassation claiming a violation of Article 13(b) of the 1980 Hague Convention and of Article 8 of the ECHR, and a failure to take into account the *child's best interests* as guaranteed by Article 3 § 1 of the CRC. In the meantime, the French authorities tried to enforce the Court of Appeal's judgment by entering the child's nursery school. The French national, the child's grandparents, and school staff physically opposed the police intervention by forming a protective barrier around the child, helped by the prompt arrival of several villagers and the village mayor himself. The operation attracted widespread media attention, nationally as well as locally. As a result, the child was placed for six months in specialist family care. Court of Appeal endorsed the child's temporary placement in care but, when ruling on the merits, ordered that she be removed from the care and returned to her father following the USA court's decision. In the end, the girl left France for the USA. Also, the Court of Cassation dismissed the appeal of the French national. The American court granted visitation rights to the French national on rigorous conditions.[37] The French national summoned the ECtHR on the alleged violation of Articles 3, 6 § 1 and 8 of the ECHR, claiming that the child's separation from mother and environment in France placed her in an *intolerable situation* because of her very young age and was contrary to her *best interests*. In this case, the ECtHR expressed the belief that the concept of *the child's best interests* was essential in the procedures provided in the Hague Convention. Moreover, this concept's integral element was the child's right not to be unlawfully taken or retained. The ECtHR wholeheartedly agreed with the philosophy underlying the 1980 Hague Convention, that this instrument was inspired by the desire to stop the increase in the number of parental abductions. The ECtHR failed to see how the interpretation of Article 13(b) of the 1980 Hague Convention by national courts was incompatible with

37 *Maumousseau and Washington v. France*, paras. 8–40.

the CRC. However, differently to the previous cases, the Court underlined that the domestic courts thoroughly examined the situation of the whole family and all factors affecting the child's situation, in particular the child's actual, emotional, psychological, material, and medical situation, and made a balanced and reasonable assessment of the interests of each person involved in the case. Then determined what would be best for the girl in the context of her return to the USA. The "in-depth examination of the entire family situation and of a whole series of factors, in particular of a factual, emotional, psychological, material, and medical nature"[38] conducted by the French authorities, meant that these best interests had been adequately taken into consideration.[39] In *Maumousseau and Washington v. France,* the ECtHR tried to achieve the correspondence of the 1980 Hague Convention with the CRC by parsing the French courts for conducting the *in-depth examination* in the given case. However, the first inaccuracy arose because, in the 1980 Hague Convention proceedings, there is no place for an *in-depth examination of the entire family situation*. Under the 1980 Hague Convention, the national court in the abduction state must examine only the premises for nonreturn. The *in-depth examination of the entire family situation* should be carried out in the state of the child's habitual residence. However, the ECtHR could not pass unconcernedly by the alleged incoherence between the national court order and the CRC. The initial enthusiastic attitude towards the *in-depth examination* expressed by the ECtHR in *Maumousseau and Washington v. France* has changed into obligation imposed on the national courts in *Neulinger and Shuruk v. Switzerland.*

In this case, the first applicant was born in Switzerland and then moved to Israel, where she met an Israeli national, and they had a son. Soon after, the Israeli national joined the Jewish "Lubavitch" movement, which the first applicant described "as an ultra-orthodox, radical movement that is known for its zealous proselytising."[40] The conflicts that arose between parties focused on belonging to the movement. The first applicant was afraid that the Israeli national would take the child to join the community abroad. Therefore she applied for a *ne exeat* order[41] to prevent the child from being removed from Israel.

38 Ibidem, para. 74.
39 Ibidem, paras. 74–76.
40 *Neulinger and Shuruk v. Switzerland*, No. 41615/07, 6 July 2010, para. 18.
41 On *ne exet* order in parental abduction cases see: L. Silberman, "Patching Up the Abduction Convention: A Call for a New International Protocol and a Suggestion for Amendments to ICARA," *Texas International Law Journal* 2003, Vol. 38, No. 41, pp. 45–48.

The Israeli court granted her the *ne exeat* and *temporary custody* of the child. The father was given visitation rights. The conflict escalated. The first applicant claimed the husband's violence. The couple got divorced. The first applicant applied to the Israeli court to annulment the *ne exeat* order prohibiting removing the child from Israel. However, she was declined because there was a severe risk that the first applicant would not return to Israel with the child after visiting her family abroad. Regardless, the mother secretly left Israel with the child. The Israeli national started looking for them, and Interpol found them a year later in Switzerland. The father applied under the 1980 Hague Convention. His application was dismissed by the Swiss court on the grounds of Article 13(b) of the 1980 Hague Convention, as there was a grave risk that the child's return would expose him to physical or psychological harm or otherwise place him in an intolerable situation. The father appealed against that decision. The court of appeal ordered an expert's report, which advised to decline the application, firstly on the base that it would be harmful to the child to go back without the mother, and secondly that the mother cannot go back since she might be subject to criminal procedure for abducting her child. The father lodged an appeal with the Federal Court claiming that the court had misapplied firstly Article 13(b) of the 1980 Hague Convention, and secondly Article 3 of the CRC. The Federal Court changed the order of the lower instances and ordered the mother to secure the child's return to Israel because the mother has failed to establish the existence of reasons that would objectively justify her refusal to return to Israel.[42] In the meantime, the district court, at the request of the first applicant, decided that the child should live with the mother in Switzerland, suspended the father's visitation rights, and granted parental authority to the mother. The court justified the decision by stating that according to case-law, the wrongful removal does not itself deter the establishment of a new habitual residence for a child in the country to which he or she has been taken. In the present case, the child had lived in Switzerland for four years. Moreover, the court stated that the father was impossible to locate, and he appeared to have lost interest in the present case.[43]

The circumstance of the case brought the ECtHR to the conclusion that a fair balance between the competing interests at stake must be reached in international child abduction cases. The competing interests are those of the child, of the two parents, and public order. This should be done within the margin

42 *Neulinger and Shuruk v. Switzerland*, para. 44.
43 Ibidem, para. 47.

of appreciation afforded to states in such matters. However, the child's best interests must be the primary consideration, as is apparent from the preamble to the 1980 Hague Convention, which provides that "the interests of children are of paramount importance in matters relating to their custody." On this basis, the ECtHR stated that there is currently a broad consensus – including in international law – supporting the idea that in all decisions concerning children, their best interests must be paramount. In other words, the concept of the child's best interests is also an underlying principle of the 1980 Hague Convention. Moreover, certain domestic courts have expressly incorporated that concept into the application of the term *grave risk* under Article 1(b) of that Convention.[44] In this paragraph of the judgment, the ECtHR touched on the nature of the best interest principle but did not consider its procedural character, which this principle has adopted in the 1980 Hague Convention. The ECtHR found the Hague proceedings as any other proceedings concerning children where the best interest principle is a substantive measure. That is especially evident in paragraph 139, where the ECtHR stated that the ECtHR

> must ascertain whether the domestic courts conducted an in-depth examination of the entire family situation and a whole series of factors, in particular of a factual, emotional, psychological, material, and medical nature, and made a balanced and reasonable assessment of the respective interests of each person, with a constant concern for determining what the best solution would be for the abducted child in the context of an application for his return to his country of origin.[45]

States were thus required to take into account "a variety of individual circumstances, in particular [the child's] age and level of maturity, the presence or absence of his [or her] parents and his [or her] environment and experiences," as well as the child's linguistic proficiency and familiarity with the new environment, wherefore an in-depth examination was necessary in each case.[46]

This reasoning was acclaimed with sharp criticism.[47] The ECtHR interpretation meant that in each Hague proceedings held in the ECHR Member States,

44 Ibidem, para. 134.
45 *Neulinger and Shuruk v. Switzerland*, para. 139.
46 Ibidem.
47 In the matter of S (a Child) [2012] UKSC 10, in where the Supreme Court of the United Kingdom expressed the opinion: "[w]ith the utmost respect to our colleagues in Strasbourg, we reiterate our conviction, as Reunite requests us to do, that neither the Hague Convention nor, surely, article 8 of the European Convention requires the court which determines an application under the former to conduct an in-depth examination of the sort described. Indeed it would be entirely inappropriate;" see

the domestic courts were obligated to examine not only the fulfilment of the nonreturn premises but also if the return is in the best interest of the child in general. That was seen as overturning the underlying presumption of the 1980 Hague Convention. Moreover, the in-depth examination of the child's situation could have led to excessive elongation of already overly elongated proceedings. However, return proceedings are urgent, and return orders should be rapidly enforced. Thou, the Hague proceeding is not a full-scale judicial procedure, but rather an initial legal response to *put out the fire* until the courts in the place of residence can deal with the child's best interests and decide upon final custody over the child.[48] However, it is quite understandable that the ECtHR, which ensures the enforcement of human rights, could not turn an indifferent eye on incoherent application of the principle, which aims to protect vulnerable parties in court proceedings.

Shortly after, the ECtHR identified the consequences of applying the best interest principle to the Hague proceedings, as described in *Neulinger and Shuruk v. Switzerland.* Therefore, the ECtHR revised their viewpoint in *X v. Latvia*. In this case, the ECtHR adopted a harmonised application of the best interest principle and the 1980 Hague Convention. That can be achieved provided that the following two conditions are fulfilled. Firstly, the circumstances capable of constituting an exception to the child's immediate return in the application of Articles 12, 13 and 20 of the 1980 Hague Convention, mainly where they are raised by one of the parties to the proceedings, must genuinely be taken into consideration by the domestic court. That court must then make a decision that is sufficiently reasoned on this point to enable the ECtHR to verify that those questions have been adequately examined. Secondly, these factors must be evaluated in light of Article 8 of the ECHR.

In consequence, the ECtHR considers that Article 8 of the ECHR sets on the domestic courts a particular procedural obligation in this respect. When assessing an application for a child's return, the courts must not only consider arguable allegations of a *grave risk* for the child in the event of a return. Still, they must also give a judgment regarding specific reasons in light of the

---

also: L. Walker, "The Impact of the Hague Abduction Convention on the Rights of the Family in the Case-Law of the European Court of Human Rights and the UN Human Rights Committee: The Danger of Neulinger," *Journal of Private International Law* 2010, Vol. 6, No. 3, pp. 649–682.

48 E. Sthoeger, "International Child Abduction and Children's Rights: Two Means to the Same End," *Michigan Journal of International Law* 2011, Vol. 32, No. 511, p. 534, [online:] http://repository.law.umich.edu/mjil/vol32/iss3/3 [available: 15.03.2020].

case's circumstances. Both a refusal to take account of objections and insufficient reasoning in the decision dismissing complaints would be contrary to the requirements of Article 8 and the aim and purpose of the Hague Convention.[49] Moreover, as the preamble to the 1980 Hague Convention provides for children's return *to the State of their habitual residence*, the courts must satisfy themselves that adequate safeguards are convincingly provided in that country, and, in the event of a known risk, that tangible protection measures are in place. Therefore, the reasoning must not be *automatic and stereotyped.*[50] The domestic court is obligate to carry out an effective examination of all allegations concerning the premises of no-return raised by the abducting party.[51] That may come to light as lowering high standards of protection of children's rights established for the proceedings concerning children in the CRC. It should not be excessive to say that the interpretation given in *X v. Latvia* can be seen as a restriction to human rights, and as any restriction to human rights, must be interpreted narrowly.[52] The question is if anything can be done to strengthen the children's rights within the limitation established in *X v. Latvia*. The child objects to being returned are one of the nonreturn premises of the 1980 Hague Convention. Therefore, it is questionable under Article 13 of the 1980 Hague Convention if the exception appears when the abducting parent claims the child's objection or the should be activated wherever the court finds that the child objects even without the parent's claim.[53] The abducting parents often reiterate that the child is not willing to go back, yet not always. Therefore, according to interpretation in *X v. Latvia,* domestic courts are obligated to examine these premises. The question arises on how the domestic court can read this premise if the court does not hear the child. Therefore, in my opinion, there are two possible methods to increase the protection of children's rights and, at the same time to adopt a dynamic interpretation of evolving standards[54] of human rights protection in the 198 Hague Convention. The first is to hear a child in the court proceedings, and the second is to provide him or her a legal representation in court.

---

49 *X v. Latvia*, No. 27853/09, 26 November 2013, paras. 106–107.

50 Ibidem, para. 107.

51 Ibidem, para. 118.

52 *Klass and Others v. Germany*, No. 5029/71, 6 September 1978, para. 42, and *Observer and Guardian v. the United Kingdom*, No. 13585/88, 12 July 1990, para. 59.

53 R. Schuz, The Hague Child Abduction Convention: A Critical Analysis" London 2013, p. 317.

54 E.g. *Tyrer v. United Kingdom*, No. 5856/72, 25 April 1978.

4. Hearing of the child

As underlined in the previous chapter, it is not clear from Article 13 whether the objections to the return should be examined only when the abducting party claims that or there is an obligation to examine if the child objects even if the abducting parent does not raise this premises. One can argue that the second solution is the only possible under Article 12 of the CRC. The CRC's protective measures have already been lowered in the Hague proceedings as to the application of Article 3 of the CRC. It would be even more irrespective of the children's rights to limit the possibility of hearing the child's view only to the situation when the abducting parent claims that. One cannot forget that raising the issue may be contrary to the abducting parent's interest as he or she may be aware that the child wants to return. However, under Article 8, the ECtHR does not interpret the right to respect private and family life as always requiring the child to be heard in court.[55] The ECtHR accepted the domestic court's decisions not to hear abducted children in the past.[56] The child's opinion, therefore, can but does not *per se* justify nonreturn.[57] Once again, the jurisprudence of the ECtHR can be seen as departing from the strict application of the CRC. In the literature, there are four main arguments given to deny the child the right to participate.[58] First is the capability argument. That argument is often followed by the question concerning the wording of Article 12 of the CRC, which states that the child capable of forming his or her views should have the right to freely express those views in all matters affecting the child. Therefore, the arguments being given due weight consideration following the age and maturity of the child. This article's wording often recalls a limitation of the right to be heard only to older children. Consequently, one can raise the question of what age the rights to participate would not be challenged. In the ECtHR case-law, the testimony of an abducted child aged three years and five months at the time of the domestic proceedings was found *non-decisive*.[59] Still, children as old as eleven

55 *Handbook on European law relating to the rights of the child*, European Union Agency for Fundamental Rights and Council of Europe, 2015, p. 42.

56 *Gajtani v. Switzerland*, No. 43730/07, Judgment of 9 September 2014, para. 112.

57 *Levadna v. Ukraine*, No. 7354/10, 27 April 2010, *Raw and Others v. France*, No. 10131/11, 07 June 2013, *Blaga v. Romania*, No. 37379/02, para. 80.

58 T. Gal, B. Duramy, *International Perspectives and Empirical Findings on Child Participation: From Social Exclusion to Child-Inclusive Policies*, Oxford 2015, pp. 2–5; see also: R. Schuz, *The Hague Child Abduction Convention...*, pp. 317–353.

59 *Maumousseau and Washington v. France*, para. 80.

were considered unable to decide for themselves what is in their best interests.[60] However, that is contrary to the interpretation of the CRC given in General Comment No. 7, which states the CRC defines a child as "every human being below the age of eighteen years unless, under the law applicable to the child, majority is attained earlier." Consequently, young children are holders of all the rights enshrined in the CRC.[61] Moreover, General Comment emphasizes that Article 12 of the CRC applies both to younger and older children. As holders of rights, even the youngest children are entitled to express their views, which should be "given due weight in accordance with the age and maturity of the child."[62] Young children are sensitive to their surroundings and rapidly acquire an understanding of their own unique identity, people, places, and routines in their lives. They make choices and communicate their wishes, feelings, and ideas in many different ways, long before talking.[63] We also cannot forget that capacity is acquired gradually. The capacity argument application can lead to a vicious circle where the child cannot be heard because he or she is found incapable of forming his or her views. Simultaneously, the child cannot prove differently because he or she cannot be heard. Therefore, the question arises of how the above-mentioned interpretation of Article 12 can be reconciled with granting the children the right to be heard in the Hague proceedings in a very narrow manner.

The second problem is the best interest consideration. The parents, judges, or child-care professionals elaborate that argument, as taking part in the decision-making process would expose children to stress, hurt them, or put them in a situation of conflict. The primary observation here is that abducted children are already in the position of conflict as the most vulnerable, passive, and unwilling participants.[64] Moreover, the conflict is often beyond the family conflict and sometimes turns into the conflict of legal cultures, doctrines, and general perception of the law. The social research shows that most children asked whether they wish to participate in the decision-making process are clear about their

---

60 *Tarkhova v. Ukraine*, No. 8984/11, Decision of 6 September 2011.

61 General Comment No. 7 (2005) Implementing child rights in early childhood, Committee on the Rights of the Child, Fortieth Session Geneva, 12–30 September 2005, CRC/C/GC/7/Rev.1, para. 3

62 Article 12 of the CRC.

63 General Comment No. 7, para. 14.

64 Z. Ponjavic, V. Vlaskovic, "Space for the Child's. . .," p. 49.

wishes to be listened to and taken seriously.[65] Also, experiencing difficulties is not necessarily the same as what experiences harm. It cannot be measured whether it would be more difficult for a child to experience difficulties related to participation or those caused by non-participating. From the developmental point of view, there are two main arguments presented: the enlightenment argument and the empowerment argument. The enlightenment argument is that children can provide valuable information about their perspectives and experience to contribute to more informed decisions and potentially more positive and workable outcomes. They can be *experts* in their own lives. The empowerment argument is that children can benefit from being involved in several ways. When they participate, they learn to make decisions and have a greater sense of control and self-esteem. They see themselves as people with interests and perspectives on the decision rather than merely as someone else's trouble.[66] Participation provides for personal development, leads to better decision-making and outcomes, contributes to preparation for civil society development, tolerance, and respect for others, and strengthens accountability.[67] One of the few published empirical studies concerning child abduction also suggests that children's lack of involvement may cause them to lose faith in the adult world. One previously abducted young person reported that the *major stress* was not moving countries, but that decisions were made without taking children seriously or giving sufficient weight to their views.[68] Moreover, in family law, irrespectively if a court or the parents make decisions, children would recognise judgments as fairer and more likely comply with them if they have had involvement in the case, at least in terms of being heard.[69]

---

65 T. Gal, B. Duramy, *International Perspectives…*, pp. 2–5, J. Cashmore, "Children's participation in family law decision making: Theoretical approaches to understanding children's views," *Children and Youth Services Review* 2011, Vol. 33, pp. 515–520; R.A. Hart, *Children's Participation: The Theory and Practice of Involving Young Citizens in Community Development and Environmental Care*, Routledge 1997, p. 43.

66 J. Cashmore, "Children's participation…," p. 515.

67 G. Lansdown, *Every child's right to be heard a resource guide on the UN Committee on the rights of the child General Comment No. 12, Save the Children UK on behalf of Save the Children and UNICEF* 2011, pp. 3–12, [online:] https://www.unicef.org/french/adolescence/files/Every_Childs_Right_to_be_Heard.pdf [available: 31.03.2020].

68 M. Freeman, *International Child Abduction the Effects, Reunite Research Centre* 2006, p. 61 [online:] http://takeroot.org/ee/pdf_files/library/freeman_2006.pdf [available: 31.03.2020].

69 J. Cashmore, "Children's participation…," p. 515.

The third argument that children should not be heard is the confrontational nature of participation.[70] As mentioned already, international parental child abduction is confrontational *per se,* and many interests are represented in this situation, not only the parties to the proceedings.[71] However, the hearing cannot lead to making the child choose between two parents[72] because that is not the question of the Hague abduction proceedings. The problem, at least in theory,[73] is to select the appropriate forum for the custody proceedings. Therefore, the hearing should concentrate on aspects of living in certain places and particular cultural surroundings, not only with certain people. When children are involved in the parental conflict, the often raised controversy is that children object to return because they are under the influence of the abducting parent,[74] which may be a fact in many cases. However, this factual circumstance should not become a prerequisite to deny the right to be heard to all children. It must be weight in the light of the fact that adult parties of the court proceeding are also often under the influences of others, and this does not limit their capability for actively presenting their views in the courtroom. When reading the case-law in the Hague abduction proceedings, one can get the impression that children are subject to higher requirements in court than people in general.[75] Even where there is evidence that children's views have been influenced, the

70 T. Gal, B. Duramy, *International Perspectives...*, pp. 2–5.

71 According to some theories of international law, state interests, such as respect for their own laws, are a key factor in state behaviour, which includes the decision to comply with international norms. Enhancing the rights of all children by promoting a mechanism to deter potential abductors-as called for by the CRC itself is a worthy primary consideration. Ensuring member states interests in maintaining the effectiveness of the 1980 Hague Convention can be viewed as a valid secondary consideration. See: E. Sthoeger, "International Child Abduction and Children's Rights...," pp. 536–537.

72 E. Pérez-Vera, *Explanatory Report...*, p. 433.

73 It should be bear in mind that the custody proceedings will not always take place in state of the habitual residence, either because of lack of willingness of the parties to conduct them or the lack of money.

74 It the case *S. v. S. (Child Abduction)* [1992] 2 FLR 31 (United Kingdom – England And Wales High Court First Instance) the court stated: "if the court should come to the conclusion that the child's views have been influenced by some other person, e.g. the abducting parent... then it is probable that little or no weight will be given to those views. Any other approach would be to drive a coach and horses through the primary scheme of the Hague Convention."

75 *Charles J in Re S (Abduction: Children's Representation)* [2008] EWHC 1798 (Fam).

court should try to assess the effect of the influence rather than ignore the child's views completely. Therefore, children's right to be heard cannot be seen as inflammatory to the conflict, but rather as a mode to reach an agreement that will be respected by all the parties to the conflict.

The fourth argument is the cost-effectiveness of children's participation.[76] That certainly is a significant issue in the Hague proceedings, as the 1980 Hague Convention sets an unrealistic time limit of six weeks for the order to be delivered,[77] which is rarely obeyed.[78] However, the effectiveness of the proceedings should not be raised as another argument to limit the children's rights within the 1980 Hague Convention. The practical exercise of the right to be heard clearly requires appropriate preparations, including simplified internal procedures within the Member States of the 1980 Hague Convention and substantive training of the judges and other professionals engaged in the Hague proceedings. Under the 1980 Hague Convention, examining the nonreturn premises is required, yet the court is obligated to conduct the parents' hearing[79] or their legal representatives. Nothing stands in the way to hear the child on the same date as the parents so that not much delay would be caused.

The problem mentioned above urges us to consider the possible methods of hearing the child. Generally speaking, in the literature, the four main

76 T. Gal, B. Duramy, *International Perspectives.*, pp. 2–5.

77 Article 11 of the 1980 Hague Convention.

78 See among others: M.M. Copertino, "Hague Convention on the Civil Aspects of International Child Abduction: An Analysis of Its Efficacy," *Connecticut Journal of International Law* 1991, Vol. 6, No. 2, pp. 715–744; E.S. Horstmeyer, "The Hague Convention on the Civil Aspects of International Child Abduction: An Analysis of Tahan and Viragh and Their Impact on Its Efficacy," *University of Louisville Journal of Family Law* 1994–1995, Vol. 33, No. 1, pp. 125–142; for the discussions on the problem of delay before the ECtHR see: P. Beaumont, "The Jurisprudence of the European Court of Human Rights and the European Court of Justice on the Hague Convention of International Child Abduction," *Recueil des cours/Académie de droit international* 2008, Vol. 335, pp. 79–80; N. Lowe, "A supra-national approach to interpreting the 1980 Hague Child Abduction Convention – a tale of two European Courts: Part 1: Setting the Scene," *International Family Law* 2012, pp. 48–52; In *López Guió v. Slovakia* App. No. 10280/12, 3 June 2014, the Hague proceedings were in breach of Article 8 ECHR because they took 22 months, however the ECtHR took two years and four months to decide the case.

79 The reformed Brussels II bis Regulation required the mandatory hearing of the left-behind parent in proceedings conducted with the EU.

approaches to determine children's views are identified.[80] The first is to commission an expert (a welfare officer, social worker, psychologist, or psychiatrist) to examine the child and then report to the court on the child's maturity and views. However, this method is criticised, as the report can be affected by personal opinions of the expert on the situation of the child in the case, but also by the general views of the expert on the application of the 1980 Hague Convention. For this reason, the expert report is not strictly in compliance with the right of the child to be heard.[81]

The other method is for the judge to meet with the child in person and interview him or her. In this method, the judge is in a better position to make an informed decision about the child's views because they can acquire a personal impression of the child. The judge may also gain insights from a face-to-face meeting, which could not be seen from reading a written report. Moreover, hearing the child express his or her views and respond to questions can give the judge a better appreciation of the child as a person and the strength with which those views are held.[82] Regarding the form in which the child must be heard, the ECtHR is relatively tolerant, p. e. it is compatible with the ECHR to listen to a child via webcam. Also, the abducted children can be heard only by the first domestic instance, and the remaining instances can make their assessment based on a protocol that makes it straightforward that there is no grave risk.[83]

The third method is to allow the child to testify in court. This method is rarely used in the Member States of the 1980 Hague Convention's jurisdiction and is seen as the most stressful for children. Thou from the best interest of the child's perspective should be omitted. The fourth method is to order separate legal representation for the child and a highly strengthen children's right to be heard, as discussed in the chapter below.

Disseminating the hearing of an abducted child to increase protection of the most vulnerable actors of the Hague proceedings needs procedural guarantees, which are not present in the 1980 Hague Convention. However, situation alerts within the European Union, where Article 11(2) of Brussel II bis Regulation stipulates that:

---

80 N. Taylor, R. M. Fitzgerald, M. Tamar, A. Bajpai, A. Graham, "International models of child participation in family law proceedings following parental separation/divorce," *International Journal of Children's Rights* 2012, Vol. 20, No. 4, pp. 645–673.

81 More on the pros and cons of this method, see: R. Schuz, *The Hague Child Abduction Convention...*, pp. 373–388.

82 R. Schuz, *The Hague Child Abduction Convention...*, p. 344.

83 *Rouiller v. Switzerland*, No. 3592/08, Judgment of 22 July 2014, para. 72.

> [w]hen applying Articles 12 and 13 of the 1980 Hague Convention, it shall be ensured that the child is given the opportunity to be heard during the proceedings unless this appears inappropriate having regard to his or her age or degree of maturity.

Therefore, the European legislator encourages to give children in the Hague proceedings *the opportunity to be heard*. That was seen as an insufficient way to protect children's rights with the European Union.[84] For this reason, reform in this aspect has been implemented. The amended version of the Regulation[85] adopted in June 2019 provides in Article 21(1):

> the courts of the Member States shall, in accordance with national law and procedure, provide the child who is capable of forming his or her own views with a genuine and effective opportunity to express his or her views, either directly, or through a representative or an appropriate body

And in Article 21(1) we read:

> [w]here the court, in accordance with national law and procedure, gives a child an opportunity to express his or her views in accordance with this Article, the court shall give due weight to the views of the child in accordance with his or her age and maturity.

Firstly, the wording has changed from "it shall be ensured that the child is given the opportunity" to the definitively more robust expression: "provide the child . . . with a genuine and effective opportunity." Secondly, under Article 26, "Article 21 of this Regulation shall also apply in return proceedings under the 1980 Hague Convention." Therefore, there is no doubt now that children should be heard in the Hague proceedings under EU law. This obligation is even strengthened by Article 47(3), which stipulates that the court can issue the certificate for recognition and enforcement of a child's return order if the child was given an opportunity to express their views under Article 21. In consequence, it would be impossible to enforce the return order within the Members States of the EU without hearing of the abducting child in the Hague proceedings.[86]

---

84 B. Ubertazzi, "The hearing of the child in the Brussels IIa Regulation and its Recast Proposal," *Journal of Private International Law* 2017, Vol. 13, No. 3, pp. 568–601.

85 Council Regulation (EU) 2019/1111 of 25 June 2019 on jurisdiction, the recognition and enforcement of decisions in matrimonial matters and the matters of parental responsibility, and on international child abduction, ST/8214/2019/INIT OJ L 178, 2.7.2019, pp. 1–11.

86 The reformed version of the Brussel II bis Regulation shall apply from 1 August 2022.

5. Legal representation for children

Literature analysis undertaken in the previous chapter points out that there is no doubt that children have the right to participate in court proceedings in cases concerning them. However, the wording of Article 12 of the CRC does not stipulates the right of the child to separate legal representation but only stipulates "the opportunity to be heard . . . either directly, or through a representative or an appropriate body" and one should agree that the right to be heard does not go so far as to establish the right to legal representation for children.[87] Nevertheless, next to the obligatory hearing, the separate legal representation for children may constitute a sufficient procedural guarantee to increase the protection of children's rights in court proceedings. This method of participation of children in the proceedings is traditionally realised through the parents who would represent the child, usually through a lawyer instructed by them.[88] The interpretation of Article 12 of the CRC by the Committee does not forbid this form of children's representation. However, one must be cautious with having parents as a representative, as there is often the risk in family law proceedings that there is a conflict between the child and the parents or between the two parents who ought to represent the child's interests jointly.[89] Thus, the only possible solution is a separate legal representation for children.

There are various forms of children's legal representation in different jurisdictions. The most popular is a legal guardian or *guardian ad litem*[90] with the legal authority and the equivalent duty to care for a minor's personal and property interests. Guardian can be a legal practitioner, but sometimes is also a person with qualifications and experience in social, health, or behavioural

87 N. Bala, R. Birnbaum, "Rethinking the role of lawyers for children: Child representation in Canadian family relationship cases," *Les Cahiers de Droit* 2018, Vol. 59, No. 4, p. 792.

88 R. Schuz, *The Hague Child Abduction Convention. . .*, p. 391.

89 *The Committee's General Comment No. 12, Committee on the Rights of the Child*, Fifty-first session Geneva, 25 May-12 June 2009, para. 36, see also: Ch. Mol, "Children's Representation in Family Law Proceedings A Comparative Evaluation in Light of Article 12 of the United Nations Convention on the Rights of the Child," *International Journal of Children's Rights* 2019, Vol. 27, p. 70.

90 *Kurator* in Article 99 of the Polish Family and Guardianship Code; *administrateur ad hoc* in Article 388-2 of the French Civil Code, *a special guardian* in Article 1: 250 of the Dutch Civil Code, *Guardian ad litem* in Article 41 of Children Act 1989, *Guardian ad litem* in Rule 17(2) of the Federal Rules of Civil Procedure in the USA.

sciences[91] or even a person whose only requirement is to be not associated with the parties to the proceedings.[92] Then there are independent children's lawyers or the independent legal representative who are legal practitioners and represent the child's interests in legal proceedings.[93] The third category is the direct (separate) legal representative, who acts on children's instructions and serves their views.[94]

In the Hague proceedings question of the separate representation for abducted children is of particular importance. The consequences of the return order can be severed for all parties engaged in the proceedings and have a deep impact on a child's life are more far-reaching than in a typical custody case. Depending on whether the abducted child will return or not, and whether the abducting parent will return with the child or not, the contact with one of the parents will be significantly reduced. The outcome of the custody proceedings in the habitual residence state is often difficult to predict, and not always the custody proceedings are initiated at all. Therefore, the Hague order can settle the child's life for many years ahead.

Despite the severe consequences of the Hague order for the child's lives, the concept of the separate representation for abducted children is often criticized. The first argument raised is that the separate representation would cause significant delay. Yet this argument is unfounded. There is no good reason why separate representation should cause a delay if ordered promptly after the proceedings' initiation. In many jurisdictions, legal practitioners are prepared to defend persons in provisional detention within hours after they get arrested, and still, the criminal defence lawyers are not seen as the cause of a delay in the proceedings. Similarly, children or family lawyers should not be seen as causing

---

91 In the Netherlands, special guardians of Article 1: 250 are lawyers or mediators, sometimes non-legal professional with backgrounds social science, e.g. psychologists.

92 See: Decision of Constitutional Tribunal of Poland of 11 February 2014, S 2/14, which recommends, that as legal guardians for children in criminal proceeding should be appointed persons qualified in law or social science and not e.g. court secretariat employees as it happened before.

93 Section 68L of the Family Law Act 1975, Australian federal law, which includes international child abduction cases, *avocat d'enfant* in certain cases of the French Civil Code, among them international child abduction cases, Section 279 of the Children's Act 2005 of South Africa provides a legal representation for children in international abduction cases.

94 New South Wales, Children and Young Persons (Care and Protection) Act 1998 and the Adoption Act 2000.

a delay in the Hague proceedings. If adequately trained lawyers are readily available, they will meet with the child and other relevant persons within a short period.

The other argument is the expenses and remuneration of the separate legal representation. The argument of cost of the proceedings is often raised as limiting the right to a fair trial in general;[95] however, in the case of children is even more complicated because children often have no financial means at their disposal. Therefore the cost of the separate legal representation would have to be bear for the Member States of the 1980 Hague Convention in either of two possible methods: in the manner adopted in the domestic law of a given state for a free legal aid or included in the costs of the proceedings and settled between the parents in the final order. Both methods cannot be seen as generating a significant increase in the cost of the Hague proceedings in general as to the limited number of abduction cases every year.

The idea of separate legal representation for children in the Hague proceedings is not widely spread, despite many voices advocating its use.[96] So far, only in two jurisdictions, there is mandatory separate legal representation for children in the Hague proceedings: South Africa[97] and Switzerland. In the second state, the reasoning behind making the representation compulsory was to prohibit repetition of the situation in divorce proceedings, where a representative was only to be designated if there is a significant need for one. Judges only accept such a designation in sporadic cases.[98]

In other jurisdictions, a separate child representative is appointed in some types of cases, p. e. Australia applies additional requirements making an appointment exceptional. In France, the child can only be assisted in their right to be heard. In the Netherlands, representation is possible in theory but in practice rarely employed due to the short timeframe available for international child abduction proceedings.[99] In Germany, an appointment of a representative for a

95 For example, in *Airey v. Ireland*, No. 6289/73, 9 October 1979, the ECtHR held that Article 6(1) had been violated because the applicant was not able to bring an action for separation against her husband due to the fact that she did not have sufficient financial means to pay for a lawyer.

96 Ch. Mol, *Children's Representation...*, p. 70.

97 Ibidem, p. 83.

98 A. Bucher, "The new Swiss Federal Act on International Child Abduction," *Journal of Private International Law* 2008, Vol. 4, No. 2, p. 150.

99 Ch. Mol, *Children's Representation...*, p. 83.

minor child usually is necessary *when the proceedings relate to removal from . . . from the spouse, the life partner, or person having access rights.*[100]

However, there are jurisdictions where children in the Hague proceedings are not represented in any circumstances. In Poland, children are not formal parties in the proceedings concerning parental authority, custody, or access rights. In consequence, they are also not formally engaged in the Hague proceedings. Accordingly, if they are not considered parties officially, they cannot be represented in any way. Polish constitutional law and polish civil procedure guarantee children the right to be heard in court proceedings concerning them; however, this right is not often executed.[101] Regardless of the voices of polish legal doctrine and both polish ombudsmen, the Commissioner for Human Rights and the Commissioner for Children Rights[102] for the reform to enable children to be formal parties to the proceedings, which in consequence would allow them to be independently represented. However, these appeals do not meet the expected reaction of the legislator. For that reason, the reform should be carried out at the level of the 1980 Hague Convention to introduce uniform procedural guarantees for all abducted children. If the introduction of compulsory representation on an international level for all abducted children would not be possible, it is necessary to discuss mandatory representation in selected categories of cases.[103] A separate child representative's appointment should be considered when a child objects to the return, when doubts arise about determining the child's habitual residence and when the claim of the grave risk is raised.

6. Conclusions

This article has provided an insight into the problem of the vulnerability of children in the Hague proceedings. Because of the procedural understanding of

100 M. Stotzel, J.M. Fegert, "The representation of the legal interests of children and adolescents in Germany: study of the children's guardian from child's perspective," *International Journal of Law, Policy and the Family* 2006, Vol. 20, No. 2, p. 202.

101 J. Słyk, "Aspekty prawne wysłuchania dziecka w postępowaniu cywilnym," *Dziecko krzywdzone. Teoria, badania, praktyka* 2015, Vol. 14, No. 4, p. 28.

102 Joint petition of the Commissioner for Human Rights and the Commissioner for Children Rights to the Ministry of Justice regarding the representative of the child of 27 June 2016, [online:] https://www.rpo.gov.pl/pl/content/jak-ochronic-interes-dziecka-gdy-dochodzi-do-konfliktu-pomiedzy-rodzicami.pdf [available: 20.03.2020].

103 R. Schuz, "The Hague Child Abduction Convention. . .," pp. 394–395.

the child's best interest principle in the 1980 Hague Convention, the problem of protecting children's rights is of particular importance because the Hague order can settle the child's life for many years ahead. The literature analysis embarked upon in this paper shows that children have the right to participate in court proceedings in cases concerning them. The question that must be answered is what form this participation should be applied in the court proceedings, emphasizing the Hague proceedings, that reduce children's legal vulnerability. Firstly, it should be mentioned that any form of participation should include the concept of minors' graduated capacity. Secondly, as was discussed above, the most effective ways of legal participation of children are hearing of the child and separate legal representation for children. To strengthen the protection of the children's rights local jurisdiction involved in the Hague Convention could follow the EU legislator and make the hearing of the child in the Hague proceedings mandatory. The question of the form of hearing, p. e., whether the hearing should always be conducted by the judges themselves or by the experts involved in the proceedings, should be, however left to the particular jurisdiction due to the multiple legal orders and traditions. It is also beyond doubt the professional lawyers representing the interest of individual children engaged in the Hague proceedings can strengthen the children's position and ensure that their voice would be heard.

Bibliography:

Bala N., Birnbaum R., "Rethinking the role of lawyers for children: Child representation in Canadian family relationship cases," *Les Cahiers de Droit* 2018, Vol. 59, No. 4).

Beaumont P. "The Jurisprudence of the European Court of Human Rights and the European Court of Justice on the Hague Convention of International Child Abduction," *Recueil des cours / Académie de droit international* 2008, Vol. 335.

Bigss H., Jones C., "Legally Vulnerable: What is vulnerability and who is vulnerable," in: Freeman, M., Hawkes, S., & Bennett, B., *Law and Global Health, Current Legal Issues*, Volume 16, Oxford University Press, 2014.

Bucher A., "The new Swiss Federal Act on International Child Abduction," *Journal of Private International Law* 2008, Vol. 4, No. 2.

Caldwell J., "Child welfare defences in child abduction cases – some recent developments," *Child and Family Law Quarterly* 2001 Vol. 13, No. 2.

Cashmore J., "Children's participation in family law decision-making: Theoretical approaches to understanding children's views," *Children and Youth Services Review* 2011, Vol. 33.

Copertino M.M., "Hague Convention on the Civil Aspects of International Child Abduction: An Analysis of Its Efficacy," *Connecticut Journal of International Law* 1991, Vol. 6, No. 2.

Fineman M.A., "The Vulnerable Subject: Anchoring Equality in the Human Condition," *Yale Journal of Law & Feminism Feminism* 2008, Vol. 20.

Freean M., *International Child Abduction Effects*, Reunite Research Centre 2006, [online:] http://takeroot.org/ee/pdf_files/library/freeman_2006.pdf.

Gal T., Duramy B., *International Perspectives and Empirical Findings on Child Participation: From Social Exclusion to Child-Inclusive Policies*, Oxford University Press, 2015.

Hart R.A., *Children's Participation: The Theory and Practice of Involving Young Citizens in Community Development and Environmental Care*, Routledge, 1997.

Horstmeyer E. S., "The Hague Convention on the Civil Aspects of International Child Abduction: An Analysis of Tahan and Viragh and Their Impact on Its Efficacy," *University of Louisville Journal of Family Law* 1995, Vol. 33, No. 1.

Ippolito F., Iglesias Sánchez S., *Protecting Vulnerable Groups: The European Human Rights Framework*, Hart Publishing, 2015.

Keller H., Heri C., "Protecting the Best Interests of the Child: International Child Abduction and the European Court of Human Rights," *Nordic Journal of International Law Journal* 2015, Vol. 84.

Kohn N. A., "Vulnerability Theory and the Role of Government," *Yale Journal of Law & Feminism* 2014, Vol. 26, No. 1.

Lansdown G., *Every child's right to be heard a resource guide on the UN Committee on the rights of the child General Comment No. 12*, Save the Children UK on behalf of Save the Children and UNICEF, 2011.

Lowe N., "A supra-national approach to interpreting the 1980 Hague Child Abduction Convention – a tale of two European Courts: Part 1: Setting the Scene," *International Family Law*, 2012.

Mol Ch., "Children's Representation in Family Law Proceedings A Comparative Evaluation in Light of Article 12 of the United Nations Convention on the Rights of the Child," *International Journal of Children's Rights* 2019, Vol. 27.

Pérez-Vera E., *Explanatory Report on the 1980 Hague Child Abduction Convention, Acts and Documents of the Fourteenth Session*, 1980, Vol. III.

Ponjavic Z., Vlaskovic V., "Space for the Child's Best Interests inside the Hague Convention on the Civil Aspects of International Child Abduction," *Revija za evropsko pravo* 2014, Vol. XVI.

Schuz R., "The Hague Child Abduction Convention and Children's Rights," *Transnational Law & Contemporary Problems* 2002, Vol. 12.

Schuz R., *The Hague Child Abduction Convention: A Critical Analysis*, London: Hart Publishing, 2013.

Silberman L., "Patching Up the Abduction Convention: A Call for a New International Protocol and a Suggestion for Amendments to ICARA," *Texas International Law Journal*, Vol. 38: 41, 2003.

Słyk J., Aspekty prawne wysłuchania dziecka w postępowaniu cywilnym, "Dziecko krzywdzone. Teoria, badania, praktyka," 2015, Vol. 14(4), p. 28.

Sthoeger E., "International Child Abduction and Children's Rights: Two Means to the Same End," *Michigan Journal of International Law* 2011, Vol. 32, No. 511.

Stotzel M., Fegert, J.M., "The representation of the legal interests of children and adolescents in Germany: study of the children's guardian from child's perspective," *International Journal of Law, Policy and the Family* 2006, Vol. 20, No. 2.

Taylor N., Fitzgerald R.M., Tamar, M., Bajpai A., Graham A., "International models of child participation in family law proceedings following parental separation/divorce," *International Journal of Children's Rights* 2012, Vol. 20, No. 4.

Ubertazzi B., "The hearing of the child in the Brussels IIa Regulation and its Recast Proposal," *Journal of Private International Law* 2017, Vol. 13, No. 3.

Walker L., "The Impact of the Hague Abduction Convention on the Rights of the Family in the Case-Law of the European Court of Human Rights and the UN Human Rights Committee: The Danger of Neulinger," *Journal of Private International Law* 2010, Vol. 6, No. 3.

Woodhouse, B. B., "A World Fit for Children is a World Fit for Everyone: Ecogenerism, Feminism, and Vulnerability," *Houston Law Review* 2009, Vol. 46, No. 3.

Katarzyna Kamińska

University of Silesia in Katowice

e-mail: katarzynakaminska@us.edu.pl

ORCID ID: 0000-0002-4438-0127

Welfare of adopted children in international legal acts in the twentieth and twenty-first century[1]

Abstract: The function of adoption is to create a family environment for the minor child, ensure care and fulfilment of everyday needs, because of the child's natural immaturity and incapability. Adoption means the establishment between the adopting person and the adopted party of a family law relationship which imitates relations between a parent and a child. It is an act of formal character, whose conclusion depends on the fulfilment of premises required by the provisions of law. However, there is still little talk of adoption in the context of welfare of the child, which this institution is supposed to serve. All of this provided the grounds for considerations on the legal standard of protection for a child adopted under international law. The purpose of this paper is to show how the welfare of an adopted child is protected under international law, based on selected international legal instruments of a universal character.

Keywords: adoption, international adoption, child welfare, international law, adopted children

1. Basic principles of adoption

Adoption (from Latin: *adoptio*), is the creation of a legal relationship between adoptive parent and adoptee that exists between parents and child. In legal language, an adoption that changes the child previous place of residence to another country is commonly referred to as foreign adoption. The statutory

1 This work was supported by grant 2019/33/N/HS5/00284, funded by the National Science Centre, Poland (Praca powstała w wyniku realizacji projektu badawczego nr 2019/33/N/HS5/00284, finansowanego ze środków Narodowego Centrum Nauki).

term of such an adoption is "international adoption."[2] In this paper, these two terms will be used interchangeably.

The essence of adoption is to create a foster care and educational environment for the child, which is as similar as possible – in terms of normative effects of his or her functioning – to the natural environment. This need arises especially when the child becomes a natural (after parents' death) or social orphan. The latter term is used to describe a situation in which at least one of the parents is still alive but does not carry out its parental responsibilities towards the child.[3]

In the judgment of August 8 1967, the Supreme Court indicated that adoption is aimed exclusively at guaranteeing the welfare of the child. It is necessary to emphasise that the child's welfare is the key principle of family law. This term exists both in the language of the law, which encompasses the text of effective regulations and in the legal language, which we use in the discussions of a juridical nature. It is also used in normal speech. However, its statutory definition is yet to be elaborated. For the purpose of this paper, I shall adopt the most representative definition of the child's welfare, presented in the polish legal literature by W. Stojanowska, who sees the child's welfare as

> a set of values of a tangible and intangible nature, required to ensure correct physical and spiritual development of the child and adequate preparation of the child for work in accordance with his or her talents. These values are determined by a number of diverse factors, whose structures depends on the content of the applied legal norm and the specific, at a particular moment in time, situation of the child, assuming that <<the child's welfare>> so understood is consistent with the social interest.[4]

This interpretation corresponds with provisions laid down in the Convention on the Rights of the Child, known as the World Constitution of the Rights of the Child, which became a point of reference for internal policies of states and detailed solutions in international law. While the Convention on the Rights of the Child does not define the child's welfare, most of its provisions entail the principle of primacy of the criterion of the child's welfare, and its scope is defined in provisions of Art. 3(2) of the Convention.

---

2 This term appears in the provisions of the Act of 9 June 2011 on Family Support and the Foster Care System which regulates pre-adoption proceedings (Journal of Laws of 2019, item 1818).

3 See J. F. Strzebinczyk, *Prawo rodzinne*, Warszawa 2016, p. 331.

4 See: W. Stojanowska, *Rozwód a dobro dziecka*, Warszawa 1979, p. 27.

Furthermore, the child's welfare is a general clause that determines the manner of exercise of parental authority.[5] In the evaluation of the child's welfare, one should take into account objective criteria such as the child's sex, his or her age, how the parents treat one another, as well as subjective ones, e.g. the child's sensitivity, feeling of safety, or bonds between the parents and children. An important element – from the point of view of the child's welfare – in addition to proper satisfaction of his or her needs associated with maintenance and upbringing, is the formation in the child's mind of a sense of family connection between the child and his or her adoptive parents, which has an important impact on the proper development of the child's consciousness and emotional sphere.[6]

2. Statistics on international adoptions

The number of adoptions in Poland has been stable for years, averaging 3000 children per year.[7] However, the number of Polish children adopted by couples from abroad has been drastically decreasing, as shown in the table 1.

5 The essence of parental authority is protection of the welfare of the child and the social interest (Art. 95 § 3 of the Family and Guardianship Code). The social interest should generally be consistent with the child's interests. After all, it is in the society's interest that harmonious families exist, with parents caring for the development of their children and thus properly preparing them for independence and work for the society. That said, analysis of relations between an individual and the society is not the subject of interest of family law. Suffice it to note that the Polish legal system, which is humanistic in its assumptions, protects with particular expediency the welfare of the individual.

6 See: judgement of the Supreme Court of 8 August 1957 (I CR 120/67, OSNC 1968, No. 12, item 210).

7 Statistical information of the Ministry of Family, Labour and Social Policy, data for 2006–2015.

Table 1: Statistics on international adoptions (number of adoption cases) in Poland in the years 2012–2018[a]

COUNTRY OF ADOPTIVE PARENTS	**2012**	**2013**	**2014**	**2015**	**2016**	**2017**	**2018**
Austria	0	0	5	0	0	0	0
Belgium	10	0	17	10	6	3	0
Canada	2	0	1	1	0	1	0
France	13	21	24	6	4	2	1
Germany	2	5	2	10	2	2	0
The United Kingdom	0	0	1	1	0	0	0
Ireland	0	0	0	0	1	0	0
Italy	156	209	176	177	124	56	11
Netherlands	13	6	5	8	1	1	1
Spain	9	21	13	17	12	4	1
Sweden	12	17	13	11	12	3	0
USA	38	44	54	85	55	26	14
TOTAL	**255**	**323**	**311**	**326**	**217**	**98**	**28**

Source: *Statistical information of the Ministry of Family, Labour and Social Policy (own research of the Policy Department of the Ministry on the basis of statistical data from reports of the Adoption Centers that organize international adoptions),* https://www.gov.pl/web/rodzina/667informacje-statystyczne [available: 19.10.2020]. Since 2003, over 4,000 children have been adopted by families from abroad; the largest number of charges of Polish orphanages have gone to Italy (2500) and the United States (almost 700).

In 2013, the number of international adoptions worldwide tripled compared to 2003, as shown in the chart.

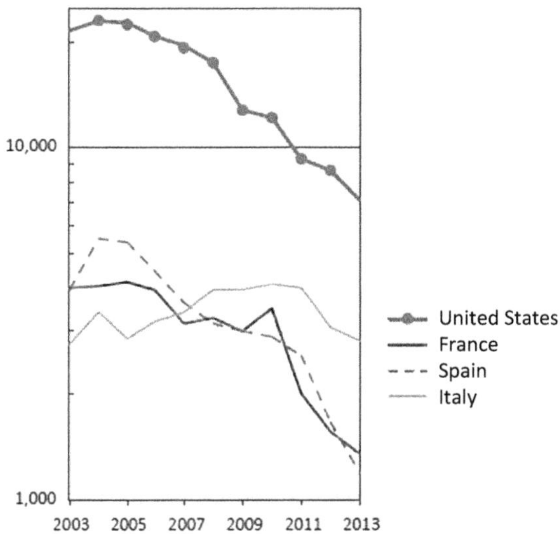

Chart 1: Statistics of international adoptions worldwide, in the main receiving countries in the years 2003–2013 (downward trend). See: P. Selman, *Key tables for intercountry adoption: receiving states 2003–2013 and States of Origin 2003–2013*, Newcastle University 2014. More on the causes of that phenomenon: J. Mignot, "Why is intercountry adoption declining worldwide?, *Population & Societies* 2015, No. 519, p. 3.

International adoptions are part of a global context of poverty and inequality. Most scientists share the view that this phenomenon could not exist in a world without global inequalities. Children who enter the international adoption system come from developing countries, while adoptive parents are from highly developed ones. The importance of international adoptions is the subject of dispute, where positions vary according to the given perspective – taking into account the context of origin or adoption. The declining number of international adoptions worldwide and increasing criticism, together with accusations of child trafficking, have contributed to a change in the adoption system from mass adoption to a more elite system, where childless couples and single people from rich countries realize their belief in the right to have a child and build a family. In this context, the question may arise as to why some countries agree to foreign adoptions, while others with similar social, political and economic circumstances do not.

At the same time, the analysis of this phenomenon indicates that it reflects the division of the world into the center and peripheries and into the system of global inequalities that drives international migration. The latter include, in particular, social and cultural gender inequalities. As the literature shows, women from developed countries (privileged and aware of their rights (e.g. concerning family planning) adopt children from countries where the cultural position of women is low and their bargaining position is weak, further exacerbated by the pressure of the difficult situation of the biological mother.[8] However, there is still little talk of adoption in the context of welfare of the child, which this institution is supposed to serve.

Most representatives of the Polish doctrine claim, that in practice, the most frequent cause of international adoption recently seem the specific needs of the child who requires medical treatment with methods not admitted in Poland, or inaccessible because of excessive costs. Other reasons occur relatively rarely, since the standards of living and civic freedoms in Poland nowadays correspond in full to the EU standards.[9]

All of this provided the grounds for considerations on the legal standard of protection for a child adopted under international law. The purpose of this paper is to show how the welfare of an adopted child is protected under international law, based on selected international legal instruments of a universal character.[10]

3. International adoption laws: A comparative analysis

Development of the international human rights protection system now also includes adoption institutions. With the respective initiatives of international character, the need for protection of the adopted person has been increasingly highlighted.[11] The first international document aimed at protecting the

---

8 See: Ł. Albański, M. Krywult-Albańska, "Adopcje międzynarodowe jako zaniedbany obszar badań nad migracjami," *Studia Migracyjne – Przegląd Polonijny* 2016, No. 3 (161), pp. 384–388.

9 S. Kalus, M. Habdas, *Family and Succession Law in Poland*, 3rd Edition, Wolters Kluwer, 2400 AH Alphen aan den Rijn – the Netherlands 2020, p. 136.

10 The legal standard of protection of human rights, and thus of an adopted human being, includes not only binding acts of international law, but also formally non-binding documents, such as declarations or resolutions. The model of protection is built on the basis of standards contained both in the treaties and other documents devoted *strictly* to human rights, as well as in some treaties of private international law that are important for the protection of human rights, see M. Balcerek, *Międzynarodowa ochrona praw człowieka*, Warszawa 1977, p. 181.

11 R. Łukasiewicz, *Dobro dziecka a interesy innych podmiotów w polskiej regulacji prawnych przysposobienia*, Warszawa 2019, p. 42.

welfare of the adopted child was the Declaration of the Rights of the Child of 13 February 1923.[12] The second point of the Declaration is worth noting, according to which an orphan or an abandoned child should be taken into care and aided. However, it is difficult to perceive such an approach as a direct and comprehensive protection of the welfare of an adopted child.[13] The Declaration of the Rights of the Child was therefore only a starting point for further, more intensive and specific protection of the welfare of a child deprived of a family environment, including an adopted child.

3.1. Declaration of the Rights of the Child

The Declaration of the Rights of the Child was revised and supplemented in 1948. Greater account has been taken of children's rights to family life and potential assistance in the cases of problems or absence of family environment. According to the respective points of the declaration, the child should be provided with assistance while preserving the integrity of the family. It should be given the opportunity for normal physical, moral and mental development, while the orphan and abandoned child should be taken care of and supported. The completed Declaration of the Rights of the Child was more focused on the issue of dysfunctionality of the child's family and on the problem of abandoned and orphaned children. This kind of approach allows the protection of the child's welfare on two extremely important levels related to the institution of adoption:

- taking the child out of an environment he or she should not be in,
- providing care for a minor who is deprived of his or her family.

12 The rights of the child became the subject of world discussion at the turn of the 19th and 20th century. It culminated in the Declaration of the Rights of the Child adopted by the General Assembly of the League of Nations on 26 September 1924, called the Geneva Declaration, [online:] https://wolnelektury.pl/katalog/lektura/deklaracja-praw-dziecka-zwana-genewska.html; http://hrlibrary.umn.edu/instree/childrights.html [available: 19.10.2020].

13 The Declaration of the Rights of the Child was of general character and consisted of five concise points. They concerned the five main problems having a negative impact on the spiritual and material development of the child, such as: hunger, illness, disability, social orphanhood or crime, see: M. Truszkowska-Wojtkowiak, "Prawa dziecka a czas wolny," *Studia Gdańskie. Wizje i rzeczywistość* 2013, Vol. 10, p. 401.

3.2. Universal Declaration of Human Rights

On 10 December 1948, the United Nations General Assembly adopted the Universal Declaration of Human Rights.[14] As indicated in the preamble, that document is undoubtedly one of UN's greatest and most enduring achievements. However, its character was more general and the welfare of the child was only one of its components. Under Article 25(2) of the Declaration, the mother and child have the right to special care and assistance. It is further stated that all children, both marital and extramarital, enjoy equal social protection. That provision covers a wide range of cases in which the best interests of the minor should be taken into account. The issue of the protection of the adopted child was therefore not a key issue to be addressed in the Universal Declaration of Human Rights.

3.3. Declaration of the Rights of the Child

Guaranteeing the protection of human rights did not sufficiently safeguard the best interests of the child and therefore the decision was made to adopt a separate declaration focusing only on the welfare of minors. Thus, on 20 November 1959, the UN General Assembly adopted the Declaration of the Rights of the Child (DRC).[15] Even its preamble stresses that a child, due to physical and mental immaturity, requires special care and attention, as well as appropriate legal care, both before and after birth. According to the second principle of the Declaration of the Rights of the Child, the child shall enjoy special protection, and legislation and other measures shall provide any and all the opportunities for his or her healthy and normal physical, mental, moral,

---

14 The fact that the Universal Declaration of Human Rights was not adopted as a binding international treaty gave rise to a broad discussion on the legal nature of its obligations. The authors of the document were aware that the document would not have a legal character. It was supposed to constitute a moral code, as well as to set the goals and aspirations of humanity in the sphere of human rights, see: J. Bucińska, "Społeczne Prawa Człowieka w Powszechnej Deklaracji Praw Człowieka," *Roczniki Nauk Prawnych* 2003, Vol. 13, No. 1, pp. 126–127.

15 During the preparatory work on the Declaration of the Rights of the Child, similarly to other human rights documents, differences of opinion and differences of approach between socialist and capitalist countries were visible. The works on the document on the rights of the child were dominated by the elements of political dispute between the East and the West, see: E. A. Hanyś, "Polska jako kraj inicjujący i współtworzący Konwencję o Prawach Dziecka," *Wrocławskie Studia Politologiczne* 2015, No. 19, p. 185.

spiritual and social development, in conditions of freedom and dignity. The laws issued for this purpose should be primarily concerned with the welfare of the child. In the context of that issue, the sixth principle of the Declaration of the Rights of the Child seems to be relevant, as it emphasizes:

- bringing up the child in a family ("he or she should grow up under the protection and responsibility of the parents"),
- not separating her or him from the mother ("in the first years of life, the child must not be separated from the mother"),
- providing special care to children without a family ("society and state authorities should provide special care to children without a family or with insufficient means of subsistence").

Protection of the welfare of adopted children is visible in two areas:

- the possibility of separating the child from the family when necessary,
- the care for children who have no family.[16]

3.4. Declaration on Social and Legal Principles Relating to the Protection and Welfare of Children

The Declaration on Social and Legal Principles Relating to the Protection and Welfare of Children, with particular emphasis on foster custody and adoption on a national and international scale (hereinafter: DSLP) of 3 December 1986 was also an important international document concerning the issue of adoption.[17] First of all, it expressed the principle of *child welfare* and *family welfare*. What was recognized was that the child's highest priority is to remain under the care of his or her own parents (art. 3 of the DSLP). Where the care of the child's own parents is unavailable or inappropriate, the care provided by the child's parents' relatives, by another – foster or adoptive – family or, if necessary, by the competent institution, should be considered (Art. 4 of the DSLP). The conditions for placing a child in foster custody and adoptive family were also specified (Articles 4–7 of the DSLP). By way of example, if the case concerns the placement of a child outside his or her natural family, the best interests of the child are paramount, in particular the need for care and the right to safety and

16 See: [online:] https://wolnelektury.pl/katalog/lektura/deklaracja-praw-dziecka.html; http://www.cirp.org/library/ethics/UN-declaration/ [available: 19.10.2020].

17 See: B. Gnel, "Prawo właściwe dla przysposobienia według nowej ustawy – Prawo prywatne międzynarodowe," [in:] *Współczesne wyzwania prawa prywatnego międzynarodowego*, ed. J. Poczobut, Warszawa 2013, p. 101.

constant custody. The Declaration introduced the preparation obligation on the entities handling the conduct in the scope of foster custody and adoption. Another important element is art. 8 of the DSLP, which confirms the protection of the inalienable right of a child to have full name, nationality and a legal representative. As for the institution of adoption, a number of detailed regulations were provided for (Articles 13–24 of the DSLP). Firstly, it was indicated that the primary purpose of adoption is to provide a child who cannot be looked after by his or her parents with a natural, stable family. Secondly, the role of the persons responsible for placing the child in an adoptive family was highlighted, as they are responsible for choosing the most appropriate environment for the child. Their task is to advise the child's parents, future adoptive parents and, where possible, the child, in deciding on his or her future.

In the analysed declaration, most attention was devoted to the issue of international adoption (Articles 17–24 of the DSLP). First of all, the principle of subsidiarity of that type of adoption was assumed. It is worth emphasizing that that principle was introduced to the provisions of the Family and Guardianship Code (hereinafter: the FGC)[18] after Poland ratified the Convention on the Rights of the Child of 20 November 1989 (hereinafter: the CRC).[19] It consists in the fact that an adoption which will result in the change of the previous place of residence to the place of residence in another state is permissible only if it is possible to provide the adopted person with an appropriate substitute family environment (Articles 114^2 and 120^1 § 3 of the FGC). In other words – only when it is not possible to organize appropriate conditions for bringing a child up in the given country, in particular based on the procedure of his/her adoption.[20]

18 The Family and Guardianship Code Act of 25 February 1964 (Journal of Laws of 2019, item 2086); on international adoption in Polish family law, see J. Ignaczewski, *Kodeks rodzinny i opiekuńczy. Komentarz*, Warszawa 2010, pp. 665–670; K. Tryniszewska, *Prawo rodzinne*, Warszawa 2016, p. 90; the resolution of seven judges of the Supreme Court of 12 June 1992 (file reference No. III CZP 48/92, OSNC 1992, No. 10, item 179); decision of the Supreme Court of 22 June 2012 (V CSK 283/11, LEX No. 1232479); decision of the Supreme Court of 5 July 2006 (reference No. IV CSK 127/06).

19 The Convention on the Rights of the Child was adopted by the United Nations General Assembly on 20 November 1989. (Journal of Laws of 1991, No. 120, item 526), [online:] http://prawo.sejm.gov.pl/isap.nsf/download.xsp/WDU19911200526/O/D19910526.pdf; https://www.ohchr.org/documents/professionalinterest/crc.pdf [available: 19.10.2020].

20 The Polish legislators have provided for certain derogations from the principle of subsidiarity of foreign adoption. It does not apply when there is a relationship of kinship

3.5. Convention on the Rights of the Child

The next step after the adoption of the DRC was preparation of a binding international agreement to introduce a standard of protecting the welfare of the child. On 20 November 1989, the UN General Assembly adopted the Convention on the Rights of the Child. The solutions included in it are, in principle, framework solutions, as they relate to fundamental aspects of the protection of the welfare of an adopted child. The Convention deals with the issue of the conflict between the welfare of the child and the interests of the child's parents and adoptive parents. This follows from Article 3(2) of the CRC, under which the States-Parties shall act to protect and care for the child in so far as is necessary for his or her welfare, taking into account the rights and obligations of his or her parents, legal guardians or other persons legally responsible for him or her and, to this end, shall take all the appropriate legislative and administrative measures. This means that, irrespective of the principle of the best interests of the child, if possible the interests of others should also be taken into account.

Article 20(2) of the CRC, under which States-Parties should provide substitute custody for a child deprived of the family environment, is worth noting. Such custody may consist, among others, in placing the child in a foster family, a *Kafala* in Islamic law, adoption or – if necessary – placement in an appropriate institution established to care for children (Article 20(3) of the CRC).

Article 21(b) of the CRC expresses the above-mentioned principle of subsidiarity of international adoption. First of all, you should consider whether it is in the best interests of the child for him or her to be placed in foster care or adopted. Only when the adoption proves to be a form more appropriate for the child, can the question be raised as to whether national or international adoption is more appropriate. This means that, before an international adoption, priority is given not only to national adoption but also to foster care, provided that it is an appropriate form of care for a particular child. Furthermore, the Convention provides for specific requirements for foreign adoption. A child adopted in another country should have a guaranteed standard of living consistent with that which would be ensured in the event of national adoption (Article 21 of the CRC).

The legitimacy of adoption should be supervised by a properly organized state apparatus that is supposed to protect the child's welfare. Article 21(a) of the CRC indicates one of the basic prerequisites for adoption, i.e. the necessity

---

or affinity between the adoptive parent and the adoptee or when the adoptive parent has already adopted a sister or brother of the adoptee (Art. 1142 § 2 of the FGC).

to obtain the consent of the persons concerned. The assumption of admissibility of adoption, assumed in the CRC, only after examining the situation of the child with regard to his or her parents, relatives and legal guardians, is important. It determines, in particular, the form of custody under which the child is to be held as well as, where adoption is justified, the choice of future adoptive parents.

When analyzing the provisions of the CRC, one can notice that a number of provisions containing general rules protecting the welfare of the child also refer to ensuring the welfare of the adopted child. For example, Article 7(1) of the CRC grants a child the right to get to know his or her parents. That provision raises some doubts in law and judicial decisions. It should be noted that Poland initially stipulated that

> the right of an adopted child to know his or her natural parents will be subject to limitation by the application of legal solutions allowing adoptive parents to maintain the secrecy of origin.[21]

Moreover, the phrase used in Article 7 of the CRC: "as far as possible" provides grounds for a broad understanding of the contents of the legal standard resulting from that provision. The impossibility in question may consist in lack of an actual possibility of finding the parents (e.g. when the child has been abandoned), as well as in the situations in which the legislator has ruled out such possibility by law. It should be pointed out, however, that the applicable Polish law, even in relation to total adoption, gives the adoptee, after reaching the age of majority, the opportunity to acquaint himself/herself with the identity of his/her biological parents. Moreover, as indicated by the Supreme Court in its decision of 6 December 2007, the best interests of the child require that adoptive parents, "as keepers of the secret of adoption," provide information to the adoptee themselves, "in due time and form, of course."[22]

---

21 That reservation was withdrawn on 4 March 2013, see: the Government Statement of 27 March 2013 on the amendment of the scope of the Convention on the Rights of the Child adopted on 20 November 1989 in New York, Journal of Laws of 2013, item 677); that issue is addressed, among others, by J. Ignatowicz and M. Nazar, see: J. Ignatowicz, M. Nazar, *Prawo rodzinne*, Warszawa 2016, pp. 493–496.

22 See: decision of the Supreme Court of 6 December 2007 (IV CSK 274/07, OSNC-ZD 2008/2/58).

3.6. Convention on the Protection of Children and Cooperation in Respect of Inter-Country Adoption

On 29 May 1993, the Convention on the Protection of Children and Cooperation in Respect of Inter-Country Adoption (hereinafter referred to as "the CPC") was drawn up in the Hague.[23] It confirmed the principle of subsidiarity of international adoptions, according to which this type of adoption is treated as an *ultima ratio* measure. Article 4 of the CPC, on the other hand, indicates the conditions for international adoption. First, the competent authorities of the country of origin must establish that the child may be adopted. This means that, first of all, it should be stated that the right environment for the child would be an adoptive family and not, for example, foster care. They, after examining the possibility of placing the child in the country of origin, those authorities have to conclude that foreign adoption will serve the best interests of the child. The welfare of the adopted child is also safeguarded by proper control of the candidates for adoptive parents. The receiving state must conclude that "prospective adoptive parents are eligible and suited to adopt," as stated in Article 5(a) of the CPC. It is worth noting that the cooperation between the authorities of the state of origin and the receiving state does not boil down only to establishing that the adoptive parents have the suitable qualifications to adopt a child in general, but it is aimed at establishing that they are suitable for a specific child.

This Convention attempts to establish a minimum standard of protection of the best interests of the child at this level. Although its general qualities are indisputable, the doctrine also points to the emerging practice of international adoption between a State-Party to the Convention and a State not being a Party to the CPC, which results in different standards of protection of the best interests of the child.[24]

One of the controversial points that emerged in the discourse over the CPC is the issue of the admissibility of foreign adoptions by monogamous sex unions. It should be stressed that adoption by same-sex couples only applies in this context only if both the country of residence of the adoptive parent and the country of origin of the child allow such adoption. It may be concluded that countries

---

23 Convention on the Protection of Children and Cooperation in Respect of Inter-Country Adoption, drawn up in the Hague on 29 May 1993. (Journal of Laws of 2000, No. 39, item 448), [online:] http://prawo.sejm.gov.pl/isap.nsf/DocDetails.xsp?id=WDU20000390448 [available: 19.10.2020].

24 A. Zieliński, "Nowa konwencja haska w sprawie przysposobienia międzynarodowego," *State and Law* 1993, No. 9, p. 7.

which do not allow adoptions by same-sex couples may challenge the eligibility of such candidates on the grounds of violation of the fundamental principles of the international law system.

As regards the secret of adoption, under Article 30(1) of the CPC, the competent authorities of the contracting state shall ensure that information in their possession concerning the child's origin be preserved, in particular concerning the identity of the child's mother and father, as well as the health of the child and his or her family. This provision addresses the important issue of access to information on the natural parents of children and the distinction between identifying and non-identifying data. In doing so, the State shall ensure that the child or his or her representative has access to this information, together with the provision of appropriate advice, to the extent permitted under its law (Article 30(2) of the CPC). However, it should be borne in mind that the legal arrangements for access to data relating to child's natural parents vary greatly from country to country. It may happen that the state of origin and the receiving state apply different rules on adoption secrecy. This may lead to a conflict associated with the fact that access to data on adoptive parents is allowed in one country and illegal in another.

4. Conclusions

The act of adoption usually provides the child with new and better living conditions, but it should also be examined in terms of the risks involved. Not all adoptions which are, in principle, considered to be for the benefit and interest of the child, prove to be like that, since, in addition to legally sanctioned adoptions, illegal child trafficking also takes place. Such trafficking translates into an assessment of the responsibility of the state for comprehensive child protection at home and abroad. It appears that close international cooperation and good coordination among the entities established to prevent and prosecute offences, and in particular clear and transparent legal provisions, guarantee effective activity in the scope of both detection and prevention of offences, and therefore of trafficking in human beings, including children.

Bibliography:

Albański Ł., Krywult-Albańska M., "Adopcje międzynarodowe jako zaniedbany obszar badań nad migracjami," *Studia Migracyjne – Przegląd Polonijny* 2016, No. 3 (161).

Balcerek M., *Międzynarodowa ochrona praw człowieka*, Warszawa 1977.

Bucińska J., "Społeczne Prawa Człowieka w Powszechnej Deklaracji Praw Człowieka," *Roczniki Nauk Prawnych* 2003, Vol. 13, No. 1.

Gnel B., "Prawo właściwe dla przysposobienia według nowej ustawy - Prawo prywatne międzynarodowe," [in:] *Współczesne wyzwania prawa prywatnego międzynarodowego*, ed. J. Poczobut, Warszawa 2013.

Hanyś E.A., "Polska jako kraj inicjujący i współtworzący Konwencję o Prawach Dziecka," *Wrocławskie Studia Politologiczne* 2015, No. 19.

Ignaczewski J., *Kodeks rodzinny i opiekuńczy. Komentarz*, Warszawa 2010.

Ignatowicz J., Nazar M., *Prawo rodzinne*, Warszawa 2016.

Kalus S., Habdas M., *Family and Succession Law in Poland*, 3rd Edition, Wolters Kluwer, 2400 AH Alphen aan den Rijn - the Netherlands 2020.

Łukasiewicz R., *Dobro dziecka a interesy innych podmiotów w polskiej regulacji prawnych przysposobienia*, Warszawa 2019.

Mignot J., "Why is intercountry adoption declining worldwide?," *Population & Societies* 2015, No. 519.

Selman P., *Key tables for intercountry adoption: Receiving states 2003–2013 and States of Origin 2003–2013*, Newcastle University 2014.

Stojanowska W., *Rozwód a dobro dziecka*, Warszawa 1979.

Strzebinczyk J.F., *Prawo rodzinne*, Warszawa 2016.

Truszkowska-Wojtkowiak M., "Prawa dziecka a czas wolny," *Studia Gdańskie. Wizje i rzeczywistość* 2013, Vol. 10.

Tryniszewska K., *Prawo rodzinne*, Warszawa 2016.

Zieliński A., "Nowa konwencja haska w sprawie przysposobienia międzynarodowego," *State and Law* 1993, No. 9.

Part IV Other faces of vulnerability

Dominika Bek
University of Silesia in Katowice
e-mail: dominika.bek@us.edu.pl
ORCID ID: 0000-0003-4560-808X

Cultural determinants of the victimization of women in the Roma community

Abstract: The Roma community has maintained its cultural distinctiveness even though it has existed in Poland since the fifteenth century. It is an internally diverse ethnic group, yet it upholds its common traditions. The aim of this study is to present those aspects of Roma culture that may favor the victimization of women. A distinction must be made between what is culturally acceptable for the Roma – conforming to the norm, and what is considered pathological in that environment – a violation of the norm. This study focuses on more traditional groups living in Poland: Polska Roma and the Kalderash. It should be noted that the Roma inhabit most countries of the world and therefore this subject-matter is of a transnational nature.

Keywords: Roma community, minority, woman, cultural offence, *romanipen*

1. Introductory remarks

"Man not only creates culture, inhabits it, he carries it around within himself – man is culture."[1] This sentence by Ryszard Kapuściński adequately conveys the strength of the ties of the individual to the culture they come from. The distinctive character of certain gestures, behavior and rules of conduct most often results from the individual growing up in a particular culture, and not from the very nature of things. It is widely known that when the deeply embedded cultural norms adhered to by an individual differ from the general culture represented in legal regulations, the attachment to the native culture may lead to a violation of the applicable regulations. The same is true when state authorities, in the name of civilizational progress, try to eradicate or modify specific traditional practices established in a given area by introducing adequate legal

1 R. Kapuściński, *Podróże z Herodotem*, Kraków 2004, p. 81.

standards. A culturally different group is then a minority in the sociological sense, that is a community not smaller in terms of numbers, but rather weaker and at risk of discrimination.[2] Tadeusz Paleczny is of the opinion that "a cultural minority in relations with other groups is aware of its own separateness resulting also from different, often discriminatory treatment by another, typically majority, cultural group."[3] The very fact of being a member of a minority group allows for the classification of an individual in the category of *vulnerable persons.*[4]

Meanwhile, an issue of fundamental importance arises in the case where the imposed provision of law breached because of reasons of culture is underpinned by an interest of special significance such as life, health, or personal or sexual freedom. In that context, reference is made to the concept of cultural offences (culturally motivated crimes) defined as acts committed by members of a cultural minority which are recognized as acts prohibited by the legal system of the dominant culture, while at the same time are tolerated, considered normal, approved and accepted, or even promoted in certain circumstances by the cultural group of the perpetrator of the act.[5] The literature review shows that typically women and children fall victim to the most serious acts of that type,[6] that is individuals generally seen as vulnerable persons.[7] In recent years, the elderly have also been increasingly identified as a particularly vulnerable group.[8] It can

---

2 Cf. J. Mucha, "Badania stosunków kulturowych z perspektywy mniejszości," [in:] *Kultura dominująca jako kultura obca. Mniejszości kulturowe a grupa dominująca w Polsce*, ed. J. Mucha, Warsaw 1999, p. 20; T. Paleczny, *Stosunki międzykulturowe. Zarys problematyki*, Krakow 2005, p. 104.

3 T. Paleczny, *Stosunki międzykulturowe*. . ., p. 105.

4 Cf. for instance in K. Mazalik, "Mniejszości narodowe i etniczne jako przykład grup szczególnie wrażliwych," [unpublished paper].

5 J. van Broeck, "Cultural Defence and Culturally Motivated Crimes," *European Journal of Crime, Criminal Law and Criminal Justice* 2001, No. 9, p. 5; cf. also A. Phillips, "When culture means gender: issues of cultural defence in English courts," *Modern Law Review* 2003, Vol. 66, No. 4, pp. 19–20. In the Polish literature: O. Sitarz, "Culture defence a polskie prawo karne," *Archiwum Kryminologii* 2007–2008, Vol. XXIX-XXX, p. 650; cf. D. Bek, "Przestępstwa motywowane kulturowo – kierunki możliwych ocen prawnokarnych," *Chorzowskie Studia Polityczne* 2015, No. 10; D. Bek, *Obrona przez kulturę. Analiza na gruncie polskiego prawa karnego*, Warsaw 2018.

6 Cf. e.g. O. Sitarz, "Culture defence. . .," pp. 650–651; S. Sykuna, J. Zajadło, "Kontrowersje wokół tzw. obrony przez kulturę," *Przegląd Sądowy* 2007, pp. 26–36.

7 Cf. for instance the contents of this volume.

8 Cf. e.g. E. Bieńkowska, "Osoby starsze grupą o podwyższonym stopniu ryzyka wiktymizacji," *RPEiS* 1999, No. 1, pp. 111–117; B. Mikołajczyk, *Międzynarodowa*

accordingly be concluded that persons perceived as vulnerable due to their sex or age, and at the same time being members of a national or ethnic minority are exposed to discrimination and harm as if twice over.[9]

The complexity of the situation of women, children and the elderly belonging to cultural minorities gives rise to numerous problems too complicated to be examined in a single study limited to several pages. Consequently, I intend to focus only on cultural considerations that may potentially be conducive to the worse treatment of individuals belonging to vulnerable groups within a given cultural minority. To illustrate that issue, I would like to take the example of the Roma ethnic minority in Poland. The roots of that group go back to India,[10] it therefore seems appropriate to seek traces of the cultural determinants of victimization in Asia.

2. An outline of the situation of women in India

The Asian continent, in particular China, India, Indonesia, Pakistan, Bangladesh, Taiwan and South Korea are recognized as areas of a particularly difficult situation of women and girls.[11] Demographers state that the terrifying phenomenon of "missing women" in the overall amount of over 90 million is especially noticeable in those countries.[12] Although that figure is derived only from demographic data, it reflects the real-life tragedies of millions of women who were not allowed to be born through the use of sex-selective abortion, or

---

ochrona osób starszych, Warsaw 2012; D. Bek, A. Jaworska-Wieloch, O. Sitarz, *Prawo karne wobec naruszeń praw i wolności osób starszych*, Warsaw 2020.

9 Cf. e.g. K. Jędrzejczyk-Kuliniak, "Podwójna dyskryminacja imigrantek w Polsce," this volume.

10 Cf. A. Fraser, *Dzieje Cyganów*, Warsaw 2001, pp. 19–35.; L. Mróz, *Geneza Cyganów i ich kultury*, Warsaw 1992, p. 38 et seq; A. Bartosz, *Nie bój się Cygana/Na dara Romestar*, Sejny 2004, pp. 19–30.

11 I. Attané, "Brakujące kobiety" w Azji," [in:] *Czarna księga kobiet*, ed. Ch. Ockrent, Warsaw 2007, p. 27. The text deliberately does not take into account the situation of woman in the Arab world since it is extensive separate subject matter which has already been covered in numerous publications. Cf. e.g. M. Afkhami, *Faith and Freedom: Women's Human Rights in the Muslim World*, Syracuse University Press, 1995; *Encyclopedia of women & Islamic cultures*, ed. S. Joseph, Vol. 1–5, Brill 2003–2007; S. Treiner, "W imię "honoru:" zbrodnie w świecie muzułmańskim" [in:] *Czarna księga kobiet*, pp. 74–94, as well as many other documentaries and media articles concerning so-called honor killings.

12 I. Attané, "Brakujące kobiety. . .," p. 28.

Table 1: Human sex ratio in selected parts of the world

	POPULATION IN 2005 (MILLIONS)	NUMBER OF MALES TO 100 FEMALES
CHINA	1303,7	105,6
INDIA	**1103,6**	**105,2**
INDONESIA	221,9	100,6
PAKISTAN	162,4	106,0
BANGLADESH	144,2	104,5
SOUTH KOREA	48,3	100,5
TAIWAN	22,7	103,8
ASIA	3905,4	103,9
AFRICA, AMERICA, EUROPE AND OCEANIA	2559,3	96,9
WORLD	6464,7	101,1

Source: I. Attané, "Asia's Missing Women," [in:] *The Black Book of Women's Condition*, ed. Ch. Ockrent, p. 29.

were killed through various forms of murder of newly born girls, or as a result of neglect of their nutritional and health needs.[13]

Multicultural India, whose female to male ratio is among the lowest in the world, brings into sharp focus various forms of discrimination against women.[14] It should be acknowledged that the authorities in India try (though with varying commitment) to combat traditional practices harmful to women, but without any great success.[15] The status of women is still very low. In addition to the methods of elimination of female children indicated above, underage girls and women are at risk of, among others, culturally conditioned forced marriages (sometimes coupled with human trafficking), rape, partner violence, including bride-burning, that is death by fire allegedly caused by accidental inflammation of the sari when the woman's dowry did not satisfy the husband's family.[16] These are only some of the most striking manifestations of

13 Ibidem, pp. 34–36.; C. Brisset, "Już od dzieciństwa…," [in:] *Czarna księga kobiet*, pp. 16–17.

14 I. Attané, "Brakujące kobiety…," p. 29.

15 Amendments to law considerably more favorable to women started in the 1950s from *Hindu Marriage Act* 1955 and *Hindu Succession Act* 1956 (acc. to M. Sach, *Ginefobia w kulturze hinduskiej. Lęk przed kobietą w dyskursie antropologicznym i psychoanalitycznym*, Krakow 2011, pp. 91 and 169).

16 Ibidem, pp. 34–35.

violation of women's rights, leaving aside the issue of discrimination in civil rights. It should be emphasized that the Indian authorities endeavor to counteract practices harmful to women, in particular among the Hindu population, but also among Muslim and Christian minorities.[17] Moreover, women's representatives have always been successful in securing a significant position among the intellectual and social elites of India.[18] This, however, does not alter the fact that the situation of a multitude of women in India is alarming.

Consideration should be given to the reasons for such mistreatment of women in India. Tradition and religion are often singled out as significant factors. The social structure is certainly unfavorable – patriarchy and patrilineality prevail as in many other cultures.[19] India is also characterized by the dominance of group interest (family, caste) over individual interest.[20] No matter what religious group they belong to, representatives of all castes of India cultivate the custom of arranging marriages and negotiating a dowry. The dowry expected by the prospective husband and his family is often such a heavy burden for the parents of a girl of marriageable age that the birth of a daughter is seen as the greatest misfortune. Hindus say that "raising a daughter is like watering your neighbor's garden," and equate having daughters with a financial disaster.[21] The reasons for this state of affairs are also seen in certain tenets of Hinduism: the birth of a son allows the parents to achieve nirvana given that only a male descendant can set fire to the funeral pyre of deceased parents, which guarantees release from a sequence of reincarnations.[22] Having only female descendants can therefore deprive the parents of property and also, according to Hindu beliefs, of eternal rest. In contrast, in the Muslim communities of India, a key role is played by often distorted Sharia law skewed against women by local authorities.[23] The permanence and strength of the above practices, which remain resistant to the legislative activities of central decision makers, is emblematic. Indian families

17 Cf. S. Khan, "Położenie kobiet w Indiach," [in:] *Czarna księga kobiet*, pp. 257–283.

18 Ibidem, pp. 263–264.

19 Cf. e.g. I. Attané, "Brakujące kobiety…," p. 37.

20 K. Dębnicki, *Konflikt i przemoc w systemie politycznym niepodległych Indii*, Warsaw 2000, p. 54.

21 Ibidem, p. 37.

22 C. Brisset, "Już od dzieciństwa…," p. 17.

23 Cf. S. Khan, "Imrana, czyli o bezpieczeństwie muzułmanek w Indiach," [in:] *Czarna księga kobiet*, pp. 112–121.

are typically marked by high conservatism, and the value system and customs are passed on to children through the generation of the grandparents.[24]

3. The situation of women from the Roma minority in Poland

Although it must be a matter of concern to the international community, the difficult situation of women in India only briefly outlined here seems far removed from the Polish reality and practice of the Polish judiciary. Following the Hindu trail, mention may be made of the Romani / Roma / Gypsies who originate from India and who have inhabited Poland for many centuries. Researchers mostly agree that Gypsies migrated from India, although it is not clear when the migration of the Romani started and whether it was a uniform group.[25] They reached the Polish territory by the end of the 15th century.[26] At present, the Romani are considered an ethnic minority in Poland.[27] Although they do not constitute a homogenous community and four basic Roma groups can be distinguished in Poland alone,[28] the ties to the culture of their Indian ancestors can still be seen. Anthropologist Ewa Nowicka made an interesting study of that relationship focusing on the European, in particular, Polish Roma and the Nepalese representing Indian culture. Her research highlights numerous similarities between the principles governing both communities: thinking in line with caste divisions or ritual purity and ritual uncleanness, the importance of the family and, finally, the position of women.[29] It therefore appears appropriate

24 K. Dębnicki, *Konflikt i przemoc...*, p. 55.

25 Cf. A. Fraser, *Dzieje cyganów...*, pp. 19–35; L. Mróz, *Geneza...*, p. 38 et seq.; A. Bartosz, *Nie bój się Cygana...*, pp. 19–30.

26 L. Mróz, *Dzieje Cyganów-Romów w Rzeczypospolitej XV-XVIII w.*, Warsaw 2001, p. 19 et seq.

27 Cf. Act of 6 January 2005 on National and Ethnic Minorities and on the Regional Language (Journal of Laws of 2017, pos. 823).

28 Polska Roma (Romowie Polscy, Nizinni), the Kalderash (Kełderasze, Kalderari, Kotlarze), the Lovari (Lovari, Koniarze), Bergitka Roma (Romowie Karpaccy, Wyżynni) – cf. L. Mróz, *Cyganie*, Warsaw 1971, p. 179 et seq., J. Ficowski, *Cyganie na polskich drogach*, Krakow 1985, pp. 21–22 and 78, A. Bartosz, *Nie bój się Cygana...*, pp. 32–35; A.J. Kowarska, *Polska Roma. Tradycja i nowoczesność*, Warsaw 2005, pp. 6–7.

29 E. Nowicka, "Związki żywe i zaskakujące. Europejscy Romowie i społeczeństwo Nepalu," [in:] *Zapomniani sąsiedzi. Studia o Romach w Polsce i w Europie*, ed. P. Borek, Krakow 2011, pp. 10–26.

to search for links between those two geographically distant communities and throw some light on the situation of Roma women in Poland.

3.1 *Romanipen*: Selected aspects of Roma customs

As given above, the Roma inhabiting Poland do not constitute a homogeneous group. Out of necessity, I intend to limit the presentation of the Romani culture only to its most representative features preserved by traditional groups: Polska Roma and the Kalderash. At the same time, I aim to focus more on those elements of their customs that may be conducive to crimes against women and girls.

The basic concept associated with the traditional customs of Gypsies is *romanipen*, or "Romani-ness," Gypsiness, which requires the observance of certain rules. The opposite is not being a gypsy, alienness known as *gadźipen*.

The point of reference for all Romani families is the multi-generational family. In general, children are the most valuable treasure and elders enjoy respect. For Gypsies, a stage of life is more important than the actual age – a person is considered old once they have grandchildren (at about 50 years of age). The principle of seniority (*phuripen*) requires particularly polite behavior and the use of polite language in the presence of elders. A person who due to their life experience has gained wisdom and is able to make the best use of it may be recognized as an authority figure. The status of an "elder" gives real power in the local community. That status may also sometimes be achieved by a post-menopausal woman (*phury daj*), as long as she enjoys an impeccable reputation. It is therefore difficult to conclude that the Romani culture is conducive to the victimization of the elderly, although women in that age group find it slightly more difficult than men to earn the respect of the Romani community. The situation of children before puberty is somewhat similar. Cultural factors seem to contribute solely to the victimization of adolescent girls, but not minor girls in general.

Moreover, *patyv* meaning mutual respect, but also hospitality, appears to be of great importance in the Romani culture. Feasts offer the Romani an opportunity to have a lavish shared meal and, at the same time, make a Rom's social position fully visible. Only venerable group members can drink from one glass and dine together. A disgraced person (*magerdo*) remains part of the group, but no one is allowed to touch them or share a meal with them.[30]

30 A. J. Kowarska, *Polska Roma…*, pp. 31–35; A. Bartosz, *Nie bój się Cygana…*, pp. 170–177.

A central institution underlying *romanipen*, in particular for the *Polska Roma* group, is *mageripen* – a system of defilements incurred by breaking the ritual and moral principles. A violation of a rule does not in itself constitute a defilement which arises once that fact is noticed by another Rom. Defilement must be pronounced by authorized elders. The highest authority among Polska Roma is held by *Śero Rom*, although village heads and respected elders may also pronounce defilements (so-called small defilements – *tykne mageripena*).[31]

Ritual uncleanness is by and large an undesirable condition, yet it is virtually inseparable from women. Women are perceived as unclean from puberty to menopause, and their defiling properties are exacerbated during menstruation, pregnancy, childbirth and confinement. The belief in the ritual uncleanness of women imposes numerous restrictions on them; although it equips them with specific powers. The so-called major defilements (*bare mageripena*) include, among others, female defilements (*dźiuvlitko mageripen*), particularly as regards their specific forms: skirt, shoes and childbirth. A woman brings defilement from the waist all the way down.[32] The prohibition on a woman staying above a man is particularly illuminating – e.g. in a multi-story building. Not only body parts are unclean, but also underwear, clothing, footwear and in fact everything that came in contact with them. In the periods of increased "uncleanness," even an accidental touch of a woman's skirt can become a source of defilement, and such a woman has no right to prepare meals, serve food to the table, or dine with others. Further, striking someone intentionally with a skirt or shoe in front of other Roma can be an effective form of defense.[33] Women's defiling nature results in a strict separation of what is male and by definition "clean" from what is female and thus "unclean." The distinctness of those two worlds is reflected in a clear division of activities intended for men and women, the division of guests at receptions by gender, separate dishes, cutlery and washing bowls for women during periods of special "uncleanness," etc. At the same time, a woman must continuously maintain relative ritual purity through modesty in clothing and virtue in behavior, which she is taught from an early age.[34] *Patyvali romni* should cover the lower parts of her body with baggy skirts, move carefully in the company of others, should not leave the house alone (even to school) given that the loss of virginity, or only such suspicion, is associated

31 A. Bartosz, *Nie bój się Cygana...*, p. 188; A. J. Kowarska, *Polska Roma...*, p. 36.
32 J. Ficowski, *Cyganie...*, pp. 175–198.
33 A.J. Kowarska, *Polska Roma...*, p. 37 and 41; E. Nowicka, "Związki żywe...," p. 22.
34 A.J. Kowarska, *Polska Roma...*, pp. 47–58.

with the conclusion of marriage.[35] A woman is obliged to stay faithful to her husband, give birth to his children and take care of the household, sometimes being in effect forced into maintaining it.[36] Women suspected of adultery and childless women live on the margins of the community. It is a man who makes the most important decisions and should hide the fact of any consultations held with his wife if they took place at all. He is a representative of the family outside and speaks on behalf of the family within the group. He has the right to go out alone and contact *gadjo* (non-Romani), including non-Romani women.[37] The cultural standards require that he should be faithful to his wife, but male infidelity is tolerated.[38]

3.2 Roma women as a vulnerable group

Given the traditional social roles outlined above, it seems that women are particularly vulnerable to behavior in breach of Polish criminal law. The question remains whether this is in fact the case. The first female-specific risk occurs when a girl reaches puberty and is beginning to look like a woman. She is then perceived as a marriageable girl and the importance attached to virginity means that marriages are still solemnized quite early, sometimes, though less frequently nowadays, before the girl reaches the age of 15. The engagement in a sexual intercourse with such a young partner violates the provision of Art. 200 of the Criminal Code which penalizes pedophilia.[39]

---

35 Ibidem, p. 45.

36 Ibidem, pp. 51–52 and 218.

37 Ibidem, p. 52.

38 Ibidem, pp. 148–149.

39 This controversial issue is discussed in a rich body of Polish literature relating primarily to the case of Kędzierzyn-Koźle: Marek K. – A Rom "husband" of a Rom minor and at the same time father of their child was convicted of the offense provided for in Art. 200 of the Criminal Code, but the court applied an extraordinary mitigation of penalty and conditionally suspended its enforcement. Cf. i.a. S. Sykuna, J. Zajadło, "Kontrowersje wokół. . .," pp. 26–36; A. Bartosz, "O nieromskiej tradycji "łupania panieneczek na sianku," *Studia Romologica* 2008, No. 1, pp. 279–284; J. Warylewski, "Zasada ustawowej określoności przesłanek odpowiedzialności karnej a kontratypy pozaustawowe," [in:] *Okoliczności wyłączające bezprawność czynu*, ed. J. Majewski, Toruń 2008, pp. 34–36; J. Bojarski, M. Leciak, "Polskie interkulturowe prawo karne (?)- niektóre aspekty tzw. obrony przez kulturę," [in:] *Nauki penalne wobec szybkich przemian socjokulturowych. Księga jubileuszowa Profesora Mariana Filara*, Vol. I, eds. A. Adamski et al., Toruń 2012, pp. 75–96; D. Bek, *Obrona. . .*, pp. 380–383.

Agnieszka Kowarska distinguishes in her monographic work between two types of arranging a marriage by the modern Romani: by a matchmaker and by abduction (*chwyteł*). In the first case, marriage is arranged by the families of the prospective bride and groom. The newlyweds-to-be, typically both at a very young age, often have not met each other before and are unaware of their parents' plans; although they are both asked to give their consent to the marriage when the boy's family pay a visit to the girl's father.[40] However, the situation of the maiden may be quite specific: in some families (in particular the Kalderash), the custom of giving gifts to the girl's family still prevails. The custom sometimes equated with "buying" a wife stems from the fact that after the marriage the girl will typically live with her husband's family and will thus no longer take care of her own parents' home. The girl's virginity is checked before the wedding, and if in doubt, she is to undergo a gynecological examination. There are also double marriage contracts – a kind of daughter exchange, possible when both families have maidens and bachelors. That arrangement makes it possible to cut costs relating to gifts and the wedding reception.[41] Such contracts without doubt bear a resemblance to human trafficking, although it is possible to put a milder interpretation on those practices. The girl's father will typically donate a large portion of *daro* for the wedding; hence, it may be regarded as a specific form of sharing the costs of the ceremony between the families.[42] Moreover, in the opinion of A. Bartosz, the sum paid is to ensure the new wife the respect of her husband's family.[43]

The second aforementioned form of concluding a marriage has seemingly even stronger criminal connotations. Abduction may take many forms. It is often the case that the "abduction" is planned jointly by the young couple, and sometimes it is arranged by the families themselves as an introduction to further marriage activities. Clearly, spending time together allows a young couple to skip the phase of matchmaking, exchange of gifts and a typical wedding, which makes the whole process less expensive.[44] There are also instances of abductions in the strict sense of the term: against the will of the girl and interested families,[45] which undoubtedly satisfies the constituent elements of deprivation of liberty, and sometimes of rape. Where both the families come to

40 A.J. Kowarska, *Polska Roma...*, pp. 103–107.
41 Ibidem, pp. 107–108.
42 Ibidem, pp. 115–116.
43 A. Bartosz, *Nie bój się Cygana...*, pp. 192–193.
44 A.J. Kowarska, *Polska Roma...*, p. 110.
45 Ibidem, p. 111.

an agreement, notwithstanding that brutal form, the marriage is considered concluded and binding upon both.

Following a more or less traditional wedding (*mangavipen*) sometimes combined with a church or civil marriage ceremony,[46] the bride becomes part of the husband's family and gains his protection. In any case, the dominant role of a man makes the life of a gypsy wife rather difficult. In one of the interviews given, Romani poet Papusza stated:

> A Gypsy can do whatever comes to his mind with his wife. He can lose his wife in a card game, smash her mouth, squeeze her throat with his foot, beat the daylights out of her.[47]

Gypsy crime researcher Albert Pawłowski confirms frequent cases of domestic violence.[48] Both opinions referred to above come from the previous political system and no recent studies are available due to the difficultly in gaining access to primary sources. A. Pawłowski made use of *The Photographic Index of Wanted Persons of Romani Nationality*, a register kept by the General Headquarters of Citizens' Militia in the 1960s. That type of registration was naturally discontinued and nowadays political correctness does not allow for collecting separate statistical data relating to the Romani. Paradoxically, the problem also lies in a sense of community within Roma groups – it is indeed very unusual for a Gypsy woman to turn to state authorities for help, and even if she does it, she will hide the real reason for denouncing her husband.[49] Denunciation is treated as so-called betrayal of Gypsies and is recognized as one of the most serious violations of customary law.[50] As regards the culture's contribution to victimization, mention should be made of A. Pawłowski's observation that an important crime factor in crimes against life and health is alcohol abuse by some Romani men, but that factor is clearly cross-cultural.[51] In addition, physical violence against women does not result from any cultural imperative and is not welcomed by Romani elders. Cases of violence are settled by the elders of the family, whilst more serious disputes are resolved by *Śero Rom*, or by common court (*kris*). It cannot therefore be said that physical violence against women is inherent in Romani culture.

---

46 Ibidem, pp. 116–124.

47 Quotation after A. Kuźniak, *Papusza*, Wołowiec 2013, p. 15.

48 A. Pawłowski, *Cyganie. Studia nad przestępczością*, Zielona Góra 1973, p. 15.

49 J. Ficowski, *Cyganie...*, pp. 160–161. and A. Pawłowski, *Cyganie...*, p. 165.

50 A.J. Kowarska, *Polska Roma...*, p. 37.

51 A. Pawłowski, *Cyganie...*, p. 163.

A separate issue is psychological abuse which members of many other communities may likely recognize in treating women as "unclean" and separating them from men. Nonetheless, that type of abuse is largely subjective and the rules of ritual purity instilled in Gypsies from birth certainly affect the mindset of Romani women.

A Romani woman should get pregnant directly after the wedding and the child is a much awaited family member raising the parents' social status.[52] The period of pregnancy, childbirth and confinement is above all ritually unclean. Nowadays, she is most often accompanied by other women to the hospital, but in extreme cases, she is left alone without support, which exposes her to the danger of loss of life and satisfies the constituent elements of not providing aid.[53]

The concern for the purity of young girls, threat of abduction, getting married and starting a family at a very young age most often prevent young women from continuing their secondary school education. Currently, there are families in which elder relatives accompany a young woman on her way to and from school, which may partially protect her from defilement.[54] In the absence of such willingness in the family, there may be instances where a young woman eager to receive education is in fact prevented from going to school by her family who limit her freedom by forcing her to stay at home, which in extreme cases may also satisfy the constituent elements of a prohibited act. Yet the traditional manner of upbringing means that such a strong desire to continue education is rather uncommon.

4. Conclusions

E. Nowicka has no doubts that "the position of a woman in the Romani world is definitely low and subordinate to a man."[55] A. Kowarska or A. Bartosz indicate that the subordination of women is not unconditional.[56] In the opinion of A. Kowarska, a Romani woman can count on support from her own and her husband's family. In the event of splitting-up from her husband, child maintenance is a given. In the case of danger from her husband or other man, a woman can always resort to the defiling powers of her skirt or shoe, which still appears

52 A.J. Kowarska, *Polska Roma. . .*, p. 59.
53 Ibidem, p. 66.
54 Cf. Ibidem, p. 213.
55 E. Nowicka, "Związki żywe. . .", p. 22.
56 A.J. Kowarska, *Polska Roma. . .*, p. 44; A. Bartosz, *Nie bój się Cygana. . .*, pp. 192–193.

to be of great importance in the community.[57] It would be grossly wrong to say that Romani culture is the main criminogenic factor in all the cases referred to above. The ritual inferiority of a woman is compounded by alcohol abuse or poverty – commonly known criminogenic factors. It seems useful to indicate that although the specifically shaped defilement system is an original feature of Romani culture, the position of a Gypsy woman does not differ substantially from the position of women of Polish origin recorded by historians and ethnographers. Poland, in particular Polish rural areas, was governed by similar laws in the nineteenth and early twentieth centuries, and their impact is apparent in modern customs to this very day.[58] An important difference lies in the fact that the Romani intent on maintaining their separateness abandon their discriminatory and oftentimes harmful practices against women and girls more slowly and with greater resistance. Moreover, they seek to solidify some of them in the name of tradition through the norms of customary law enforced by elders.

On a more general level, a traditional belief in the inferiority of women to men, their objectification and the related exposure of women to various forms of discrimination, as well as other more drastic behavior that violates the norms of criminal law may be encountered in numerous cultures. Some of those practices seem justified in the eyes of women themselves who recognize the validity of the traditions they belong to. Having regard to that separateness, it must be stressed that only equal access to education and development of social awareness of women can give them an opportunity to adequately assess their situation and make fairly independent life choices. Therefore, in cases where a woman carries a sense of grievance and rejects, completely or only partially, the tradition she comes from, she certainly should not be left alone without the help of state authorities, and the justification for the above situations by invoking the specificity of culture should not take place.

---

57 A.J. Kowarska, *Polska Roma...*, p. 215; E. Nowicka, "Związki żywe...," p. 23. Notably, A. Pawłowski, *Cyganie...*, p. 165, correctly claims that the degree of defilement weakens in the case of an intoxicated man who can control his behavior only to a limited extent due to the influence of consumed alcohol.

58 Cf. e.g. W. Mędrzecki, "Konwenans wiejski i nowe wzorce zachowań kobiet na wsi w Królestwie Polskim na przełomie XIX i XX wieku," [in:] *Kobieta i kultura życia codziennego. Wiek XIX i XX. Zbiór studiów*, eds. A. Żarnowska, A. Szwarc, Warsaw 1997, pp. 71–87, in particular p. 72. and M. Stawiak-Ososińska, *Ponętna, uległa, akuratna... Ideał i wizerunek kobiety polskiej pierwszej połowy XIX w. (w świetle ówczesnych poradników)*, Krakow 2009, pp. 49–50.

Bibliography:

Afkhami M., *Faith and Freedom: Women's Human Rights in the Muslim World*, Syracuse University Press, 1995.

Attané I., "Brakujące kobiety" w Azji," [in:] *Czarna księga kobiet*, ed. Ch. Ockrent, Warsaw 2007.

Bartosz A., *Nie bój się Cygana/Na dara Romestar*, Sejny 2004.

Bartosz A., "O nieromskiej tradycji "łupania panieneczek na sianku," *Studia Romologica* 2008, No. 1.

Bek D., Jaworska-Wieloch A., Sitarz O., *Prawo karne wobec naruszeń praw i wolności osób starszych*, Warsaw 2020.

Bek D., *Obrona przez kulturę. Analiza na gruncie polskiego prawa karnego*, Warsaw 2018.

Bek D., "Przestępstwa motywowane kulturowo – kierunki możliwych ocen prawnokarnych," *Chorzowskie Studia Polityczne* 2015, No. 10.

Bieńkowska E., "Osoby starsze grupą o podwyższonym stopniu ryzyka wiktymizacji," *Ruch Prawniczy, Ekonomiczny i Socjologiczny* 1999, No. 1.

Bojarski J., Leciak M., "Polskie interkulturowe prawo karne (?) – niektóre aspekty tzw. obrony przez kulturę," [in:] *Nauki penalne wobec szybkich przemian socjokulturowych. Księga jubileuszowa Profesora Mariana Filara*, Vol. I, eds. A. Adamski et al., Toruń 2012.

Brisset C., "Już od dzieciństwa. . .," [in:] *Czarna księga kobiet*, ed. Ch. Ockrent, Warsaw 2007.

Broeck J. van, "Cultural Defence and Culturally Motivated Crimes," *European Journal of Crime, Criminal Law and Criminal Justice* 2001, No. 9.

Dębnicki K., *Konflikt i przemoc w systemie politycznym niepodległych Indii*, Warsaw 2000.

Encyclopedia of women & Islamic cultures, ed. S. Joseph, Vol. 1–5, Brill 2003–2007.

Ficowski J., *Cyganie na polskich drogach*, Krakow 1985.

Fraser A., *Dzieje Cyganów*, Warsaw 2001.

Jędrzejczyk-Kuliniak K., "Podwójna dyskryminacja imigrantek w Polsce," this volume.

Kapuściński R., *Podróże z Herodotem*, Krakow 2004.

Khan S., "Imrana, czyli o bezpieczeństwie muzułmanek w Indiach," [in:] *Czarna księga kobiet*, ed. Ch. Ockrent, Warsaw 2007.

Khan S., "Położenie kobiet w Indiach," [in:] *Czarna księga kobiet*, ed. Ch. Ockrent, Warsaw 2007.

Kowarska A.J., *Polska Roma. Tradycja i nowoczesność*, Warsaw 2005.

Kuźniak A., *Papusza*, Wołowiec 2013.

Mazalik K., "Mniejszości narodowe i etniczne jako przykład grup szczególnie wrażliwych," [unpublished paper].

Mędrzecki W., "Konwenans wiejski i nowe wzorce zachowań kobiet na wsi w Królestwie Polskim na przełomie XIX i XX wieku," [in:] *Kobieta i kultura życia codziennego. Wiek XIX i XX. Zbiór studiów*, eds. A. Żarnowska, A. Szwarc, Warsaw 1997.

Mikołajczyk B., *Międzynarodowa ochrona osób starszych*, Warsaw 2012.

Mróz L., *Cyganie*, Warsaw 1971.

Mróz L., *Dzieje Cyganów-Romów w Rzeczypospolitej XV-XVIII w.*, Warsaw 2001.

Mróz L., *Geneza Cyganów i ich kultury*, Warsaw 1992.

Mucha J., "Badania stosunków kulturowych z perspektywy mniejszości," [in:] *Kultura dominująca jako kultura obca. Mniejszości kulturowe a grupa dominująca w Polsce*, ed. J. Mucha, Warsaw 1999.

Nowicka E., "Związki żywe i zaskakujące. Europejscy Romowie i społeczeństwo Nepalu," [in:] *Zapomniani sąsiedzi. Studia o Romach w Polsce i w Europie*, ed. P. Borek, Krakow 2011.

Paleczny T., *Stosunki międzykulturowe. Zarys problematyki*, Krakow 2005.

Pawłowski A., *Cyganie. Studia nad przestępczością*, Zielona Góra 1973.

Phillips A., "When culture means gender: Issues of cultural defence in English courts," *Modern Law Review* 2003, Vol. 66, No. 4.

Sach M., *Ginefobia w kulturze hinduskiej. Lęk przed kobietą w dyskursie antropologicznym i psychoanalitycznym*, Krakow 2011.

Sitarz O., "Culture defence a polskie prawo karne," *Archiwum Kryminologii* 2007–2008, Vol. XXIX-XXX.

Stawiak-Ososińska M., *Ponętna, uległa, akuratna... Ideał i wizerunek kobiety polskiej pierwszej połowy XIX w. (w świetle ówczesnych poradników)*, Krakow 2009.

Sykuna S., Zajadło J., "Kontrowersje wokół tzw. obrony przez kulturę," Przegląd Sądowy 2007.

Treiner S., "W imię "honoru:" zbrodnie w świecie muzułmańskim," [in:] *Czarna księga kobiet*, ed. Ch. Ockrent, Warsaw 2007.

Warylewski J., "Zasada ustawowej określoności przesłanek odpowiedzialności karnej a kontratypy pozaustawowe," [in:] *Okoliczności wyłączające bezprawność czynu*, ed. J. Majewski, Toruń 2000.

Ilona Delekta
University of Silesia in Katowice
e-mail: ilona.delekta@us.edu.pl
ORCID ID: 0000-0002-8341-246X

Senior consumer's dilemma: what does my warranty actually say? Or, once again, on exclusion and warranty readability

Abstract: The article is devoted to the consumer warranty, elderly consumers, it also examines how easy or difficult it is for them to understand. It is a sociolinguistic analysis presenting (a) document setting (b) its target reader – senior and (c) selected text variables influencing text quality and readability. Assumptions and conclusions presented here are based on the literature and the corpus analysis of 100 consumer warranties conducted using two readability formulas. Despite the small corpus size, the study revealed some tendencies, characteristics and potential problem areas related to the consumer warranty. Texts in the corpus varied significantly in many ways but majority of them shared one common characteristic indicated by readability test: text difficult to read. The article attempts to show linguistic and non-linguistic sources of problems, provide some remedies to make the consumer warranty a more readable and accessible document, and indicate further research direction.

Keywords: senior consumer, consumer warranty, document readability

1. Introductory remarks

This article presents selected aspects related to the consumer warranty and senior consumers. It is based on my doctoral research aimed at investigating consumer's warranty as a genre. Thus, linguistic perspective dominates in this study. This kind of research, however, cannot be narrowed down to strictly linguistic issues as this kind of document also has a strong social context that also needs to be taken into consideration. Presumably, majority of consumers of various backgrounds and all ages worldwide are familiar with this document as it has been one of the oldest text genres. Due to the need for some trade standards, product warranty was created as one of trade practices. The warranty has played an important role since the beginnings of human civilization and it covered various products and services ranging from sale of cattle or slaves in ancient times to modern electronic devices and other products currently. For a long time, there had been no one clear-cut definition or characteristics for warranty. Researchers investigating its history (Loomba, 1995) trace its history back to the times of the Hammurabi Code.

This article is continuation and expansion on my preliminary research into this area conducted and described in my earlier article on this subject (Delekta, 2013). Due to its complexity the consumer warranty can be analysed from different perspectives (a) people's perspective: producers/sellers vs. purchasers, (b) topical perspectives: legal, economic, statistical, engineering, insurance, consumerist as well as marketing, psychology, computer data processing, publishing (traditional and on-line), sales or even current changes in the market or the Internet. etc.). As there had not been any research into its language, I decided to add to a linguistic perspective based on qualitative and quantitative analysis of warranty documents using methods of the corpus linguistics. The disciplines, however, cannot be analysed separately since even linguistic or sociolinguistic perspective is connected in varying degrees with the abovementioned areas. Thus, the focus of this study is put on linguistic aspects but is not and cannot be analysed in a complete separation from the abovementioned areas since they have a significant impact on the syntax, lexis and registers present in this genre (e.g. legal or technical terminology).

In this article I focus on the consumer's warranty readability and usefulness, particularly in relationship to vulnerable groups like senior citizens who seem to be one of the 'silent' groups whose voice and opinions are hardly heard or seen in media or public life in comparison to other 'more and better seen' groups fighting for their rights and unlike these groups they do not hold demonstrations, debates or other activities aimed at protection of their rights and provision of appropriate care. Seniors organisations tend to focus on arranging free time activities or solving their everyday problems rather than on for fighting for their rights at higher levels. Also, for example, families with children are taken better care of in terms of legal, institutional or other solutions in comparison with senior and their families.

2. Research description

In my main research I have adopted a multi-perspective approach including a few of the abovementioned disciplines to provide a broader context for this text genre to see how and to what extent extralinguistic factors influence text quality. In this study the warranty analysis is limited to presenting its social context as well as selected research findings of the ongoing research.

For the purpose of this study, I have used the context analysis based on the context model schema and its three categories suggested by van Dijk (2008) slightly modified for this analysis:

- Setting (time, place),
- Participants: warranty authors: producers, sellers and warranty 'readers' (purchasers),
- Communicative event (analysed warranty documents, actual documents and their characteristics)

3. Warranty research: sample selection, accessibility, participants, document setting, time framework

3.1 Sample selection

Small corpus of original warranty texts collected in 2017–2019 has been analyzed, texts come from producers' or sellers' websites or from scans of traditional printed warranties attached to purchased products. Unexpectedly, this initial stage revealed the first issues encountered by prospective or existing consumers: in some cases, it is difficult or impossible to find the current warranty version, most producers and sellers provide one warranty for several products, so their content is too general and not all the information applies to specific products. It also turned out that it is a very dynamic genre during this time the warranties were reviewed or even removed from websites. Changes also affected producers due to their transformation e.g. mergers with other companies, ownership changes or other structural or organizational changes caused by their economic situation.

3.2 Accessibility

There is no official obligation for producers or sellers to issue the warranty, it is an element of good practice and, in reality, in some cases only a short very general document is attached to a product, typically it gives information about the website providing more details concerning warranty, servicing, repairs and other issues concerning the product. On websites it is typically found in support section but sometimes without a separate section or heading, which makes it difficult to find it. Surprisingly, in some cases the document is available after the purchase of the product, accessing it on-line requires a unique code, which does not allow the prospective customer to compare warranty conditions for similar products offered by the competition and limits their consumer's choice. Thus, this preparation stage revealed that the consumer needs to have good analytical skills to be able to make a claim or take a decision concerning prospective purchases on the basis of the producer's or seller's warranty terms. To do this, they also need reasonably good computer skills as well as equipment and good Internet connection allowing consumers to make a claim. To conclude, finding correct documents and information can be one of the potential sources of exclusion.

3.3 Participants: warranty authors and senior consumers

3.3.1 Authors

While constructing and analyzing the corpus one should also take into consideration some sociolinguistic variables concerning text authors (Meyer, 2007) such as: age, gender, level of education as well as social contexts and relationships. In the analysed corpus it was virtually impossible to find authors:' names, age, gender, nationality, or information on professional or educational background. Thus it is hardly possible or impossible to infer if the collected documents were written by e.g. native or non-native speakers or maybe only translated into English; engineers, lawyers, translators or other producer's/sellers employees (more or less proficient in English – judging by the quality of texts, some of them seem to have been done by means of not very good translation software). The level of English fluency varies from B1 level (according to the CEFR criteria[1] for language fluency levels) to C2 (native speaker level) with highly complex and specialised lexis and syntax related to legal or technical issues, which can pose serious problems even for native speakers of any language. What should be emphasised is that there are hardly any guidelines as to the warranty content and how such a document should be drafted. In the EU legislation consumer sale warranties are regulated by the Consumer Sales Directive[2] (where it is referred to as 'guarantee' not 'warranty'). However,

1 Council of Europe, *Common European Framework of Reference foe Languages,* [online:] https://www.coe.int/en/web/common-european-framework-reference-languages/level-descriptions [available: 15.07.2020].

2 Directive 1999/44/EC of the European Parliament and of the Council of 25 May1999 on certain aspects of the sale of consumer goods and associated guarantees, Official Journal L171, 07.07/1999, pp. 0012–0016, [online:]

as Wiewiórowska-Domagalska (2011) suggests "the legislation of the Directive regarding the content of the guarantee is very modest," and adds that "under the Directive the guarantor is free not only to offer a guarantee but also to determine the contents of his undertaking." There are only very general suggestions with no more specific guidelines for guarantors as to the guarantee content, it only mentions what can include: information for making claims, guarantor's name and address and the document should be legible and in plain intelligible language thus allowing for different interpretations.

3.3.2 Senior consumers

When it comes to the social context, one conspicuous feature stands out – imbalance or asymmetry of power in the producer/seller – consumer relationship where the former one has more power and holds a superordinate position in contrast to the subordinate consumer. Consumers have no influence on the content of the warranty or a way it is written nor have they knowledge of legal regulations concerning sales or technical specifications or functionalities of the product they have already bought or intend to buy. As a consequence, they only receive a non-negotiable document and, deprived of any choice, they are forced to accept it. Due to the development of consumer organisations and campaigns consumers can get some assistance in case they have problems with defective products. In this article, however, the focus is put on the senior consumer because of ageing population and a growing number of older people in the European Union. According to the Eurostat data (2019)[3] currently in the EU there are 101.1 million people aged 65 or more and it is estimated that in 2050 the number will reach the level of 149.2 million people (28 % of the whole EU population). There is no one clear-cut definition specifying the threshold for age when exactly people get old, for some marketing agencies it is even age of 55, while others (employers or some institutions) commonly associate seniors with those aged approximately 65 and a beginning of their retirement. Now, with time, as Vernon indicates in his article (2017)[4] due to increasing longevity

---

https://eur-lex.europa.eu/legal-content/EN/TXT/HTML/?uri=CELEX:31999L0044&from=LT [available: 16.07.2020].

3 Eurostat (2017), *A look at the lives of the elderly in the EU today*. 2017. Ec.europa.eu, [online:] https://ec.europa.eu/eurostat/cache/infographs/elderly/index.html [available: 20.07.2020].

4 S. Vernon, What age is considered 'old' nowadays?, [online:] https://www.cbsnews.com/news/what-age-is-considered-old-nowadays [available: 17.07.2020].

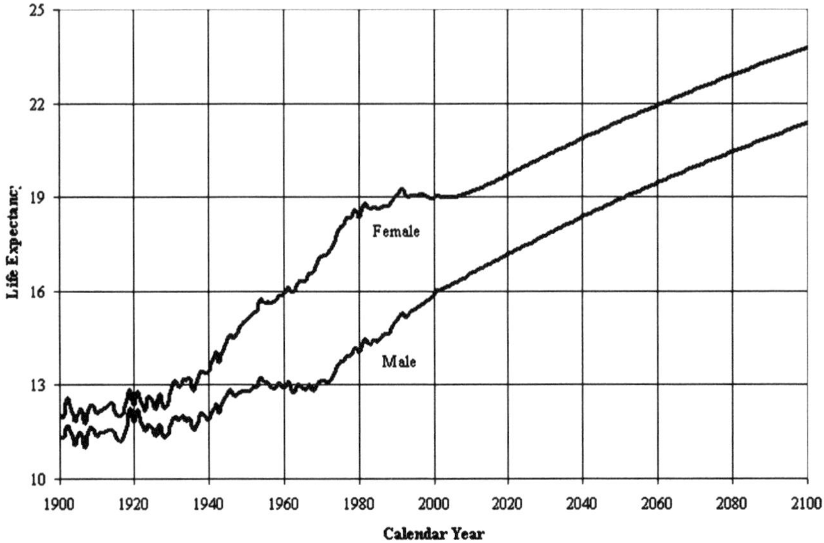

Figure 1: Life expectancy at age 65 by sex and calendar year (based on period tables). LIFE TABLES FOR THE UNITED STATES SOCIAL SECURITY AREA, [online:] https://www.ssa.gov/OACT/NOTES/as120/LifeTables_Body.html#wp1173782, [available 19.07.2020].

observed over the past decades. The term 'old' is related to the mortality risk and rate. Figure 1 illustrates the changes in life expectancy at the age of 65 and shows its significant increase within last decades both for males and females in 1900 for men it was 11.3 and in 2001 rose to 15.7 and for women 12 in 1900 and 18.8 in 2001 respectively. The graph below illustrates this difference.

So, for example, in 1920s a 55-year-old man who was regarded as old is now regarded as middle-aged and gets old at the age of 70.

However, age is not the only criterion for defining this group. The research shows that this group is not a homogenous unity,[5] it indicates a segmentation of this group and the necessity of taking into account other variables like: life experiences, health status, financial conditions, attitudes towards others and

5 G. Guido, M. Pichierri, G. Pino & R. Conoci, R., "The Segmentation of Elderly Consumers: A Literature Review," *Journal of Customer Behaviour* 2018, Vol. 17, No. 4, pp. 257–278, [online:] https://doi.org/10.1362/147539218x15445233217805 [available: 20.07.2020].

many other characteristics reflecting their actual needs and consumption behaviours.

Generally, research focuses on adult consumers and it showed that the warranties are not particularly consumer-friendly texts due to their accessibility described earlier and complexity which is described in more detail later on in the article. While describing senior consumers one should also bear in mind their declining physical and/or mental health and cognitive abilities in varying degrees affects their daily activity, may limit their options, abilities or decisions and with increasing age lead to their exclusion. Other crucial issues to be considered are the Internet access and seniors' digital literacy. Eurostat also indicates that 45 % of the elderly consumers in the EU use the internet at least once a week.[6] The reach of the internet continues to expand: not only are an increasing number of users online, but there is a growing number of devices connected to the Internet. While analysing statistics for the EU countries one can easily observe marked differences in the access to the Internet and the ways it is used, in terms of activities and computer literacy, which in turn can positively or negatively influence their access to some products and/or services (that are sometimes available only on-line) as well as other strongly computerised areas like on-line banking, health and financial issues or searching for all kinds of information needed to solve everyday problems. That also applies to some consumer warranties that are available only in an e-version.

4. Warranty: qualitative and quantitative text analysis, findings and their interpretation

In order to investigate the warranty in more depth I decided to conduct a quantitative and qualitative analysis of corpus of a 100 on-line consumer warranties or scans of warranty documents attached to products with broadly understood and frequently bought electronic goods including minor and major household goods including cooking, cooling and cleaning appliances, e.g. dishwashers, refrigerators, food processors, coffee makers, juice extractors, vacuum cleaners), phones and smartphones, tv and entertainment equipment, photography, computer equipment and PC accessories and health, beauty and personal care products. The rationale for the selection of the corpus analysis is the fact that it analyses a real language and its actual samples thus enabling to identify similarities, differences and other text characteristics and also to

6 Eurostat (2017).

conduct a quantitative analysis of the collected texts. The corpus fulfils criteria for a small, specialized corpus,[7] which means that it is large enough to provide a representative picture of this genre not only at the linguistic level.

The texts were analyzed using the Word tool for checking readability statistics, it provided text descriptive components including: number of words and sentences in each text, average sentence length, number of words in the longest sentence in the text, amount of passive voice (expressed in percent). The analysis has shown a significant difference in the warranty length as it ranges from 58 words to 3,459 words in the longest document. The shortest text consists of only two sentences, the longest one of 129 sentences. What is worth highlighting is the fact that the longest sentences are usually found in the exclusions section – in 79 texts out of 100 in the corpus. Many warranties contain numerous long sentences about 80 words. Their length, complex syntax with the combination of legal and technical jargon have a significant impact on the level of text difficulty as the consumer has difficulty in understanding what is or is not covered by the warranty.

Kohl (2008) in his guidelines for writing clear, translatable documentation claims that "Short sentences are less likely than long sentences to contain ambiguities or complexities that impede translation and reduce readability." He also suggests limiting sentence length to 20 words for procedural (task-oriented) information and around 25 for conceptual information since lengthy sentences pose interpretation problems both for native speakers and translators. Long sentences can lead to main interpretation problems: (a) sentences contain a lot of detailed information, is grammatically correct but this legalese language contains complex lexis and syntax typical of specialized languages; (b) texts are poorly drafted or translated and include various language or translation mistakes. Poorly drafted source or translated texts as they may generate and multiply further mistakes in subsequent documents (e.g. translated into other languages) and be a source of misinformation. Both types can be confusing for consumers. Many of the collected texts contain too much of legal terminology, some fixed old-fashioned expressions or formulas used mostly by lawyers.

However, it does not mean that long sentences are to be completely eliminated from the document, using longer sentences might occasionally be acceptable

7 S. Goźdź-Roszkowski, "Korpusy a języki specjalistyczne," [in:] *Podstawy Językoznawstwa Korpusowego*. Łódź 2005, pp. 174–200; M. Nelson, "Building a written corpus: What are the basics?," [in:] *The Routledge Handbook of Corpus Linguistics*, eds. A. O'Keeffe and M. McCarthy, London, New York 2010, pp. 53–64.

provided that (a) there is a logical link between them, (b) sentence is divided into clauses, but no more than two, (c) they conform to other rules of the plain language postulated by the Plain English Campaign members attempting at making documents more readable for the public.

What might work with long sentences is appropriate text organization and dividing it into short paragraphs, presenting information chunks with e.g. bulleted lists as well as following postulates of the Plain English movement which would help eliminate legalese from consumer warranty and other documents and make them more readable.

As for the passive voice ratio, various style guides e.g. Google developer documentation style guide (2020)[8] give a number of guidelines for those writing for a global audience and recommend limiting the use of the passive voice as "The subject of the sentence is the person or thing performing the action. With passive voice, it's often hard for readers to figure out who's supposed to do something." For example: *This procedure must be completed.* It is hard to decide who should deal with this procedure: consumer, producer, seller or someone else. Using active voice will enable the author to write a text of better quality by reducing a number of words this will make the message more concise, which will in turn reduce the cost of translation. The amount of passive voice in the corpus ranges from 0 to 66 %. Michigan University (2007)[9] in its guidelines for students recommends that the passive voice in their written documents is limited to 10–15 % of the document. Only seven texts in the corpus fulfil this criterion.

In the next stage, all the texts were checked with two readability formulas: Flesch Reading Ease (FRE) and Flesch-Kincaid Grade Level. It is estimated that there are more than 200 different formulas for testing text readability and scoring the text difficulty. Originally they were used to test level of textbooks and check if they were appropriate at a specific grade or level. Nowadays they are also used for testing readability of documents, manuals, websites or other texts in various areas of everyday life (e.g. insurance, health service, banking and others), particularly in informative texts. The FRE scale indicates how easy or difficult written English texts are to understand. It measures word length and sentence length and number of syllables in 100 words.

8 *Writing for a global audience*, Google Developers, 2020, [online:] https://developers.google.com/style/translation [available 17.07.2020].

9 *BIOSYSTEMS. Technical Writing Guide*, Msu.edu, 2007, [online:] https://msu.edu/course/be/485/bewritingguideV2.0.pdf [available: 17 July 2020].

Score and difficulty level	Number of analyzed texts in this score range
90–100 very easy	0
80–89 easy	0
70–79 fairly easy	0
60–69 standard	0
50–59 fairly difficult	6
30–49 difficult	69
0–29 very confusing	25

Table 1: FRE scores for the analyzed texts.
Source: own research.

The scores range from 0 to 100, the higher score the easier the text is. The table above shows score ranges and corresponding readability levels and readability scores for the analyzed texts in the corpus:

The scores reveal that all the texts in the corpus are very difficult to understand because of long complex sentences and words.

Another testing tool used in the readability analysis was the Flesch-Kincaid Grade Level based on the US school grade level which shows for example that text with a score of 7 can be understood by an average 7th grader. The scores obtained in this test range from 8.5 to 20.8 and majority of texts (79) indicate that college graduate level of education is needed for correct understanding of the warranty text.

What should be stressed, however, are numerous criticisms related to using the formulas for assessing texts since they do not measure other crucial text parameters like layout, content and its organization (headings, paragraphs, lists, use of visuals, style etc.). The formulas have been used among others by marketers, policy or instruction writers, scientists presenting their research to a non-specialist audience or even the US navy for testing readability of their training manuals to mention but a few. Before discussing some drawbacks of the readability tests, I would like to test a text fragment using a few formulas. To show their usefulness let us have a look at the fragment of the Huawei's warranty concerning limitation of liability

Flesch Reading Ease	13.2 impossible to comprehend
Flesch-Kincaid Grade Level:	32.1 college graduate and above
Gunning Fog	27.7 extremely difficult to read
The Coleman-Liau Index	12 twelfth grade
The SMOG Index	22.9 graduate college
Automated Readability Index	36.2 college graduate
Linsear Write Formula	50.2 college graduate and above
Readability Consensus based on 7 formulas	Grade level: 31
	Reading level: impossible to comprehend Reader's age: college graduate

Table 2: Test scores obtained in seven on-line readability tests for the text below
Source: own research

Text sample
HUAWEI'S LIMIT OF LIABILITY UNDER THIS LIMITED WARRANTY SHALL BE THE ACTUAL CASH VALUE OF THE PRODUCT AT THE TIME PURCHASER RETURNS THE PRODUCT FOR REPAIR, AS DETERMINED BY THE PRICE PAID BY THE PURCHASER FOR THE PRODUCT LESS A REASONABLE AMOUNT OF USAGE. HUAWEI SHALL NOT BE LIABLE FOR ANY OTHER LOSSES OR DAMAGES SUCH AS SPECIAL, INCIDENTAL, CONSEQUENTIAL, OR PUNITIVE DAMAGES (INCLUDING BUT NOT LIMITED TO LOSS OF ANTICIPATED BENEFITS OR PROFITS, LOSS OF SAVINGS OR REVENUE, LOSS OF DATA, LOSS OF USE OF THE PRODUCT OR ANY ASSOCIATED EQUIPMENT, COST OF CAPITAL, COST OF ANY SUBSTITUTE EQUIPMENT OR FACILITIES, DOWNTIME, ANY COSTS OF RECOVERING, REPROGRAMMING, OR REPRODUCING ANY PROGRAM OR DATA, ANY FAILURE TO MAINTAIN THE CONFIDENTIALITY OF DATA STORED ON THE PRODUCT, THE CLAIMS OF ANY THIRD PARTIES, INCLUDING SUBSEQUENT PURCHASERS, AND INJURY TO PROPERTY, RESULTING FROM THE PURCHASE OR USE OF THE PRODUCT OR ARISING FROM BREACH OF THIS WARRANTY, BREACH OF CONTRACT, NEGLIGENCE, STRICT LIABILITY, OR ANY OTHER LEGAL OR EQUITABLE THEORY, EVEN IF HUAWEI KNEW OF THE LIKELIHOOD OF SUCH DAMAGES). HUAWEI SHALL NOT BE LIABLE FOR DELAY IN RENDERING SERVICE UNDER THE LIMITED WARRANTY, OR LOSS OF USE DURING THE PERIOD THAT THE PRODUCT IS BEING REPAIRED.

On-line FRE test score for this text is 13.2 and was rated: impossible to understand. To verify this negative score, I also used other readability formulas[10] for the same fragment. Table 2 above shows scores and their interpretation (comprehension difficulty and in some cases grade level).

10 Further information on the applied formulas can be found at: On-line readability calculator, [online]: https://readabilityformulas.com/freetests/six-readability-formulas.php.

Total number of words in this fragment is: 205, 2 sentences, first sentence: 178 words. Long words i.e. with three or more syllables account for 23 % of the text (48 words). After removing the company name from the list 44 words. Three-syllable words are regarded as difficult words. However, one must approach critically such words as not all them are difficult (e.g. limited), it is advisable though to check these words. For the above fragment the FRE analysis showed the following hard words:

> LIABILITY | LIMITED | WARRANTY | ACTUAL | PURCHASER | DETERMINED | PURCHASER | REASONABLE | LIABLE | INCIDENTAL | CONSEQUENTIAL | PUNITIVE | INCLUDING | LIMITED | ANTICIPATED | BENEFITS | REVENUE | ASSOCIATED | EQUIPMENT | CAPITAL | SUBSTITUTE | EQUIPMENT | FACILITIES | RECOVERING | REPROGRAMMING | REPRODUCING | CONFIDENTIALITY | INCLUDING | SUBSEQUENT | PURCHASERS | INJURY | PROPERTY | RESULTING | ARISING | WARRANTY | NEGLIGENCE | LIABILITY | EQUITABLE | LIKELIHOOD | LIABLE | RENDERING | LIMITED | WARRANTY | PERIOD |

At this stage author (producer or seller) might consider replacing difficult words with their easier equivalents, shortening sentences and reorganizing the text to make it more consumer-friendly. More in-depth analysis, however, requires taking into account text features that cannot be measured automatically and will provide a more informative feedback. Using formulas is a tool for non-philologists who would like to write a (more) readable text for clients or consumers.

My initial research objective was to describe the genre and present a typical warranty and its characteristics. With time it revealed numerous differences in various text aspects like 'moving' it to the Internet and increasing or limiting its accessibility for different groups of consumers or changing its form. Traditional warranty was a separate document attached to the purchased goods, dedicated to one product with warranty terms related to it. Now the warranty is a part of a bigger document, very often for a group of various producer's/seller's products, sometimes difficult to find between various language versions with instructions, technical specifications and other information. Short warranties consisting of only a few sentences are not particularly informative, the long ones, on the other hand, can be confusing since it is very unlikely that a consumer will read a-few-pages long document, written in small font, before buying, for example a vacuum cleaner. Even the name of the document differs (or is even absent and only informs the consumer what to do in case a product is defective) and it is called: *warranty, guarantee, guarranty, warranty conditions, warranty information, warranty statement, warranty policy, warranty & repairs, warranty and service after purchase*. Also, other factors have been investigated in the warranty research which are not discussed here, they refer to other text features like cohesion or specific sentence components or lexis and their impact on text functions and their effect on the target reader.

The current research analyses 100 documents but the original collection of texts was much bigger and also included warranties for other types of goods like: clothing, stationery, various non-electronic household goods. What strikes most about them is:

- varied content because of its length (too long or too short);
- too complex or simplistic syntax and vocabulary contributing to reader's comprehension of the text;
- the longest and most difficult text is typically found in exclusions; Is this by chance? This is a common characteristic of almost all warranty texts;
- all sorts of layout with or without: visuals, titles, subtitles, sections, lists; in some cases, all the text is in one paragraph and on top of that squeezed into a very small space among several other language versions;
- according to the applied readability formulas only a few were reasonably easy to read
- that they are being increasingly moved to the producers' websites.

5. Remedies for improving texts quality and readability

To sum up, there seems to be some steps taken to tackle the issue. Firstly, the producers and sellers should be provided with more specific guidelines for drafting warranty documents. They should also be more aware of the consumer (the target reader – here senior but also other groups like teenagers) who reads their documents and is not necessarily a lawyer or another highly-educated professional, might not have access to the Internet or only limited access and appropriate equipment for using it and require help of others to find out about their consumers rights. Thus, traditional paper and electronic version should be used. Also, some companies, as a part of good practice, write two document versions: one including detailed information for professionals – necessary for "official" purposes and plain language version for average consumers. So, in case a dispute arises, there is also possibility to consult a specialist. Also, increasing its accessibility would matter i.e. possibility of reading it before the purchase and finding quickly the correct version on the website (providing appropriate dates and/if this document is binding in your country). Knowing potential target consumer producers or sellers should not take it for granted that all the consumers can and will register their products on-line to make their warranty valid. That refers not only to seniors but also to other digital emigrants of different ages that are also excluded in many ways due to the lack of Internet access. Secondly, consumer organizations emphasize the necessity of raising consumers' awareness in various age groups and thus empowering them and providing vulnerable groups with better protection. Finally, whether or not any changes to the existing consumer law are needed might be a topic for separate research.

6. Conclusions

The article provides new insights into the character of the consumer warranty due to employing a linguistic perspective in the analysis of this text genre. Existing research focused predominantly on law and various legal aspects, the consumer law makes only brief references to the language to be used in documents and suggests using a clear style but does not expand on this by giving any specific guidelines for document authors or translators. The study is devoted mainly to the discourse analysis of various text features using a corpus of authentic warranty documents as well as qualitative and quantitative analysis conducted by means of software testing text readability. Findings revealed potential difficulty areas and indicated the difficulty level of the analyzed texts whose target readers are seniors. Research focus is narrowed down to elderly consumers, but it would be worthwhile to further investigate this group as well as other groups and compare results and test whether or to what extent the 'problems' with texts overlap. What is to be emphasized a pragmatic aspect of these findings as it is based on actual documents: their linguistic and non-linguistic features like layout, numbering etc. This combination of linguistic and non-linguistic factors gives a broader and more practical perspective on the analyzed genre than it would have been in the case of a purely theoretical linguistic analysis focused only on strictly textual features dealing with syntactic or semantic patterns, text cohesion etc. without taking into account the social and psychological context. Adopting the broader perspective allowed for assessment of text readability and indicate problem areas, which would in turn provide guidelines for drafting documents that are more senior-consumer friendly. By no means is the description complete, it is to be treated rather as a starting point for further discussion and research oriented towards improving on the quality of the warranty as well as other documents. Further research might investigate psycholinguistic aspects focusing on document perception in vulnerable consumer groups. Analysis could also extend their scope to other consumer documents and/or other kinds of documents received by senior citizens from various institutions and test their communication ease and effectiveness in terms of their correct interpretation by target readers.

Bibliography:

BIOSYSTEMS. Technical Writing Guide, Msu.edu, 2007. [online:] https://msu.edu/course/be/485/bewritingguideV2.0.pdf [available: 17 July 2020].

Delekta I., "Consumer Warranty as a genre," *Comparative Legilinguistics* 2013, Vol. 15, No. 15, pp. 7–17.

Dijk T., *Discourse and Context: A Sociocognitive Approach*, Cambridge 2008.

Goźdź-Roszkowski S., "Korpusy a języki specjalistyczne," [in:] *Podstawy Językoznawstwa Korpusowego.* Łódź 2005, pp. 174–200.

Guido G., Pichierri M., Pino G., Conoci R., "The Segmentation of Elderly Consumers: A Literature Review," *Journal of Customer Behaviour* 2018, Vol. 17, No. 4, pp. 257–278 [online:] https://doi.org/10.1362/147539218x15445233217805 [available: 20.07.2020].

Kohl J., *The Global English Style Guide: Writing Clear, Translatable Documentation for a Global Market,* New York 2008, pp. 34–35.

Loomba A., "Historical Perspective on Warranty," [in:] *Product Warranty Handbook 1st ed.*, eds. W. Blischke, D. Murthy, New York 1996.

Meyer C., *English Corpus Linguistics: An Introduction,* Cambridge 2007.

Nelson M., "Building a written corpus: What are the basics?," [in:] *The Routledge Handbook of Corpus Linguistics*, eds. A. O'Keeffe and M. McCarthy, London, New York 2010, pp. 53–64.

Wiewiórowska-Domagalska A., "Consumer sales guarantees in the European Union," unpublished PhD thesis, 2011, p. 71 [online:] https://dspace.library.uu.nl/bitstream/handle/1874/235592/wiewiorowska.pdf [available: 15.07.2020].

Writing for a global audience, Google Developers, 2020 [online:] https://developers.google.com/style/translation [available 17.07.2020].

Jolanta Klimczak

University of Silesia in Katowice

e-mail: jolanta.klimczak@us.edu.pl

ORCID ID: 0000-0003-1167-2921

Dorota Nowalska- Kapuścik

University of Silesia in Katowice

e-mail: dorota.nowalska-kapuscik@us.edu.pl

ORCID ID: 0000-0003-4224-3257

Local senior policy as a tool of combating discrimination of the elderly on the basis of the situation in Bogucice district.

Abstract: Ongoing process of ageing of society results in transformation of population structure and growing share of the elderly, in combination with decrease of share of people in working age, in total population. In Poland, just like in other EU countries, demographic slowdown causes growth of the percentage of people who are above 65. It is estimated that in 2030, the elderly will constitute 23,8 % of society. The growth of the percentage of the elderly in population is perceived as a problem phenomenon; it results in tendency to create negative attitudes, prejudices and stereotypes causing marginalization, exclusion and even discrimination of seniors. A tool to fight with ageism should be a coherent senior policy, Department of Senior Policy in the Ministry of Labour and Social Policy is responsible for this policy in the national dimension, however, the scale of negative consequences of the process of ageing of society requires mobilization also in the local dimension. Taking regional diversity of the level of old age and dynamics of process of ageing into account, as well as specificity of socio-economic transformation of particular provinces of Poland, such actions seem to be justified. The discussion on senior policy in the cities has just begun, therefore, it is necessary to coordinate and constantly monitor the state of implementation of human rights with reference to the elderly in Poland. It will allow not only to objectively assess current actions, but also to create a basis to formulate conclusions and recommendations within the scope of necessary changes.

The goal of the article is to analyse the assessment of actions preventing ageism taken within regional senior policy implemented in Katowice and confront declared effects with experiences of exclusion and resilience strategies of older inhabitants. An empirical basis of presented theses and conclusions is qualitative research conducted with the use of free-form and standardized interview with the elderly and analysis of documents and legacy data.

Keywords: ageism, discrimination, senior policy

1. Introductory remarks

A lot of attention has recently been paid to the issue of old age, which is the result of demographic transformations expressing in general population growth and progressing process of ageing of world population. Despite global character of unfavourable demographic tendencies, dynamics of changes is uneven in particular countries, which causes that the degree of advancement is spatially diverse. The pace of ageing of humankind is determined by many factors, especially by the higher level of development and living standard, better medical and social care, growth of longevity, decrease of fertility, as well as – broadly understood – modifications of the patterns of consumerist behaviours, evolution of beliefs and lifestyle. It results in reorganization of a structure of a given society causing the upset of balance between people of working age and beyond their retirement age[1] that can have negative impact on stability of public finances. In the long-term perspective, it means that radical changes must be made, connected not only with providing universal access to health care services of good quality, modification of pension system and social base, but also with coordination in all fields of economy so it would correspond to diverse economic behaviours of the society.

The awareness of necessity of changes is now constant subject of discussions, both in the sphere of politics and in media and public discourse. The need to develop fast and effective working methods is particularly emphasized in highly developed regions such as Europe, North America (without Latin part), Australia with New Zealand, Japan, in which the process of ageing of society– in accordance with the determinants mentioned above – can be regarded as advanced.

An estimation for Europe[2] and above all for European Union member states is particularly alarming. For these countries, the percentage of population at

1 D. E. Bloom, D. Canning, J. Sevilla, *Economic Growth and the Demographic Transition*, Cambridge, National Bureau of Economic Research, 2001, [online:] https://www.nber.org/papers/w8685 [available: 22.06.2020].

2 Eurostat Statistics Explained, *Population structure and egeing*, 2019, [online:] https://ec.europa.eu/eurostat/statisticsexplained/index.php?title=Population_structure_and_ageing [available: 22.06.2020].

the age of 65+ in 2050 will be 28.1 % (according to data of January 1, 2018, this percentage was 19.7 %). It means growth by 8.4 process points within 32 years. It must be emphasized that the growth of population at senior age will be associated with decrease of population of working age, which may cause that the group of professionally inactive people will increase until 2060 by about 19 million, by 14 million in the Eurozone.[3] It is estimated that until 2060, life expectancy of men in EU countries will increase to 84.8; and to 89.1 for women (for comparison, now it is 77.7 for men, 83.1 for women).[4] The comparison of percentage of people at young and retirement age shows that number of the elderly of non-working age with reference to people of working age will be constantly increasing. It will have impact on the budgets of specific countries that will be obliged to increase social expenditure, in the form of pensions, health care, institutional or private. As a result, ageing of society – apart from external and internal migrations – is treated as the most notice able demographic phenomenon in modern Europe, as an issue of strategic importance.

From among European Union member states, the worst changes in demographic structure occurred in Italy and Germany; Poland, according to the report of the European Commission[5] is also one of these countries that will have to face serious consequences of these changes.

Although the works on solving the problems are done both from the perspective of European Union authorities and authorities of specific European countries, the role of regional policy that can (and should) be treated as the main subject responsible for the shape and execution of pro senior actions is more and more often emphasized. It seems that this concept is correct, taking into account the fact that the scale and strategies of coping with the effects of the issue that we are interested in, strongly depends on economic, political and social capabilities of a given region. Taking regional differences along with their specificity and cultural resources into account, allows not only better understand the needs of the seniors, but also allows proper management of economic, residential, tourist etc. potential of a given region. Decentralization of power and subsidiary has opened the commune the path to design a regional

3 *The 2015 Ageing Report European Economy* (EU), 2015, [online:] https://ec.europa.eu/economy_finance/publications/european_economy/2015/pdf/ee3_en.pdf [available: 22.06.2020].

4 "The 2015 Ageing Report," *European Economy* 2015, Vol. 3.

5 Eurostat Statistics Explained, *Population structure and ageing*, 2019, [online:] https://ec.europa.eu/eurostat/statisticsexplained/index.php?title=Population_structure_and_ageing [available: 22.06.2020].

policy in terms of specific local community. It is particularly important in the case of the elderly, for whom local environment is often the most important (or the only) area of their activity.

The article is focused on the actions taken within the framework of preventing discrimination that – due to their age – is experienced by the in habitants in one of the districts of Katowice-Bogucice.

2. Old age in theoretical perspective

The terms "old age" and "ageing" are analysed in many ways. These phenomena include biological, demographic, economic or social aspects, which gives them interdisciplinary character, resulting in abundance of various definitions and theoretical concepts. It would be expected that the development of appropriate definition of old age is significant for all of us as people being subject to the process of ageing; however, digressions on semantic structure of this word are usually made in the context of developing effective tools applied in a pension system or health care.

Therefore, the definitions of old age are the result of consensus developed as a result of mixing three areas of the process of ageing: biological, mental and social. It is completely understandable because according to Gorman so it can be taken that a biological age reference is not sufficient to classify someone as 'old' or 'elderly.' The ageing process is of course a biological reality which has it down dynamic, largely beyond human control. However, it is also subject to the constructions by which each society makes sense of old age. In the developed world, chronological time plays a paramount role. The age of 60 or 65, roughly equivalent to retirement ages in most developed countries, is said to be the beginning of old age. In many parts of the developing world, chronological time has little or no importance in the meaning of old age Other socially constructed meanings of age are more significant such as the roles assigned to older people; in some cases, it is the loss of roles accompany in physical decline which is significant in defining old age. Thus, in contrast to the chronological milestones which mark life stages in the developed world, old age in many developing countries is seen to begin at the point when active contribution is no longer possible."[6]

6 M. Gorman, "Development and the rights of older people," [in:] *The Ageing and Development Report: Poverty, Independence and the World's Older People*, London, Earths can Publications Ltd., eds. J. Randel, 1999, pp. 3–21.

It is hard to precisely estimate when old age begins; it is determined by many individual factors, mental and physical health, lifestyle and economic conditions can be regarded as particularly important. Many attempts have been made to accept appropriate "age scales" that – at least approximately – would allow to adopt certain frameworks. One of the propositions of division was presented by the WHO:

- The phase of older age– between 60 and 75 years old;
- The phase of old age– between 75 and 90 years old;
- The phase of deep old age– more than 90 years old.[7]

This division results from preference differences applied in the selection of old age criteria. It also shows heterogeneity of population of the seniors. It is diverse both in terms of socio-demographic features and physical and mental health condition, and above all, quality of life understood as:

> individual way of perceiving by the individuals of their life position in cultural context and system of values, in which an individual lives, and with reference to tasks, expectations and standards determined by environmental determinants.[8]

The "scales" of old age proposed by the WHO are quite large, which allows to determine and define old age corresponding to national conditions and shape of social policy towards the elderly.

> Most developed world countries have accepted the chronological age of 65 years as a definition of 'elderly' or older person. While this definition is somewhat arbitrary, it is many times associated with the age at which one can begin to receive pension benefits. At the moment, there is no United Nations standard numerical criterion, but the UN agreed cut off is 60+ years to refer to the older population. Although there are commonly used definitions of old age, there is no general agreement on the age at which a person becomes old. The common use of a calendar age to mark the threshold of old age assumes equivalence with biological age, yet at the same time, it is generally accepted that these two are not necessarily synonymous.[9]

---

7 WHO, 2014, *Revision of the World Urbanization Prospects,* [online:] http://www.un.org/en/development/desa/publications/2014-revision-world-urbanization-prospects.html, 2014 [available: 12.04.2018].

8 The World Health Organization Quality of Life assessment (WHOQOL): "Position paper from the World Health Organization," *Social Science & Medicine* 1996, Vol. 41, No. 10, p. 1403–1409.

9 WHO, 2014, *Revision of the World Urbanization Prospects,* [online:] http://www.un.org/en/development/desa/publications/2014-revision-world-urbanization-prospects.html, 2014 [available: 12.04.2018].

In Poland, retirement age is diverse due to sex and it is 60 years old for women and 65 years old for men (for comparison: in the years 2013–2017, retirement age was the same for everyone and it was 67 years old).

The determination of retirement age is not tantamount to determination of the moment of commencement of old age, of which proof can be a thresh old of 60 years of age applied in the statistics as a moment of "commencement" of old age. Based on statistical data,[10] we can see that the number of in habitants at the age of 60 and older is increasing every year (in 2018, the number of in habitants in this age range was 9508.4 thousand people and it was higher by 214.8 thousand in comparison with 2017). According to the prognosis, the number of people at the age of 60 and older will be increasing, however, it is obvious that this growth will not progress in the same way in all age groups. The highest values will be reached for the oldest group, that is, people at the age of 90 and older, the lowest values will be reached in two younger age groups: 60–64 and 65–69. Until 2050, among the elderly (over the age of 60), the highest share of people will be in the oldest age group.

An analysis of data that includes sex and place of residence allows to formulate a hypothesis that women will still be the majority in all older age groups. In general, for population of people above the age of 60, it will be 16.7 % (women) to 12.3 % (men). Much more old people will be living in the cities the (prognosis for 2030) and it will be about 18 % of all seniors. It shows that there may be a demographic crisis, which may result in excessive welfare expenditure for people of working age. The solution to above demographic problems can be focusing on the actions aiming at radical transformation within the scope of demand for care or social services, as well as reorganization of expenditure on infrastructure and organization of urban space to adjust to new social stratification. The key seems to be a consolidation in the sphere of economy, social policy, health and social care responsible for formation of negative, unjust stereotypes about seniors.

2.1 Discrimination of the elderly: Between theory and practice

Despite the fact that the number of old people is growing, it has not made social position of this group stronger. It is assumed that satisfying ageing means: low level of disability, independent physical and mental functioning, as well as active involvement and interest in life. More and more often, social participation

10 GOV, [online:] https://stat.gov.pl/obszary-tematyczne/osoby-starsze/osoby-starsze/sytuacja-osob-starszych-w-polsce-w-2018-roku,2,1.html [available: 23.06.2020].

is added to the factors mentioned above. "Social participation, defined as socially oriented sparing of individual resources, is often regarded as an import ant criterion of quality of life in old age."[11]

However, the elderly often with draw to the margin of social life, or – what seems to be practiced more often – they are simply pushed there.

> While on average we are living longer, this prospect does not seem to generate much joy. Perhaps given its proximity to death, few of us are eager to achieve 'senior' status. Furthermore, ageism – prejudice on the grounds of age – renders the status and prospect of old age unattractive, and restricts the opportunities available in this phase of life. While it is experienced on a personal level, 'old age' is defined and constructed by society at large. One of the main social influences here is the custom of 'retirement.' In historical terms, the idea of retirement is a recent invention. Retirement draws a chronological in across our lives, so making 'old age' an absolute as well as a relative concept. Retirement itself is paradoxical. The greater productivity of our society now allows folk to be put out to 'leisure.' However, the very same productivity often renders older workers redundant, thus – for some at least – removing their purpose, role, and meaning in life.[12]

> A key feature of any definition of discrimination is its focus on behaviour. Discrimination is distinct from racial prejudice (attitudes), racial stereotypes (beliefs), and racism (ideologies) that may also be associated with racial disadvantage. Discrimination may be motivated by prejudice, stereotypes, or racism, but the definition of discrimination does not presume any unique underlying cause.[13]

In the case of the elderly, we can observe two fundamental dimensions of discrimination. The first one is related to creation of barriers in the access to employment, health care, education, financial services and social participation. The second area is related to, above all, mental sphere that is based on a stereotype of an infirm, scruffy individual, which is fuelled by the mass media and public opinion. It translates in to growing negative attitude towards the elderly, marginalizing this social group, causing social exclusion and disrespect. Such perception of the seniors is an effect of the lack of consciousness and proper interpretation of the needs of the seniors, which leads to perceiving the elderly from the angle of additional challenges that are related to satisfaction of their needs, and not resources and potential that they have.

---

11 A. Bukov, I. Maas, T. Lampert, "Social Participation," *The Journals of Gerontology Series B* 2002, Vol. 57, No. 6.

12 D. Wiles, "Who Is Old? Defining Old Age," *Australian Journal on Ageing* 1987, Vol. 6. No. 4.

13 L. Quillian, "New approaches to understanding racial prejudice and discrimination," *Annu. Rev. Sociol.* 2006, Vol. 32, pp. 199–328.

2.2. The challenges of regional senior policy: The theoretical aspect

The issue of observance of civil rights of all age groups is becoming a significant element of a model of social policy, creating a challenge for the entities appointed to execute tasks resulting from legal regulations. In Poland, due to its membership in the European Union, there is an issue of adjustment of national legal regulations to the requirements of the European Council, while respecting the principle of equal treatment of all citizens as a dominant directive.

The shape of Polish senior policy a consequence of the actions of public administration of all ranks, as well as other organizations and institutions doing the work for the seniors. Recently, the role and importance of regional policy of development has increased and there is a chance to implement solutions appropriate to the specificity of a given community. It is justified when we take into account the fact that although the whole country must face the problem of ageing of population, the growth of percentage of the elderly in population is regionally diverse. It creates an opportunity to flexible adjustment of the cities/communes to evolving needs and expectations of the seniors in accordance with the concept of friendly city that includes participation of the seniors "in social, economic, cultural, spiritual and civil life."[14]

In accordance with WHO recommendations[15] eight key areas of functioning of the city/commune have been defined, creating proper conditions for an idea of dignified ageing. They include: external spaces and buildings, especially public utility buildings, transport, housing conditions: public and private, participation in social life, respecting the rights and social inclusion, participation in civil life and on the labour market within employment, communication and information, medical services and networks of support of local community.

In regional senior policy of Silesian Voivodeship, the seniors are supported based on the main types of social participation: collective, productive and political participation. It is in conformity with the rules of social participation:

> Social participation occurs in the conduct of actions in which individuals share (a part of) their resources with others. On the one hand, through socially oriented sharing, resources are contributed to the social environment. Self-oriented sharing, on the other hand, entails resources being taken from the environment. The socially

14 The World Health Report 2002, *Reducing Risks, Promoting Healthy Life*, [online: https://www.who.int/hiv/whr_press/en/ [available: 22.06.2020], p. 12.

15 The World Health Report 2007, *Global Age-friendly Cities: A guide*, [online:] www.who.int [available: 23.06.2020].

oriented sharing of individual resources represents the genuine phenomenon of social participation.[16]

The most important goals within this scope were defined in the Strategy of Social Policy of Silesian Voivodeship in 2006–2020. Revision of 2015.[17] In the document mentioned above, it was determined as significant:

> supporting and strengthening the potential of the elderly and their active participation in social life, identification, reduction, prevention and countering the barriers making life of the elderly more difficult, shaping the image of the elderly and improvement of cross-generational relationships, as well as adjustment of the system of support to the needs of ageing society.[18]

The improvement of living conditions and quality of life of people exposed to social exclusion and socially excluded, including direction of actions providing equal opportunities in the access to health care in the subregions and provision of uniform standard of health safety was regarded as a strategic goal in social policy of Katowice. Particular emphasis was put on the actions related to supporting seniors in their mobilization, including professional activation, supporting families, including care of people that need it, eliminating consequences of the process of demographic ageing of society, as well as broadly understood actions, including health promotion, prevention and education. Taking formal regulations into account, the authors made an attempt to check how the projects observing the rules of senior policy are evaluated. We were interested in both projects run by public institutions (local government units, Municipal Cultural Centers, MOSiR, MOPS and others), and by non-governmental organizations (associations, foundations, non-profit institutions). A merging link that was necessary to qualify a given project for the research was its subject, not the source of financing. It must be emphasized that not the very projects that were assessed; the research was focused on the attempt to check whether evaluation is treated as a significant tool allowing to verify

16 G. Schmied, *Schenken: Über eine Form sozialen Handelns,* Opladen 1999.

17 Strategy of Social Policy of Silesian Voivodeship in 2006–2020. Revision of 2015 Resolution No. 183/239/V/2018 of the Board of Silesian Voivodeship of 31.01.2018, p. 243.

18 Strategia Polityki Społecznej Województwa Śląskiego na lata 2006–2020. Aktualizacja 2015 [Social Policy Strategy of the Silesian voivodeship for 2006–2020. Updated 2015] (Uchwała nr 183/239/V/2018 Zarządu Województwa Śląskiego z dnia 31.01.2018 r.), pp. 243–244.

the value of a given project. The research conducted for this purpose[19] allowed to get answers for the most important issues related to conducting evaluation in Katowice. The questions were composed in accordance with previously established criteria, consisting of not only issues related to the subject scope of evaluation, but also the whole process of its organization. In the research tool, particular emphasis was put on the recommendations, conclusions, which were both the summary of the project and starting point for development of different actions for the community of the elderly. The results allow to formulate a few fundamental conclusions:

1) In the majority of analysed projects, no financial resources were allotted for evaluation research. Despite that, the initiators of the projects made the attempts to sum up the results of the projects. SWOT analyses conducted in this way allowed, at least partially, to determine desire do run desired direction of actions. It also allowed to make decisions about potential continuation of the projects. This practiced "substitute" solution may be treated as a good starting point to develop knowledge and propagate the necessity to use professional methodology of evaluation research and use it to critically assess senior policy;
2) The demand for continuation of regional senior policy run in specific districts is increasing. It can be clearly seen in the statements of the respondents who emphasized that mobilization of the seniors in their place of residence has created a safe space for such actions, providing sense of security, as well as support from the neighbours or inhabitants. However, trans district communication and coordination of actions is required so as to people from other districts or estates would also take part in the actions having higher budgets;
3) The actions taking place in the homes of the seniors should also be considered so as to effectively combat marginalization of disabled people or people having limited physical activity.

19 The research was conducted using qualitative method and interview questionnaire containing instructions for questions. The research was conducted in the period between October 2019 and January 2020. Finally, a basis for analyses is material collected in 20 districts of Katowice.

3. Senior urban policy

In Katowice, the inhabitants at the age of 65+ constitute 21 % of population, at the age of 59+, this number increases to 25,2 %, and within the next few years, large category of nearly 40 % of people of non-mobile working age will enter the period of occupational deactivation (GUS 2017). For the city, it means not only demographic change of a dominant profile of the inhabitants, but also the change of expectations and needs, especially social and residential ones. "Urban Strategy of Solving Social Problems in 2016–2022" partially refers to it. In this strategy, we can find words indicating the need of "strengthening resources for health and active participation *of the elderly* in social life [italic from the author]" (BIP 2015). However, ageing is a spatially diverse process, and specific areas of the city–along with their history, cultural identity, resources of the inhabitants – create various (but not equal) opportunities and conditions for activity or health services. Southern part of Katowice has average or lower than average share of older in habitants in population structure, there are city areas, in which accumulation of the elderly is very high and value of rate of ageing exceeds 217 pts, not saying that most people at the age of 75+ live in four historically the oldest districts (Śródmieście, Brynów- Osiedle Zgrzebnioka, Dąb and Koszutka).

The awareness of spatial accumulation of the elderly in Katowice seems to be present in local policy because we can find in the "Local Program of Renewal of the City of Katowice in 2016–2022" on the fifth page of the document that:

> An integrated approach is the answer to the challenges resulting from character and scale of socio-economic problems identified in particular degraded subareas of Katowice, referring to: depopulation, *ageing of community* [italics from the author], unemployment, professional activity, poverty and social exclusion, low enterprise and low level of public safety in the identified crisis areas (BIP 2018: 5).

However, the document says that among all districts that are supposed to be renewed, only in the case of the Downtown, the program of changes and formulated goals says about the elderly and actions for this group of in habitants (BIP 2018: 31–35). In the remaining areas covered by the renewal, the goals focus either on other social categories, or *implicate* include problems of the elderly in the program called "preventing social exclusion," for example, in the district that is an area of our research.

Old age as a subject of our research: A methodological note
Creating anti-discrimination regional policy is a challenge for the whole voivodeship or city; we should pay particular interest in the actions taken in the places beyond mainstream. One of such places is one of the districts in Katowice – Bogucice– situated

nearly 2 km to the north-east from the city centre.[20] This district, both in perception of the very inhabitants and people living in other areas of Katowice, is neglected, undercapitalized, devastated, there are mostly "familok" buildings. The lack of Local Spatial Development Plan for the part of area of a former mine (Katowice mine), low activity of the inhabitants, as well as bad occupational and demographic structure have caused that this district is exposed to marginalization and exclusion and it is slowly transforming into "poverty ghetto." The idea of the initiators of the project was to diagnose the situation and needs of the elderly in the district, as well as collection of data about the level of social participation of the seniors. These research were conducted in 2018. In 2020, we returned to Bogucice to check how educational, cultural and care offer was assessed by our respondents. The method applied in the research, having all the hallmarks of longitudinal studies, allowed to observe development, behaviour, direction of changes in the research group, providing unique knowledge about the factors shaping local senior policy, providing valuable arguments about how to improve and coordinate the actions of the bodies of local administration and other organizations and institutions, leading to provision of conditions of extending activity, both professional and social, and healthy, safe and independent life of the elderly.[21]

3.1 Senior policy in the district in the eyes of the elderly

The oldest part of in habitants of Bogucice has lived in the district for at least few decades. Some of them were born here or have become its inhabitants, finding a job in local industry or entered the state of matrimony with a partner living here. So, they are connected with this city space not only by material, but also personal bonds; it is anointer subjective cultural landscape founded on family memory and memories of former ethos of a mining estate.

Due to closing "Katowice" mine, this district, along with its inhabitants, has experienced dramatic infrastructural and socio-cultural degradation. In 2018,

20 They are inhabited by over 16,000 people. The whole is composed of 2 parts: 1) it consists of the old 19th century part; 2) a few new settlements.

21 The research were conducted among seniors living on the following streets: Katowicka, Modrzewiowa, Leopolda, Kopalniana, Kowalska, Ryszarda, Markiefki, Krakusa, Piotra, Zofii Koniarkowej, Węglana, Brunona Żogały, Księdza Franciszka Ścigały, Grabowa, Kręta, Nadgórników, Grabonia, Sztygarska, Wróblewskiego, Krzysztofa Mieroszewskiego, Księdza Norberta Bończyka, Ignacego Kraszewskiego, Normy, Nowa). The research were multi-stage: in the first stage of the research (2018) focus study with local leaders, 131 questionnaire interviews and 30 individual interviews were conducted; in the second stage of the research (2020), 78 questionnaire interviews and 10 individual interviews were conducted.

the seniors said about forgetting, abandoning Bogucice, using a metaphor of death and dying. 29 % of the respondents assessed its district as worse than other districts of Katowice, degraded and affected by social pathologies and infrastructural ruins.

The perspective of the seniors has changed now. None of the respondents assessed their district as worse than others, whereas, the number of the respondents assessing their district as "better" has increased (from 34 % to 43 %). More than half of the respondents has perceived positive changes in their place of residence in short two-year period after previous research. What, according to the inhabitants, justifies growing valorisation of their place of residence? What has objectively changed in social space of the district that externalization of social me so world caused the growth of positive assessments of old Bogucice?

The respondents most often said about investments in residential infrastructure (new residential blocks, repairing a few tenements and Municipal Cultural Center). Aestheticization of physical space and attempt to create the foundations of urban order have given inhabitants the hope of resuscitation of the district and its development. However, renewal of the park has become a local symbol. We paid a lot of attention to this space in previous research (2018). Following the tracks indicated by the inhabitants, we have discovered multidimensional structure of collective memory rooted in Bogucice Park, collective practices related to mining culture becoming a thing of the past, celebrating community and individual memories about affections, bonds and youth. It is what park also triggered – in the narratives of the respondents – the context of civil objectification of inhabitants by local authority, and broader, criticizing the way of not implementing/implementing the program of district renewal. In 2019, this space was returned to the inhabitants and has again become a central point on the map of not only activity of the seniors, but was also added to the catalogue of arguments for improvement of quality of life in the district. What is important, we could feel the pride in their words from achieving success of renewal of the park for the seniors, and this success is largely attributed to the inhabitants of the district and their involvement in exerting social pressure on execution of this part of a plan of city renewal: "we have a beautiful park now, this park was once neglected, squalid, it was scary to go there. But people rebelled and demanded renewal, and they were right because this park was really neglected" [W_K_79]. It is a very significant dimension of this project and its implementation because the seniors have started having the sense of authorship, which is the key in organizing every local environment, and in the case of the seniors, it is also a foundation of their group empowerment.[22]

The second reason of growing number of positive assessment of the changes occurring in old Bogucice has direct connection with senior policy, which has not existed or was only declarative in the last few years. However, in the last two years, it has entered a phase of institutional implementation thanks to Local Activity Program in the district and orientation of its activity to mobilization of the seniors. Municipal Cultural Center has also developed its offer addressed to the elderly and created a space friendly and open to local initiatives taken by senior environment: "it was nothing here a few years ago, there were no events . . . We also have needs and some of us do not want only stay at home . . . luckily everything moves forwards and something is finally going on . . . so I am happy that I can participate in something like that" [W_K_76]. In general, institutional actions dedicated to the seniors allow to broaden the spectrum of daily activity of the elderly. For some of them, it is a motivation to simply go out: If it was not [Local Activity Program] here, I wouldn't go out [W_K_67]; for others it is a chance for participation in dissemination of culture (cinema, operetta) or having fun: "I like going there [Municipal Cultural Center] with my friends to dancing, but there were also St Andrew's eve party and Miner's Day party organized" [W_K_72]. A very important aspect is also these forms of mobilization that make the elderly feel needed: "we are going to the kindergarten to read fairy tales or rhymes and then make art works based on them. When we had read a rhyme about a snowman, we stuck little snowman on the little pieces of paper. It was such a fun. These kids gave us so many hugs. We are like their grandmas" [W_K_74]. Thanks to social networks rooted institutionally, the elderly also involve as the volunteers in the actions addressed to all inhabitants of the district: "when a lady from the Local Activity Program was organizing a run, we also helped her" [W_K_68]. A very important dimension of functioning of educational and cultural institutions in Bogucice is creating bonds and offering in formal social support by the participants; "I meet with my friends here to drink coffee and gossip, to spend a nice time with people" [W_K_66]. It is not only about educational and cultural offer stimulating cognitive or kinetic resources, but also social and emotional ones. These institutions are a substitute of coffee houses or restaurants unavailable in the district, a place of informal meetings and satisfying affiliation needs.

22 J. Jacobs, *The Death and Life of Great American Cities*, New York: Random House, 1961.

However, the presence and offer of the Local Activity Program has not resulted in spectacular growth of activity of potential beneficiaries in the institutional actions, although it is treated by the elderly as a sign of changes in perception and treatment of the seniors: "they have finally noticed that we're here" [W_M_78]. Higher involvement of the seniors is limited – apart from lifestyle –by two fundamental factors: lack of information (source of knowledge are friends) and health problems ("I would go to the Local Activity Program, but it's too far for me" [W_K_81]). It is especially a problem of people from two old subcategories of old age (74+), that is, those who seem to be neglected the most in urban social policy. Short time of functioning of this institution: 2018–2020 is also a problem.

3.2 Old age in the experiences of the oldest inhabitants of the district

Daily life of the seniors is shaped by psychophysical and social specificity that makes older inhabitants of the district similar in experiencing somatic changes and emerging problems. For our respondents, old age means, above all, combating diseases: "Old age would be beautiful if not all these diseases" [W_K_81]. Although seniors have access to local clinics, their health condition requires treatment from the specialists from various fields of medicine. They can be found in centres located outside old Bogucice and journey to these places requires to use public transport and help of a family. Old age also means loneliness, when a person becomes a widow/widower, when there is no social support of family and friends: Since my wife has died, I spend all days alone at home, I rarely go out, I do not know what's going on, I have nobody" [W_M_72]. Old age means also struggle with health care system, institutional mechanisms of access selection and bureaucratic procedures*:*

> If not the help of my son, I would have been dead by now. They did not want to operate this tumour because I'm too old, and I have just six months more to live . . . I would give up without the help of my son. An old man alone in the hospital has no chance. He can die in the waiting room . . . it was four years ago [W_M_75].

The seniors said about contending with decrease of income, after becoming a widow/widower, when they had to become financially self-sufficient and bad health makes it impossible to find a temporary job. The situation is dramatic especially when they are not supported by the family:

> my daughter and granddaughter went to Holland. When my husband was alive, we had supported her financially . . . I am poor myself now, I have to pay the bills, I don't even have the money to visit her [W_K_65].

For the disabled seniors, one of the key limitations–apart from the ones mentioned above – are architectural barriers: buildings without elevators, lack of driveways, unevenurface, not adapted service premises, distant bus stops. It does not only discourage, but also make using public space, maintaining social relationships, activity outside the house and independent life impossible.

Meanwhile, care services available for the seniors in the district are assessed negatively due to the quality of services: the carers are changing, they are sometimes unpunctual and have low social competences "No one came to me for three weeks. One day, someone rang the doorbell, I asked "who's there?" and I heard the male voice. I got scared. No one warned me that instead of a woman, an unknown man would come to me and after such a long time! Then, I found out that the company does what it wants and even MOPS can do nothing about that . . . that company won a tender because its offer was the cheapest, but also the worst . . . nothing can be done until the next tender . . . and everything at the cost of older people" [W_K_76].

3.3 Ageism in the experience of the oldest inhabitants of the district

Ageism is a term evolving in scientific discourse due to increasing interest of social science indiscrimination of the elderly. Its author, Robert Butler defined it as "the systematic stereotyping of and discrimination against people because they are old, just as racism and sexism accomplish this with skin colour and gender. Old people are categorized as senile, rigid in thought and manner, old fashioned in morality and skills . . . age is mallows the younger generation to see older people as different from themselves; thus they subtly cease to identify with their elders as human beings."[23] Talking about modern ageism, the researchers emphasize a few dimensions of this phenomenon. Firstly, we can deal with both negative and positive stereotypes, prejudices and discrimination due to chronological age or perception of people as old (older);" secondly, ageism can be open or hidden and functions at the micro, meso and macro level; thirdly, it can be conscious or unconscious and finally fourthly, it can be manifested at the individual, social and institutional level.[24]

In our research, the exploration of this phenomenon seemed to be very important. Both in questionnaire and individual interviews and focus studies,

---

23 R.B. Butler, M.L. Lewis, *Aging and Mental Health*, 1973, p. 35.

24 T.N. Iversen, L. Larsen, P.E. Solem, "A Conceptual Analysis of Ageism," *Nordic Psychology* 2009, Vol. 61, No. 4, pp. 12–15.

our respondents described practices that were our research material, which was further analysed.

Let us look at the remarks formulated by the respondents about health care system. The seniors said about the issue of their health and treatment that:

- the elderly are treated as patients not worthy of investing money and time "because their days are numbered anyway" (F_M);
- subsequent specialist doctor's offices in the district are liquidated, not caring about inhabitants who, due to their age and progressing infirmity, have difficult access to other parts of the city, in which medical services are available (F_K);
- the elderly are treated with contempt and they are not informed about cancelling examination early enough so as not to expose them to unnecessary efforts and waste of time: "I had waited two months for a medical appointment, and the doctor said that her apparatus was broken. I became irritated because she could call me and she said that I have a lot of free time at my age!" (F_M);
- no one takes care of minimal comfort of patients in the hospital waiting room "People from all over Poland come to this oncological hospital, waiting even several dozen hours, crowded like cattle, and then they find out that there will be no medical appointment" (F_M).

The second area, in which the elderly say that their age is an excluding factor, is the labour market. What this criticism come from if the participants of the research have a status of old-age pensioners? The reason is failed attempts to find a temporary job or to return to a former job, made mainly due to economic reasons, but also passion connected with professional activity and prestige of such job. The seniors said that:

- their job applications lose with applications of younger people "I went there in the morning because there was a recruitment for people like me, having disability category. It turned out that they prefer younger people. I lost half a day. I have to manage somehow. I don't have too much money and I need to work" (W_M_);
- despite full physical fitness and willingness to continue work by an older employee, an employer does not extend a contract due to the age of his/her employee "I really liked my job. I was an academic teacher my whole life ... but I had to quit. My employer has not agreed to extend my contract. I was forced to retire ... I miss contact with my students" (W_M_).

The third issue that triggers descriptions of practices showing the manifestations of discrimination, is local policy:

- "I have been fighting for this fragment of a road for a few years, I even invited a journalist to write about that. And what? Nothing. This journalist lost her job after writing that article and there is no normal crossing there, these three meters. They are saying that there is nothing they can do. And when the winter will come, people will be falling down there and disabled people, like my friend without a leg, won't be able to cross at all" (F_M)
- "the housing cooperative sold a plot near the building, its owner has fenced everything in and my neighbour can't drive on the driveway. They won't do anything. They don't care about us" (F_M);
- "it was once a beautiful place, but everything is deteriorating now. When I had reported that pavement must be repaired because we can all die here, they said that it falls outside their competence. I had sought help in the housing cooperative, they sent me back to the city council, and again. There is no one who can help me" (W_M);
- "the tenement is falling apart, we live like in the nineteenth century, no one does anything here. They are waiting for all us to die" (W_K_).

The sense of being a person that is treated worse due to old age also express descriptions of dangerous situation and loss of security in the district:

- when the interviewed person mentioned an assault that she was a victim of and stealing her bag "I was walking along Markiefka street and hooded man pushed me and took my bag . . . I was helpless, no one helped because there were only old people. It was scary" (W_K_16);
- or when the senior feels anxious during evening walks with her dog. "These men wearing hood shave no respect for older people, I have a dog that must be taken for a walk on the evening sand I am really afraid walking next to them. . . they sit at the gate and call you the worst names . . . I lower my head and go home as fast as I can" (W_K_17).

Generally, although our respondents do not refer directly their experiences to discrimination due to age, they seem to know that as seniors, they belong to a category of *vulnerable persons,* that is, people "particularly exposed to be hurt, having to face with difficult situations."[25]

---

25 B. Mikołajczyk, *Międzynarodowa ochrona praw osób starszych*: Warszawa, Wolters Kluwer, 2012, p. 38.

The signs of discrimination present in the experiences of the seniors are, above all: not being recognized, sepization, showing disrespect, being neglected, segregation, isolation, bodily abuse, condescension.

Not being recognized is manifested by "invisibility" of the seniors and their needs. The respondents said that they are "dying along with the district," in which space is unfriendly: bus shelters, benches, lighting are liquidated, no one takes care of the pavements, building ruins are tolerated, specialist medical services are moved to other districts, market offer is diminishing etc.

It is associated with sepization, that is, hiding problems of the seniors and the whole district through renewal discourse. This discourse invalids protests and complaints of the inhabitants, marginalizing the importance of the needs of local community that are not satisfied. It imposes its own spatial valorisation and orients renewal in to actions that are spectacular from the point of view of city image, in the form of Bogucice Park –the space that was once symbolically significant for local environment–heralded for years as a reconstitution of a *genius loci*. Therefore, material renewal is created as an antidote to all "problems of the district" (F_K).

The seniors taking anti-sepization actions, through publicizing their needs and opinions, have to face condescension. Protesting against destruction of a band shell, pointing out on the fact that this shell was included in the register of monuments, or appealing to collective frame works of social memory, are ignored, silenced, the arguments of the "experts" win with the arguments of the inhabitants: "We play together in an orchestra, so I took him to the park and said: look, what acoustics you will have now?! None! That band shell had beautiful acoustics and that what is now is very bad. How could you allow to destroy that?!" (F_M).

The seniors from Bogucice also feel ignored and marginalized as social actors in the actions of their local political representatives. Having no contact with the councillors, lack of information about their work for the district and inhabitants, administrative impossibilism, are some of the charges. The seniors also feel treated like objects: "Mr Kocurek lived here a few year ago, but he is dead now. He was the deputy mayor of Katowice and he was trying to do something here. There were various meetings. But now, some young person came here because he wanted to run for office. I just saw him once. He was elected and has never reappeared. There are no meetings with us. He only cared about my signature" (W_M_14).

Being neglected is a manifestation of discrimination that is particularly emphasized in the interviews with the seniors because according to them, "Nothing has changed here for thirty years. That's the truth" (W_M_14). They feel deprecated, there is low-quality service offer: "what do we have here? all these all-night shops? There are no such things in normal countries, bad people wander around here . . . it is not nice to enter such shop or walk next to it. . . . we live like in the Middle Ages." The needs of socio-cultural character are particularly neglected, the seniors said about organization of free time and social integration: "Instead of such shop, there should be a coffee house, day-care room. Something that would liven up the seniors, a place to go with friends to, sit and listen to music, play billiards . . . of course at the decent level." (W_M_14).

The need of common, public space for the elderly, the space not too formalized, allowing to maintain interpersonal relationships and spending of free time is strengthened by the sense of segregation, that is, living in an area, in which seniors are particularly large category, and due to decrease of their mobility, also condemned to live in their own environment. However, such segregation is not of exclusive character like in other districts, in which middle class seniors live (Koszutka, Bażantów etc.), it's just the opposite. Here segregation means exclusion from attractive urban space, cultural or sport offer[26]and "being an island" (F_M), around which everything is blooming and developing, and it is a "graveyard" (W_M_).

The sense of segregation is additionally strengthened by intergenerational disintegration resulting in social isolation. The elderly feel threatened by the presence and activity of young people, uncertain about the rules of mutual social coexistence, anxious about consequences of meeting them. "I feel sad. It's not a nice view, these boys in the hoods, falling down, taking designer drugs or different drugs. . . . This view is revolting when a young boy lies on a bench" (W_M_14); "it is better not to get out at night. These youth gangs, hooligans, drug addicts (F_K).

Social isolation is justified by the sense of threat from young people (young men) and helplessness in the face of their aggression. And we do not say only about potential, anticipated events, but about real experiences of our respondents who said about the acts of violence against them (theft, assault).

26 "This park here is a mini park . . . mainly mud and smashed bottles. Nothing is going on here. There aren't any pitches. There are not true pitches" (W_M_14).

Table 1: The manifestations of discrimination of the seniors in the district

The manifestations of discrimination	Signs	Type of discrimination
Not being recognized	Lack of infrastructure necessary for improvement of quality of life of the seniors	Institutional
Sepization	Hiding everyday problems of older inhabitants of the district by "propaganda of success" in the form of the so-called renewal	Institutional
Condescension	Pretending to cooperate with local social actors, "fake" dialogue and public consultations, lack of diagnosis of the resources and needs of the inhabitants of the district	Institutional
Showing disrespect	Treating seniors like objects for purposes not serving to them	Institutional
Being neglected	Neglecting the needs of the seniors related to spending free time and security	Institutional
Segregation	Territorial concentration of the elderly	Institutional
Isolation	Intergenerational disintegration	Institutional Individual
Bodily abuse	The acts of violence against he elderly	Individual

Source: own elaboration.

4. Research conclusions

Living space is very important for the quality of life of the elderly. Going into retirement resulting in occupational deactivation,[27] reduces the area of routine mobility and eliminates (at least partially and gradually) the sphere of social relationships based on professional role. With time, living environment is becoming the main or the only social space allowing activity and providing formal and in formal support. Therefore, psychophysical well-being of the elderly depends on activity, the number of interpersonal relationships and

27 Not every old-age pensioner resigns from professional work. Therefore, we think here only about such people who become professionally passive after going into retirement.

quality of social bonds. Therefore, socio-economic structure of neighbourhood and broader – habitat, are determinants (but not the only one) of quality of life and ageing. This relation between the features of living space and ageing should imply such actions in the area of senior policy (social, urban) that would eliminate the processes of social disruption, and also transform social space towards inclusiveness and subject participation. Whereas, in the case of old Bogucice, for many years, we would say about concentration of negative phenomena: heterogeneity of local community was increasing, which was caused, among others, by location of social flats in this area; instability of living resulting from infrastructural dismantling and vanishing of various social functions of the district was increasing; impoverishment of the households was cumulating and crime rate was increasing: "social climate" of the district was dominated by the sense of having no authorship and social confidence and assessment of the district as a social environment of low quality. The researchers connect these rates of social disruption with higher risk of mortality[28] and incidence,[29] as well as with deterioration of mental health[30] and health self-assessment[31] and environmental stress. They also said that the quality of infrastructure may curb social interactions, and heavy traffic, noise, in appropriate lighting and devastated pavements may discourage to physical activity (mainly the elderly).[32]

Only since 2018, we have observed the change of viewpoint in implementation of the principles of urban policy that includes the needs of (the oldest) older inhabitants of the district. Spatial environment, degenerated by restructuring changes requires revival of social capital, preventing exclusion and

28 A.V. Diez Roux, Ch. Mair, "Neighborhoods and Health," *Annals of The New York Academy of Sciences* 2010, 18 February, https://doi.org/10.1111/j.1749-6632.2009.05333.x.

29 A.V. Diez Roux, L.N. Borrell, M. Haan, S.A. Jackson, R. Schultz, "Neighborhood environments and mortality in an elderly cohort: Results from the cardiovascular health study," *Journal of Epidemiology and Community Health* 2004, Vol. 58, No. 11, pp. 917–923.

30 C. Aneshensel, R. Wight, D. Miller-Martinez, A. Botticello, A. Karlmangla, T. Seeman. "Urban Neighborhoods and Depressive Symptoms Among Older Adults," *Journal of Gerontology: Social Sciences* 2007, Vol. 62B, pp. 52–59.

31 K.A. Cagney, C.R. Browning, M. Wen, "Race and self-rated health at older ages: what difference does the neighborhood make?," *Journal of Gerontology: Social Sciences* 2005, Vol. 60B, No. 4, pp. S193–S194.

32 J.K. Balfour, G.A. Kaplan, "Neighborhood environment and loss of physical function in older adults: evidence from the Alameda County Study," *American Journal of Epidemiology* 2002, Vol. 155, No. 6, pp. 507–515.

passivity. The sense of security, axiological and normative order, social confidence, feeling of community and identity must be restored. The effectiveness of this process depends on people creating the vision of changes and people who experience these changes, therefore, we need social dialogue and participation of(potential) beneficiaries of urban policy in contribution to and execution of the project of changes. The seniors living in Bogucice constantly mention (just like respondents two years ago) about: hooliganism, drunkenness and vandalism; public transport not adapted to the needs of the seniors (the number and arrangement of bus stops, timetables and routes of buses); pedestrian communication with a large number of barriers (dimly lit pavements, pavements packed with cars, high kerbs, lack of benches allowing to rest);municipal services that do not maintain order (mainly garbage lying not only in the containers, but also on the lawns, pavements and courtyards). Apart from physical and social space, the barriers are also of institutional character: low level of care services; the lack of access to specialist health care (high deficit of geriatrics).

5. Conclusions

The Bogucice district has social potential that, supported institutionally, is a resource allowing to rebuild the local community. To improve the quality of life of the elderly, spatial accumulation of the seniors may be an advantage, provided that barriers in integration of this age group will be eliminated. The research showed that co presence of the elderly and mutual relationships and bonds makes assessment of the quality of own health better, improve mental state and protect against premature death during dramatic random incidents (disasters) and after death of a husband/wife.[33] The district may create opportunities for such positive influences through the presence of institutions (understood as physical places for organized social activity), around which social networks of the seniors are created.[34]

Although attachment to the district is increasing with age and area of mobility is limiting, ageing in a place of residence is associated with activity in the environments beyond a place of residence and it also (to a various degree) affects the quality of life of the elderly. Apart from senior policy at the level

33 S.V. Subramanian, F. Elwert, N. Christakis, "Widowhood and Mortality Among the Elderly: The Modifying Role of Neighborhood Concentration of Widowed Individuals," *Social Science & Medicine* 2008, Vol. 66, No. 4, pp. 873–884.

34 A.R. Hochschild, "Emotion Work, Feeling Rules, and Social Structure," *American Journal of Sociology* 1979, Vol. 85, No. 3, pp. 551–575.

of district, political actions organizing the life of the city are also important. Whereas, Katowice was classified in the 14th place (out of 18) in the ranking of large Polish cities in terms of senior policy.[35]

An initiative of the Council of Seniors to join the network of the Ageing-Friendly Cities has also not been implemented. There is a need of critical reflection on also mobilization paradigm that local senior policy is founded on and deficit in social policy: in such districts as old Bogucice, with accumulation of the inhabitant sat senior age and the problems related to the process of ageing, it' sin vestment in the development of institutions providing formal long-term care, home care and medical geriatric services should be an element of urban and senior policy equally emphasized as social mobilization.

Bibliography:

Aneshensel C., Wight R., Miller-Martinez D., Botticello A., Karlmangla A., Seeman T., "Urban Neighborhoods and Depressive Symptoms Among Older Adults. Journal of Gerontology," *Social Sciences* 2007, Vol. 62B, pp. 52–59.

Balfour J.L.; Kaplan G.A, "Neighborhood environment and loss of physical function in older adults: evidence from the Alameda County Study," *American Journal of Epidemiology* 2002, Vol. 155, No. 6, pp. 507–515.

Brańska A., *Raport Najlepsze miasta dla seniorów 2019* [online:]https://www.ikalkulator.pl/blog/raport-najlepsze-miasta-dla-seniorow-2019/ 27.11.2019 [available: 20.03.2020]

Bloom D.E., Canning D., Sevilla J., *Economic Growth and the Demographic Transition*, Cambridge 2001.

Bratt Ch., Abrams D., Swift H., Vauclair C. M., Marques S., "Perceived Age Discrimination Across Age in Europe: From an Ageing Society to a Society for All Ages," *Developmental Psychology* 2018, Vol. 54, No. 1.

Bukov A., Maas I., Lampert T., "Social Participation in Very Old Age: Cross-Sectional and Longitudinal Findings From Base," *The Journals of Gerontology Series B* 2002, Vol. 57, No. 6.

Butler R. B., Lewis M. L, *Aging and Mental Health*, Mosby 1973.

Butler R.N., "Ageism: Looking back over my shoulder," *Generations* 2005, Vol. 3.

35 A. Brańska, *Raport Najlepsze miasta dla seniorów 2019* (https://www.ikalkulator.pl/blog/raport-najlepsze-miasta-dla-seniorow-2019/ 27.11.2019.

Cagney K.A., Browning C.R., Wen M., "Race and self-rated health at older ages: what difference does the neighborhood make?," *Journal of Gerontology: Social Sciences* 2005, Vol. 60B, No. 4.

Diez Roux A.V., Borrell L.N, Haan M, Jackson S.A., Schultz R., "Neighborhood environments and mortality in an elderly cohort: Results from the cardiovascular health study," *Journal of Epidemiology and Community Health* 2004, Vol. 58, No. 11, pp. 917–923.

Diez Roux A.V., Mair Ch., "Neighborhoods and health," *Annals of the New York Academy of Sciences* 2010 (18 February), https://doi.org/10.1111/j.1749-6632.2009.05333.x [available: 20.03.2020].

European Commission Economic and budgetary projections for the 28 EU MemberStates.

"The 2015 Ageing Report," *European Economy* 2015, Vol. 3.

Gorman M., "Development and the rights of older people," *The Ageing and Development Report: Poverty, Independence and the World's Older People*, eds. J. Randel et al., London, Earth Scan Publications Ltd. 1999.

Hochschild A.R., "Emotion Work, Feeling Rules, and Social Structure," *American Journal of Sociology* 1979, Vol. 85, No. 3, pp. 551–575.

Iversen T. N., Larsen L., Solem P. E., "A conceptual analysis of Ageism," *Nordic Psychology* 2009, Vol. 61, No. 4.

Quillian L., "New approaches to understanding racial prejudice and discrimination," *Annu. Rev. Sociol.* 2006, Vol. 32.

Schmied, G., *Schenken: Über eine Form sozialen Handelns*, Opladen1996.

Subramanian S. V., Iwert F. E., Christakis N., "Widowhood and mortality among the elderly: The modifying role of neighborhood concentration of widowed individuals," *Social Science & Medicine* 2008, Vol. 66, No. 4, pp. 873–884.

Wiles D., "Who is old? Defining old age," *Australian Journal on Ageing* 1987, Vol. 6. No. 4.

"The World Health Organization Quality of Life Assessment (WHOQOL): Position Paper from the World Health Organization," *Social Science & Medicine* 1995, Vol. 41, No. 10.

Authors

(in alphabetical order)

Grażyna Baranowska, PhD, Poznań Human Rights Center, Polish Academy of Sciences

Dominika Bek, PhD, University of Silesia in Katowice

Ilona Delekta, PhD Candidate, University of Silesia in Katowice

Aleksandra Gliszczyńska-Grabias, PhD, Poznań Human Rights Center, Polish Academy of Sciences

Justyna Gumuła-Kędracka, PhD Candidate, University of Silesia in Katowice

Anna Jaworska-Wieloch, PhD, University of Silesia in Katowice

Katarzyna Jędrzejczyk-Kuliniak, PhD, University of Wrocław

Katarzyna Kamińska, PhD Candidate, University of Silesia in Katowice

Joanna Klimczak, PhD, University of Silesia in Katowice

Samanta Kowalska, PhD, The President Stanisław Wojciechowski Academy in Kalisz

Joanna Markiewicz-Stanny, PhD, University of Zielona Góra

Elżbieta H. Morawska, Prof., Cardinal Stefan Wyszynski University

Małgorzata Myl, PhD, University of Silesia in Katowice

Dorota Nowalska-Kapuścik, PhD, University of Silesia in Katowice

Magdalena Półtorak, PhD, University of Silesia in Katowice

Olga Sitarz, Prof., University of Silesia in Katowice

Barbara Stępień, PhD, Iberoamerican University (Universidad Iberoamericana) in Mexico

Aleksandra Szczerba, Prof., The Jacob of Paradies University in Gorzów Wielkopolski

Ilona Topa, PhD, University of Silesia in Katowice

Urszula Torbus, PhD, University of Silesia in Katowice

Agnieszka Wedeł-Domaradzka, PhD, Kazimierz Wielki University in Bydgoszcz

Lex et Res Publica
Polish Legal and Political Studies

Edited by
Anna Jaroń

Vol. 1 Anna Jaroń: Socio-Economic Constitutional Rights in Democratisation Processes. An Account of the Constitutional Dialogue Theory. 2012.

Vol. 2 Stanisław Filipowicz: Democracy – The Power of Illusion. 2013.

Vol. 3 Teresa Dukiet-Nagórska (ed.): The Postulates of Restorative Justice and the Continental Model of Criminal Law. As Illustrated by Polish Criminal Law 2014.

Vol. 4 Agnieszka Kupzok: Enforcement of Patents on Geographically Divisible Inventions. An Inquiry into the Standard of Substantive Patent Law Infringement in Cross-Border Constellations. 2015.

Vol. 5 Alicja Jagielska-Burduk / Wojciech Szafrański: Legal Issues in Cultural Heritage Management. A Polish Perspective. 2016.

Vol. 6 Maciej Mataczyński (ed.): The Takeover of Public Companies as a Mode of Exercising EU Treaty Freedoms. 2017.

Vol. 7 Maciej Barczewski (ed.): Value of Information. Intellectual Property, Privacy and Big Data. 2018.

Vol. 8 Pawel Smoleń, Marcin Burzec: Introduction to Polish Tax Law. 2018.

Vol. 9 Łukasz Pohl, Konrad Burdziak: Judicial Interpretation of the 1997 Criminal Code Provisions on Self-Defence. 2019.

Vol. 10 Adam Szot: Judicial Review of Administrative Discretion. The Influence of Court Decisions on Administrative Actions. 2019.

Vol. 11 Michał Peno / Konrad Burdziak (eds.): The Concept of Modern Law. Polish and Central European Tradition. 2019.

Vol. 12 Leszek Leszczyński / Bartosz Liżewski / Adam Szot (eds.): Potential of Precedent in the Statutory Legal Order. 2019.

Vol. 13 Łukasz Bolesta: In Search of a Model for the Legal Protection of a Whistleblower in the Workplace in Poland. A legal and comparative study. 2020.

Vol. 14 Paweł Chmielnicki / Adam Sulikowski (eds.): New Perspectives on Legislation. A Comparative Approach. 2020.

Vol. 15 Marcin Burzec / Beata Kucia-Guściora / Paweł Smoleń (eds.): Agricultural Activity in Poland: A Fiscal and Legal Study. 2020.

Vol. 16 Magdalena Półtorak / Ilona Topa (eds.): Women, Children and (Other) Vulnerable Groups. Standards of Protection and Challenges for International Law. 2021.

www.peterlang.com

www.ingramcontent.com/pod-product-compliance
Ingram Content Group UK Ltd.
Pitfield, Milton Keynes, MK11 3LW, UK
UKHW021830100926
8556IPUK00004B/260

9 783631 841525